Jesus, Paul, and the Law

Jesus, Paul, and the Law

STUDIES
IN
MARK AND GALATIANS

James D. G. Dunn

Westminster/John Knox Press
Louisville, Kentucky

First American edition

Published by Westminster/John Knox Press
Louisville, Kentucky

PRINTED IN THE UNITED STATES OF AMERICA
9   8   7   6   5   4   3   2   1

Library of Congress Cataloging-in-Publication Data

Dunn, James D. G., 1939–
    Jesus, Paul, and the law : studies in Mark and Galatians / James
D. G. Dunn. — 1st American ed.
        p.   cm.
    Includes bibliographical references.
    ISBN 0-664-25095-5

    1. Jesus Christ—Views on Jewish law.   2. Paul, the Apostle,
Saint—Views on Jewish law.   3. Bible.   N.T.   Mark—Theology.
4. Bible.   N.T.   Galatians—Theology.   5. Jewish law.   6. Law
(Theology)—Biblical teaching.   7. Law and gospel—Biblical
teaching.   I. Title.

BS2417.L3D85 1990
241'.2'09015—dc20   90-32703
                                                                    CIP

To

Hans Hübner
Heikki Räisänen
and
Ed Sanders,

partners in dialogue

Contents

Abbreviations

AnBib	Analecta Biblica
ABR	*Australian Biblical Review*
ANRW	*Aufstieg und Niedergang des romische Welt*
BAGD	W. Bauer, *A Greek-English Lexicon of New Testament and Other Early Christian Literature*, ET, ed. W. F. Arndt and F. W. Gingrich; 2nd ed. rev. F. W. Gingrich and F. W. Danker (University of Chicago 1979).
Bib	*Biblica*
BJRL	*Bulletin of the John Rylands University Library of Manchester*
BZ	*Biblische Zeitschrift*
CBQ	*Catholic Biblical Quarterly*
CD	K. Barth, *Church Dogmatics*, ET G. W. Bromiley and T. F. Torrance (Edinburgh: T. & T. Clark, 1975)
CNT	*Commentaire du Nouveau Testament*
ConBNT	*Coniectanea biblica, New Testament*
EB	Études bibliques
EKK	Evangelisch-katholischer Kommentar zum Neuen Testament
EncJud	Encyclopedia Judaica
ETL	*Ephemerides theologicae lovanienses*
HNT	Handbuch zum Neuen Testament
HTR	*Harvard Theological Review*
HUCA	*Hebrew Union College Annual*
ICC	International Critical Commentary
ITQ	*Irish Theological Quarterly*
JB	Jerusalem Bible
JBL	*Journal of Biblical Literature*
JETS	*Journal of the Evangelical Theological Society*
JJS	*Journal of Jewish Studies*
JQR	*Jewish Quarterly Review*
JR	*Journal of Religion*
JSJ	*Journal for the Study of Judaism in the Persian, Hellenistic and Roman Period*
JSNT	*Journal for the Study of the New Testament*
JSNTSupp	*JSNT Supplement Series*
JSOT	*Journal for the Study of the Old Testament*
JTS	*Journal of Theological Studies*
KD	*Kerygma und Dogma*
KEK	H. A. W. Meyer, *Kritisch-exegetischer Kommentar über das Neue Testament*

LSJ	H. G. Liddell and R. Scott, *A Greek-English Lexicon*, rev. H. S. Jones (Oxford: Clarendon, 1940; with supplement, 1968)
MM	J. H. Moulton and G. Milligan, *The Vocabulary of the Greek Testament* (London, Hodder, 1930)
MTZ	*Münchener theologische Zeitschrift*
NCB	New Century Bible (new ed.)
NEB	New English Bible (NT 1961; OT and Apoc. 1970)
NICNT	New International Commentary on the New Testament
NIGTC	New International Greek Testament Commentary
NIV	New International Version (1978)
NovT	*Novum Testamentum*
NTSupp	Supplement to *NovT*
NTD	Das Neue Testament Deutsch
NTS	*New Testament Studies*
OGIS	W. Dittenberger, ed., *Orientis Graeci Inscriptiones Selectae* (Leipzig, 1903–5)
PTMS	Pittsburgh (Princeton) Theological Monograph Series
RSR	*Recherches de science religieuse*
RSV	Revised Standard Version (NT 1946, OT 1952, Apoc. 1957)
SBL	Society of Biblical Literature
SBLDS	SBL Dissertation Series
SBLSBS	SBL Sources for Biblical Study
SBM	Stuttgarter biblische Monographien
SEÅ	*Svensk exegetisk årsbok*
SJT	*Scottish Journal of Theology*
SNTSMS	Society for New Testament Studies Monograph Series
ST	*Studia theologica*
Str-B	H. Strack and P. Billerbeck, *Kommentar zum Neuen Testament*, 4 vols. (Munich: Beck'sche, 1926–28)
TDNT	G. Kittel and G. Fredrich, eds., *Theological Dictionary of the New Testament*, 10 vols., ET (Grand Rapids: Eerdmans, 1964–76)
THNT	Theologischer Handkommentar zum Neuen Testament
TQ	*Theologische Quartalschrift*
TZ	*Theologische Zeitschrift*
USQR	*Union Seminary Quarterly Review*
VF	*Verkündigung und Forschung*
VT	*Vetus Testamentum*
WBC	Word Biblical Commentary
WMANT	Wissenschaftliche Monographien zum Alten und Neuen Testament
WTJ	*Westminster Theological Journal*
WUNT	Wissenschaftliche Untersuchungen zum Neuen Testament
ZNW	*Zeitschrift für die neutestamentliche Wissenschaft*
ZRG	*Zeitschrift für Religions- und Geistesgeschichte*
ZTK	*Zeitschrift für Theologie und Kirche*

Acknowledgements

I wish to express my thanks and give due acknowledgement to the various publishers involved for their permission to reproduce the following:

Chapter 1 – 'Mark 2.1—3.6: A Bridge between Jesus and Paul on the Question of the Law', *NTS* 30 (1984), pp. 395–415;

Chapter 2 – 'Jesus and Ritual Purity. A study of the tradition history of Mk 7, 15', *A cause de l'évangile, Mélanges offerts a Dom Jacques Dupont*, Lectio Divina 123 (Saint-André: Editions du Cerf, 1985), pp. 251–76;

Chapter 3 – 'Pharisees, Sinners, and Jesus', *The Social World of Formative Christianity and Judaism, Essays in Tribute to Howard Clark Kee*, ed. J. Neusner, P. Borgen, E. S. Frerichs and R. Horsley (Philadelphia: Fortress Press, 1988), pp. 264–89;

Chapter 4 – ' "A Light to the Gentiles": the Significance of the Damascus Road Christophany for Paul', *The Glory of Christ in the New Testament, Studies in Christology in Memory of George Bradford Caird*, ed. L. D. Hurst and N. T. Wright (Oxford: Clarendon Press, 1987), pp. 251–66;

Chapter 5 – 'The Relationship between Paul and Jerusalem according to Galatians 1 and 2', *NTS* 28 (1982), pp. 461–78;

Chapter 6 – 'The Incident at Antioch (Gal. 2: 11–18)', *JSNT* 18 (1983), pp. 3–57;

Chapter 7 – 'The New Perspective on Paul', *BJRL* 65 (1983), pp. 95–122;

Chapter 8 – 'Works of the Law and the Curse of the Law (Galatians 3.10–14)', *NTS* 31 (1985), pp. 523–42;

Chapter 9 is a much-revised version of the paper which appeared in first draft as 'The Theology of Galatians', *SBL 1988 Seminar Papers* (Atlanta: Scholars Press, 1988), pp. 1–16.

Introduction

During the 1980s one of the main controversies among New Testament scholars and researchers into Christian origins has focused on the attitudes towards the Jewish law within earliest Christianity. Most of the issues are of long standing, of course, but in the preceding generation, debate was not very vigorous and most of the contributions seem to have occasioned little discussion.[1] But since the more polemical treatments of H. Hübner[2] and E. P. Sanders,[3] the debate has proceeded apace, particularly in relation to Paul. Especially prominent has been H. Räisänen.[4] An indication of the interest aroused is the number of review articles on the debate which have appeared in the last few years,[5] including the recent major study by S. Westerholm.[6]

It has been my privilege to participate in this debate. Since for most of the period I was working on my commentary on Romans,[7] I would have found it necessary to engage with the several issues anyway. In particular, it quickly became clear that in order to understand Romans it was essential to have a clear perspective on Paul's earlier letter to the churches in Galatia. Moreover, Sanders' *Paul and Palestinian Judaism* had opened up such a fresh perspective on Paul over against his Jewish background, or, as I prefer, within his Jewish context, that it had become a matter of first priority for me to work through the key Pauline material which illuminated Paul's understanding of his Jewish heritage. This research has engaged me for about ten years, and as my work on Paul begins to move into a new phase it seems appropriate to gather together the various contributions I have offered in this area, since they all hang together and provide what I hope may be regarded as a sufficiently coherent collection.

The essays have been ordered in a natural sequence from Mark to and through Galatians. But it may well be helpful for readers to bear in mind the chronological sequence in which they were written. For one thing there is some progression from one to the other: the later essays build on and refine the earlier. I will attempt to draw attention to this in the notes, lest any fall into the mistake of taking an earlier formulation as a 'final' expression of my views. For another, it might just be of interest to some to read the essays in order of composition, to see how my particular slant or theses developed over the period. Some of the essays have also drawn

1

critical fire, and I have taken the liberty of adding an Additional Note at the end of most of the following chapters to clarify my position and respond. In that sense this volume contains what may properly be called a second edition of these essays. In this way I hope to continue the dialogue already begun in these exchanges, since it is only by such dialogue that each of us will be able to refine and sharpen our several hypotheses.

The earliest essay is 'The Incident at Antioch (Gal. 2:11–18)' – here Chapter 6. This was first conceived in 1979, which included a period of research in Israel/Palestine and Tübingen, although at that time my main concern was to complete *Christology in the Making*.[8] It had long been obvious to me that the Antioch incident was a crucial episode in Paul's career.[9] The question was, How crucial? How crucial for the Gentile mission, for Paul's understanding and expression of the (his) gospel, and for his relationships with Jerusalem? To answer these questions it was important to clarify as precisely as possible what was at issue in the Antioch incident; what it was that the 'certain men from James' demanded, and why; what it was that Peter and the other Jewish Christians withdrew from, and why. But the episode also had the virtue of exposing the complexity of relationships between Jews and Gentiles, and of Jewish (including Jewish Christian) attitudes towards such relationships. It thus provided an ideal agenda for an initial exploration of these relationships and of the considerations which must have been decisive for the Jewish Christians at Antioch. The article drew some immediate responses (in the same issue of the journal) from J. L. Houlden and D. Cohn-Sherbok, responses which have been cited as often as 'Incident'. The Additional Note at the end of Chapter 6 attempts to further the dialogue with them, and also with T. Holtz and P. F. Esler, whose critical responses followed later. I am grateful to them all for their critiques, and not least for the way in which they have helped to sharpen some of the central issues; such is the benefit of these dialogues. From the notes to the Additional Note it will be apparent how much of my subsequent research in this area has been an attempt to check the key provisional findings of the original essay, to dig deeper foundations and refine where necessary.

One of the issues raised by that study and requiring fuller study was the relationship between Paul and the church in Jerusalem before and up to the Antioch incident. Interest in the earlier parts of Galatians 1–2 had already been aroused by a splendid New Testament postgraduate seminar at Nottingham on these chapters which ran for two terms, interacting particularly with the then recent commentary of H. D. Betz. This proved highly instructive on the central issue (the relationship between Paul and Jerusalem) and convinced me that prior to the Antioch incident Paul had been much less independent of Jerusalem than subsequently – hence the somewhat defensive tone of Galatians 1.10—2.10. A briefer version of the paper, entitled 'The Relationship between Paul and Jerusalem according to Galatians 1 and 2' (ch. 5 of this volume) was delivered at the annual meeting of the Society of New Testament Studies (SNTS) in Rome in 1981. One major response to this paper, by O. Hofius, focused on Galatians 1.18,[10] and I have appended my response to it as an Additional Note. I regret, however, that the major thesis of the 'relationship' paper, that Galatians 1–2 reflects a transition in Paul's relationship with Jerusalem, has attracted so little attention,[11] since it is an integral part of the overall picture of Paul's theology and its development which I have attempted in these essays to build up. If I am right, Chapter 5 underscores the fulcrum character of the Antioch incident, strongly suggests that the Antioch incident marked a crucial stage in the development of Paul's theology, or at least in the formulation of his gospel and theology of justification by faith, and so also provides an important underpinning for the more specific arguments of the essays which followed.

The essay which really marked my entry into the debate about the law was 'The New Perspective on Paul' (ch. 7 of this volume). Professor Lindars, who did me the honour of inviting me to deliver the Manson Memorial Lecture in 1982, was initially less than enthusiastic about yet another Manson lecture on Paul. But I was by this time sufficiently convinced that the work of E. P. Sanders, in his *Paul and Palestinian Judaism*,[12] had made a decisive breakthrough in Pauline studies which had not yet been properly acknowledged and which deserved further exposure. Along with others, I was most impressed by Part One on Palestinian Judaism (the bulk of the book) and a good deal less impressed by Part Two on Paul. Professor Sanders, however, was kind enough to let me have a copy of the manuscript of his follow-up book on *Paul, the Law, and the Jewish People*,[13] and this made it possible for me to use the Manson lecture for a fuller statement of 'the new perspective' and to offer a fuller response to Sanders than would otherwise have been possible.

Because my lecture appeared in print before Sanders' book, some apparently thought that I had anticipated him in some of the points he makes on the topic. It should have been clear from the published Manson Lecture[14] that I both attribute 'the new perspective' to Professor Sanders and was interacting with his *Paul, the Law, and the Jewish People* (albeit in manuscript form). Some of my German colleagues, on the other hand, think I am too much won over by Sanders' views, and no doubt our critique of the classic Lutheran exposition of Paul on 'justification by faith' needs a good deal more refinement and nuancing. But it should be clear from 'The New Perspective' that I both follow Sanders in recognizing that the Judaism from which Paul came has been distorted in much Protestant exegesis,[15] and criticize him for failing to pursue that important insight fully and consistently enough in his exposition of Paul. Against Sanders, I have to say that Paul's reaction to and theological critique of what he saw as the typical (or Pharisaic) Judaism of his day, particularly with regard to the law, is much more coherent and internally consistent than Sanders allows. The paper brought responses or critical footnotes from a number who have become caught up in the debate. The Additional Note to Chapter 7 is therefore devoted to responses to H. Räisänen, H. Hübner, P. Stuhlmacher, E. P. Sanders, F. F. Bruce and T. R. Schreiner.

'The New Perspective' essay was the first statement of my specific thesis regarding 'works of the law' – that in that phrase Paul has in mind particularly circumcision, food laws and sabbath, as the characteristic marks of the faithful Jew, so recognized and affirmed by both Jew and Gentile. That exposition was critized by some of those just mentioned (ch. 7, Additional Note, points 6 and 11). And with some justification. In 'The New Perspective' I did not make it clear enough that 'works of the law' do not mean *only* circumcision, food laws and sabbath, but the requirements of the law in general, or, more precisely, the requirements laid by the law on the Jewish people as their covenant obligation and as focused in these specific statutes. I was glad, therefore, to accept an invitation to contribute a paper on Galatians 3 for the Seminar on 'Paul and Israel' at the 1984 SNTS annual meeting, since it gave me the opportunity to clarify my position and to dig its foundations more deeply. (Räisänen made his response to 'The New Perspective' essay at the same seminar.) In this paper (ch. 8 below) I have been able to develop what seems to me the important point regarding 'the social function' of the law – that is, the law functioning to mark out Israel's distinctiveness as the people of God, both in terms of Jewish self-identity (the people who delight and boast in the law – cf. Rom. 2.17–20, 23), and as forming a boundary between Jews (those 'inside the law') and Gentiles (those 'outside the law'). It is within this context that it becomes clear *why* circumcision, food laws and sabbath were in the event so important – precisely as crucial identity and boundary markers. The Additional Note here contains a response to R. Y. K. Fung, and seemed also to be the most suitable place to respond in a little detail to Westerholm.[16]

From this point the line of my research bifurcated. I had intended to review Professor S. Kim's *The Origin of Paul's Gospel* since its first appearance in 1981,[17] and this seemed an opportune time. For not only did Kim's conclusion about the significance of the Damascus road conversion/commissioning for Paul in terms of

4

Christology cut somewhat across my earlier *Christology in the Making*,[18] but also his thesis claimed that Paul's conversion led him to reject the law (Christ as 'the end of the law'). This popular conviction I had in effect been putting to question in my own conclusion that Paul's (explicit) views in Galatians (and Romans) were the result of a period of development, in which the Antioch incident had played an important part. Moreover the study of Galatians 3.10–14 had suggested that the more immediate deduction in Paul's mind, by reason of his conversion/commissioning, was from the cursed but vindicated Jesus to the (with)out-law but now acceptable Gentile (Galatians 3.13–14), rather than to 'the end of the law' which had pronounced such a curse on Jesus. A welcome invitation to contribute to the George Caird memorial volume, with its intended focus on 'the glory of Christ', provided the ideal opportunity to explore this further with special reference to Galatians 1.15–16 (ch. 4 below). The Additional Note here extends the debate to C. Dietzfelbinger, whose study of Paul's calling had focused much more on the issue of the law than Kim's, and, once again, to H. Räisänen, whose own response to Kim also focused on the issue of Paul's view of the law. To highlight this emphasis and to bring out the essay's coherence with the overall theme of this volume of essays I have taken the liberty of modifying the original title by adding a few words.

At the same time I had become uncomfortably aware that the line of my inquiry into Paul and the law was raising increasingly pressing questions about Jesus and the law. I had always wondered at Ernst Käsemann's ability to hold together both the claim that Jesus and Paul had the same attitude to the law and the claim that Paul was not dependent on Jesus on this matter, and had attempted to pin him down on the point during his visit to Nottingham earlier in the 1970s. Unfortunately Professor Käsemann was too tired at the end of a gruelling lecture tour and my German was not equal to the demands of a very technical discussion. Since then the issue had become pressing for me. Clearly the more development one detects, whether in Paul's implicit or only in his explicit view of the law, the more difficult it would be to argue that Paul's full-blown views of the law were just the same as those of Jesus. So, what was the position with regard to Jesus and the law? In particular, it seemed highly significant that key episodes in the Gospels focused on two of the three Jewish distinctives which had assumed such prominence in my earlier studies – food laws and sabbath. In addition, as part of my new lecture load at Durham I was having to prepare lectures on Mark.

In consequence, one of my first projects, as soon as time permitted following the transition to Durham, was a careful study of the traditions preserved in the fascinating section of Mark 2.1–3.6.

5

Here it became evident, on the one hand, that the historical context of and concerns expressed in the episodes were such as we might expect within Palestinian Judaism at the time of Jesus; and on the other, that the communities who preserved these traditions were probably Hellenistic Jewish, evidencing, in other words, a transition phase between Jesus himself and the greater questioning of sabbath laws evident in Paul. Hence the title of the essay (ch. 1 below). In the following year a thorough study of the same section of Mark appeared in the monograph by J. Kiilunen, which runs counter in part to the findings of my Chapter 1. The Additional Note therefore responds to Kiilunen in some detail, and also, once more, to H. Räisänen, whose critique of my essay took Kiilunen's work as his starting-point.

Shortly afterwards, a much appreciated invitation to contribute to the Dom Jacques Dupont Festschrift gave me the opportunity to tackle the still more demanding issue of Mark 7.15 (ch. 2 below). The central problem of this passage is that if Jesus treated the law as Mark 7.15 indicates, then he seems to have been every bit as dismissive of a central element of the law as Paul (the law on clean and unclean foods). In which case the conservatism of the earliest Jerusalem church on the issue (Acts 10.14!) becomes scarcely credible – a point made much of by both Räisänen and Sanders, whose book on *Jesus and Judaism*[19] reached me just in time for me to include an initial reaction to it.[20] Here the key seems to be the recognition that Matthew's and Mark's versions of the tradition are probably *both* legitimate ways of taking Jesus' original words. Which may help explain what would otherwise be the puzzle as to why Paul's view on the matter was not more widely shared. In this case the Additional Note briefly reviews the monograph on the same passage and theme by R. P. Booth, since although Booth was not able to refer to my essay, his findings provide an interesting counterpoint to my own. It also interacts with the more recent essay by B. Lindars.

These essays had involved further debate with Hübner and Räisänen, who had both concerned themselves in this area. But Sanders' new blockbuster, *Jesus and Judaism*, raised many other questions and required a much fuller response than had been possible in Chapter 2. A public debate with Professor Sanders on his book in November 1985 at Birmingham, under the masterful and provocative chairmanship of Michael Goulder, had allowed me only enough time and opportunity to develop a preliminary critique. But his argument, in particular, that there was no significant disagreement between Jesus and the Pharisees, including his radical reassessment of who were the 'sinners' with whom Jesus was associated, would, if true, have undermined any attempt to construct 'a bridge between Jesus and Paul' and thus warranted a much more detailed response. The gladly received invitation to contribute to the Festschrift in honour of Howard Clark Kee provided the opportunity and stimulus.

This essay (ch. 3) comes at the same range of issues from a different angle. But the result is an important insight into the factionalism of the Judaism of Jesus' day, which Sanders has entirely ignored. Equally important, it provides another bridge between Jesus and Paul. For if Jesus broke down the boundaries which factionalism had erected within Israel between the 'righteous' and 'sinners', then it becomes all the more understandable that Paul's encounter with this Jesus should lead him to break down the boundaries between righteous Jew and 'Gentile sinner' (Galatians 2.15–16). Since this essay has only recently appeared the Additional Note refers simply to further literature relevant to its theme. I have expanded my initial critique of Sanders[21] on another major point of disagreement in my contribution to the Festschrift for George Beasley-Murray.[22] But that is on Matthew 12.28/Luke 11.20 and not really on the law; so I have excluded it from this collection.

The final essay (ch. 9) is a revised version of my contribution to the Pauline Theology Group at the SBL Conference in Chicago, November 1988. As part of that valuable ongoing seminar, which is working through the Pauline letters in chronological sequence, it was my brief to write on the theology of Galatians in its own right, without reference to other Pauline texts.[23] This seemed the ideal opportunity to attempt to sum up my work so far on Galatians, so that Chapter 9 provides a natural conclusion to the volume. As the most recent expression of my views, themselves developing as my exegetical inquiry has proceeded, this can be regarded as the clearest expression of where I have so far reached on the question of Paul and the law in Galatians, refining and clarifying, as it does, some of the earlier essays at important points. I wish to express my gratitude to the other members of the Chicago Seminar, particularly my respondent, Lou Martyn, who drew my attention in discussion to various deficiencies of the first draft, which I have attempted to remedy in preparing Chapter 9 for publication. I have also used the opportunity for revision to include more substantial interaction with others who are actively engaged in the debate about Paul and the law, particularly F. Watson and J. M. G. Barclay.[24]

This is not to say that my study of either Galatians or of Paul and the law has come to a conclusion. On the contrary, my work on Romans required a different summing up on the question of Paul and the law as background to the commentary proper.[25] And a paper to the first meeting of the Durham-Tübingen Research Symposium on Earliest Christianity and Judaism in Tübingen in

7

September 1988 gave me a chance to attempt further clarification – with particular reference to Romans 2 this time.[26] Moreover, I am already committed to further work on Galatians, principally for the Black Commentary on Galatians, and for a series on the Theology of the New Testament, which I am editing for Cambridge University Press, and I confess to looking forward to the opportunity of carrying through a sustained exegesis of the letter to see whether and how much of my conclusions so far can be sustained.

Since so much of the last ten years has been spent in friendly and frank debate with Hans Hübner, Heikki Räisänen and Ed Sanders, it gives me a particular pleasure to dedicate the volume to them. I am also grateful to Judith Longman of SPCK for her ready willingness to accept the collection for publication and for her advice on what to include.

James D. G. Dunn
University of Durham
March 1989

Notes

1. e.g. R. J. Banks, *Jesus and the Law in the Synoptic Tradition*, SNTSMS, Cambridge University (1975); C. E. B. Cranfield, 'St Paul and the Law', *SJT* 17 (1964) 43–68; A van Dülmen, *Die Theologie des Gesetzes bei Paulus*, SBM 5, Stuttgart: KBW (1968); O. Kuss, 'Nomos bei Paulus', *MTZ* 17 (1966) 173–226; R. N. Longenecker, *Paul: Apostle of Liberty*, New York: Harper & Row (1964).
2. H. Hübner, *Das Gesetz bei Paulus*, Göttingen: Vandenhoeck (1978, ²1980) = *Law in Paul's Thought*, Edinburgh: T. & T. Clark (1984); note also his earlier *Das Gesetz in der synoptischen Tradition*, Witten: Luther (1973).
3. E. P. Sanders, *Paul and Palestinian Judaism*, London: SCM (1977); also *Paul, the Law, and the Jewish People*, Philadelphia: Fortress (1983).
4. H. Räisänen, *Paul and the Law*, WUNT 29, Tübingen: Mohr (1983); also *The Torah and Christ*, Helsinki: Finnish Exegetical Society (1986), shortly to be published in England by Sheffield Academic Press.
5. R. H. Gundry, 'Grace, Works, and Staying Saved in Paul', *Bib* 66 (1985) 1–38; B. Reicke, 'Paulus über das Gesetz', *TZ* 41 (1985) 237–57; A. J. M. Wedderburn, 'Paul and the Law', *SJT* 38 (1985) 613–22; J. M. G. Barclay, 'Paul and the Law: Observations on Some Recent Debates', *Themelios* 12.1 (1986) 5–15; also *Obeying the Truth: A Study of Paul's Ethics in Galatians*, Edinburgh: T & T. Clark (1988); J. Lambrecht, 'Gesetzesverständnis bei Paulus', *Das Gesetz im Neuen Testament*, ed. K. Kertelge, Freiburg: Herder (1986) 88–127; D. J. Moo, 'Paul and the Law in the Last Ten Years', *SJT* 40 (1987) 287–307; F. F. Bruce, 'Paul and the law in recent research', *Law and Religion. Essays on the Place of the Law in Israel and Early Christianity*, ed. B. Lindars, Cambridge: James Clarke (1988) 115–25; G. Klein, 'Ein Sturmzentrum der Paulusforschung', *Verkündigung und Forschung* 33 (1988) 40–56; T. R. Schreiner, 'The Abolition and Fulfilment of the Law in Paul', *JSNT* 35 (1989) 47–74.
6. S. Westerholm, *Israel's Law and the Church's Faith. Paul and his Recent Interpreters*, Grand Rapids: Eerdmans (1988).

7. J. D. G. Dunn, *Romans*, WBC 38A and 38B, Dallas: Word (1988).
8. London: SCM/Philadelphia: Westminster (1980).
9. See my brief treatment in *Unity and Diversity in the New Testament*, London: SCM/Philadelphia: Westminster (1977) 253–4.
10. O. Hofius, 'Gal. 1.18: ἱστορῆσαι Κηφᾶν', *ZNW* 75 (1984) 73–85.
11. But see N. Walter on p. 128 below and now also P. von der Osten-Sacken, *Die Heiligkeit der Tora. Studien zum Gesetz bei Paulus*, München: Kaiser (1989) 125–6, 129–30, 133.
12. See above, n. 3.
13. See above, n. 3
14. *BJRL* 65.2 (Spring 1983); and below, ch. 7.
15. The point has been acknowledged by Westerholm (above, n. 6), even though the main thrust of his book is directed to a defence of the classic Lutheran position.
16. Above, n. 6.
17. Tübingen: Mohr; subsequently by Eerdmans.
18. Above, n. 8.
19. London: SCM (1985).
20. See below, ch. 2, n. 66.
21. In very brief compass in my review of *Jesus and Judaism* in *JTS* 37 (1986) 510–13.
22. 'Matt. 12.28/Luke 11.20 – a word of Jesus?', *Eschatology and the New Testament. Essays in Honor of George Raymond Beasley-Murray*, ed. W. H. Gloer, Peabody: Hendrickson (1988) 29–49.
23. Other papers each year attempt syntheses of the letters so far examined.
24. F. Watson, *Paul, Judaism and the Gentiles. A Sociological Approach*, SNTSMS 56, Cambridge University (1986), and Barclay, *Obeying* (above, n. 5).
25. Dunn, *Romans*, lxiii–lxxii.
26. J. D. G. Dunn, 'What was the Issue between Paul and "Those of the Circumcision"?', *Paulus als Missionar und Theologe und das antike Judentum*, hrsg. M. Hengel, Tübingen: Mohr (1990).

1
Mark 2.1—3.6: A Bridge between Jesus and Paul on the Question of the Law*

1 PAUL, THE LAW AND THE JESUS-TRADITION

V The problem of continuity between Jesus and Paul is an old one, not least with regard to their respective attitudes towards the law. For example, in a private conversation some years ago Ernst Käsemann maintained a typically provocative position: (1) that Jesus' attitude to the law lies very much at the heart of Jesus' distinctiveness; (2) that Paul's attitude to the law was in fact the same; and (3) that Paul was independent of Jesus at this point. The conversation unfortunately had to end before we could pursue such further questions as whether in that case Paul was as religiously significant (distinctive? unique?) as Jesus. But it highlights an important problem: if Paul's attitude to the law, with its co-ordinate teaching about grace and justification, is central to the Christianity of the Gentile mission, then in what sense or degree is his teaching continuous with or dependent upon the traditions which stemmed from Jesus – if at all?

A large part of the problem, of course, is the difficulty of gaining a clear appreciation of what it is we are comparing. What are the 'attitudes' of Jesus and of Paul to the law? Is Jesus the Jesus of Mark 7, who denies that anything outside a man is able to defile him and who thus defines all foods as clean (Mark 7.15, 18–19)? Or is Jesus the Jesus of Matthew 5, who declares the inviolability of jots and tittles and the importance of even the least commandments (Matt. 5.18–19; 23.23)? Or do both Mark and Matthew present tendentious portraits of Jesus which obscure the 'real' Jesus beyond restoration?

And what of Paul? The traditional Lutheran view portrays Paul in head-on conflict with the law, and speaks of Paul rejecting the law or breaking with the law. But, as Krister Stendahl pointed out,

---

* An earlier draft of this paper was presented to the SNTS Seminar on *Traditionen im Corpus Paulinum* at the University of Kent in August 1983. I wish to express my gratitude to members of the Seminar for their comments on that earlier draft, particularly to Prof. K. Kertelge who made the chief response. I am also grateful to Prof. R. A. Guelich for permitting me to see the first draft of this section of his *Mark*. WBC 34a, Dallas: Word (1989).

this portrayal has been too much influenced by Luther's own experience of grace,[1] set as it was against the background of the medieval Church's doctrine of merits and of salvation as something which could be paid for in instalments. The natural reflex was to read Paul's experience of grace in the light of Luther's, and to identify what Paul rejected with that which Luther rejected. But it has become increasingly apparent in recent years, particularly since E. P. Sanders' *Paul and Palestinian Judaism*,[2] that the stereotype of earning salvation by the merit of good works simply does not fit first-century Judaism; it is an inaccurate summary of the faith of the typical first-century Jew as we know it from other sources. On the contrary, the devout Jew rested on God's choice of his people and understood salvation in terms of the covenant given to Israel with its provision of law to regulate his conduct and of atonement to cover his sins.

If the stereotype of striving for works-righteousness usually drawn from Paul does not fit first-century Judaism, the obvious alternative is to test the reverse correlation: Does the Jewish doctrine of salvation as outlined by Sanders provide a closer 'fit' with the views Paul rejected? I believe the answer is Yes, and have tried to make a beginning to arguing the case in the 1982 Manson Memorial Lecture.[3] My conclusion there is that what Paul was objecting to was not the law *per se,* but the law seen as a proof and badge of Israel's election; that in denouncing 'works of the law' Paul was not disparaging 'good works' as such, but observances of the law valued as attesting membership of the people of God – particularly circumcision, food laws and sabbath. The theological rationale opposed by Paul was straightforward and firmly rooted in the Scriptures: Israel was the elect nation; the covenant promises were given to the decendants of Jacob; forgiveness and atonement were provided for the people of God through the law of Moses. Therefore to be a beneficiary of God's righteousness, the saving acts covenanted to his people, it was necessary to be a member of that covenant people. That meant, in the first place, circumcision – the terms of the covenant with Abraham left no room for dispute about that (Gen. 17.9–14). But membership of the elect people also meant life-long observance of the law, particularly those regulations which characterized and marked out the Jews in their distinctiveness as the people of the one God – among which food laws and sabbath held places of particular prominence both in Jewish self-consciousness and in Greco-Roman perception of the Jews as a people.[4]

It was this understanding of the law from which Paul broke away when he objected to works of the law. That is to say, he objected to works of the law as limiting the grace of God, *not* because they constituted impossible merit-earning demands, but because they

11

were so firmly identified as distinctive marks of the Jewish nation and so in effect confined the grace of God to members of that nation. This is basically the position Paul maintained at and in the light of the Antioch incident (Gal. 2.11–18) and the case he subsequently elaborated in Romans 3—4 and 9—10.[5]

That is the thesis put forward in the Manson lecture noted above (n. 3). It has yet to be scrutinized by my peers, and even if it is basically sound it will have to be established more firmly than I have so far had time to do and will no doubt have to be modified in various ways.

One possible test of the thesis, however, is to examine whether this perspective on Paul makes any better sense of the question of continuity/discontinuity between Jesus and Paul. Is there, in other words, in the Jesus-tradition any indication of a similar or related attitude to the law which might help to explain the background to and possibly also the emergence of Paul's view? There is, after all, a considerable *a priori* plausibility in the working hypothesis that there was *some* bridge between Jesus and Paul, some group of individuals through whom at least some of the Jesus-tradition was mediated to Paul, whether we specify the Hellenists in particular,[6] or include also Peter (Gal. 1.18)[7] and other unnamed disciples. And if we need a test-piece, Mark 2.1—3.6 at once offers itself as a candidate for such an examination: the character and cohesion of Mark 2.1—3.6 as pre-Markan (in large part at least) has long been recognized (though see below); it deals with two issues (table-fellowship and the sabbath law) which we know from Galatians (2.11–18 and 4.10) and elsewhere (particularly Rom. 14) were sensitive issues for the first Christians; and the earlier thesis of H. W. Kuhn has already given grounds for thinking that Mark 2.1—3.6 might well have played a role in expressing Christian views on these issues in the tunnel period between Jesus and Paul's known contribution.[8]

We will begin by briefly reviewing the case for seeing a pre-Markan unit within 2.1—3.6 and the extent of the pre-formed material. We will then focus on the issues at stake in the elements of that pre-formed material and seek to show how well they fit into the pattern of Palestinian Judaism as documented by Sanders. And finally we shall ask whether the pre-Markan unit does indeed fill out our knowledge of the tunnel period between Jesus and Paul. The conclusions which emerge can properly be seen as a refinement of Kuhn's thesis.

2 THE SCOPE OF THE PRE-MARKAN MATERIAL IN MARK 2.1—3.6

While there is widespread agreement as to the pre-Markan nature of the traditions utilized by Mark in 2.1—3.6, there is more dispute about the extent of the Markan redaction, and, more important for present purposes, dispute too about the extent to which these traditions had already been grouped to form a cohesive unit prior to Mark.

2.1 The considerations which point to a pre-Markan unit of greater or less extent can be summarized briefly.

(a) The coherence of the material within 2.1—3.6. All five of the narrative sections focus on controversies between Jesus and his critics, particularly the Pharisees. In all five the principal issue seems to be the authority claimed by Jesus, implicitly or explicitly, in matters of healing and forgiveness, consorting with sinners, fasting and the sabbath, a claim disputed or obviously disallowed by Jesus' critics on legal grounds. The variation in the ways in which both this criticism and the authority of Jesus are expressed in no way lessens but rather enriches the thematic unity of the whole. Moreover, evidence of Markan editorial work on the connecting-links between the narratives is lacking.[9]

(b) Mark 3.6 seems to provide a fitting conclusion to the sequence as a whole. It is not that the verse provides a climax to a steadily mounting spiral of opposition.[10] More to the point is the fact that the earlier confrontations are left in a state of unresolved suspension which only achieves resolution in the dramatically final decision that Jesus must die. This portrayal of Jesus putting forward a series of controversial claims, which result in such a final solution on the part of the guardians of Judaism's religious (and political) heritage, makes 2.1—3.6 a miniature *Vorlage* of Mark's Gospel as a whole, a well-rounded unit of tradition which can quite readily be conceived as having a distinct and separate identity of its own.

(c) Mark has incorporated this unit as a whole even though in doing so he has set up some tension with the rest of his narrative – particularly the sharpness with which the section is set off from its surrounding context where Jesus' popularity with the crowd is stressed by Mark,[11] and the degree of incoherence which results from 2.1 being set immediately after 1.45,[12] the somewhat surprising appearance of the two Son of Man sayings so distinct and isolated from the others used by Mark, and the slight awkwardness of both 2.20 and 3.6 coming so early within the overall development of Mark's 'plot'.

All of which strongly suggests that what we have in 2.1—3.6 (in whole or part) is a thematic unit, rather than a chronologically linked sequence, built up ultimately out of historical memories which probably spanned a much lengthier proportion of Jesus' ministry. The question of what the linking theme was is one we shall have to return to below.

There has, of course, been much dispute on points of detail.

Most would accept, for example, that 2.13–14 were added to the unit subsequent to its formation, probably by Mark himself.[13] Opinions differ regarding 2. 21–22.[14] And there is a continuing debate as to whether all of the verses 2.25–28 were part of the original grouping.[15] None of these issues, however, are determinative for the questions which motivate this enquiry (though see further below §§4.3–4), so we need not attempt a resolution of them before proceeding.

2.2 More important is the debate about larger issues. Was the whole section (2.1–3.6) a completely pre-formed unit before Mark took it over? Or do we need to distinguish more than one redactional layer prior to Mark? For half a century after M. Albertz's initial analysis the tendency was to take 2.1–3.6 as a whole, with the main variation focused on the possibility of discerning a larger block of pre-Markan material of which 2.1–3.6 was only part, with 12.13–17 providing the most obvious further extract.[16] Since then, however, the opposite tendency has predominated, with most commentators concluding that the pre-formed unit is more limited in scope, with either the first or the last of the five episodes, or both, being distinguished from the rest as later additions, probably by Mark himself, who supplemented the smaller block of three or four episodes with other traditional material on his own account.

Kuhn offered the first major refinement of Albertz's earlier thesis, by arguing that the pre-Markan unit comprised only 2.1–28. The fulcrum-point on which the whole discussion swung for Kuhn was 3.6. He accepted the views of those who regarded 3.6 as a redactional formulation of Mark, principally on the grounds that the verse fits well with Mark's special interest in the passion of Jesus.[17] However, the question has to be asked whether consistency with a Markan interest is a sufficient criterion for distinguishing tradition used by Mark from Markan redaction. To which the answer must be, No. On the contrary, precisely such consistency is what Mark would have been looking for in the material he took over, otherwise either he would not have used the material or he would have modified it. Indeed, if anything the reverse would be true: a significant element of tradition might well be expected to have influenced Mark's own perspective and vocabulary in some degree.[18] The question therefore is not one of compatibility with Markan motifs evidenced elsewhere in the Gospel, but whether Mark would have expressed this motif at this point in these terms if he had been an entirely free agent.[19] Nor is it sound analysis to distinguish 3.6 from the preceding narratives because of its 'biographical interest'.[20] A biographical interest, as exemplified in other biographies of the period,[21] cannot be excluded from the

14

preceding narratives; and, as we shall note later, 3.6 is entirely of a piece with these controversy stories in the way it underlines the seriousness of these controversies by highlighting their outcome. The distinctive elements in the vocabulary of v. 6,[22] and the degree of awkwardness in producing such an advanced element in the plot at this early stage, remain, and continue to indicate that Mark was more bound by his tradition at this point than Kuhn allows.[23]

The probability that 3.6 serves as the conclusion to the pre-Markan collection strengthens the likelihood that 3.1–5 was also part of the pre-Markan unit. The fact that the opponents are not identified and their opposition is not expressed in words[24] is of no great significance. Uniformity of form is not a *sine qua non* of any known collection of Jesus-traditions, large or small; form was always determined in greater or less degree by the content of the earliest memories when they came to be formulated. Indeed it is precisely because of what has preceded this episode that the hearer or reader does not require such information about Jesus' critics and their criticism. He knows well who 'they' were (3.2) – the Pharisees, of course (2.16, 18, 24). By this stage the narrator can assume such an understanding. And the echo of 2.24 in 3.4[25] only serves to bind the two sabbath incidents more closely, by underscoring the fact that the issue is the same in each case – what is lawful on the sabbath. To argue that Mark himself was responsible for these links between the two sabbath episodes requires the corollary that Mark was much freer with his tradition at this point than the evidence otherwise indicates. The lack of a more explicit Christological emphasis in 3.1–5, however, is an item to be pondered, and we will return to it (§5).

The most obvious solution to our problem (the extent of the pre-Markan unit), if criteria of form and content were to be strictly applied, is that only the three central episodes are of sufficient homogeneity to be seen as a single piece. In each the opponents are clearly identified as Pharisees. In each the disciples of Jesus are integrally involved. In each the criticism is formulated openly. And in each the issue is one of customary Jewish practice. The first and fifth episodes can then be seen as matching brackets, providing an opening and closing to the smaller unit, since they are of a similarly mixed form (healing and controversy stories), with objection unexpressed, and no mention of the disciples.[26]

However, the case presented above for seeing 3.1–5 and 3.6 as part of the earlier collection weakens this otherwise attractive schema. Even with the parallel between 2.1–12 and 3.1–5, and the link between the two Son of Man references (2.10, 28), 2.1–12 is not so closely integrated with the succeeding episodes as 3.1–5 is with 2.23–8. Moreover, the καὶ γίνεται of 2.15, which may well suggest the beginning of traditional material,[27] and the insertion of

15

2.13–14, both serve to distance 2.1–12 from the traditional unit more than 3.1–5. If anything, the more plausible reconstruction is to recognize the earlier unit as 2.15–3.6, with 2.1–12 added at a later stage, though still quite probably at a stage prior to Mark. The elements within the earlier unit which would have attracted 2.1–12 would be the parallel with 3.1–5 in form and the homogeneity with the other three episodes in overt Christological emphasis.

We will bear this hypothesis in mind as we proceed and see if our further analysis sheds any more light on it or its alternatives.

3 THE *SITZ IM LEBEN* OF THE PRE-MARKAN UNIT – THE LAW AS AN ISSUE

3.1 Why should such a collection of Jesus-traditions be put together? The standard form-critical deduction is that such material was preserved because of its value to the earliest Christian communities. The presumption is that the pre-Markan unit functioned as a mini-manual of instruction for the communities' members and/or as a vehicle or model for their own attempts to explain or defend themselves against criticism from without. Can we be more precise?

It was as an answer to this question that Kuhn's thesis made its most valuable contribution. Kuhn noted that all the episodes (that is, for Kuhn, 2.1–28) have the same *Sitz im Leben* of the *Auseinandersetzung* between church and Judaism. Or, more precisely, the *Sitz im Leben* is an internal dispute within earliest Christianity, a dispute with the Judaism of Jewish Christianity, with the Judaism inside the community.[28] The point comes out most clearly in regard to the pericope on table-fellowship (2.15–17), where the parallel with Galatians 2.11–18 in particular shows that in the most plausible *Sitz im Leben* of the pre-Markan unit the 'sinners' in view would be Gentile Christians (cf. Gal. 2.15). The pericope would therefore be used in reference to the relationship of Jewish Christians with Gentile Christians and as a justification for unrestricted table-fellowship, particularly at the Lord's Supper, within a mixed community.[29]

Here we would have evidence that the Jesus-tradition was used with reference to the kind of questions which played a part in the formulation of Paul's views on the law. The difference of opinion over the scope of the pre-Markan unit (2.1–28 or 2.15–3. 6) does not affect the central thesis itself, though, as we shall see, it has relevance in any attempt to define the tradition-history of the unit more carefully.

3.2 More important, however, is the point that when we view the pre-Markan material in the light of Palestinian Judaism as presented by Sanders, Kuhn's thesis is both illuminated and clarified. This point can quickly be demonstrated. In view of the uncertainty as to whether 2.1–12 belonged to the original pre-Markan unit we will focus the discussion on the other four pericopes. The significant feature in each case is that the pericope affords us an insight into Pharisaic *halakah* at the time of Jesus and the first Christians.

(a) *Mark 2.15–17*. The issue here is what the Pharisees would have seen as Jesus' disregard for the law, in this case the laws governing table-fellowship – particularly clean and unclean foods, tithes, and ritual purity. We know from rabbinic tradition how central these concerns were for the Pharisees already before AD 70.[30] It was just these laws which preserved Israel's holiness as the people of God in the eye of the Pharisees – hence their elaboration of them in their concern to avoid breaching them. And it was disregard for these laws in particular which merited the dismissive and condemnatory epithet 'sinner' from the Pharisees.[31] Jesus in eating with such 'sinners' would be seen by the Pharisees to show the same disregard for these laws. Hence their accusing question: 'Why does he eat with tax collectors and sinners?' (2.16).

(b) *Mark 2.18–20(22)*. The issue here too is the questioners' concern that the law should be complied with as fully as possible. The concern would be the same therefore whether it was a major fast which was in view (e.g. the Day of Atonement or one of the other great fasts), or a personal fast expressing repentance, or the regular weekly fasting practised by the Pharisees (cf. Tob. 12.8; Ps.Sol. 3.9; Matt. 6.16; Luke 18.12).[32] Once again Jesus is shown as coming under fire because of insufficient commitment to and discipline regarding matters which devout Jews of his day evidently saw as important aspects of covenant righteousness, integral elements of the *halakah* which emerged directly from the law of the covenant.[33]

(c) *Mark 2.23–28*. On this occasion the point of friction is the law of the sabbath. The criticism is that Jesus' disciples did what the law forbade for the sabbath – that is, they engaged in reaping and grinding on the sabbath.[34] Presumably, therefore, the Pharisees had already elaborated the basic prohibition against working on the sabbath to cover such transgressions. We need not assume a *halakah* so developed as the fuller elaboration of the Mishnah (*m.Sab*. 7.2 – the prohibition against working· broken down into thirty-nine categories of forbidden actions).[35] We know from Jubilees that concern to protect the sabbath was already well developed more than a hundred years before Jesus (Jub. 2.29–30; 50.6–13), and from the Damascus Document that that concern had already been given a very rigorist interpretation by the time of Jesus (CD 10.14—11.18). The degree of concern and development of *halakah* reflected here is just what we might expect for the less rigorous Pharisees at a stage roughly halfway between Jubilees and the Mishnah.

The point is that so far as the Pharisees were concerned, Jesus' disciples were in breach of the law. For them the sabbath law was a fundamental part of Israel's covenant relationship with God (Exod. 20.8–11; Deut. 5.12–15; Neh. 13.15–22; Ezek. 20.16). Observance of the sabbath was one of the practices which marked Israel out as the peculiar people of the one God (cf. Isa. 56.6; Jub. 2.17–33, particularly vv. 19 and 31). For Jesus to show such disregard for Israel's covenanted obligation was tantamount to denying Israel's election and abrogating the covenant.

(d) *Mark 3.1–5*. The echo of 2.24 in 3.4 reveals not only that the two episodes interlock within the larger unit (2.15—3.6), but also that the issue is the same in each case – what is lawful on the sabbath, what the sabbath law permits and forbids. The Pharisees no doubt already recognized that danger to life overrode the sabbath law (cf. *m.Yoma* 8.6). But the handicapped individual concerned in this instance was evidently in no danger to his life. Consequently a devout Jew able to help the man in his disability could show his respect for the law by delaying his help till the evening or till the following day (cf. Luke 13.14). With such a short delay the man would hardly have been inconvenienced very much. The cause of offence in this case was that Jesus was not willing to show even that fairly minimal level of respect for one of the fundamental laws regulating God's covenant with Israel. (*Mk.2.13*)

We can see then how sharply relevant all these episodes in the Jesus-tradition would have been in the context of first-century Palestinian Judaism as we know it from both Jewish and Christian (and indeed from other Greco-Roman) sources. Each issue as remembered here touched sensitive nerves in the self-understanding of the typical devout Jew of that period – his identity as a member of the people specially chosen by God to be his people, an identity expressed and embodied in his obedience to the law. It is no doubt precisely because Jesus was remembered as challenging that self-understanding of his own people's faith that these incidents were preserved as a single unit. But if that is the case, it means that the issues confronting Jesus with regard to Pharisaic *halakah* were not so very different from those confronting Paul. The possibility that the Jesus-tradition here serves as a bridge between Jesus and Paul becomes still stronger. Can we go further?

4 THE STAGE IN THE CONTROVERSY OVER THE LAW REFLECTED IN THE PRE-MARKAN UNIT

4.1 Still to be clarified are two issues. First, is the pre-Markan unit also a pre-Pauline unit? If the Gospel of Mark reflects in any degree Pauline influence,[36] might the same not be true of the pre-Markan material utilized by Mark? The degree of correlation just noted between the situation confronting Paul and those confronting Jesus in Mark 2.15—3.6 could be explained by the fact that Pauline influence was a factor in both the collection and shaping of the pre-Markan unit. In which case our material ceases to provide a bridge between Jesus and Paul, and our knowledge of Jesus at this point becomes critically obscure.

Second, is Kuhn correct when he argues that the pre-Markan unit reflects an internal dispute within the earliest communities? – a 'dispute of the church with the Judaism within the community'?[37] Who represents 'the church' in this case? – Hellenists, Gentile Christians? If such sharp polarization has already taken place is this not indicative of a situation in which Paul was already active? – as we might say, pre-Markan, but post-Galatians? Or should we speak rather of a controversy between Jewish Christianity and Judaism, as A. J. Hultgren has argued in critique of Kuhn? – on the grounds, particularly, that 'the disciples' are shown as a single group over against the Pharisees, and that a positive evaluation is placed on such 'Jewish' practices as fasting and the sabbath.[38] In which case we are presumably still some distance from Paul in his championing of the rights of Gentile Christians, and our bridge may not stretch quite far enough.

A consideration of the four key sections of the pre-Markan unit with these questions in mind is clearly called for.

4.2 *Mark 2.15–17.* As already noted, the issue here is closely parallel to that confronting Paul at Antioch in Galatians 2.11–18 – the issue of table-fellowship, and the propriety of eating with those regarded by devout Jews as 'sinners' (Gal. 2.15). At the same time, it is generally accepted that the tradition is firmly rooted in the earliest historical memories of Jesus' openness to 'tax collectors and sinners' as expressed particularly in table-fellowship (cf. especially Matt. 11.19/Luke 7.34).[39] It is hard, then, to believe that the memory of such an episode and its accompanying Jesus-saying played no part in the earliest communities' wrestling with the equivalent questions of their own day. Particularly in a situation where 'sinners' was more or less synonymous with 'Gentiles' (Gal. 2.15; cf. Mark 10.33 with 14.41, and Matt. 5.47 with Luke 6.33), the pericope's applicability when the issue of table-fellowship between Jewish and Gentile believers began to emerge as an issue must have been obvious.

On the other hand, it remains a factor of some importance that in this episode and saying only sinners *within* the nation of Israel are in view. However freely creative individuals or groups may have been with regard to the Jesus-tradition, no attempt has been made here to include Gentiles within the 'sinners', and no attempt made to show Jesus at this point eating with Gentiles. However relevant the tradition was to the kind of situation recalled by Paul in Galatians 2.11–18, the needs of such a crisis have not been allowed to determine the form and content of the tradition.

Indeed, in the form in which it was passed down (having only sinners within Israel in view) it was quite possible to interpret the pericope simply as justifying a less scrupulous attitude towards less devout fellow Jews, without necessarily drawing the further conclusion that Jesus thereby dismissed all covenantal distinction between Jew and Gentile (cf. Matt. 10.5–6; 15.24). Moreover, it should be noted that Jesus does not speak of 'the righteous' in a negative or disparaging way.[40] The concern reflected in both episode and saying is not to play down the strength of the Pharisaic commitment to God through the law. The concern of Jesus is rather that their commitment excludes others, that they have restricted God's acceptance to the devout within Israel.

Here then we may say we have an element of the Jesus-tradition which provided a growing point for interpreting the breadth of the gospel of Jesus Christ. As it stands here it emphasizes the breadth of Jesus' appeal to the whole nation, particularly to those regarded as apostates and self-disqualified by the Pharisees – an interpretation strengthened by Matthew's addition of the quotation from Hosea 6.6 (Matt. 9.13), which implies that Jesus' saying is to be understood in alignment with the prophetic criticism of the cult within Judaism. But the saying in Mark also stands open to an interpretation which regarded Jews as 'the righteous' and Gentiles as 'sinners' and which called for an abolition of the distinction through the gospel. At the stage of tradition-history at which this episode was included within the collection of Mark 2.15—3.6 we seem to be nearer the beginning of that process of reinterpretation of the Jesus-tradition. But any group which cherished this collection of Jesus-traditions must have found it invaluable as they wrestled with the questions which the earliest outreach to Gentiles began to pose for Jewish self-understanding as the elect of God.

4.3 *Mark 2.18–22.* The material presented here is striking for the way in which the strong sense of newness, validating departure from old practices, is combined with respect for the practices themselves. 2.18–19 provided the first Christians with sufficient justification for non-fasting. Yet 2.20 clearly implies that the post-Easter communities of Jesus' disciples nevertheless maintained a practice of fasting (cf. Matt. 6.16–18; Did. 8.1).[41] Similarly the two mini-parables of 2.21–22 provide a vivid expression of the tension between old and new. Yet at the same time it would be inaccurate to say that they pose an antithesis between old and new. Indeed, we can even say that the parables show some concern for the preservation of the old – the concern to prevent a worse tear in the old fabric, the concern to preserve wineskin as well as wine. Presumably it was because the two elements (vv. 18–20 and 21–22) exemplify the same tension that they were initially brought together. And since the common factor is tension between old and new rather than antithesis, that linkage probably happened sooner rather than later – at the time when the collection (2.15—3.6) was compiled or even earlier.[42]

At the same time, the material here could obviously be interpreted as having wider relevance than the case in point. Indeed the linking in of the two mini-parables to the particular case of fasting invites hearer and reader to focus on the principle enshrined in these verses – that the coming of Jesus set up a tension between the lifestyle of Jesus' followers and the accepted practices of hallowed tradition. Even though they did not require the saying of Jesus about fasting to justify disregard for the practice of fasting, the sayings of Jesus about fasting, together with his mini-parables about new patches on old cloth and new wine in old wineskins, could serve to justify *other* departures from accepted tradition among the Jewish believers.

So here too there is a degree of ambiguity in the Jesus-tradition on matters of law and traditional *halakah*. Clearly there is preserved here a consciousness of eschatological newness which almost certainly stems from Jesus himself. And also an awareness of a degree of incompatibility between this eschatological new and the traditional old. But the debate is still at the stage of asking how the two can be retained together without the one destroying the other (or both), and there is a concern that the two should somehow coexist – illustrated perhaps also by the Christian communities' readiness to return to the tradition of fasting after Jesus' death (2.20). So here too the addition of this material into the collection 2.15—3.6 seems to mark a fairly early stage in the Christian wrestling with such questions, but the tradition itself could readily be taken to justify a much more radical departure from old patterns and customs hitherto regarded as typical of Jewish piety.

4.4 *Mark 2.23–28.* In both this and the following episode we see a similar tension between an ancient, still-respected national institution and statements of principle which could be interpreted as undermining that institution.

On the one hand, both of these episodes (2.23—3.5) presuppose a life-setting for the tradition in which the significance of the sabbath was still taken for granted. In these accounts it is not yet an issue as to *whether* the sabbath needs to be observed; the issue is rather *how* the sabbath is to be observed, how its significance is to be recognized and expressed – by meeting need and doing good, or by refraining from unnecessary labour. That is to say, they presumably presuppose an early Palestinian setting – before the view expressed in Romans 14.5 (all days are alike) became a factor, and the Sunday a clear alternative to the sabbath. Moreover, since these two episodes provide the climax to the sequence of confrontation stories, the implication must be that the *unit* was put together for the benefit of communities for whom the obligation of the sabbath was still assumed and the only issue was how it should be observed.

On the other hand, verse 27 indicates clearly that a principle was seen to be involved, and not simply an exception to the normally accepted rules governing the sabbath.[43] Jesus is remembered as expressing the principle which governed his attitude to the sabbath law: the sabbath was given for man's benefit, not the other way round. The Pharisees could no doubt express themselves in similar terms (cf. Mekilta on Exod. 31.14); but the fact remains that their way of enjoying the sabbath was through the avoidance of anything that could be called work, with exceptions only envisaged in cases of danger to life.[44] Jesus is remembered as saying something quite different: the incident in the cornfield is not an exception, not even an exception to be justified by exceptional need; rather it is the way in which the sabbath should be observed. To act in that freedom is to express the principle that the sabbath is for man, not man for the sabbath.[45]

The tension is heightened by verses 25–6, whether part of the original pericope or added later (though still probably at the pre-Markan stage). For the citing of a scriptural precedent is typically Jewish, though *haggadic* rather than *halakic* in character;[46] the debate is an 'in-house' debate between Jews. Yet the precedent cited – David eating the bread of the Presence when fleeing from Saul (1 Sam. 21.1–6) – has nothing to do with the sabbath. Matthew evidently felt this lack and added a more appropriate and rabbinically proper precedent for breach of the sabbath law (Matt. 12.5–6).[47] The point of connection was presumably seen to be the disciples' hunger: Jesus citing a precedent in which hunger was regarded as sufficient justification for the breach of important rules governing the cult. The logic seems to be that God regards relief of hunger as more important than cultic propriety. Matthew highlights the point once again by having Jesus cite the further justification of Hosea 6.6 – 'I desire mercy, and not sacrifice'. The fact that different breaches of the law were involved (sabbath, holiness of the cult) was presumably taken as an indication that Jesus was prepared to extend this principle quite far.

The tension is heightened still more by the further incongruity between the cornfield episode and the precedent cited, an incongruity which devout Jews would hardly miss. For both need and justification are out of proportion in the incidents held up for comparison. Compared with the need of David and his followers, the need of Jesus' disciples seems much less weighty – David fleeing for his life, the disciples of Jesus simply on the move from one place to another. And, in 1 Samuel 21 David justifies the use of the bread of the Presence by assuring the priest that he and his followers were in a state of purity (1 Sam. 21.5). The attitude of Jesus as presented in this passage is remarkably casual in comparison, and might well have seemed to most Pharisees quite irresponsible. The implication is probably sound, therefore, that the principle encapsulated here was understood not simply as human need justifying an occasional breach of laws which otherwise retained validity. Rather the point seems to be more about the liberty of the new age of God's favour: in the new age brought in by Jesus, faith and piety are not bound to or dependent on such rulings. The community which treasured such a story must have felt justified in exercising a considerable liberty with respect to the sabbath and other important matters of Pharisaic *halakah*.

Here then is an important statement on a matter which must have exercised the Christian communities even before the Gentile mission and the more libertarian attitudes of Romans 14.5 appeared. It is hard to believe that such a tradition did not influence attitudes as the Christian mission spread outwards; on the contrary, treasured no doubt for its continuing relevance, it must surely have prepared the way for the acceptability within Christian circles for just such a discounting of all holy days as we find in Romans 14.5. The sensitivity of the Jewish churches on the issue is probably indicated by Matthew's omission of verse 27, so that all told the liberty expressed in the episode is aligned with prophetic emphases already within the scriptures (Hos. 6.6) and limited to the Christological assertion of the Son of Man's lordship over the sabbath.

4.5 *Mark 3.1–5.* A similar point of principle lies at the heart of the final episode. In it Jesus responds to the test case of performing an unnecessary healing in breach of the sabbath by challenging the understanding of the sabbath presupposed by the critical onlookers. As verse 4 sums it up, the question for Jesus was whether doing something which is obviously good can be ruled out on the sabbath, whether saving life should be treated as merely an exception for the sabbath.

The implication of the encounter is that Jesus was remembered as approaching the whole question of sabbath law from a quite different angle from the Pharisees – and by extension, not only the sabbath law, but the law as a whole.[48] The Pharisees saw the law as having a first claim on the good Jew – the law being the God-given rule for life within the covenant. Where particular laws seemed to be in conflict, the concern must be to resolve the conflict without damage to the law. But the Jesus-tradition here enshrines a case where basic human relationships were being hindered rather than helped by giving the law priority over human need. For Jesus there was evidently a higher responsibility than the sabbath law – his obligation to help someone in need whose need he could meet. In short, the episode illustrates how Jesus extracted from the breadth of the law one overriding principle – love your neighbour; and, by implication, he resisted any tendency to expand that principle into a multiplicity of specific rulings.

In preserving this account, the Christian groups who did so indicate to us that they wanted to follow Jesus by living in accord more with this principle than in terms of multiplied *halakoth*. In some contrast, Matthew shows himself to be less sympathetic to such freedom from particular laws, for he replaces Jesus' statement of principle with a more rabbinic argument (Matt. 12.11–12). That is to say, instead of an open-ended principle he cites a specific case (a sheep falling into a pit on the sabbath) and argues in good rabbinic style *a minori ad maius*. By implication then Mark preserves the tradition more in the form in which the story would have been told in the Hellenistic churches from which Paul emerged.

4.6 We can now answer the questions posed at the beginning of this section (§4.1) with some confidence. In the first place, there are good grounds for concluding that the material in 2.15—3.6 was brought together at a pre-Pauline stage – that is, before the issues which Paul confronted and answered had surfaced. Above all, we have the clear implication that the pre-Markan unit was primarily servicing an internal Jewish discussion. Respect for traditional Jewish praxis is still prominent (fasting, old garment/wineskin, sabbath), even though points of principle are raised which, from a later perspective, almost inevitably undermined that praxis. At the stage of the pre-Markan unit's formation, however, the extent of these principles' application and the degree of undermining involved was far from clear. Matthew's use of the same tradition taken over from Mark is sufficient indication that the discussion of such questions was by no means curtailed by Mark's use of the pre-formed unit.

Secondly, we can now see that both Kuhn and Hultgren are partially right and partially wrong. The pre-Markan unit does not yet clearly envisage a Gentile dimension to the controversies and principles presented; there is no indication that the pre-Markan unit as such had been formed or taken over by Gentile Christians

24

to serve as ammunition in a Gentile–Jew confrontation. Yet, at the same time, it is difficult to see here simply the apologetic tool of a united Jewish Christian community against pre-70 Pharisaism. There is sufficient indication in the tensions within the pericopes, confirmed also by the Matthean redaction, that the internal Jewish debate was also an internal Jewish Christian debate, that while the unit would serve as Jewish Christian apologetic over against non-Christian Jews, it would also function as a crucial 'text' in the Jewish Christians' attempt to formulate their own self-identity. Indeed we can go so far as to say that the formation of the pre-Markan unit probably reflects a stage within the maturing Jewish Christian self-understanding, within the Jewish Christian attempt to achieve self-definition, where the interpretation of the tradition could either stay within the terms provided by covenant and law, however radical and eschatological that interpretation might otherwise be, or could move firmly in the direction of Paul, the spokesman for the Gentiles.

5 A SECOND STAGE IN THE TRADITION-HISTORY OF THE PRE-MARKAN UNIT?

Before summing up and drawing any further conclusions we should pause to follow through an immediate corollary which bears upon the issue of whether 2.1–12 formed part of the original unit.

5.1 The immediate corollary is that it was primarily concern about the law and the Pharisaic *halakah* which motivated the linking of the four episodes in 2.15—3.6. The unifying thread is the issues posed, the example given, the principles enacted by Jesus in a sequence of confrontations with the chief exponents of the law in its bearing on members of the people of God. That conclusion seems to be at odds with the complete sequence of controversy stories as we now have it in 2.1—3.6. There the predominant emphasis seems again and again to be Christological – particularly Jesus' ability to read men's thoughts, his power as the Son of Man to forgive sins, his mission to call sinners, the warning of the bridegroom's impending departure, and his authority as the Son of Man over the sabbath. Should we not say, then, that the primary unifying thread is the Christology embodied in these episodes?

Several factors, however, point away from the deduction: (1) There is no particular pattern to the Christological emphases in the unit, whereas the common themes and tensions of 2.15—3.6 serve to bind these pericopes closely together. (2) An overt Christological thrust is lacking altogether in the concluding episode (3.1–5), however much it may be implicit.[49] This was one of

25

the factors which led Kuhn and others to omit 3.1–5 from the pre-Markan unit. Likewise it is the viewing of 3.6 from such a Christological perspective which justifies it being set aside as too 'biographical' (see above n. 20). But when Jesus' controversy with the Pharisees over Torah and *halakah* is seen to be the unifying theme, 3.1–5 can easily be seen to fit well with the preceding three episodes, and 3.6 fits too as showing the seriousness and fundamental sharpness of the controversy, since it was an immediate cause of Jesus' rejection and death. Seen thus, 3.6 is a fitting conclusion to a unit (2.15—3.6) with a relatively limited scope and purpose.[50] (3) There is some possibility that the Christology of 2.15—3.6, as it now stands, became more overt or was given sharper profile in the course of the material's tradition-history. This possibility is clearest with respect to 2.28: it may well have exemplified an original non-titular *bar 'enasa* usage ('. . . so that the son of man [= eschatological? man] is lord of the sabbath'), which has been transformed into a Christological title in the course of the tradition process.[51]

This, of course, is not to say that there was no Christological content in the earliest form of these traditions, or that there was no Christological concern in the initial linking of these traditions. On the contrary, the authority claimed by Jesus provided one pole of the controversy. It was precisely because Jesus himself provoked such controversy, and raised such points of principle on the basis of his own conception of his mission, that such fundamental questioning of Jewish (or Jewish Christian) self-identity could arise. It was the eschatological newness which he himself embodied in his own praxis and teaching which made such a radical reappraisal necessary for his disciples. The character of the pre-Markan unit itself constitutes an appeal to Jesus as the primary normative authority. Nevertheless, all that being true, the point still remains that it was not primarily a Christological concern to present Jesus as the bridegroom,[52] or as the Messiah of David's line,[53] or as the Son of Man[54] which binds the pre-Markan unit together. The linkage is controversy over points of law and *halakah,* the controversy initiated by Jesus and still troubling his disciples. Thus the Christological emphasis on Jesus' authority is fundamental to the controversy collection, but is is the *controversy,* remembered and still continuing, which occasioned the drawing together of the pre-Markan unit. Too much emphasis on the Christology of the material at the Markan level should not be permitted to obscure this point so basic to any clear understanding of the scope and function of the pre-Markan unit.

5.2 What of 2.1–12? The more this discussion has continued, the more distinctive 2.1–12 appears. For here the issue is not a point of *halakah*: as the pericope now stands the issue is authority to forgive sins. And the focal point is the Christological assertion that Jesus laid claim to and enacted such authority. One might argue that according to 2.5 the issue was the right to declare sins forgiven (divine passive),[55] outside the cult, without reference to the usual means of forgiveness laid down in the law and enacted by the priest.[56] Also the case could again be made that underlying the titular Son of Man lay a non-titular *bar 'enasa* form, of much less clear-cut Christological force.[57] But even so, it is impossible to soften the Christological force of 2.7 and 10: Jesus is able and has authority to forgive sins, not merely to declare them forgiven. In other words, in so far as 2.1–12 is linked with 2.15—3.6 it is clearly the Christology which provides the link. It is not possible to uncover a form of the story where the issue is a point of *halakah*.[58]

∨ The possibility which emerges from all this (I put it no more strongly than that), is that two levels or stages of tradition-history can be discerned within the unit 2.1—3.6. The first stage would have been the grouping of 2.15—3.5, with the conclusion of 3.6 added, both to show how Jesus' controversies with the Pharisees resulted in a final breach between Jesus and the guardians of Israel's heritage, and to provide guidance and authoritative tradition for very early Jewish Christian attempts to find their own identity over against the same guardians of Israel's heritage. The second stage would have been greater concentration on the Christological emphases in the same stories as a result of which or as part of which 2.1–12 was added. Since this suggestion does not bear directly upon the principal thesis of this paper I need speculate no further. It is enough for present purposes that we have demonstrated sufficient grounds for setting 2.1–12 to one side and for focusing on the controversies over points of law and *halakah* which bonded 2.15—3.6 into the pre-Markan unit.

∨ 6 CONCLUSIONS

6.1 The grouping of these four Jesus-traditions affords us a fascinating glimpse into the early history and development of Jewish Christianity. For the four episodes must have been put together by followers of Jesus concerned to understand the bearing of such controversies between Jesus and the Pharisees on their own faith and life. The collection must have been particularly valued by those Jewish believers in Messiah Jesus who began to wrestle seriously with the possibility and implications of an outreach beyond the confines of Palestine and of the covenant people as such. In such circumstances these episodes and sayings of Jesus would have been treasured not so much because of particular points of practice, valuable as these were, but because of the

27

attitude of Jesus to the law which they enshrine – that is, Jesus' attitude to features of Israel's faith and life which expressed the devout Jew's conviction and assurance of Israel's election and of God's continuing covenanted favour towards his people – purity of food and table, the fundamental importance of the sabbath, and tension between the eschatological new and traditional old in such matters as fasting.

In these traditions the attitude of Jesus to the law is not so very different from that of Paul. The chief difference is that by the time Paul wrote Galatians the issue of Gentile membership of God's people had come to the fore, and the principal focus of dispute had become circumcision, the even more basic mark of the covenant. But the fundamental issue remained the same – what Sanders calls 'covenantal nomism', that is obedience to the law as the primary distinguishing mark of the people of God. And within these different contexts both Jesus and Paul give the same answer – No: the primary distinguishing marks of those favoured by God are faith and love. Paul in effect was arguing for an extension of the principles Jesus enunciated, as documented in the pre-Markan unit 2.15—3.6.

6.2 Can we therefore be more precise with regard to the life-setting of the original unit grouping the Jesus-traditions of Mark 2.15—3.6? (1) The unit is clearly pre-Pauline in its scope. No questions regarding circumcision or Gentiles are included. It is still an internal Jewish dialogue. The presuppositions are still clearly Jewish, and the stage which the discussion of these particular issues has reached seems to be earlier rather than later. Any line of influence between Paul and the Jesus-traditions at this point, therefore, more probably runs from the Jesus-tradition to Paul than vice-versa. (2) On the other hand, the episodes clearly illustrate a liberty with regard to the law which seems to be at some remove from the piety of the Jerusalem-based believers (cf. Acts 11.2–3; 21.20). Those who cherished such traditions were evidently wrestling with questions of law and *halakah* in a way which seems to anticipate Paul to at least some degree. Not least of significance is the fact that Matthew in writing for a more consistently Jewish audience of Christian believers takes such care to stifle or diminish some of the more radical implications which follow from the Markan form of the tradition.

If these observations are sound, we are driven to hypothesize a Hellenistic-Jewish Christian life-setting. It is likely indeed that the grouping of traditions preserved in Mark 2.15—3.6 was first put together as an aid to those Hellenistic-Jewish Christian communities which were beginning to wrestle with questions of law and *halakah* for themselves. What bearing did the Jesus-tradition have on such issues? The grouping of the four episodes from Jesus' ministry provided a very pertinent answer.

6.3 Why did Paul not cite such a Jesus-tradition in his own disputes? Possibly because Jewish presupposition still determined the formulation of the tradition, and the principles enshrined were not entirely clear-cut (as Matthew's redaction reminds us); as already noted, what Paul was arguing for was in effect an extension of those principles. Possibly also because at the stage where the issue arose most sharply for Paul (around the time he wrote Galatians) it was a point of principle for him to rest his primary authority on the revelation given him directly, rather than on the tradition received from Peter and others (Gal. 1).

There is no evidence, then, that the traditions behind Mark 2.15—3.6 influenced Paul directly. Yet we do well to recall that Paul was not the first to break through the Jewish presuppositions in terms of which the gospel was initially expressed. Indeed Paul, we might say, was only consolidating and extending the earlier breach achieved by the unknown Hellenists who first took the gospel to the Gentiles at Antioch without requiring circumcision or the yoke of the Torah (Acts 11.19–26). Surely the tradition behind Mark 2.15–3.6 must have had some influence on the thinking and vision of these unknown precursors of Paul. Without such authorization from the Jesus-tradition it is difficult to see how such a departure gained the acceptance it did within the earliest Christian communities of Palestine. At the very least, then, we can say that the initial collection of the Jesus-traditions preserved in Mark 2.15—3.6 indicates the way the collectors were thinking and explains how it was that the Hellenists could make such a radical departure from traditional Judaism in the name of Jesus.

In short, the tradition behind Mark 2.15—3.6 provides an invaluable bridge between Jesus and Paul and shows a little of the development in Christian thinking on the law which must have prepared the way for the decisive contribution of Paul.

Notes

1. K. Stendahl, 'The Apostle Paul and the Introspective Conscience of the West', *HTR* 56 (1963), pp. 199–215; reprinted in his *Paul Among Jews and Gentiles* (SCM 1977), pp. 78–96.
2. SCM 1977.
3. 'The New Perspective on Paul', *BJRL* 65 (1983), pp. 95–122 (ch. 7 below), in which Sanders' findings are referred to more fully.
4. For documentation on these points I must refer to my 'The Incident at Antioch (Gal. 2.11–18)', *JSNT* 18 (1983), pp. 3–57, particularly pp. 12–25 (ch. 6 below); also 'New Perspective' (n. 3) pp. 107–9 (ch. 7 below).
5. See further chs. 8 and 9 below, and my Introduction.
6. cf. the conclusion of M. Hengel: 'We owe the real bridge between Jesus and Paul to those almost unknown Jewish-Christian "Hellenists" of the group

around Stephen ...; this was the first to translate the Jesus traditions into Greek and at the same time prepared the way for Paul's preaching of freedom by its criticism of the ritual law and the cult' ('Zwischen Jesus und Paulus', *ZTK* 72 [1975], p. 206; ET in Hengel, *Between Jesus and Paul* [SCM 1983], p. 29). This essay is also in effect an attempt to fill out Hengel's claim from within the Jesus-tradition itself.

7. See my 'The Relationship between Paul and Jerusalem according to Galatians 1 and 2', *NTS* 28 (1982), pp. 461–78, particularly pp. 463–6 (ch. 5 below, particularly pp. 110–113).

8. H. W. Kuhn, *Ältere Sammlungen im Markusevangelium* (Vandenhoeck 1971), pp. 53–98.

9. V. Taylor, *The Gospel according to St Mark* (Macmillan 1952), p. 92; N. Perrin, *The New Testament: an Introduction* (Harcourt 1974), p. 145.

10. Kuhn (n. 8) pp. 20f., against particularly M. Albertz, *Die synoptischen Streitgespräche* (Trowitzsch 1921), pp. 5–16.

11. J. Dewey, *Markan Public Debate: Literary Technique, Concentric Structure, and Theology in Mark 2.1—3.6,* SBL Dissertation Series 48 (Scholars 1980), pp. 17, 42, 54.

12. Even if Mark is responsible for specifying the location (Capernaum), as, e.g., R. Bultmann maintains (*The History of the Synoptic Tradition* [ET Blackwell 1963], pp. 64, 340–1), the following story implies an event which took place in a centre of population, and it is this fact which causes the slight jarring with 1.45.

13. See, e.g., A. J. Hultgren, *Jesus and his Adversaries* (Augsburg 1979), p. 161; E. Best, *Following Jesus: Discipleship in the Gospel of Mark, JSNTSupp.* 4 (Sheffield University 1981), p. 175.

14. cf., e.g., Hultgren (n. 13) p. 161 and n. 55 and R. Pesch, *Das Markusevangelium. 1. Teil* (Herder ²1977), p. 170.

15. See particularly F. Neirynck, 'Jesus and the Sabbath: Some Observations on Mark 2.27', in *Jésus aux Origines de la Christologie,* ed. J. Dupont (Leuven 1975), pp. 227–70, especially pp. 254–68.

16. See Kuhn's brief survey (n. 8) pp. 22–3; Dewey (n. 11) p. 47.

17. Kuhn (n. 8) pp. 19–20.

18. πῶς αὐτὸν ἀπολέσωσιν in 11.18 might well be an echo of ὅπως αὐτὸν ἀπολέσωσιν in 3.6, as Kuhn acknowledges (p. 20 n. 46).

19. These methodological considerations apply with equal force to Dewey's attempt (n. 11) to argue against the existence of a Markan unit.

20. Bultmann (n. 12) p. 12.

21. G. N. Stanton, *Jesus of Nazareth in New Testament Preaching* (Cambridge University 1974), ch. 5, especially p. 122.

22. Pesch (n. 14) pp. 195–6.

23. See also Taylor (n. 9) pp. 220–1; K. Kertelge, *Die Wunder Jesu im Markusevangelium* (Kösel 1970), p.83; and on the Herodians (3.6) Hultgren (n.13) pp.154–6.

24. Kuhn (n. 8) p. 88.

25. 2.24 – τί ποιοῦσιν τοῖς σάββασιν ὃ οὐκ ἔξεστιν;
3.4 – ἔξεστιν τοῖς σάββασιν ἀγαθὸν ποιῆσαι ...

26. So J. Gnilka, *Das Evangelium nach Markus 1. Teil.* (EKK 1978) pp. 131–2.

27. Pesch (n. 14) p. 164 and n. 2.

28. Kuhn (n. 8) pp. 82–5.

29. Kuhn (n. 8) pp. 91–5.

30. See particularly J. Neusner, *From Politics to Piety* (Prentice-Hall 1973), pp. 80, 83–90, and further ch. 3 below.

31. See my 'Antioch Incident' (n. 4) pp. 27–8, and further ch. 3 below.

32. See further I. Abrahams, *Studies in Pharisaism and the Gospel* (First Series, Cambridge University 1917), pp. 121–8; Strack-Billerbeck IV pp. 77–114.

33. If the references to the Pharisees were inserted into an original tradition of comparison simply between the disciples of the Baptist and the disciples of

Jesus, as is quite possible, the insertion must have taken place at the stage when the tradition was meshed into the other traditions to form the complete unit – Taylor (n. 9) p. 210; E. Schweizer, *Das Evangelium nach Markus* (NTD 1), 1967, p. 36.

34. Taylor (n. 9) p. 215.
35. As a too casual reference to the rabbinic evidence like that of Taylor (n. 9) might imply.
36. See particularly Schweizer (n. 33) pp. 210–14; R. P. Martin, *Mark: Evangelist and Theologian* (Paternoster 1972), pp. 156–62.
37. Kuhn (n. 8) p. 85.
38. Hultgren (n. 13) pp. 162–5.
39. See particularly J. Jeremias, *New Testament Theology, Vol. I: The Proclamation of Jesus* (ET SCM 1971), pp. 118–21; but also ch. 3 below.
40. H. Kruse, 'Die "Dialektische Negation" als semitisches Idiom', *VT* (1954), pp. 385–400. On the historicity of the saying within Jesus' ministry see e.g. Taylor (n. 9) pp. 207–8; Pesch (n. 14) pp. 167–8.
41. We need not discuss here the ultimate origin of vv. 19b–20 or the intended reference of 'on that day'.
42. cf., e.g., the views of Kuhn (n. 8) pp. 71–2; Schweizer (n. 33) pp. 36–7; Pesch (n. 14) p. 177; Gnilka (n. 26) p. 111.
43. I assume, with most commentators who address the quesion of the pre-Markan unit, that v. 27 at least was attached to vv. 23–4 by the time the sequence of controversy episodes was put together.
44. Strack-Billerbeck I p. 623; II p. 5.
45. I need not go into the relation of v. 28 to v. 27, which complicates the point being made here but does not diminish it (cf. n. 51 below).
46. D. Daube, *The New Testament and Rabbinic Judaism* (Athlone 1956), pp. 67–71; D. M. Cohn-Sherbok, 'An Analysis of Jesus' Arguments concerning the Plucking of Grain on the Sabbath', *JSNT* 2 (1979), pp. 31–41.
47. See the discussions in n. 46 above.
48. cf. L. Goppelt, *Theology of the New Testament*, Vol. I (ET Eerdmans 1981), pp. 93–5.
49. But see Goppelt (n. 48).
50. Against Dewey (n. 11) p. 47.
51. cf. e.g. J. Roloff, *Das Kerygma und der historische Jesus* (Vandenhoeck 1970), pp. 61–2; G Vermes, *Jesus the Jew* (Collins 1973), pp. 180–1. We should note that the transition to a titular sense need not have coincided with translation of the Jesus-tradition from Aramaic to Greek, however much the unfamiliarity of the form in Greek may (must) have helped forward the process.
52. Since there is no real indication that Judaism had already used the image of the bridegroom for any messianic figure, probably the eschatology of 2.19 was originally more to the fore than the Christology as such (see J. Jeremias, *TDNT* IV pp. 1101–3; also *The Parables of Jesus* [ET SCM revised 1963], p. 52).
53. Despite particularly Roloff (n. 51), pp. 56–8, there is no clear indication of any desire to equate David and Jesus – for, apart from anything else, it was the disciples and *not* Jesus who plucked the grain, whereas it was David and *not* his followers who took the bread of the Presence.
54. See above n. 51 and below n. 57.
55. See e.g. Jeremias (n. 39) p. 114.
56. cf. Kuhn (n. 8) p. 56, n. 20; E. P. Sanders, *Jesus and Judaism* (SCM 1985). pp. 206–7, 273–4.
57. Most recently B. Lindars, *Jesus Son of Man* (SPCK 1983), pp. 44–7.
58. If 2.5b–10 are to be regarded as redactional – so Bultmann (n. 12) pp. 14–15; Taylor (n. 9) p. 191; Gnilka (n. 26) p. 96 – the links which might be said to be bind 2.1–12 to 2.15—3.6 vanish completely.

Additional Note

The most significant treatment of Mark 2.1—3.6 since the publication of the above article has been the thorough and well-argued thesis of J. Kiilunen, *Die Vollmacht im Widerstreit. Untersuchungen zum Werdegang von Mk 2.1—3.6*.[1] Its central purpose is to examine the various hypotheses of a pre-Markan collection and its principal conclusion is that, although Mark was drawing on older material, there was *no* pre-Markan collection. Rather it is Mark himself who brought the material together (the five pericopes) and gave the section its thematic unity within the larger context of his Gospel as a whole.

Since Räisänen has made Kiilunen the basis of his brief critique of my argument in Chapter 1 (see below) it is necessary to pay some attention to Kiilunen's discussion, at least to the extent that it bears on the argument of Chapter 1 above.

1. Kiilunen puts considerable weight on his demonstration of the coherence of 2.1—3.6 within the context of the Gospel. (a) He denies (pp. 28–30) that there is any jarring between 1.45 and 2.1, since the implication is that Jesus entered Capernaum οὐ φανερῶς, δι' ἡμερῶν, and since 2.1–2 fits well with 1.33. Nevertheless some jarring remains. 1.45 envisages a level of popularity which made it necessary for Jesus to remain 'outside in deserted places'; whereas the next two episodes are set in areas of population (2.1ff., 15ff.). In contrast, there is no such jarring in Mark's later equivalent summary or linking passages (3.7–12; 6.53–6). The implication remains strong that had Mark been solely responsible for the connection between 1.45 and 2.1–2 it would not have been so awkward.

(b) Kiilunen's argument almost wholly depends on his thesis regarding 3.6, so great weight is put by Kiilunen on his conclusion that it is redactional (pp. 250–1, 259–61). Certainly he succeeds (pp. 35–49) in showing how well it fits into Mark's passion theme (cf. particularly 11.18, 12.12 and 14.1), though otherwise he recognizes how evenly balanced the arguments are (pp. 230–2). But he does not really move the argument beyond what was discussed briefly above (pp. 14–15 = *NTS*, p. 399), and the awkwardness of such an advanced element of the plot (cf. precisely 11.18, 12.12 and 14.1!) remains.

2. Kiilunen's discussion of the relationship of 2.9 and 10 strengthens the likelihood of an early form of 2.1–12, less Christological in focus (pp. 108–10), but otherwise makes little difference to the conclusion drawn in Chapter 1 above.

3. On 2.15–17, Kiilunen recognizes the Palestinian Jewish context, and though he tries to drive a wedge between 2.17b and 17c, once 2.16b has been reckoned as part of the pericope's 'raw material', the point fundamental to my reconstruction of the *Sitz im Leben* of the original form has been granted. He himself argues that 2.17c ('I came not to call the righteous, but sinners') is a refutation of the Jewish 'pure community' ideal (p. 161). But once it is recognized that the purity of the meal table was a key factor in that ideal (cf. Qumran and ch. 1, n. 30 above), and that 'sinner' was precisely the epithet which many Pharisees would use for those who made light of such concerns (see ch. 3 below), the logic of the argument developed above (pp. 19–20 = *NTS*, pp. 404f.) retains its force.[2]

4. The discussion of 2.18–20 (Kiilunen, ch. IV.3) surprisingly takes no account of the tradition preserved in Matthew 11.18–19//Luke 7.33–5 (or Matt. 11.16–19//Luke 7.31–5), with its confirmative testimony that Jesus' 'celebratory' lifestyle was seen to contrast with John the Baptist's asceticism and drew forth negative comment on Jesus' frivolity or lack of spiritual seriousness. This provides a more realistic historical context for a basic unit consisting of 2.18–19, to which 2.20 was subsequently added for obvious reasons (Jewish Christians who drew the conclusion that fasting was appropriate now that the bridegroom was absent), in contrast to Kiilunen's more strained attempts to find a context for an original unit consisting of 2.19–20 (an antithetical proverb). This in turn strengthens the conclusion that basic to the unit is the issue of comparison and contrast between Jesus' disciples and more traditional Jewish praxis. But even if we were to accept that 2.19–20 points to an earlier intra-Christian discussion, the fact remains that as soon as 2.18 is added the issue becomes one of Christian explaining and defending Christian practice over against Jewish, so that the unit functions as an intra-Jewish (Christian and non-Christian Jews) dispute about *halakah* (see further above pp. 20–21 = *NTS*, pp. 405–6).

5. On 2.23–8 Kiilunen concludes that the earliest unit, 2.23–6, was used by the Jewish Christian church in defending its free-er sabbath practice over against Pharisaic sabbath *halakah*. 'What is proclaimed is not freedom *from* the sabbath, but freedom *on* the sabbath' (p. 220). Here again we are in cordial agreement. Kiilunen however thinks that verse 27 was added by Mark and that verse 28 is a Markan creation.

As to verse 27, καὶ ἔλεγεν αὐτοῖς does look to be typically Markan (pp. 206–7); but the hypothesis of a free-floating saying (v. 27) which stems from a quite different but unrecalled sabbath controversy (p. 217) seems rather strained, particularly as the attitude to the sabbath in verse 27 is the same (above pp. 21–3 = *NTS*, pp. 406–7). It is more likely that verse 27 was already attached to the preceding episode at an early Palestinian-Jewish Christian stage of the tradition than that verses 23–6 functioned on their own, a rather unfinished torso, or that Mark (writing when freedom *from* the sabbath was more the issue) should have first made the link. If we have to weigh stylistic considerations against *Sitz im Leben* considerations, the latter seems to be more persuasive here and the former can be accounted for readily enough by assuming Markan editing *within* preformed material (cf. after all the typically Markan εὐθύς, and Kiilunen's own findings with regard to 3.1–6).

As to verse 28, Kiilunen does not really address the issue of whether 'the son of man' there originated from *bar 'enasa* = 'man', 'eschatological man', or 'a human being like me' (above p. 26 = *NTS*, p. 410). In that case verse 28 too would stem from pre-Markan tradition, and it becomes highly plausible to see verse 28 as already the conclusion to the whole pericope at a later, but still pre-Markan stage. To be noted now is the article by P. M. Casey,[3] who demonstrates how well the whole episode goes back into Aramaic more or less as it stands, and also that the controversy is intelligible only if we make assumptions which would have been normal for a Jew in Palestine. Since the question of how the sabbath should be observed was not a major flashpoint in early church disputes, Casey justifiably concludes that 'the only feasible *Sitz im Leben* for this dispute is in the life of Jesus' (pp. 20–21). Contrast D. J. Doughty,[4] who works too exclusively at the level of Markan redaction and who fails to allow methodologically for a distinction between Markan 'composition' and Markan use or adaptation of older material.

6. Kiilunen rightly concludes that the earliest *Sitz im Leben* of 3.1–5 is early Jewish Christian self-defence against Pharisaic sabbath *halakah* (pp. 244–8), against the hypothesis of J. Sauer,[5] that the passage reflects *Gentile* Christian opposition to Jewish *Christians*. However, he also sees considerable Markan redaction without giving enough weight to the indications that the two sabbath episodes interlock: particularly the tie-in between 2.24 and 3.4 (which Kiilunen sees as the core of the tradition),[6] and the fact that the opponents of verse 2 do not need to be identified since it can be assumed they are the same as in the previous episode (2.24); whereas Kiilunen's reconstruction of a pre-Markan unit (lacking 3.2) leaves the question of 3.4 wholly in a void. Such a *reductio ad absurdum* conclusion should be recognized as evidence that too much weight is being given to methodologically questionable evidence of redaction.

7. Kiilunen's conclusion (pp. 249–66) is that although there is evidence of a lengthy process of tradition-history in the individual pericopes, and although some of them share a very similar *Sitz im Leben*, the exegetical evidence of redaction points too firmly to Markan editing as that which bound the units together in the first place.

(a) I naturally welcome the extent of our agreement: my suggestion that the material reflects a stage within 'maturing Jewish Christian self-understanding' 'can be considered as right (*zutreffend*)' (pp 256f., n. 24). But the point goes further. For even on Kiilunen's reconstruction, the last four units of 2.1–3.6 are all in one degree or other, and at one stage or other in their pre-Markan form, attempts by Jewish Christians to explain and defend their lifestyle over against criticism from within Judaism. Since Mark himself reflects a much sharper breach of Christianity from traditional Judaism (cf. only 7.19), that must mean that all these pericopes provide evidence of similar attempts of early Jewish Christianity to achieve self-definition in relation to traditional Judaism (see further below).

(b) The coherence of these four pericopes as reflecting 'a stage of maturing Jewish Christian self-understanding' *prior* to the stage of Mark himself suggests a grouping of these pericopes for mnemonic or apologetic or catechetical purposes prior to Mark.[7] It is highly unlikely that the teachers in the early congregations, upon whom lay the responsibility for retaining and retelling the community's oral tradition, would have remembered it all in a random series of individual forms. Much more probable that they grouped the individual traditions and strung them together in a connected way and retold many of them with a sense of their dramatic character. Despite Kiilunen, the degree to which 2.1—3.6 fits that very plausible *Sitz im Leben* is too strong to be set aside. We need not assume that such groupings and retellings of the tradition were independent of other groupings. Of a surety, there were not teachers who specialized in miracle stories, and others in controversy stories, others in parables, others in passion narrative. The suggestion would be absurd.

But the coherence and roundedness of 2.15—3.6 and 2.1—3.6 (at different stages in the tradition-history process) is too striking to be dismissed so readily as does Kiilunen.

(c) Against all this the evidence of Markan redaction is neither so conclusive, nor, if agreed, so decisive in favour of a collection first made by Mark. I continue to think the evidence of correlation at a pre-Markan stage is strong (see more detailed comment above; and the degree to which 3.6 provides a conclusion to the whole, a summing up of the controversial impact of Jesus' ministry and its inevitable conclusion). But even if Kiilunen is right and it was Mark who stitched these stories together in their present form, the likelihood is that he was able to draw on a grouping already available in the churches' remembering and tradition, a grouping put together at the time when the early Jewish Christians were having to defend themselves from Pharisaic criticism, and remembered in that grouping thereafter.

H. Räisänen in turn has added a further brief critique in his treatment of 'The "Hellenists"–a Bridge between Jesus and Paul?', *The Torah and Christ*.[8] In so far as his critique is dependent on the thesis of his pupil Kiilunen, the above response must suffice.

However, he makes two further points. (a) My suggested *Sitz im Leben* 'makes the "unit" unbelievably early ... early on in the thirties? Perhaps already in Jerusalem?' (pp. 296–7). And (b) 'in most of them [the pericopes] there is no law-critical substance at all' (p. 297).

(a) The first point of criticism derives from a tendentious reading of my argument. In the tunnel period from the first Easter and Pentecost till the emergence of the issue of circumcision and foods (Gal. 2.1–14) there is no real indication (outside this passage) that such matters were an issue in the spreading Hellenistic-Jewish Christian outreach. My point is that the stories preserved in 2.15—3.5(6) reflect a stage along that way, when Jewish Christians had to explain and defend themselves by means of these stories. And in so doing they prepared the way for the more radical stands taken by Paul and Gentile believers and reflected by Mark. When the Hellenistic-Jewish Christians reached that stage we cannot say. The fact that the issues of circumcision and food laws took so long to blow up (some fifteen to twenty years) makes it likely, if anything, that the issues reflected in Mark 2.15—3.6 only came to sharp and polemical focus in the period prior to and leading up to the fundamental controversies reflected in Galatians 2.[9]

(b) I agree that there is 'no law-critical substance' in most of the pericopes in 2.1—3.6. This is only a criticism for Räisänen because he thinks Paul opposes the law as such. In contrast, I see both the material in 2.15—3.5(6) and Paul as wrestling (at different stages and in different contexts) with the same issue – the attempt to define and express this new movement over against a Judaism concerned to maintain Jewish prerogatives and distinctives, as expressed not least in questions of table-fellowship with 'sinners' (cf. Mark 2.15–17 and Gal. 2.11–15) and of special days (cf. Mark 2.23—3.5 with Gal. 4.10). But here we enter the much larger debate with Sanders[10] and Räisänen to which most of the following chapters are addressed (see particularly chs 3, 7 and 8).

35

Notes

1. Helsinki: Suomalainen Tiedeakatemia (1985).
2. cf. D. Lührmann, *Das Markusevangelium*, HNT 3, Tübingen: Mohr (1987) 59.
3. 'Culture and Historicity: the Plucking of the Grain', *NTS* 34 (1988) 1–23.
4. 'The Authority of the Son of Man (Mk 2.1—3.6)', *ZNW* 74 (1983) 161–81.
5. 'Traditionsgeschichtliche Überlegungen zu Mk 3.1–6', *ZNW* 73 (1982) 183–203.
6. Note the observation of Lührmann, *Markusevangelium* 66: in the parallel passage, 1.21–8, no conflict about the sabbath emerges (despite Mark's introduction setting it on the sabbath), thus showing 'that the controversy about the sabbath was no longer an actual problem at the time of Mark'.
7. So also D. Lührmann, 'Die Pharisäer und die Schriftgelehrten im Markusevangelium', *ZNW* 78 (1987) 169–85 (here 180); also *Markusevangelium* 56 and 67.
8. Helsinki: Finnish Exegetical Society (1986) 242–301 (here 295–7).
9. Räisänen 297, n. 1, plays off my talk of a 'pre-Pauline stage' against my talk of 'Helleistic-Jewish Christian communities beginning to wrestle with questions of law and *halakah* for themselves'. 'The later formulation suggests Antioch, the former ... a still earlier date'. But, of course, 'pre-Pauline' = prior to the formulation/appearance of the distinctive notes of Paul's teaching/theology, *not* prior to his conversion.
10. Räisänen cites Sanders to demonstrate the historical unrealism of Mark 2.23–8. But see ch. 3 below.

2

Jesus and Ritual Purity: A Study of the Tradition-History of Mark 7.15

'Christ, the end of the law' is a much-used slogan in studies of Christianity's beginnings, particularly in relation to the Judaism of that period.[1] Understandably so, since it highlights one of the major issues in the first generation of the new movement which caused the two great religious streams emerging from first-century Judaism (Christianity and rabbinic Judaism) to diverge and separate. The credit (or blame) for forcing or occasioning this divergence is usually laid at the door of Paul, the apostle to the Gentiles. Again understandably so, in view of his treatment of the law, particularly in his letters to the Galatians and Romans, and its lasting influence – despite the renewed debate as to what his attitude to the law really was.[2] But lurking in the background is the potentially more important question: Should Paul be given *all* the credit (or blame) for this breach between Christianity and Judaism on the issue of the law, or should we rather see Paul as simply broadening a breach or crystallizing an emphasis already made before Paul? The Hellenists against whom Paul directed his pre-Christian persecuting zeal are obvious candidates for this earlier role.[3] Even more important, however, is the issue of whether the breach really began with *Jesus*. It is more important, because if it was indeed the breach with the rest of Judaism over the law which determined that Christianity would be a separate religion and helped form its distinctive character, and if it was Paul who almost single-handedly achieved this breach, then it follows that Wilhelm Wrede was right after all, on this point at least: Paul was 'the second founder of Christianity' who, 'compared with the first, exercised beyond all doubt the stronger ... influence'![4] In other words, the issue which has haunted New Testament scholarship since Reimarus is still with us: To what extent was the Christianity which emerged true to 'the intention of Jesus'?[5] To what extent can Christianity claim the authority of Jesus' own teaching for one of its most striking departures from the long-established understanding of God's revealed will for his people?

The question, Did Jesus teach or encourage his disciples to ignore or abandon the law? comes to clearest focus, of course, in the Synoptics,[6] particularly in the contrasting treatments of Matthew and Mark, and nowhere more sharply than in Mark 7.1–23, specifically verses 15 and 19.[7] For if Jesus actually said, 'There is nothing from outside a man entering into him which is able to defile him' (Mark 7.15), then the comment of 7.19b is sound ('declaring all foods clean'), and the conclusion is unavoidable that Jesus denied the necessity of treating some foods as 'unclean' and so in effect called for the abolition of the important sequence of laws dealing with unclean foods (Lev. 11; Deut. 14).[8] If Mark 7.15 is part of the authentic core of Jesus' teaching, then the breach with Judaism *did* begin with Jesus![9] The importance of this logion has been fully recognized in recent discussion,[10] but results of previous investigations are strongly disputed, and the passage itself is so crucial for our understanding of the emergence of Christianity in relation to Judaism (an investigation which has itself become more contentious in recent years),[11] that a further analysis is not hard to justify.

II

Since the advent of form-critical and tradition-history analyses of the Jesus-tradition no clear consensus regarding Mark 7.15 has emerged, although, as we shall see, aspects of the analysis of the complete passage (7.1–23) have won greater support. From Bultmann onwards a strong body of opinion has been very ready to trace the saying back to Jesus himself. The principal reason which has weighed most heavily, also with scholars not particularly noted for such 'conservative' conclusions, is the radicalness of the saying itself. By the criterion of dissimilarity with the rest of Judaism it must be accounted part of the historical Jesus' teaching. 'Mark 7.15 is ... completely without parallel in either rabbinic or sectarian Judaism, and, more than this, it completely denies a fundamental presupposition of Jewish religion: the distinction between the sacred and the secular ... This is perhaps the *most radical* statement in the whole of the Jesus-tradition, and, *as such, it is certainly authentic.*'[12]

Unfortunately, however, it is precisely at a point like this that the overrated 'criterion of dissimilarity' becomes methodologically suspect. For it is precisely the radical nature of the saying, and its comparative isolation in its radicalness within the Jesus-tradition, which engenders the counter-suspicion that here we have a case where Gentile Christian influence has sharpened a less radical saying;[13] we may compare the 'Christological heightening' which many scholars have perceived in sayings like Mark 13.32 and Matthew 11.27.[14] The same consideration tells against varying uses of the criterion of coherence: there is nothing quite so radical as this; it would 'cohere' more readily in a less radical form.[15] Furthermore, if the other half of the criterion of dissimilarity is called upon (dissimilar from early Christian, post-Easter teaching), the case becomes even more precarious. For not only does Romans 14.14 ('nothing is unclean in itself') come into play, but it also becomes quite possible to argue that Mark was more influenced by Paul at this point (or more carefully, that the Markan tradition was more influenced by the insights and theology of the Gentile mission as expressed in Rom. 14) than that Paul was influenced by Jesus.[16]

Not surprisingly then, there has been a strongly maintained minority view that Mark 7.15 cannot be traced back to Jesus. The most important consideration here has been its striking absence from any of the controversies which disturbed the early Gentile mission, particularly when we recall that these were controversies between fellow Christians (who *ipso facto* might be expected to treasure a word of Jesus on this issue), and about the Jewish food laws (to which Mark 7.15 speaks so directly). If Jesus had spoken so clearly and unequivocally as Mark 7.15 claims ('nothing from outside can render a man unclean'), how could Peter and the Jerusalem believers have been so hostile to the thought of eating something unclean (Acts 10.14; 11.3)? How could the confrontation at Antioch (on the same issue of ritual purity and food laws) have been carried through without a single reference to such an important teaching of Jesus (Gal. 2.11–18)? On another crucial facet of the same debate there is at least some evidence that Stephen and the Hellenists were influenced by the Jesus-tradition (cf. Acts 6.14 with Mark 14.58 and John 2.19). But that such a pointed saying as Mark 7.15 could remain submerged and without influence till a relatively late stage of the formulation of the Synoptic tradition is certainly hard to comprehend and difficult to accept.[17]

The same line of reasoning has been the main motivation behind various attempts to argue for a mediating position between the two extremes (wholly attributable to Jesus, wholly later in formulation). Perhaps the saying's lack of influence on the controversies between Jerusalem and the emerging Gentile mission is to be explained by the fact that the saying was preserved in Galilee and only emerged into the general stream of Jesus-tradition at a date subsequent to these controversies.[18] But this is a counsel of near despair (as well as an argument from silence), and it ignores the fact both that the Jerusalem leadership was Galilean and that Paul in all his disputes with or acknowledgement of debt to Palestinian Christianity never once suggests that there was an alternative source of authoritative tradition other than Jerusalem. Alternatively, we should give fuller consideration to the possibility that the present Greek version of Mark 7.15 is more radical than its earlier formulations (in Greek and/or in Aramaic), and that the earlier version lacked the cutting edge of the verse as it now stands. The problem is that most of the suggestions along this line remain as suggestions and have not been fully worked out,[19] or are vulnerable to the charge of being too speculative.[20] And the more considered and sophisticated attempts at reconstruction have found some difficulty in working back from 7.15 itself to the proposed earlier form.[21]

Thus the issue of how Mark 7.15 contributed to the earliest Christian understanding of the role of the law can hardly be said to have achieved satisfactory resolution. Hence too the larger question of how far the breach between Christianity and Judaism over the law can be attributed to Jesus' own teaching remains obscure at a crucial point. Despite all the attention given to the passage, therefore, a further examination is necessary – particularly with regard to the crucial tradition-history of the text.[22] The question which chiefly motivates the present study is thus not so much the simple, Can the verse be traced back to Jesus in its present form?, but, What light does a clearer appreciation of the tradition-history of the verse, including its relation to its present context, throw on the process by which the breach between Christianity and Judaism over the law became unavoidable?

III

Analysis of the tradition-history of Mark 7.15 has several facets; there are a number of aspects from which the limited amount of information available to us can be examined. A major weakness of previous treatments of the passage is that they have failed either to take sufficient account of one or more of these aspects or to co-ordinate the information gleaned into a fuller picture of the tradition-history process.[23] Even if we succeed in doing so, we may, of course, still be unable to draw firm conclusions; but at least we should be clearer as to the greater or lesser viability of the different hypotheses currently canvassed.

A. Redactional elements in Mark 7.15

Any tradition-history analysis of a text is wise to start with this issue: it is one of the more easily testable aspects of the text; and if editorial elements can be ascertained the analysis is given an immediate boost.[24] In this case the initial signs are not hopeful: the possibility of the verse being redactional in whole or part seems to have been given little consideration in the past fifty years or so.[25] One exception is Vincent Taylor's suggestion that εἰσπορευόμενον εἰς αὐτὸν and ἐκπορευόμενα are 'explanatory additions, for they are detachable and are characteristic of Mark's vocabulary.'[26] But this is a case where a merely statistical account can be misleading, since although Mark does use the verbs more than Matthew or Luke, the characteristic Markan usage denotes physical movement from place to place.[27] More recently Jan Lambrecht has noted that οὐδέν ... ἀλλά is a frequent construction in Mark and that δύναμαι is also characteristically Markan and often redactional.[28] Moreover, the ἔξωθεν seems to answer to the ἔσωθεν which is very probably redactional in verses 21 and 23, and may be intended to provide a variation on the 'outside' theme which Mark uses so effectively elsewhere (particularly 3.21–2 and 4.11).

Heikki Räisänen accepts the possibility that the wording of the text has been 'slightly changed' at these points in the course of transmission, but then comments that such changes do not necessarily imply that a 'major modification of *meaning*' must have taken place.[29] This is more than a little surprising, because it is precisely these elements which give the Markan text its polemical sharpness. It is the assertion that *nothing* coming *from outside* is *able* to render a person unclean which distinguishes the Markan version of the saying from the Matthean form, and which makes the *rejection* of the Jewish food laws an inevitable corollary for the person who holds this view (cf. 1 Cor. 10.25–6; Rom. 14.14,20).[30] It is this fact which makes the possibility that just these elements of the text are redactional so interesting and potentially so important. The case for attributing them to a later stage of the text's tradition-history is hardly strong in itself, but the possibility that just these elements are redactional when judged in terms of Markan style and emphasis is certainly present and certainly has to be borne in mind when all the evidence and arguments are brought together in a final assessment.

B. *An Aramaic* Vorlage

Here is another point in tradition-history analysis of the Jesus-tradition where we may entertain good hope of gaining some purchase on the issue. All the more puzzling is it, therefore, that the question of a Semitic form of the saying at issue is often not asked, although one would naturally assume that any attempt to trace the tradition-history of a Jesus-logion was bound to ask whether the text could reasonably be explained as a translation from Aramaic. And even when this task is taken on board it is often envisaged in too narrow terms and attempted too woodenly — as though the case depended on being able to demonstrate word-for-word correlation between the Greek and the postulated Aramaic version. But, of course, no one needs to be reminded that translations from one language to another can be quite free, and a properly idiomatic rendering (where the translator is familiar with

the idioms of both languages) can be significantly different from
that achieved by a word-for-word correlation. The determinative
question, therefore, is not so much whether the Greek of Mark
7.15 can be put back directly into Aramaic, but whether we can
envisage an Aramaic form which a good translator might well have
rendered into our present Greek.

In the case of Mark 7.15 the probabilities are very strong: the
antithetic parallelism

        going into a man   not defiling
        coming out of a man   defiling

is characteristic of Hebrew poetry or proverbial speech;[31] ἄνθρωπος
= τις may well translate the Aramaic *bar 'enāšā*;[32] κοινόω in the
sense 'make common' = 'defile' is certainly a Semitism;[33] and the
saying as a whole is a typical Jewish proverb or *mashal*, such as
evidently was also characteristic of Jesus' own teaching style.[34] It is
true that the πᾶν . . . οὖ of verse 18 is closer to the typical Hebrew
. . . *lā* . . . *kol*, than the οὐδέν ἐστιν of verse 15.[35] But here is a case
where the consideration outlined above may well apply, since the
οὐδέν ἐστιν form makes the same point in more elegant Greek and
could therefore quite properly have been chosen by a translator to
render the same Aramaic *Vorlage*. At the same time, the fact that
the Matthean version of the text goes back into a Semitic form a
good deal more easily than the Markan version[36] should give us
cause for pause, and certainly raises again the question as to
whether the distinctive Markan features belonged to the earliest
form of the text.

C. *Alternative forms*

Where there are alternative or parallel forms for a particular saying
we are in much better position to detect the forces and concerns
which played upon that saying in the course of its transmission.
Here we can speak of three alternative forms to the version
preserved in Mark 7.15: Matthew 15.11, *Gospel of Thomas* 14 and,
we should not forget, Mark 7.18b, 20.

Mark:	*Matthew:*
There is nothing from	Not what
outside a man entering into	enters into
him which is able to defile	the mouth defiles a man,
him; but those things which	but what comes forth
come forth from a man are	from the mouth, that
what defile a man	defiles a man.

There are two possible reasons for the differences between these
versions. One is that Matthew, conscious of the polemical and at
least potentially 'antinomian' sharpness of Mark's version, refor-
mulated it precisely in order to soften its harshness for those who

still regarded the Torah as binding on their conduct in all its rulings. This would certainly be consistent with the way Matthew treated the Markan tradition on sensitive legal issues here and elsewhere (Mark 12.1–14//Mark 2.23—3.6; Matt. 15.17//Mark 7.18–19; Matt. 19.3–12//Mark 10.2–12).[37] The other is that Matthew has preserved the earlier form of the saying and that the differences are due primarily to Markan redaction[38] – a possibility strengthened by both of the previous findings.

It may be, however, that we do not need to choose between these possibilities. To reduce the discussion to the sole issue of direct literary dependence between Matthew and Mark is to make the unjustified presumption that by this time oral tradition and written tradition were mutually exclusive modes of transmitting the Jesus-tradition, that when oral tradition had once been committed to writing somewhere within the wide range of Christian congregations it *ceased* to exist in oral form anywhere else as an inevitable corollary. But that is obviously a ridiculous assumption. The initial writing down was only the literary crystallization of a tradition which would already be known much more widely in many churches in oral form, and which would continue to be remembered and used and circulated in that form. It is *a priori* likely that across the spectrum of churches already in existence in the second half of the first century, the sayings of Jesus were known in various groupings and collections in both oral and written form. And although we are well into the stage of the written tradition by the time Matthew's Gospel was composed, it is antecedently highly probable that the Jewish Christian congregation(s) within which 'Matthew' himself moved were familiar with a good range of Jesus-tradition in the oral form of a living celebration, catechesis and worship. The fact that Matthew chose to follow Mark's structure and order probably indicates that Mark's was the most structured and ordered account available to Matthew. It does *not* follow that the *only* access Matthew had to that tradition at particular points was the Markan version.[39]

This *a priori* likelihood is strengthened by the indication that Matthew's redaction of Mark seems regularly to omit features of the Markan narrative which appear to have been introduced to the tradition by Mark.[40] In other words, again and again Matthew shows himself to be alive to the fact of Markan elaboration of the tradition. And that probably means that in many of these cases he was aware of a different form of the tradition, that his own transmission of the written tradition was determined in part at least by reference to the oral tradition he was most familiar with.

At this point we can call in the other versions of Mark 7.15. The importance of *Gosp. Thos.* 14 in the present discussion is that it is much closer to the Matthean than to the Markan version:

43

Matthew:	Thomas:
Not what enters into the mouth defiles a man, but what comes out from the mouth, that defiles a man.	For what will go into your mouth will not defile you, but what comes out of your mouth, that is what will defile you

The two forms of the saying are so close that it must mean one of two things: either *Gosp. Thos.* 14 is dependent on Matthew, that is on Matthew's redaction of Mark; or *Gosp. Thos.* 14 is a witness together with Matthew 15.11 to an alternative form of the logion, that is to a form lacking the radicalizing features of the Markan version. Tradition-history analysis of the *Gospel of Thomas* would tend to support the latter, since so much of the Thomas material stems originally from Q tradition, or perhaps more precisely, from tradition also preserved in Q.[41] The rest of *Gosp. Thos.* 14 itself points to a variant summary version of the subject matter of Matthew 6.2–6, 16–18, and evidences knowledge of the commissioning tradition preserved in Q and Luke (Luke 10.8; Matt. 10.8// Luke 10.9). Moreover, since the nearest parallel to the purity logion within the Jesus-tradition also comes in Q material (Matt. 23.25–6//Luke 11.39–40), it must be judged quite likely that Matthew 15.11//*Gosp. Thos.* 14 is itself Q material (which Luke's omission of the whole unit has hidden from us), with the direct second person address of *Gosp. Thos.* 14 possibly preserving the Q version of the saying more closely than Matthew.[42] The presence of Matthew 15.12–14 is further evidence that Matthew was in touch with other traditions at this point, including Q material (Luke 6.39) also known to Thomas (*Gosp. Thos.* 34, 40).

A somewhat similar conclusion may also be indicated by the other variant version – Mark 7.18b, 20. For the same paradox is present as in Matthew 15.11: the form of 7.18b, 20 presupposes 7.15 and yet is more immediately Semitic in character than 7.15.[43] In addition, while 7.18b clearly echoes 7.15 in its Markan form (*'everything* which is *from outside* entering into a man *can not* defile him'), 7.20 is closer to the *Matthean* version of our saying ('what comes out from a man, that defiles a man'). Both features suggest that the explanatory elaboration of 7.15 using 7.18b, 20 was carried through either in knowledge of the Aramaic original or idiom underlying 7.15 which could be rendered in different Greek versions, or in knowledge of a different Greek version of the saying known also to Matthew.[44] Either way we have some further indication that the different versions of Mark 7.15 are not to be explained solely as elaborations or redactions of Mark 7.15 as such, but in part at least also as evidence that the original underlying Mark 7.15 was itself different from the present form of Mark 7.15.

D. *The pre-Markan context of Mark 7.15*

A tradition-history analysis of Mark 7.15 is bound to inquire after the tradition-history of its context, that is, the context in which and with which it circulated prior to Mark's use of it. Such an inquiry need not exclude the possibility that the saying circulated as an independent *mashal*, or circulated *also* as an independent saying of Jesus.[45] But if there is evidence that it was remembered and used in some particular context, then that must shed some light on the significance perceived in it at these earlier stages.

Tradition-history analysis is a hazardous enterprise: the more detailed a reconstruction seeks to be the more hostages it gives to fortune and the less agreement is it likely to command.[46] In this case, however, the broad lines of development are sufficiently clear and command a large measure of consensus. We will be able to proceed without the necessity of resolving too many questions of detail.[47]

As the text stands at present verse 15 is related backwards and forwards to the larger unit 7.1–23: verse 15 responds to the question of verse 5, and is itself elaborated in verses 17–23. It is also clear that this unit is directed towards a Gentile audience: verses 3–4 explain Jewish customs ('all the Jews'!);[48] and most commentators agree that verse 19c ('cleansing all foods') is designed to point out or serve as a reassurance to Gentile believers that the Jewish food laws were not obligatory for them. This orientation of the pericope as a whole is confirmed by the fact that in Mark it leads into and obviously serves as introduction to a period of ministry by Jesus among the Gentiles (7.24—8.10). It is hard to dispute, then, that the final form of the context of 7.15 has been shaped by concern for the Gentile mission; we need not inquire in more detail as to whether or to what extent this final shape was provided by Mark or was taken over by Mark.

The presence of such obviously explanatory additions as verses 3–4 and 19c also indicates that there was earlier material to be thus interpreted. What can we say of it? The material to which verses 3–4 were added obviously focuses on the issue raised in verses 1–2, 5 – the fact that some of Jesus' disciples ate with unwashed hands. This material was probably already linked to verse 15, since otherwise the Pharisees' question ('Why do your disciples ... eat bread with defiled hands?') would have been left unanswered; within the earliest Christian tradition it is hardly likely that such a question would have been remembered without Jesus' answer attached.[49] At this stage we are clearly dealing with an internal Jewish debate: it is an argument with one of the sub-groups within the Judaism of the period, the sub-group closest to and evidently most threatening to the new movement of Jesus' followers – the

Pharisees; and the Pharisees in turn are presented as having grounds for expecting that Jesus' disciples should observe their *halakic* rulings.[50] Moreover, κοινός in the sense 'impure, defiled' ('defiled hands') is indisputably a Jewish usage (it too has to be explained to the wider Greek readership – v. 2).[51] The fact that only '*some* of Jesus' disciples' are criticized may also suggest that there was some diversity of practice among the Christians who preserved the Pharisaic criticism in this form.

We do not need to decide whether verses 6–8 or 6–13 were already linked with verses 1–2, 5, 15 in whole or part at this earlier stage.[52] But the possibility is quite strong: the use of περιπατέω ('walk') as a description of praxis is characteristically Jewish;[53] (τὸν) ἄρτον ἐσθίειν is a semitism;[54] and talk of conducting one's life in accordance with 'the tradition of the elders' expresses a typical Pharisaic concern in not untypical Pharisaic language (cf. Gal. 1.14; *m. Abot* 1.1).[55] Posed thus (v. 5), the question invites some such distinction between human tradition and divine law as that which follows (both vv. 6–8 and vv. 9–13). If, then, that material in whole or part was already linked with verse 15 prior to the construction of the complete unit 7.1–23, it would simply confirm that an internal Jewish discussion was in view, where obedience to the law could be assumed as a *desideratum* on both sides and where Jews who followed Jesus used Jesus' own appeal to law and prophet to respond to Pharisaic criticism of their conduct.

On the other side of verse 15, it is an obvious deduction that verse 19c was inserted into a unit where the elaboration contained within verses 17–19 or 17–23 had already been appended to verse 15, although we would have to allow that the πᾶν and δύναται which make verse 18b so radical could have been added by Mark if he also inserted them in verse 15 itself.[56] The force of this elaboration is clearly to explain the logic of verse 15 – why what enters a man does not (cannot) defile him. But the important point is that in so doing it puts beyond doubt that what is in view in verse 15 is the eating of food.[57] This strongly suggests that the elaboration reflects the concerns of mixed (Jewish and Gentile) Christian congregations (cf. Gal. 2.11–14) or of Jewish Christians already open to missionary possibilities among the Gentiles (cf. Acts 10.28–9, 34–5) – whereas the earliest Palestinian congregations do not seem either to have known these concerns or to have provoked the same sort of Pharisaic criticism (cf. again Acts 10.14; 11.3; Gal. 2.12; Acts 21.20). That Mark 7.15 was thus seen to encourage and validate an openness to Gentile mission in Jewish Christian circles receives striking support from the fact that the missionary overtones of 7.15 were evidently also recognized elsewhere – not just by Matthew, who retains the Markan 'Gentile sequence' even though he feels free to introduce modifications (Matt. 15.1–28//Mark

7.1–30), but also by *Gosp. Thos.* 14, where the purity logion is linked with words drawn from Jesus' commissioning for mission.

Thus even before the material within 7.1–23 had been directed overtly to Gentile Christians and their situation we have some indication that the previous stage already reflected Jewish Christian concern with the issue of ritual purity – a stage at which Jewish believers found in Jesus' words (7.15) defence not only against Pharisaic criticism but also justification for missionary outreach without regard for questions of ritual purity and food laws. The discussion involved is still an internal Jewish one: it concerns the conduct required of God's people by God's law. And the same conclusions may not have been reached by all who reflected on Jesus' words about purity: the fact that only 'some' of Jesus' disciples are remembered as provoking the Pharisees' criticism (v. 2) reminds us that Hellenistic-Jewish Christians sided with the stricter (Pharisaic?) line at Antioch (Gal. 2.11–14). But at this stage it certainly appears as though 7.15 was understood to validate a disregard for Pharisaic purity concerns and an acceptance of open table-fellowship with Gentiles.

What, finally, of the earliest level of the traditions grouped round verse 15? That Jesus should have clashed with Pharisees over the question of ritual purity must be judged highly likely, and ritual purity and purity of food were such closely integrated issues that verse 15 can hardly be judged an inappropriate response to verse 5.[58] Either as a single incident or as two separate incidents amalgamated in one strand of Christian recollection from the first (although, as already noted, 7.15 may also have been remembered as an independent proverb), the original form of verses 1–2, 5, 15 attests Jesus' criticism of Pharisaic purity concerns. On the other hand, it does appear likely that the original core of verses 17–19 does *not* go back to Jesus but emerged as an interpretative expansion of 7.15 within a Hellenistic-Jewish Christian circle beginning to wrestle with the fact of the new movement's increasing attractiveness to Gentiles and with issues which do not seem to have disturbed the first Palestinian believers prior to the emergence of the Gentile question.[59] That such an interpretative addition should have become so firmly attached to and cherished along with verse 15 demonstrates the high value placed on verse 15 in these circles and is probably sufficient to confirm that verse 15 itself goes back to Jesus. It also strengthens the likelihood that the original form of verse 15 was less radical (above III, A), with the original elaboration of verses 17–19 providing the first step towards a more radicalized interpretative rendering of the saying itself.[60]

E. Historical context

A final area of investigation is the *Sitz(e) im Leben* of Mark 7.15; that is, the question whether we can throw further light on the social world(s) within which the saying had significance during the course of its transmission. We have already drawn in some considerations from this area of inquiry, particularly in the previous section, but it has most potential when we are able to draw in other information and material from outside the narrower circle of our concerns hitherto. In this case we can call on several further sources which illuminate this broader historical context.

First, a general point. It is now an accepted insight, established by social anthropological studies, that purity rituals are a group's way of marking itself off from others – boundary defining acts.[61] This was true in the period with which we are concerned, particularly of the ritual purifications by which the pious Jew kept himself/herself undefiled by the impurity of the wider world (e.g. Judith 12.7; *Sib. Or.* 3. 591–592).[62] The explanatory note added in Mark 7.3–4 in fact treats ritual purifications in just this way, as boundary markers, defining the identity of the Jews as a people ('all the Jews') in distinction from everybody else. But it was also true of the ritual washings by which groups *within* Judaism marked themselves off from other Jews (not least the Essenes at Qumran).[63]

In particular it was true of the rabbis and their predecessors. Jacob Neusner's tradition-history analysis of the rabbinic traditions which were formulated in the Mishnah round about AD 200 comes to the important conclusion that one of the principal motivations among the precursors of the rabbis in the period before AD 70 was ritual purity. 'The Mishnah before the wars begins its life among a group of people who are joined together by a common conviction about the eating of food under ordinary circumstances in accord with cultic rules to begin with applicable .. to the Temple alone.'[64] In earlier studies he had made the point even more emphatically:

> The Pharisees were Jews who believed one must keep the purity laws outside of the Temple ... Therefore, one must eat secular food (ordinary, everyday meals) in a state of ritual purity *as if one were a Temple priest* ... Of the 341 individual Houses' (of Shammai and Hillel) legal pericopae, no fewer than 229, approximately 67 per cent of the whole, directly or indirectly concern table-fellowship.[65]

This is striking confirmation that in the period before AD 70 (that is certainly during the early days of the Gentile mission, but also probably already during the time of Jesus' own ministry) the sort of issues bound up in Mark 7.15 and posed directly in 7.5 would have been of central concern to the Pharisees. Moreover, it should be noted that these were concerns of the Pharisees in particular, or at least of many Pharisees, not of 'the Jews' as a whole.[66] Of the circles and sub-groups within the Judaism of his time with whom Jesus and his disciples would have come most frequently into contact, it was precisely the Pharisees who were most likely to have criticized Jesus and to have disputed with his disciples on matters of ritual purity. Furthermore, while the features of Jewish praxis characteristic of Judaism as a whole were well known to non-Jewish observers in the wider Greco-Roman world (particularly circumcision, sabbath and food laws), the more scrupulous concern for ritual purity reflected in Mark 7.1–2, 5 has not attracted such comment. Finally we may add the observation that the Pharisees do not seem to have had any missionary concern, no ambition to convert non-Jews;[67] rather such concern as they had in this direction seems to have been to ensure that other Jews, particularly converts (proselytes), were properly faithful to the law, had fully taken the yoke of the law upon themselves (cf. Acts 15.5 with Matt. 23.15 and Josephus, *Ant.* 20.38–48).

All this evidence hangs together and builds into a coherent picture in which the issues of Mark 7.5 and 15 fit perfectly as expressions of an intra-mural Jewish dispute whose roots and early tradition-history must have been in Palestine or at least in areas where Pharisaic influence was strong.

Further confirmation that ritual purity was a bone of contention between Jesus and other Jews of Pharisaic persuasion, and that the issue of Jesus' attitude to ritual purity was a matter of some concern within Jewish Christian churches, is provided by the small cluster of material preserved in Matthew 23.25–6//Luke 11.39–40 and Matthew 23.27–8 (the only other passages outside Mark 7 where the theme of cleanliness and the antithesis ἔξωθεν/ἔσωθεν appears in the Gospels), and by the tradition found in *P. Ox.* 840.[68]

Of the other evidence within the New Testament, we have already alluded to Acts 10–11 and Gal. 2.11–14, both of which indicate that Jerusalem believers were conservatively traditional, at least on the very basic purity issue of clean and unclean foods, and that there were other Jewish believers who had begun to disregard these laws. This has to say something about the earliest tradition-history of Mark 7.15, and strengthens the likelihood that some at least of the tensions evident within that tradition-history are to be explained by disagreement within the new Christian groups as to the significance of Jesus' teaching with regard to ritual purity.[69]

The testimony of Romans 14 is more tantalizing. It certainly shows that purity concerns were also subjects of some dispute within the new Christian congregations of the diaspora. Here too it is the basic legal distinction between clean and unclean foods which is now at issue, an important question for any congregation which regarded the heritage from its Jewish past as constitutive in any degree (cf. Rom. 1.2; 4.1; 9.4). But how much light does Romans 14 yield for our immediate inquiry? The fact that Paul does not cite Mark 7.15 or its equivalent in any form remains a puzzle.[70] It must mean either that Paul did not know the saying in its present Mark 7.15 form, or if he did so he chose not to use it for some reason. On the other hand, the assertion of Romans 14.20 seems to be very close to the interpretative addition of Mark 7.19c:

Mark 7.19c – καθαρίζων πάντα τὰ βρώματα
Rom. 14.20 – πάντα (βρώματα) μὲν καθαρά.[71]

The two features together are perhaps most simply explained by the hypothesis that Paul knew not Jesus' teaching itself but the interpretative line of theologizing which grew from it, which we see retained in Mark 7.17–19 and 19c – that is, not that we can necessarily draw a direct line of dependence between Mark and Paul, or Paul and Mark, but that both together attest a line of theological reflection which (as Mark shows) grew out of Jesus' teaching on purity, particularly purity of foods.[72] It seems also to have been a feature of Paul's pneumatic, interpretative use of the Jesus-tradition that he rarely saw a need to cite the authority of Jesus explicitly for a teaching which the Synoptic tradition shows to have stemmed from Jesus.[73] It is quite likely, therefore, that Paul in speaking so forthrightly as he does in Romans 14.14 ('I know and am convinced in the Lord Jesus that nothing is unclean in itself') and 14.20 ('everything is clean') was consciously evoking that whole train of thought which Jesus' words on purity had sparked off, and that had he been challenged on the point his line of response would not have been so very different from that contained in the argument of Mark 7.15–19.

IV

What emerges from all this? What conclusions can we draw? It has to be admitted at once that not all the lines of argument cohere: we cannot deduce both that οὐδέν ... ἀλλά is a Markan construction (III, A) *and* that οὐδέν ἐστιν is a possible rendering of an underlying Aramaic *Vorlage* (III, B); the ἔξωθεν/ἔσωθεν antithesis can be taken as a sign of Markan redaction in Mark (III, A), but it features also in the most closely related Q material (III, E); the indications from *within* the Jesus-tradition of reflection on a saying of Jesus about purity (III, C, D) remain difficult to square with the relative *lack* of indications from *outside* the Jesus-tradition that reflection played much part in shaping earliest Christian thinking on the subject.

Nevertheless, each of the above lines of investigation (III, A-E)

53

50

has suggested the possibility that lying behind Mark 7.15 is an earlier, less radical saying whose point has been sharpened in the course of its transmission. And in each case such considerations as the evidence called forth have served to show that this hypothesis has a fair degree of plausibility. Indeed, since the same hypothesis was suggested by all five areas of our inquiry we can speak of a *convergence of plausibilities* which greatly increases the overall probability of the hypothesis. As the hypothesis which makes best sense of all the available data it ought to have commanded greater support than it has. In other words, it seems most likely that the earliest form of Jesus' saying on purity is reflected most closely in Matthew 15.11, that Mark 7.17–19b preserves a stage of reflection on that earlier saying in which its application to the issue of unclean foods was spelled out more forcibly, and that the final form of 7.15 is an interpretative rendering of that earlier saying which embodies the more radical interpretation found also separately in 7.19c.

This leaves us with a saying of Jesus whose original form was less radical and more ambiguous than Mark has it, a saying which could be most straightforwardly rendered as Matthew has in fact rendered it – though the variations possible in translating from Aramaic to Greek and probably also reflected in some measure in the different versions of Matthew 15.11 and Mark 7.18, 20 mean that we cannot be finally certain what were the actual words used by Jesus, including in particular whether he said 'all'. At that earliest stage the 'not . . . but . . .' antithesis need not be understood as an 'either . . . or', but rather with the force of 'more important than', a form of 'dialectical negation', as in the other most closely related confrontation parallel (Mark 2.17 and parallels).[74]

This initial conclusion, however, simply revives the original question: If Jesus himself did not justify the abandonment of the laws of clean and unclean foods, do we not have to conclude that the subsequent abandonment of these laws, and so in effect of the law as such as rule of faith and life, cannot be credited to Jesus but only to the claims of later revelation (whether Acts 10.15 or Rom. 14.14 or whatever)? If Matthew's rendering of Jesus' saying on purity more accurately reflects Jesus' own teaching, can Mark's rendering properly claim the authority of Jesus? Was Christianity's subsequent break out from Judaism an inadmissable distortion of Jesus' own vision and intention? Can we advance the discussion on this more crucial point? Our investigation suggests that we can, and that the issue expressed thus poses the alternatives (Jesus/Paul, Mark/Matthew) too sharply, too much as alternatives.

From the various considerations adduced above it begins to become clear that the weight given to Jesus' words inevitably depends on their force *within a particular context* – on the one hand the context of Jesus' own larger teaching, and on the other the context in which they were remembered. The point about the context of his own teaching can be readily illustrated from the fact that the other famous Jewish teachers of this time were also remembered as having made equally radical-sounding statements about important points of law.[75] Yet they were never remembered as having quite such a radical reputation, because within the context of their teaching as a whole (as it has come down to us) it is clear that individually provocative statements should not be interpreted in such a radical way – a radical interpretation of a particular saying would ill accord with the tenor of their teaching as a whole. But the radical character of a saying which set inward purity antithetically against ritual purity is fully of a piece with Jesus' teaching as a whole. Jesus is generally remembered as one whose teaching on the law and on human relations as governed by the law was characteristically searching and radical in one degree or other. This is as true of Matthew's presentation as it is of Mark's (cf. Matt. 5.38–48; 8.10–12; 11.16–19). Within the terms of Jesus' own proclamation and teaching Jesus certainly appears as one standing fully within the Judaism of his time, but simultaneously as one who questioned and challenged the normal understanding of (Palestinian) Judaism on boundary issues, that is, on the sensitive questions of who and what were acceptable or unacceptable on religious grounds.[76] The picture of Jesus' teaching as new wine in old wineskins belongs to Matthew as much as to Mark (Mark 2.22//Matt. 9.17).

Equally important is the point about the context in which Jesus' teaching was remembered. When Jesus' words were recalled by those who stayed firmly within the boundaries of Judaism as they were then defined, Jesus' saying on purity could be recalled in a still controversial but non-threatening sense. This presumably helps explain its lack of 'bite' in the earliest stages of the controversy about the food laws within the fledgling Christian communities.[77] But when the boundaries themselves began to come more into question, in that context the saying would be seen in a new light and its significance as itself actually calling the boundary (of the food laws) in question would become clearer – as we see in Romans 14 and Mark 7. In other words, Mark 7.15 is a good example of a saying whose significance partakes in some degree from the context to which it is heard to speak. Nor, of course, should we overemphasize the contrast between Mark and Matthew at this point. For all the Jewishness of Jesus, the Judaism which emerged from the disaster of the Jewish revolts has no place for him, not even as a challenging and forthright teacher of 'dialectical negations'. Even in its milder form, Matthew 15.11 was too radical in its implications. Even the teaching of Jesus according to Matthew bursts the wineskins of Judaism.

We are therefore led to the important conclusion that Matthew and Mark can *both* justifiably claim to have been faithful to Jesus' insight and emphasis at this point, simply because neither the actual form in which the saying was recalled nor the interpretation put upon it was independent of the contexts in which it was both uttered and thereafter remembered. Where food laws were not an issue (within Jewish Christian congregations), but only the greater demands for ritual purity of the Pharisees, in that situation Jesus' word to them was Matthew's version. But where the food laws had become an issue of boundary defining significance, in that situation it became clear that the negative thrust of Jesus' word had a more than merely dialectical force. Where the issue of the relative weight to be given to spiritual purity and cultic purity was becoming more than a matter of relative weighting, the antithetical form of Jesus' utterance was seen to have a more radical 'either-or' sharpness. In this way we gain a clear insight into how early Christian hermeneutic operated within the living process of remembering and understanding and handing on the Jesus-tradition. In this way we see the word of Jesus being heard afresh as the living word of God.[78]

Notes

1. Note, e.g., the number of titles using this phrase from Rom. 10.4 in the last fifteen years: G. E. Howard, 'Christ the End of the Law. The Meaning of Rom. 10, 4ff.', in *JBL* 88 (1969), pp. 331–7; P. Stuhlmacher, 'Das Ende des Gesetzes. Über Ursprung und Ansatz der paulinischen Theologie', in *ZTK* 67 (1970), pp. 14–39; A Sand, 'Gesetz und Freiheit. Vom Sinn des Pauluswortes: Christus des Gesetzes Ende', in *TGL* 61 (1971), pp. 1–14; F. Mussner, 'Christus (ist) des Gesetzes Ende zur Gerechtigkeit für jeden, der glaubt (Röm. 10.4)', *Paulus–Apostat oder Apostel?* Pustet, Regensburg, 1977, pp. 31–44; G. S. Sloyan, *Is Christ the End of the Law?*, Westminster, Philadelphia, 1978; P. W. Meyer, 'Romans 10. 4 and the "End" of the Law', in *The Divine Helmsman, L. H. Silberman FS*, New York, 1980, pp. 59–78; W. S. Campbell, 'Christ the End of the Law: Romans 10. 4', in *Studia Biblica 1978* III, E. A. Livingstone ed., JSOT, Sheffield, 1980, pp. 73–81; R. Badenas, *Christ the End of the Law: Romans 10.4 in Pauline Perspective, JSNTSupp* 10, JSOT, Sheffield, 1985.
2. See, e.g., J. W. Drane, *Paul: Libertine or Legalist?*, SPCK, London, 1975; H. Hübner, *Das Gesetz bei Paulus*, Vandenhoeck, Göttingen, 1978, ²1980; C. E. B. Cranfield, *Romans* II, ICC, T. & T. Clark, Edinburgh, 1979, pp. 845–62; H. Räisänen, *Paul and the Law*, Mohr, Tübingen, 1983; E. P. Sanders, *Paul, the Law and the Jewish People*, Fortress, Philadelphia, 1983; J. D. G. Dunn, 'The New Perspective on Paul', in *BJRL* 65 (1983), pp. 95–122; also 'Works of the Law and the Curse of the Law (Gal. 3. 10–14)', *NTS* 31 (1985), pp. 523–42; both reprinted below, chs. 7, 8.
3. See particularly M. Hengel, *Between Jesus and Paul*, SCM, London, 1983, pp. 22–6, 53–8; S. Kim, *The Origin of Paul's Gospel*, Mohr, Tübingen, 1981, pp. 44–8; but see also my critique of Kim, 'A Light to the Gentiles: the Significance of the Damascus road Christophany for Paul', in *The Glory of Christ in the New*

Testament, G. B. *Caird Fs.*, L. D. Hurst and N. T. Wright ed., Oxford, 1985, pp. 251–66, reprinted below, ch. 4.

4. W. Wrede, *Paul*, Philip Green, London, 1907, pp. 179–80.
5. *Reimarus: Fragments*, C. H. Talbert ed., SCM, London, 1971.
6. In the Fourth Gospel the older controversies over law and sabbath have been subsumed within John's Christological assertions; see S. Pancaro, *The Law in the Fourth Gospel*, NT Supp. XLII, Brill, Leiden, 1975.
7. The sharpness of the antitheses in Matt. 5.33–42 is blunted in the Matthean context at least by the prolegomena to the antitheses (Matt 5.17–20). In Mark 2.1–3, 6 the issues are not posed so sharply; but see my 'Mark 2.1–3.6: A Bridge between Jesus and Paul on the Question of the Law', in *NTS* 30 (1984), pp. 395–415, reprinted above, ch. 1.
8. On the importance of these laws see further Dunn, 'New Perspective', pp. 192–3, ch. 7 below.
9. C. E. B. Cranfield, *St. Mark*, Cambridge University, 1959, does not hesitate to draw the conclusion: 'Jesus speaks as the one who is, and knows himself to be, τέλος νόμου (Rom. 10.4)', p. 244.
10. See the literature cited by H. Räisänen in his sequence of studies: 'Zur Herkunft von Markus 7, 15', in *Logia: les paroles de Jésus*, J. Delobel ed., Leuven University, 1982, pp. 477–84, reprinted in *The Torah and Christ*, Finnish Exegetical Society, Helsinki, 1986, pp. 209–18; also 'Jesus and the Food Laws: Reflections on Mark 7.15', in *JSNT* 16 (1982), pp. 79–100, reprinted in *Torah*, pp. 219–41; also *Paul*, 245–48.
11. See n. 2 above.
12. N. Perrin, *Rediscovering the Teaching of Jesus*, SCM, London, 1967, p. 150 (my emphasis); see also particularly R. Bultmann, *The History of the Synoptic Tradition*, Blackwell, Oxford, 1963, p. 105; E. Käsemann, 'The Problem of the Historical Jesus', in *Essays on New Testament Themes*, SCM, London, 1964, p. 39; also 'The Canon of the New Testament and the Unity of the Church', in *Essays*, p. 101; E. Haenchen, *Der Weg Jesu*, Topelmann, Berlin, 1966, pp. 265–7; H Braun, *Jesus: Der Mann aus Nazareth und seine Zeit*, Stuttgart, 1969, p. 73; H. F. Weiss, *TDNT*, 9, p. 41; J. Gnilka, *Markus*, EKK, Benziger, Zürich, 1978, pp. 277–8. J. Dupont notes 'l'accord, pratiquement unanime, des exégètes qui reconnaissent dans cette sentence une des expressions les plus caractéristiques de la pensée personnelle de Jésus lui-même', *Les Béatitudes*, III, EB, Paris, 1973, p. 579. Similarly M. J. Borg, *Conflict, Holiness and Politics in the Teachings of Jesus*, Edwin Mellen, New York/Toronto, 1984, p. 96, speaks of the 'virtual unanimity among all schools of criticism that this saying is authentic'. Other references in J. Lambrecht, 'Jesus and the Law: an Investigation of Mark, 7, 1–23', in *ETL* 53 (1977), pp. 29–30, n. 10; survey of earlier research in H. Merkel, 'Markus 7, 15 – das Jesuswort über die innere Verunreinigung', in *ZRG* 20 (1968), pp. 341–50.
13. Most of those mentioned in the preceding note would argue that Mark, as well as Matthew, has weakened or restricted the force of the saying by appending what follows. But the thesis trades to an uncomfortable extent on the old Liberal picture of Jesus as the pronouncer of sweeping moral principles (cf. the much quoted words of C. G. Montefiore, *The Synoptic Gospels*, London, ²1927, I, pp. 152–3). And the *more* radical was Jesus' original saying, the *more* difficult it is to make sense both of the tradition-history of the saying itself and of the Torah conservatism of the earliest Palestinian congregations. Merkel's argument that only 7.15a is original and 7.15b is redactional ('Markus 7, 15', pp. 352–60) is particularly vulnerable to the charge of operating with an idealized picture of Jesus. A typical Jewish *mashal* would have balancing clauses.
14. See, e.g., those referred to and the discussion in J. D. G. Dunn, *Jesus and the Spirit*, SCM, London, 1975, pp. 27–35.
15. See further Räisänen's critique ('Food Laws', pp. 83–6) particularly of W. G.

Kümmel, 'Äussere und innere Reinheit des Menschen bei Jesus', in *Heilsgeschehen und Geschichte*, Band 2, Elwert Marburg, 1978, pp. 117–29.

16. So particularly Räisänen, 'Herkunft', p. 480–3; also 'Food Laws', pp. 87–9; J. Koenig, *Jews and Christians in Dialogue: New Testament Foundations*, Westminster, Philadelphia, 1979, pp. 75–6. Cf. the implausible thesis of Y. Ronen, 'Mark 7, 1–23 – "Traditions of the Elders"', in *Immanuel* 12 (1981), pp. 44–54, that Mark is dependent on Luke. Against the improbable suggestion of K. Berger, *Die Gesetzsauslegung Jesu*, Teil. I, Neukirchener, Neukirchen-Vluyn, 1972, that Mark 7.15 stems from Hellenistic Judaism (pp. 464–75) see H. Hübner, 'Mark 7, 1–23 und das "Judisch-Hellenistische" Gesetzes Verständnis', in *NTS* 22 (1975–6), pp. 319–45 (particularly pp. 337ff.) and III,E below.

17. See, e.g., E. Percy, *Die Botschaft Jesu*, Gleerup, Lund, 1953, p. 118; Räisänen, 'Herkunft', pp. 479–82; also 'Food Laws', pp. 87–9; also *Paul*, p. 248; others cited by Kümmel, 'Reinheit', p. 117, n. 3. E. P. Sanders, *Jesus and Judaism*, SCM, London, 1985 thinks that 'this great fact . . . overrides all others' (p. 268).

18. cf. H. Hübner, *Das Gesetz in der synoptischen Tradition*, Luther, Witten, 1973, pp. 171–5; U. B. Müller, 'Zur Rezeption Gesetzeskritischer Jesus-überlieferung im frühen Christentum', in *NTS* 27 (1980–1), pp. 168–82; Räisänen, 'Food Laws', p. 89.

19. B. W. Bacon, *Studies in Matthew*, Constable, London, 1930, p. 354; B. H. Branscomb, *Jesus and the Law of Moses*, Smith, New York, 1930, p. 176; also *Mark*, Moffatt, Hodder, London, 1937, pp. 126–7; D. E. Nineham, *Saint Mark*, Pelican, Penguin, Harmondsworth, 1963, pp. 191–2.

20. Räisänen, 'Food Laws', p. 81, justifiably criticizes C. E. Carlston, 'The Things that Defile (Mark 7.15) and the Law in Matthew and Mark', in *NTS* 15 (1968–9), pp. 75–96 – 'Jesus might have appealed beyond the commandment to the will of God by some statement like "what truly defiles a man comes from within, not from without"' (p. 95).

21. Both W. Paschen, *Rein und Unrein*, Kösel, München, 1970, pp. 173–7 and Hübner, *Gesetz*, pp. 165–8 argue that vv. 18b and 20b preserve elements closer to the underlying Aramaic than v. 15 – particularly v. 18b's πᾶν . . . οὐ in contrast to v. 15's οὐδέν ἐστιν, and the *casus pendens* of v. 20b, which is more common in Hebrew and Aramaic then in Koine Greek (M. Black, *An Aramaic Approach to the Gospels and Acts*, Clarendon, Oxford, ³1967, pp. 151–5).

22. cf. Räisänen, 'Das entscheidende Problem ist jedoch das der *fehlenden Wirkungsgeschichte* des Wortes in der frühen Christenheit' ('Herkunft', p. 477).

23. Of the two most recent thorough treatments, Lambrecht excludes the Matthean version of Mark 7.15 and *Gosp. Thos.* 14 from consideration, since he is concerned primarily with the question of Markan redaction of earlier tradition ('Jesus', p. 27) – but see III, C below; and Räisänen does not pay sufficient attention to the *Sitz im Leben* question ('Food Laws') – but see III, E below.

24. cf. N. J. McEleney, 'Authenticating Criteria and Mark 7, 1–23', in *CBQ* 34 (1972), pp. 431–60 (here, p. 432).

25. E. J. Pryke's review of the discussion, *Redactional Style in the Marcan Gospel*, SNTSMS 33, Cambridge University, 1978, does not even consider 7.15 as a possible example of redaction in whole or part.

26. V. Taylor, *Mark*, Macmillan, London, 1952, p. 343, citing J. C. Hawkins, *Horae Synopticae*, Oxford University, ²1909, p. 12; followed by Paschen, *Rein*, p. 174. So also Merkel, 'Markus 7, 15', pp. 353–4.

27. See further Kümmel, 'Reinheit', p. 121; Räisänen, 'Food Laws', p. 80–1. On Merkel's suggestion that 7.15b is redactional, see n. 13 above.

28. Lambrecht, 'Jesus', pp. 24–82 (here, p. 59). I would dispute McEleney's claim that δύναμαι in vv. 15, 18 has a weak force and is almost an auxiliary verb ('Criteria', p. 450, citing C. H. Turner); but cf., e.g., Mk 1.40; 2.7; 6.5; 10.38–9.

29. Räisänen, 'Food Laws', p. 81.

30. As Räisänen himself notes in the following paragraph ('Food Laws', p. 82).

Similarly Lambrecht: despite having pointed up the possibility of redactional elements in 7.15 ('considerably altered' – 'Jesus', p. 60), he does not really address the question of whether the redaction (precisely the redaction he suggested) might have radicalized a less radical saying.

31. C. F. Burney, *The Poetry of our Lord*, Clarendon, Oxford, 1925, pp. 20–1, 74; J. Jeremias, *New Testament Theology*, SCM, London, 1971, pp. 14–20; see further Paschen, *Rein*, p. 177.

32. Black, *Aramaic Approach*, pp. 106–7; but see also E. C. Maloney, *Semitic Interference in Marcan Syntax*, SBL Dissertation 51, Scholars, Chico, 1981, pp. 131–4.

33. See H. G. Liddell and R. Scott, *Greek-English Lexicon*, κοινόω; Paschen, *Rein*, p. 168; J. D. G. Dunn, *Romans* WBC 38, Word, Dallas, 1988, pp. 818–19, and further n. 51 below.

34. Bultmann, *Tradition*, p. 105; B. Gerhardsson, *The Origins of the Gospel Traditions*, SCM, London, 1979: 'He was ... a *moshel*, a parabolist' (p. 70).

35. See n. 21 above.

36. Räisänen compares F. Delitzsch's: 'quite literal Hebrew rendering of Matt. 15.11 with his handling of Mark 7.15 which produces some ten deviations from the Greek wording' ('Food Laws', p. 96, n. 60).

37. See e.g., Carlston, 'Things that Defile', pp. 86–8; J. D. G. Dunn, *Unity and Diversity in the New Testament*, SCM, London, 1977, pp. 247–8.

38. cf. E. Lohmeyer, *Markus*, KEK, Vandenhoeck, Göttingen, ¹¹1951, pp. 141–2; Cranfield, *Mark*, p. 230; R. Banks, *Jesus and the Law in the Synoptic Tradition*, SNTSMS 28, Cambridge University, 1975, pp. 139–40. The view is contested vigorously by Kümmel, 'Reinheit', p. 119 and Hübner, *Gesetz*, p. 167.

39. R. H. Gundry, *Matthew* (Eerdmans, Grand Rapids, 1982) treats the question of Matthean redaction of Mark as though Matthew had only Mark's text to take account of (here pp. 305–6). See more generally my *Testing the Foundations*, Durham University, 1984, pp. 19–21.

40. e.g. Mark 1.14b, 34c; 2.13, 18b; 3.23a, 30; 4.1a, 2b, 13c, 23, 34, 40, etc.

41. See, e.g., Dunn, *Unity*, p. 284 and n. 39.

42. cf. Matt. 5. 3–12//Luke 6.20–3, where Matthew may also have put second person Q beatitudes into third person; though see the full discussions of Dupont, *Les Béatitudes*, I, pp. 272–97; R. A. Guelich, 'The Matthean Beatitudes: "Entrance-Requirements" or Eschatological Blessings?', in *JBL* 95 (1976), pp. 415–34.

43. See n. 21 above.

44. This seems more likely than that Matthew should choose to create 15.11 by arbitrary combination and free adaptation of Mark 7.15 and 7.20.

45. Some insist that Mark 7.15 can only have circulated as an independent saying (e.g. Kümmel, 'Reinheit', pp. 120–1; Hübner, *Gesetz*, pp. 169–70; Gnilka, *Markus*, p. 277).

46. See further the cautionary remarks in my *Foundations*, pp. 16–18.

47. The most recent detailed study is that of Lambrecht, 'Jesus'; he reviews the previous discussion on pp. 28–39.

48. See, e.g., Lambrecht, 'Jesus', p. 70. To speak of the 'aggressive character' of vv. 3–4 is an overstatement; so J. Ernst, *Markus*, Pustet, Regensburg, 1981, p. 203; against Gnilka, *Markus*, p. 277.

49. Against those who think it was Mark who first moulded the material of vv. 1–13 and 14–23 into a single unit – e.g. R. Pesch, *Markusevangelium*, 1. Teil, Herder, Freiburg, 1976, who overemphasizes the differences between the two purity issues (p. 367). But in Pharisaic thinking purity of hands and utensils would have been bound up with the purity of food in the context of the meal table (see further III, E).

50. See n. 65 below.

51. Hauck, *TDNT* 3, 791; Paschen, *Rein*, pp. 165–8; see also above at n. 33.
52. See the discussion in Lambrecht, 'Jesus', pp. 48–56.
53. See, e.g., Taylor, *Mark*, p. 336; Dunn *Romans*, pp. 315–16. Only here in Mark does περιπατέω have this sense (Gnilka, *Markus*, p. 281).
54. Pesch, *Markus*, p. 372, n. 15.
55. cf. Strack-Billerbeck 1, pp. 691–4.
56. See III, A above.
57. The 'into the mouth', 'out of the mouth' of Matthew's version has the same effect and probably also attests the same concern to put the saying's reference to the eating of food beyond dispute.
58. cf. Hübner, *Gesetz*, pp. 159–65; see n. 49 above.
59. cf. Taylor, *Mark*, 'The two sayings are Christian targums . . .' (p. 343); Pesch, *Markus*, p. 384; and particularly Lambrecht, 'Jesus', p. 65, with discussion of vv. 17–23 in pp. 60–6.
60. Interpretation could be either appended to or incorporated within the rendering of a sacred text as we know from the hermeneutical practice of the time; see e.g., E. E. Ellis, *Paul's Use of the Old Testament*, Eerdmans, Grand Rapids, 1957, pp. 139–47; Dunn, *Unity*, pp. 91–3.
61. M. Douglas, *Purity and Danger*, Routledge, London, 1966.
62. For further data see particularly G. Alon, 'The Levitical Uncleanness of Gentiles', in *Jews, Judaism and the Classical World*, Magnes, Jerusalem, 1977, pp. 146–89; S. Westerholm, *Jesus and Scribal Authority*, Coniectanea Biblica, Lund, 1978, pp. 62–7.
63. J. Riches, *Jesus and the Transformation of Judaism*, Darton, London, 1980, pp. 112–28.
64. J. Neusner, *Judaism: the Evidence of the Mishnah*, University of Chicago, 1981, p. 70.
65. J. Neusner, *From Politics to Piety*, Prentice-Hall, Englewood Cliffs, 1973, pp. 83–6. See also Westerholm, *Jesus*, pp. 73–4. Sanders' criticism of Neusner (*Jesus and Judaism*, p. 388, n. 59) does not affect the key point – that ritual purity as it affected the daily life of the meal table was a matter of great concern to the Pharisaic precursors of the rabbis.
66. Note the corrective provided by E. P. Sanders, 'Jesus and the Sinners', in *JSNT* 19 (1983), pp. 5–36, particularly pp. 13–14, elaborated in *Jesus and Judaism*, chap. VI. I cannot go into the important issues raised by Sanders, including the question of whether or to what extent 'the Pharisees' who are presented as Jesus' opponents were in fact *haberim* (associates). Suffice it to say that if it be accepted that the tradition of vv. 1–2, 5 belongs to the Palestinian stage of the story (see III, D above), then it provides clear testimony that the Christians concerned felt the need to defend *themselves* against Pharisaic criticism – which hardly squares with the view that the Pharisees (or *haberim*) were concerned only for their *own* ritual purity and quite unconcerned about that of non-Pharisees (or non-*haberim* = '*amme ha-aretz*) within the wider Jewish community. It would be surprising if a group who were so zealous for the law did *not* criticize those who in their view were being too careless with regard to the law (cf. Gal. 1.13–14; Phil. 3. 5–6). Indeed, the closer we see Jesus and his immediate disciples to be to the Pharisees, the more likely it is that the Pharisees would have looked for distinguishing features to mark themselves off from Jesus, features whose lack in Jesus and his disciples they could draw attention to – it being a well-known sociological observation that it is the group which is *closest* to another which most threatens that other group's boundaries, identity and constituency. See further ch. 3 below.
67. 'There was in Palestine no active propaganda to further the cause of proselytism', D. Flusser, *The Jewish People in the First Century*, S. Safrai & M. Stern ed., Van Gorcum, Assen, vol. II, 1976, p. 1095.

68. *P. Ox.* 840 is reproduced at the end of the section Mark 7.1–23 in the Aland, *Synopsis* and discussed by J. Jeremias, *Unknown Sayings of Jesus*, SPCK, London, ²1964, pp. 47–60.
69. See further ch. 6 below.
70. See section II above.
71. See n. 16 above.
72. This seems a sounder line of argument than Westerholm's claim that in Rom. 14.14 Paul was actually referring to Jesus' *mashal* (*Jesus*, pp. 81–2).
73. See further L. Goppelt, 'Tradition nach Paulus', *KD* 4 (1958), pp. 213-33; K. Wengst, 'Der Apostel und die Tradition', in *ZTK* 69 (1972), pp. 145–62; Dunn, *Unity*, pp. 67–9, 78; also *Romans*, p. 745.
74. H. Kruse, 'Die "Dialektische Negation" als semitisches Idiom', *VT* (1954), pp. 385–400; Westerholm, *Jesus*, p. 83; see further p. 20 above. Cf. Gnilka, 'Jesus setzt mit seiner Kritik die Linie der Profeten fort', *Markus*, p. 280.
75. The saying attributed to Yohanan ben Zakkai has been frequently quoted in comparison: 'By your life! It is not the corpse that pollutes or water that purifies . . .'; see, e.g., Jeremias, *Theology*, p. 211 (a saying 'astounding in its boldness'). E. E. Urbach, *The Sages*, Magnes, Jerusalem, ²1979, points out the radical implication of Hillel's saying that *every* act can be done in the name of heaven: if so 'then something is abstracted from the absolute value of the precept and a way is opened for the nullification of the worth of (the) ritual laws . . .' (p. 341).
76. cf. Westerholm, *Jesus*, pp. 67–71, and particularly Riches, *Jesus*, pp. 133–44, though he operates only with the saying of Jesus as a radical repudiation of the whole notion of purity, which the subsequent tradition softened (cf. n. 13 above). Nevertheless, the absence of any ritual boundary (no baptism, the openness of his table-fellowship) is a striking feature of Jesus' ministry, and in striking contrast to the other Jewish groups of the time. See further ch. 3 below.
77. cf. Westerholm, *Jesus*, p. 82. Gnilka also justifiably points out that we actually know very little about the Jewish Christianity of Palestine (*Markus*, p. 286).
78 See further J. D. G. Dunn, *The Living Word*, SCM, London, 1987.

Additional Note

The monograph by R. P. Booth, *Jesus and the Laws of Purity: Tradition History and Legal History in Mark 7*,[1] analyses the whole chapter (Mark 7.1–23) in a similar way and with very similar conclusions. So far as verse 15 is concerned, he concludes that εἰσπορευόμενον εἰς αὐτόν and ἐκπορευόμενα are redactional, in the sense that Mark has substituted them for synonyms in the tradition (pp. 46–7, 53; see my n. 26). He also maintains that ἔξωθεν is a redactional elaboration of ἔξω (p. 68; see above p. 41 = *A cause de l'évangile* p. 259 top). His conclusions as to Aramaic *Vorlage* are also similar (pp. 96–7, 114; see above pp. 41–2 = *Cause*, pp. 259–61).

On the larger structure of the passage, he recognizes that the account of a dispute over handwashing must have originated in Palestine (pp. 113–14), and thinks that the earliest form of the question in verse 5 consisted only of a question about handwashing (pp. 62–5) and that in the tradition the original reply is given at verses 14–15 (pp. 65–8), with the following verses (vv. 18–22) added in at the 'Hellenistic Gentile' stage of the tradition-history (pp. 68–73) – conclusions which also accord to a marked degree with those reached above (pp. 45–7 = *Cause*, pp. 264–8).[2]

Booth's main contribution is his attempt to clarify the matter still further by use of 'historico-legal criticism', that is, whether the purity dispute is credible in the light of the then current views on purity law (Part II). His conclusion is that 'the Pharisaic question is credible in the time of Jesus on the basis that the Pharisees concerned were *haberim* who did wash their hands before *hullin* (meat that can be eaten), and were urging Jesus and his disciples ... to become *haberim*' (p. 202). Here again there is strong accord with my own relatively very sketchy treatment of the historical context (above pp. 48–50 = *Cause*, pp. 269–73, including n. 66). The major difference would be that in my judgement Pharisaic *haberim* might well disapprove and criticize those outside the boundaries of their own group without actually expecting them to become *haberim*. In chapter 3 below we note how characteristic it was for factions of this period within Judaism to castigate other Jews outside their faction or (implicity) critical of their faction as 'sinners'.

Perhaps the most striking agreement between Booth's study and the above chapter is Booth's conclusion that the reply of Jesus in verse 15 was originally a matter of 'relative depreciation of external defilement generally in favour [*sic*] of ethical defilement' (p. 219). Jesus' reply he renders as, 'Nothing outside a man defiles him as much as the things coming from him' (p. 219). The depreciation is not restricted to unclean food, but was intended in a wider sense: 'cultic impurity *in toto* does not harm a man as much as moral impurity' (p. 219). With much of this I am in accord, particularly on the conclusion that the original saying of Jesus was less radical in the antithesis it drew. Our disagreement can be focused on two points.

(a) Booth concludes that Matthew 15.11 provides no testimony to a form of the saying earlier than Mark 7.15, because it is derived by Matthew solely from Mark (p. 98). This conclusion depends on a too simplistic view of the transmission of Jesus-tradition in the early churches round the eastern end of the Mediterranean. I refer to the discussion above (p. 43 = *Cause*, p. 262). When the probability that Matthew had his own (churches') version of much at least of the tradition also used by Mark, and the other indications of a pre-Markan *Vorlage* of Mark 7.15 somewhat closer to Matthew's version are added together, the conclusion becomes difficult to avoid that Matthew 15.11 has been drawn not simply from Mark but from Matthew's knowledge of a different version.[3] In which case the argument of pp. 42–4 above (*Cause* pp. 261–4) would add further weight to Booth's conclusions.

(b) Consequently I am also less happy with Booth's conclusion that Jesus' original words were directed to the idea of cultic impurity *in toto*. This seems to me an unjustified abstraction from all the known forms of the saying and immediate parallels elsewhere in the New Testament, where the focus is consistently on the issue of unclean food. Moreover, it gives too little weight to the evidence from the historical context that at least some Pharisees not only regarded the maintenance of cultic purity as of first importance in everyday life but also focused that concern on the purity of the meal table.

B. Lindars, 'All Foods Clean: Thoughts on Jesus and the Law',[4] agrees with the main thrust of my discussion, with the following important variation.

59

He thinks the Markan form of the saying is closer to the original saying of Jesus. His attempts to retranslate Mark 7.15 back into Aramaic produced a text which, on inspection, was more literally represented by Mark 7.18b and 20b. From which he deduces that 'verse 15 is a slightly polished version of the saying, which is best preserved in verses 18b and 20b' (p. 63). The case for seeing Matthew's version as closer to the original he disputes by arguing that 'Matthew's version of verse 15 is a typical Matthean conflation, using the text of verses 18 and 20, which are then subsequently abbreviated' (p. 63). This, however, is a more contrived explanation of the data than is either necessary or probable.

(a) It presupposes that Matthew's only access to this tradition is through Mark. But then why not simply use Mark 7.15 and redact to requirement? Just as he seems to have redacted verses 18 and 20 a few lines later.

(b) Conflation of sources is certainly characteristic of Matthew's editorial style (cf. Matt. 12.31–2 as a conflation of Mark 3.28–9 and the Q tradition preserved by Luke in 12.10). But to derive a saying from two Markan texts which are then used again in abbreviated form a few verses later can hardly be described as 'typical Matthean conflation'.

(c) Lindars also argues that the original form of the Markan saying throws all the weight on to the second half, thus changing the terms of reference from ritual defilement to spiritual defilement (pp. 64–6). Consequently the saying is ambiguous, and indicates no intention on the part of Jesus to abrogate the law (pp. 66, 68). But in that case more needs to be said about Matthew's derivation of the saying. For Matthew did not derive it from the *pre-Markan* form, but, on Lindars' reconstruction of events, from Mark as it now stands. The problem there is that on the most radical point, verse 18 is as 'hard' as verse 15 – '*nothing* from outside *is able* to defile' (v. 15 – οὐδέν ... ὅ δύναται; v. 18 – πᾶν ... οὐ δύναται). Was Matthew's redaction of Mark, then, simply a piece of unscrupulous manipulation of the Jesus-tradition by one Christian faction against another, with no more justification than its disagreement with the clear meaning of the saying? Or did Matthew know that Mark (or his tradition) had already interpreted the Jesus-tradition in a more radical way? The evidence of Matthew's omission of Markan redaction elsewhere (above n. 40) points towards the latter alternative. That, together with the other evidence reviewed above, still points for me to the conclusion that Matthew knew a form of the saying independent of Mark.

Notes

1. *JSNTSupp* 13, Sheffield: JSOT (1986).
2. cf. D. Lührmann, *Das Markusevangelium*, HNT 3, Tubingen: Mohr (1987) pp. 125–6, 128.
3. I. M. Zeitlin, *Jesus and the Judaism of His Time*, Cambridge: Polity (1988) pp. 78–9 also regards Matthew's version as earlier than Mark's.
4. *Law and Religion. Essays on the Place of the Law in Israel and Early Christianity.* ed. B. Lindars, Cambridge: James Clarke (1988) pp. 61–71.

3
Pharisees, Sinners, and Jesus

One of the most striking features of the study of Christianity's beginnings in the past ten years or so has been the reassessment of Jesus' relationship with his native faith, particularly with the Pharisees, and the increasing impact of the reassessment. It is, of course, part of a much larger reappraisal of the relationship between Christianity and Judaism, a central element of which has been a growing realization that Christian attitudes towards Judaism have been deeply tainted and indeed warped by centuries of misunderstanding and prejudice. Already before the Second World War individual voices had been raised in protest on the non-Jewish side.[1] But the horror of the Holocaust forced a much wider circle of Christians to re-examine the nature and roots of anti-Semitism and to face up to the stark issue of whether, and if so to what extent, anti-Semitism is endemic to Christianity and rooted in its own sacred Scriptures.[2] Since the Pharisees are the most immediate predecessors of rabbinic Judaism, which became Judaism's enduring form (and so the object of anti-Semitism through the centuries), it was inevitable that Christian perception of the Pharisees, not least in the Gospels, would have to come under particularly close scrutiny. And since Jesus is the founder of Christianity, which came to display such regrettable antagonism towards its founder's ancestral faith, it was equally inevitable that Jesus' relationship to the Pharisees should be a crucial issue within the larger debate.

As the reassessment of Jesus' relationship with the Pharisees has gathered strength a number of important claims have been staked out:

1. The Pharisees, the contemporaries of Jesus, have been misrepresented in at least some degree in the Gospels, particularly in Matthew and John, which reflect the growing antagonism between Christianity and rabbinic Judaism after 70 CE. This judgement would now command a widespread consensus within New Testament as well as Jewish scholarship.[3]

2. The Pharisees were not responsible for and had no part in the death of Jesus – a view long championed by Jewish scholars (H. Maccoby: the 'Jewish view of Jesus').[4]

3. Pharisees would not have been hostile to Jesus. Indeed, on the Jewish side the claim is quite often made that Jesus, far

from being an opponent of the Pharisees, was himself a Pharisee.[5]

The high-water mark, so far, in this tide of re-evaluation is the work of E. P. Sanders. In his *Jesus and Judaism*[6] he re-expresses all the claims so far outlined in his own terms and develops especially the last. In Sanders' judgement there was no substantive point of disagreement between Jesus and the Pharisees. In particular, the Pharisees would not have regarded the ordinary people ('*am ha-aretz*) as 'sinners' beyond the pale of the law and would not have criticized Jesus for associating with them. The Pharisees did not have the power to exclude others from the social and religious life of Judaism. And the depiction of the Pharisees as super-bigots attacking Jesus for offering forgiveness to the common people is ridiculous and offensive.[7]

All this can be summed up under the head of Jewish-Christian rapprochement: on the one hand, the Jewish attempt to reclaim Jesus; on the other, the Christian attempt to demonstrate the Jewishness of Jesus.[8] The proponents on both sides are usually well aware of the corollary: that the 'blame' for any anti-Jewish element within the Christian Scriptures is to be shifted well beyond Jesus to a later stage – to Paul (as in Maccoby), or beyond 70 CE (as in Sanders).[9] The problem and consequences of thus separating Jesus from subsequent Christianity, however, have not been fully worked out. Nor has it been sufficiently appreciated that to replace the wedge between Jesus and Judaism with a wedge between Jesus and Gentile Christianity has an unnerving echo of the equivalent attempts at the turn of the last century to isolate Jesus as a purveyor of a purer and less offensive gospel from the 'Hellenization' begun by Paul and his successors.[10] Before the echoes of the last Jesus-v.-Paul debate have died away there seems to be a growing need for a re-match.

Obviously there are too many issues caught up in the whole affair to be dealt with in a single essay. Here we can look at only one: the question of Jesus' relationship with the Pharisees as posed most recently and most challengingly by Sanders. In particular, is it the case that opposition between Jesus and the Pharisees as portrayed in the Gospels is all a retrojection of later controversies, without historical foundation within the ministry of Jesus? And is it the case that the 'sinners' Jesus was criticized for befriending were the 'truly wicked'?[11] These are only two of the many issues raised by Sanders' important work, but they provide a sizeable enough agenda for the moment.

PHARISEES ...

Despite repeated studies of the Pharisees there are still an astonishing number of disputed claims and unresolved questions on the subject. Here we confine ourselves to the single issue of the Pharisees' character and influence in the period prior to 70 CE, with the years of Jesus' ministry particularly in mind. Only if we can gain a reasonably clear picture here will we be in any position to answer our question as to whether the opposition between Jesus and the Pharisees as portrayed in the Gospels reflects the historical realities of Jesus' ministry. We have in fact *four* potential sources from which to glean the relevant information: the rabbinic traditions themselves, Josephus, Paul, and the Gospels.

The Pharisees from the Perspective of the Rabbinic Traditions

Here we are bound to start with the work of Jacob Neusner. Whatever issues he has left unresolved, and however one may dispute particular findings, it cannot be denied that he has made a decisive beginning in the too long delayed task of providing a tradition-historical analysis of the amazingly rich and diverse traditions of the rabbis.[12] In particular, we must refer to his careful study of the traditions regarding the Pharisees before 70 CE.[13] These traditions naturally have a first call on our attention, if only for the important fact that they provide *a picture of the Pharisees as the later rabbis chose to remember them.*

Neusner's findings are very striking. The traditions about the Pharisees before 70 CE specifically attributed to individuals or houses (the houses of Hillel and Shammai) consist of approximately 371 separate items. 'Approximately 67% of all legal pericopae deal with dietary laws: ritual purity for meals and agricultural rules governing the fitness of food for Pharisaic consumption.'[14] In his numerous subsequent writings, Neusner has continued to maintain the same point: this much-repeated concern with rules on agricultural tithes and ritual purity all focuses on table-fellowship; the attempt to maintain in everyday life the purity laws designed for the temple was most at risk at the meal table.[15] The pre-70 strata of the Mishnaic law bear witness to a group where food taboos were the chief mode of social differentiation by which they maintained their continued existence as a group:

> The Mishnah before the wars begins its life among a group of people who are joined by a common conviction about the eating of food under ordinary circumstances in accord with cultic rules to begin with applicable ... to the Temple alone. This group, moreover, had other rules which affected who might join and who might not ... [which] formed a protective boundary, keeping in those who were in, keeping out those who were not.[16]

Sanders, however, finds Neusner's analysis of the rabbinic texts 'unpersuasive' and 'made especially dubious by the evidence from

Josephus'. In more detail, Sanders' objection is that Neusner's conclusions are drawn only from the tradition explicitly assigned to individuals or to houses. 'The summary does not reflect the numerous anonymous laws which probably represent *common* belief and practice, including large bodies of law on civil matters, worship, feasts and the temple cult.' And Josephus shows the Pharisees to be simply lay experts in the law and says nothing about their having peculiar food and purity laws.[17]

There is some force in both points. But Neusner is by no means so vulnerable to the criticism as might at first appear. In his original treatment of the tradition attributed to the houses he had allowed the possibility that they were 'relatively small and constituted only one part of the Pharisaic group in Jerusalem, a still smaller segment of Pharisaism as a whole'.[18] And in *Judaism* he is scrupulously careful not to identify this early stage of the Mishnaic tradition with a particular named group. In the face of Josephus' silence regarding any concern on the part of the Pharisees for the purity of the meal table, he had made the important observation that on this point the Pharisaic group were different from the Qumran covenanters (not to mention the Christians latterly). For they 'evidently did not conduct table-fellowship meals *as rituals*. The table-fellowship laws pertained not merely to group life, but to daily life quite apart from a sectarian setting and ritual occasion.'[19] Consequently, they would be less distinctive for a readership looking at Judaism from outside, for whom the Jewish food laws would be striking enough,[20] so that the refinements of subgroups within Judaism would be lost on them (cf. Mark 7.3: '... the Pharisees and *all* the Jews ...'). Besides this, Josephus with his strong Roman contacts would be well aware of Roman suspicion that special dietary laws were an indication of strange cults[21] and would not be anxious to highlight this aspect of Pharisaism in writings that take such pains to conceal the less acceptable (in Roman eyes) features of Pharisaism (see below).[22]

∨ As for Sanders' former criticism, no doubt many of the unattributed traditions do go back to the pre-70 period. But even so, that should not be allowed to detract so much from Neusner's findings. It may simply mean that there was a strand of Pharisaism which, among other things, emphasized dietary rules at the daily meal table. But in fact the evidence calls for a stronger conclusion. For despite Sanders, it must be significant that such a high percentage of the attributed traditions focus upon one main aspect of practical piety. It strongly suggests that these rulings were sensitive matters or matters of dispute among the predecessors of the rabbis, so that relevant rulings were remembered by the post-70 dominant party by their attribution to leading figures of the past or as part of the houses' disputes. The clear implication is that the purity of table-fellowship was thus remembered as a matter of great importance within pre-70 Pharisaic circles or by a group or faction of Pharisees.[23] And whatever their numerical size in that period, they were strong enough not only to survive the castastrophe of 70 CE but also to stamp their authority on the tradition preserved by the rabbis.

In short, the evidence of the rabbinic traditions points clearly to the conclusion that *the purity of the meal table was an important concern among many of the Pharisees of Jesus' time,* or at least within a significant faction of the Pharisees.

The Pharisees in Josephus

Here the main question is twofold: how to account for the differences in the pictures of the Pharisees which emerge from Josephus and from the rabbinic traditions; and what weight to give to the different emphases present in the various accounts of the Pharisees provided by Josephus himself.

The answer to the first is probably fairly straightforward, as we have already suggested. Josephus writes of the Pharisees, as on other matters, with an eye to his wider readership in sophisticated Greek-speaking society. This is particularly clear in what is his most consistent emphasis when he makes a point of describing the Pharisees: they are a 'philosophy' (*War* 2.119, 166; *Ant.* 18.11); their beliefs are described in philosophical terms (*War* 2.163; *Ant.* 13.172); they resemble quite closely (παραπλήσιος) the Stoic school or sect (*Life* 12). Clearly evident here is a deliberate and sustained strategy of commending the Pharisees as a philosophical school. Josephus was hardly likely to put that strategy in jeopardy by also presenting the Pharisees in the contrasting and much less appealing terms of a foreign superstition.[24]

When we consider the internal tensions between Josephus' various references to the Pharisees, particularly as between the *War* and *Antiquities,* the issue that comes to the fore is whether and, if so, to what extent the Pharisees were a significant influence on the religious and political life of the nation. The issue is posed by M. Smith:

> In the *War* [Josephus] says nothing of the Pharisees having any influence with the people . . . In the *Antiquities,* however, written twenty years later, the picture is quite different. Here whenever Josephus discusses the Jewish sects, the Pharisees take first place, and every time he mentions them he emphasizes their popularity . . .[25]

From this Neusner concludes, 'We must discount all of [Josephus's] references to the influence and power of the Pharisees [in the Herodian period].'[26] They *had* been deeply involved in politics during the Hasmonean period, but at the time of Jesus they were a relatively small sect concerned primarily with matters of ritual purity.

This position must, however, be regarded as something of an over-statement. For one thing, the contrast between *War* and *Antiquities* is not so marked as Smith argues. *Whenever* Josephus mentions the three sects of the Jews, he always names the Pharisees 'first', with Sadducees 'second' and Essenes 'third', in *War* as much as in *Antiquities*, as also in his *Life* (*War* 2.119, 162, 164; *Ant.* 13.171; 18.11; *Life* 10). On this point Josephus is again consistent: the Pharisees were the leading or most important of the different factions within first-century Judaism.

As to the difference in emphasis between *War* and *Antiquities* on the matter of the Pharisees' popularity and influence, an obvious explanation lies near to hand here too. In the immediate aftermath of the Jewish revolt (assuming the consensus view that *War* was published in the 70s), it would hardly be wise for Josephus to highlight the political influence of the Pharisees in the period leading up to the revolt. In fact he does note that 'distinguished Pharisees' were consulted as the crisis deepened (*War* 2.411). And in his later writings it is not only the Pharisees' popularity with the people on religious matters of which he speaks (as in *Ant.* 18.15, 17) but also of Pharisaic involvement in the revolt against Rome (*Ant.* 18.4; *Life* 21, 191, 197; note also *Ant.* 18.23). It would be unwise, therefore, wholly to discount the *Antiquities*' picture of Pharisaic influence and popularity: it is as likely that such an emphasis has been suppressed in *War* as that it has been exaggerated in *Antiquities;* apologetic considerations would play an important role in both cases. The truth probably lies somewhere in between.[27]

In short, the strong impression given by Josephus is that the Pharisees were the most important of the three or four main factions in Jewish social and religious life, outside the temple, of this period, and that the Pharisees were divided among themselves on the question of active involvement in the growing political crisis, with some leading Pharisees having influence in the highest Jewish councils and others active in the developing resistance. Even if the depiction of Pharisaic influence in *Antiquities* is exaggerated, therefore, the Pharisees cannot be discounted as a merely quietistic, purity sect without significant influence beyond their own circles. On the contrary, if we can speak of them as a coherent sect (as not only Josephus consistently does but also Acts 15.5; 26.5), we have to recognize *the likelihood that their influence reached well beyond their own ranks.*[28]

In addition, we should note the point made by A. I. Baumgarten: that when Josephus speaks of the Pharisees he regularly describes them as the party of ἀκρίβεια (*War* 1.110; 2.162; *Ant.*

17.41; *Life* 191; cf. *Ant.* 20.201, and note again the striking correlation in Acts 22.3; 26.5). The word denotes 'exactness or precision', and when used in connection with 'law' is most naturally taken in a sense like 'strictness or severity' (*Greek-English Lexicon,* ed. H. Liddell and R. Scott). So when we read, for example, in *War* 2.162, that the Pharisees interpreted the laws or customs μετ' ἀκριβείας, the implication is clear that *they were well known as those who interpreted the law with scrupulous exactness and strictness in detail.*[29] This strongly suggests that the Pharisees also saw themselves in an important sense as *guardians of the law and of the ancestral customs (Ant.* 13.297, 408; 17.41; *Life* 198). Moreover, if Josephus, the self-confessed Pharisee, is any guide, they naturally wished to commend such 'strictness' to others (*Ant.* 1.14; 4.309; 5.132; 8.21; 18.345; *Ap.* 2.149, 187, 227–8). The implications of this for their relationship to a movement like that of Jesus are potentially important, but the picture is too incomplete to say more at this stage.

Paul the Pharisee

It is very surprising that in such discussions the potential evidence of Paul is rarely taken into account.[30] For Paul is the only first-century Pharisee apart from Josephus from whom we have any first-hand evidence. And Paul is the only Pharisee who speaks to us with his own voice from the period under scrutiny. Of course, Paul's testimony has to be discounted to some extent at least, since he can be regarded as a 'hostile witness'. But the testimony should certainly not be ignored or disparaged out of hand.[31]

The passages which obviously call for consideration are the two where he speaks of his own pre-Christian past: Galatians 1.13–14; Philippians 3.5–6. In addition, however, there are one or two passages where he speaks of his fellow Jews and where the most obvious interpretation is that he is thinking of the Judaism he knew best: especially Romans 10.2–3, but also Romans 2.17ff. In Galatians 1.13–14 he briefly describes his 'way of life when he was in Judaism' in three clauses: he persecuted the church of God καθ' ὑπερβολήν; he progressed in Judaism beyond many of those of his own age among his people; he was much more of a zealot (ζηλωτής) for the traditions handed down from the fathers. In Philippians 3.5–6 the most relevant part again has three elements: in terms of the law, a Pharisee; in terms of zeal (ζῆλος), a persecutor of the church; in terms of righteousness which is in the law, blameless (ἄμεμπτος). In Romans 10.2–3, Paul bears personal testimony (no doubt on the basis of his own experience) to Israel's zeal for God (ζῆλον θεοῦ) and concern 'to establish their own righteousness'.

There are two features which recur in each description and which are worthy of special note. One characteristic of Judaism which Paul recalls and most naturally thinks of as typical of Judaism is 'zeal' – zeal for God, zeal for the traditions of the fathers. In Jewish circles the classic examples of such zeal were well known: Simeon and Levi (Gen. 34; Jth. 9:4; *Jub.* 30.5–20), Phinehas (Num. 25.10–13; Sir. 45.23–4; 1 Macc. 2.54; 4 Macc. 18.12), Elijah (Sir. 48.2; 1 Macc. 2.58), and the Maccabees (1 Macc. 2.19–27, 50, 58; 2 Macc. 4.2; Josephus *Ant.* 12.271). It is notable that in each case this zeal led to taking the sword to maintain Israel's distinctiveness as God's covenant people. It is certainly just such zeal which motivated the Zealots, and it was also such zeal which Paul had in mind in Philippians 3.6 ('in terms of zeal a persecutor') when he recalled his own past.[32] But Galatians 1.14 indicates that 'zeal for God', 'zeal for the law', could be a relative thing ('much more a zealot') and could therefore presumably express itself in dedication to observing and maintaining the law as the mark of Israel's distinctiveness without necessarily resorting to the sword (cf. 1QS 4.4; 9.23; 1QH 14.14; *T. Ash.* 4.5). The implication is that Paul was comparing himself with his fellow students or younger Pharisees as all 'zealous', but he much the more so because he resorted to the sword.

The other feature of these Pauline passages is the strong conviction of a secure status sustained not least by such zeal – of a progress beyond others (Gal. 1.14), of a righteousness sustained without reproach (Phil. 3.6), of a confidence of possessing light and knowledge to higher advantage than others by virtue of having the law (Rom. 2.17–20, 23). All this is most naturally understood as tied into and as a corollary to the 'strictness' which, according to Josephus, characterized the Pharisees. The point seems to be confirmed beyond reasonable dispute by the corroborative evidence of two other witnesses: Acts 22.3 confirms that 'zeal for God' and 'strictness' in observing the ancestral law are closely synonymous concepts in the description of a Pharisee; and in *Ant.* 17.41, Josephus provides the nearest parallel to what Paul implies in the passages cited – that the Pharisees were a group of Jews who prided themselves on the strict observance (ἐξακριβώσει) of their ancestral law(s).

⌄   The picture which emerges from Paul, therefore, is what one might fairly call a Pharisee's view of Judaism. Or to be more precise, in such passages Paul recalls his self-understanding as a Pharisee and uses language and sentiments which must have been characteristic of the Pharisee as 'sect' (and which, of course, Paul now regards as mistaken). This should *not* be taken as evidence for the old interpretation of Pharisaism as boastful of self-achievement and consumed with meritorious point-scoring. In speaking of his life as a Pharisee as 'blameless' (Phil. 3.6), Paul most likely meant that he had lived to the full in the terms laid down for members of the covenant people ($\kappa\alpha\tau\grave{\alpha}$ $\delta\iota\kappa\alpha\iota\sigma\sigma\acute{\upsilon}\nu\eta\nu$ $\tau\grave{\eta}\nu$ $\grave{\epsilon}\nu$ $\nu\acute{o}\mu\omega$), including the law's provision for atonement and forgiveness.[33] And in talking of Israel's 'seeking to establish its own righteousness' (Rom. 10.3), the thought is of *Israel's* righteousness – not available to those outside the covenant people – not of a righteousness achieved by Paul ($\tau\grave{\eta}\nu$ $\mathring{\iota}\delta\acute{\iota}\alpha\nu$ $\delta\iota\kappa\alpha\iota\sigma\sigma\acute{\upsilon}\nu\eta\nu$).[34] Nor does it follow that Paul speaks in these passages for all Pharisees, or for Pharisees alone. But he probably does speak as a Pharisee and express views typical of Pharisees of his own day. From such evidence, therefore, we may fairly conclude that *in the middle decades of the first century, Pharisees were characterized by zeal for the law and concern to practise that pattern of life which maintained the righteousness of the covenant and Israel's status as the people of God.*

The Pharisees in the Synoptic Gospels

On this issue, Sanders is at his most confrontational: 'It is incorrect to make purity the issue between Jesus and his critics.' 'Jesus' eating with the sinners probably did not involve him in a dispute with a superscrupulous group (whether called *haberim* or Pharisees).' 'It is very probable that the issues of food and Sabbath are so prominent in the Gospels because of the importance which they assumed in the church.' 'There was no substantial conflict between Jesus and the Pharisees with regard to Sabbath, food, and purity laws.'[35] A repeated claim is that the stories of such conflict are 'obviously unrealistic'.

> The extraordinarily unrealistic settings of many of the conflict stories should be realized: Pharisees did not organize themselves into groups to spend their Sabbaths in Galilean cornfields in the hope of catching someone transgressing (Mark 2:23–4), nor is it credible that scribes and Pharisees made a special trip to Galilee from Jerusalem to inspect Jesus' disciples' hands (Mark 7:1f). Surely stories such as these should not be read as describing actual debates between Jesus and others.[36]

There are a number of issues here to which we must come in due course (particularly the identity of the 'sinners' and the likelihood of Pharisees seeking to influence religious practice in Galilee). For the moment, however, we will confine ourselves to the issue of whether the Synoptic testimony, and if so how much of it, can be admitted as evidence for Pharisaic attitudes in the period before 70 CE, and particularly in regard to Jesus.

There is no question that many of the references to 'Pharisees' in the Synoptic accounts are redactional: we need think only of such passages as Matthew 3.7; 5.20; 9.34; 12.24; 21.45; Luke 5.17, 21; 7.30; 19.39; not to mention the strong sequence of references found only in one of the evangelists (particularly Matt. 23 passim; Luke 14.1, 3; 15.2; 16.14; 18.10–11). Few would dispute that at least a considerable portion of this testimony has to be read in the light of the increasing conflict between Christianity and rabbinic Judaism in the 80s of the first century, and that traditions have been shaped and particularized to make them more serviceable for congregations (usually Jewish Christian congregations) who felt themselves under threat from the successors of the Pharisees. But that still leaves a core of references strongly attested in the triple tradition, that is, including Mark – particularly Mark 2.16, 18, 24 pars.; 7.1 pars. And it is a good deal more difficult to treat these as the product of disputes of the post-70 period.

1. It is of course arguable that Mark was written after 70 CE,[37] though most scholars find the late 60s more compelling.[38] But even if a post-70 date for Mark should be accepted, that may still be inadequate for the case. In the aftermath of the destruction of Jerusalem the rabbinic school at Jabneh did not immediately leap into prominence. The probability is that they took time to find their feet and that their influence took many years to spread.[39] The hypothesis that rabbinic pressure on the Christian congregations of the post-70 period left its imprint on the Jesus-tradition used by Mark probably requires a date for Mark into the early 80s before it becomes realistic. Such a date is not impossible, but the later Mark has to be dated the weaker the hypothesis becomes.

2. Few would want to argue that the material in Mark 2.15–28 and 7.1–5 was created *de novo* at the final stage of the Gospel. Apart from anything else, there are too many indications of editorial work on a pre-formed tradition: in particular, Mark 2.20 as a qualification added in the light not least of the Christian congregations' continuation (or resumption) of the practice of fasting some time after Jesus' death; and Mark 7.3–4 as added to explain Pharisaic practice to a Gentile readership, making it necessary for 7.5a to recapitulate the introduction (7.1–2). There is clear evidence in these chapters of Mark's having taken over an *earlier* tradition in which Christian congregations in the period before 70 CE felt it necessary to defend themselves from criticism particularly on matters of table-fellowship, ritual purity, and sabbath observance, and in which the criticism is explicitly attributed to Pharisees.[40]

3. Looked at from a slightly different angle, the same evidence also indicates that at the pre-Markan level of the tradition it is *internal Jewish* disputes which are in view: a dispute over *how* the sabbath should be observed, not yet *whether* it should be observed (Mark 2.27–8; contrast Rom. 14.5), and a dispute where the indisputably Jewish use of κοινός in the sense of 'impure, defiled' has also to be explained to Gentiles (7.2). The indication again is of *Jewish* Christian congregations, who from within Judaism or as

part of Judaism felt the need to explain and defend themselves to other Jews.

4. This evidence accords well with other indicators of intra-Jewish concerns in the period prior to 70 CE (apart from those already reviewed above). On the one hand there is the evidence of both *Jub.* 2.29–30, 50.6–13 and CD 10.14—11.18 that concern to protect the sabbath by means of particular *halakoth* was already well developed before the time of Jesus.[41] On the other there is the strong testimony of Galatians 2.11–14 that pressure was exerted on the Antioch congregation from within the Jerusalem leadership anxious to maintain the traditional dietary laws. Mark's portrayal of Pharisees concerned about issues of sabbath observance and ritual purity fits much more closely into the period of Jesus' ministry than Sanders allows,[42] as does Mark's depiction of Pharisees' high regard for ancestral traditions (Mark 7.3, 5; cf. Gal. 1.14; Josephus *Ant.* 13.297, 408; 17.41; *Life* 198).

To sum up, when the four strands of testimony regarding the Pharisees examined above are put together, a remarkably coherent picture emerges of Pharisees as a sufficiently clearly defined group to be described as a 'sect', αἵρεσις, whose most characteristic concern was to observe the law and ancestral traditions with scrupulous care, with a deep desire to maintain Israel's identity as the people of the law, as expressed not least in developing *halakoth* regarding the sabbath and particularly ritual purity. To attempt to undermine this picture by setting Neusner's findings aside, by failing to follow through the logic of Josephus' description of the Pharisees as ἀκρίβεις, by ignoring the testimony of Paul, or by banishing all the evidence of the Synoptics to as late a date as possible must be counted a policy of desperation. It is not necessary to argue that the picture applies equally to all Pharisees ('the Pharisees'). Nor does the precise relation of the *haberim* in particular to the Pharisees in general (or of Pharisees/*perushim* to sages, or of scribes to Pharisees) need to be resolved.[43] But *that there were at the time of Jesus a number of Pharisees, and probably a significant body of Pharisees, who felt passionately concerned to preserve, maintain, and defend Israel's status as the people of the covenant and the righteousness of the law, as understood in the already developed* halakoth, *must be regarded as virtually certain.*

... SINNERS ...

The thrust of Sanders' attack on older positions, however, is that the Pharisees would not have been critical of those who did not observe the law in the way and to the degree they accepted as their own obligation. In particular, they would not have condemned the ordinary people as 'sinners' because they failed to observe all the

71

halakoth they took upon themselves. The 'sinners' with whom Jesus consorted were genuinely 'wicked' and 'traitors'.[44] And contraction of impurity did not constitute one a 'sinner' or exclude from the covenant; it simply prevented participation in the temple cult for the period of impurity, and lack of concern about impurity outside the temple simply made one a non-*haber*.[45] Here again Sanders is justified in reacting against overstatements by too many New Testament scholars about Pharisaic hostility to the ordinary people [46] But here too the question has to be asked whether Sanders in turn has *over*-reacted and tried to push the pendulum too far in the opposite direction.

The Role of Social Conflict in Group Self-Definition

We may consider, first of all, the insights of sociology and social anthropology into the nature of groups and their self-definition. Once we realize that the social identity of a group depends to a large extent on the distinctiveness of its practices and beliefs, it also becomes evident that the corollary of 'identity' is 'boundary', that self-definition involves self-differentiation.[47] In all this, ritual as a visible expression of social relationships usually plays a particularly important role.[48] Moreover, wherever there are other groups whose distinctives differ, each group is liable to be particularly protective of its identity and react strongly to any perceived threat to its boundaries.[49] Indeed, group conflict can play an important role in binding a group more closely together[50] and will often cause it to put still greater emphasis on the distinctiveness of its rituals. And particularly where groups are close to one another in origin or character or distinctives, the conflict is liable to be all the more intense·[51] it is the brother who threatens identity most ('sibling rivalry'); it is the party most like your own which threatens to draw away your support and undermine your reason for existence as a distinct entity.

Such generalized observations provide a remarkably close fit with the data we have already gleaned: the Pharisees as a distinct 'sect' whose distinctives included particularly their zeal for scrupulous interpretation and observance of the law and, for at least a large proportion of their number, concern to maintain temple purity at the meal table (the 'separated ones').[52] It is inherently likely that such zeal would cause friction with other groups, not least with the other main 'sects' of the time – Sadducees and Essenes. And so the evidence indicates, as we shall see. But it would also be unsurprising if at least some Pharisees refused to settle quietly behind their boundaries or opt merely for self-defence but sought to maintain their identity by taking the offensive. This was all the more true when there was any sense of conviction that what the Pharisee or *haber* practised was what God

72

required of Israel as a whole.[53] Certainly wherever the zeal of a Phinehas or a Mattathias was lauded and the concern of such heroes to preserve Israel's integrity as the people of God was taken as an ideal, a highly likely corollary would be a sharp criticism of any who seemed to threaten Israel's birthright or to deny Israel's obligation under the covenant – if not outright persecution of the offenders. None of this goes beyond the evidence already examined. On the contrary, the portrayal of the Pharisees in Mark 2 and 7 is shown to have considerable plausibility, and Paul's persecuting zeal to be not necessarily exceptional. The alternative of a quietistic group wholly absorbed in their own affairs and completely uncritical of others becomes increasingly unrealistic.[54]

Finally/we should note that Sanders' argument is in danger of rebounding on him. For the effect of arguing that Jesus was very close to the Pharisees, not least on matters of the law, is to *increase* the likelihood of tension between Jesus and the Pharisees, not to lessen it. A Jesus who sat wholly loose to the law would pose little threat: he was self-condemned. But a successful Jesus who was observant of the law and yet not a Pharisee or *haber* was bound to be regarded as some sort of competitor and to cause some friction and conflict.[55] And a Jesus who was as loyal to the covenant but who had different ideas of what covenant loyalty involved would almost certainly pose a threat to Pharisaic self-understanding and identity. In particular, where issues such as sabbath or purity *halakoth* were put in question by Jesus' conduct, critical and defensive questions were bound to arise for those who prized such *halakoth*.

In short, given the data we have regarding the Pharisees in the period prior to 70 CE, it would be very surprising had they *not* been critical of Jesus and his disciples.

Who Were the Sinners?

But what about the 'sinners'? Was the 'offence' of Jesus at this point that he consorted with the wicked and promised them the kingdom even though they remained unrepentant of their wickedness?[56] Certainly Sanders is on good ground when he questions the too simplistic equation of 'sinners' and 'people of the land'. In the Old Testament the word ($\dot{\alpha}\mu\alpha\rho\tau\omega\lambda\acute{o}s$) occurs most frequently in the Psalms, almost always translating רָשָׁע, and the rendering 'wicked' is wholly appropriate. Similarly with the word's most common use in the apocryphal writings (Sirach). But Sanders ignores the fact that the word is also used in a *factional* context to denote those outside the boundary of the group who use it, where wickedness, by definition, is conduct outside the boundary, conduct unacceptable to those inside.[57]

The most obvious example of this is where 'sinner' is used more or less as a synonym for 'Gentile' (Ps. 9.17; Tobit 13.8(6); *Jub.* 23.23–4; *Pss. Sol.* 1.1; 2.1–2; Luke 6.33 = Matt. 5.47; Mark 14.41 pars.; Gal. 2.15). In such passages the unifying concept is not that Gentiles are by definition murderers and robbers. Rather it is that their conduct lay outside the boundary of the law. They were literally lawless: they did not have the law because they did not belong to the covenant people, the people of the law. And so, not knowing the Torah, naturally they did not keep it.

More to the present point, however, is the fact that boundaries could also be drawn *within* the people of Israel, with 'sinners' used to describe those of whom a particular faction disapproved. So in the case of 1 Maccabees, where the 'sinners and lawless men' (1.34; 2.44, 48) certainly at least include those whom the Maccabeans regarded as apostate Jews, as Israelites who had abandoned the law.[58] Of course, what is in view here is no mere breach of sabbath or purity *halakoth* but full-scale apostasy, conduct no longer contained within the bounds of the covenant. Nevertheless, the fact remains that this is a factional viewpoint: 'sinners' is language used by one group of Israelites to describe another.

What is at issue here is the definition of what conduct proper to the covenant actually involves and who determines it. In the case of 1 Maccabees the issue was fairly clear cut, at least for the Maccabeans: the Syrian sympathizers among the Jews had departed too far from the Torah. But in the subsequent period the issue became more blurred as different heirs of the first wave of Maccabean resistance sought to define in their own terms what walking in the ways of the Torah meant. For example, *Jubilees* shows that the calendar became an important bone of contention. The implication is clear: that observance of a festival or ordinance whose date had been wrongly computed was regarded (by those for whom *Jubilees* speaks) as *non*observance, as failure to maintain the covenant, as walking in the errors of the Gentiles (particularly *Jub.* 6.32–5; also 23.16, 26).[59] *Jubilees* does not use the pejorative 'sinner' in the context, but the connotation is the same: those Jews who disagreed on the calendar showed disregard for the law of festivals and so put themselves outside the covenant, made themselves like Gentile sinners.

A similar attitude is evident in the earliest parts of the *Enoch* corpus and provides further evidence of a bitter calendrical dispute which divided Judaism probably in the second century BCE. 'The righteous', 'who walk in the ways of righteousness', clearly marked themselves off from those who 'sin like the sinners' in wrongly reckoning the months and the feasts and the years (82.4–7).[60] Less specific is the accusation of *1 Enoch* 1–5, where again a clear line of distinction is drawn between the 'righteous/chosen' and the 'sinners/impious' (1.1, 7–9; 5.6–7). But here too an internal Jewish

74

factional dispute is clearly in view: the sinners are addressed directly and roundly rebuked – 'You have not persevered, nor observed the law of the Lord' – 5.4). 'Sinners' here are Jews who practised their Judaism differently from the 'righteous'.[61]

A more virulent usage of the same kind occurs regularly, as we might have expected, in the Dead Sea Scrolls. Again and again the political and religious opponents of the sectarians are attacked as the wicked, the men of the lot of Belial, who have departed from the paths of righteousness, transgressed the covenant, and suchlike (e.g., CD 1.13–21; 1QS 2.4–5; 1QH 2.8–19; 1QpHab 2.1–4; 5.3–8). And again and again it is clear that the touchstone which divides 'righteous' from 'sinner' was not what the typical non-Essene would regard as blatant wickedness but the Torah as interpreted within the community (e.g., CD 4.8; 1QS 5.7–11; 1QH 7.12) – that is, a sectarian interpretation which would doubtless have been disputed at many points by the nonsectarians, who were categorized in turn as 'those who seek smooth things' and 'deceivers' (1QH 2.14–16; 4.6–8; 4QpNah 2.7–10). If we follow the usual view of these opponents, such denunciations were directed particularly against the Pharisees:[62] in this case it is the Pharisees themselves who are the 'sinners'! The point, however, is that once again we have clear evidence that in the period leading up to the time of Jesus, and in a community in existence during Jesus' ministry and beyond, 'sinner' was used as a sectarian word to denounce those outside the bounds of the sect itself.[63]

A further example is the *Psalms of Solomon,* written less than a century before Jesus' ministry. They too clearly have been composed by those who regarded themselves as the 'righteous', the 'devout' (e.g., 3.3–7; 4.1, 8; 9.3; 10.6; 13.6–12; 15.6–7). But the 'righteous' are not the covenant people as a whole; the usage is again clearly factional and amounts to a claim that only this faction properly 'live in the righteousness of [the Lord's] commandments' (14.2). Similarly with the obverse in the repeated attacks on 'sinners'. Once again 'sinners' are not synonymous with Gentiles or the blatantly wicked. On the contrary, 'sinners' often refers to the Jewish opponents of the 'devout', probably the Hasmonean Sadducees who had usurped the monarchy and defiled the sanctuary (1.8; 2.3; 7.2; 8.12–13; 17.5–8, 23).[64] According to 4.1–8 they sit in the Sanhedrin, they live in hypocrisy, they try to impress the people, they deceitfully quote the law. They do not maintain proper standards of ritual purity (8.12).[65] In the reckoning of the devout, such sinners have no part in Israel's inheritance: the promise was not made to them (17.5, 23). Here, then, is another case where 'sinners' was used by Jews for other Jews who did not live by the standards of righteousness which the devout held before themselves.

A similar internal Jewish polemic is evident in the document which of all the 'intertestamental' literature is usually dated (in its present form) closest to the time of Jesus: the *Testament* (or *Assumption*) *of Moses*. In *T. Mos.* 7 (set in the final author's own time) there is a forthright attack on 'godless men, who represent themselves as being righteous', 'with hand and mind' they 'touch unclean things' even though they themselves say, 'Do not touch me, lest you pollute me' (7.3, 9–10). In view of our earlier findings we may well have to recognize here another attack on the Pharisees themselves, where different interpretations of ritual purity requirements were at the heart of the dispute.[66]

It should not escape notice that we have just reviewed a sequence of documents which include those having the strongest claim to represent attitudes of Jewish groups in Palestine contemporaneous with Jesus. And a common feature of them all is a factional conflict within the Judaism of their time. In view of this evidence we may well have to conclude that no period of ancient Judaism was so riven with factional dispute as the time of Jesus. Nor should we regard those labelled 'sinners' simply as 'apostates'[67] – those who in the eyes of all Jews had abandoned the covenant. That they *had* done so is certainly the view of the various authors; but that is simply to underline the factional character of these documents. From the perspective of those with a narrower definition of what covenant righteousness required it was natural to accuse those who disagreed with that definition of having abandoned the covenant. Such has been the attitude of rigorists and traditionalists throughout the ages. But those (i.e., sinners) who viewed things from *outside* the circle of the 'righteous' would doubtless have a different understanding of the matter.

Against this background it has to be said that the Gospel usage of 'sinners' makes perfect sense. It is wholly plausible to see 'sinners' functioning in the Gospels as a *factional term*, describing those whose conduct was regarded as unacceptable to a sectarian mentality – that is, not just the blatantly wicked but those who did not accept the sect's interpretation of the law or live in sufficient accord with that interpretation. This fits too well with what we have learned of the Pharisees to be easily ignored. It is precisely those who were 'scrupulous' in their adherence to the law and the ancestral customs who would be most liable to criticize others whose observance was, in their eyes, significantly less scrupulous (= *un*scrupulous). It is precisely those who were earnest in their practice of ritual purity who would be most likely to count others as sinners who did not share that zeal or who blatantly disregarded matters of purity. The fact that 'tax collectors' are linked with 'sinners' in the Synoptic testimony (Mark 2.15–16 pars.; Matt. 11.19//Luke 7:34) should not be counted as evidence that 'sinners' meant blatant lawbreakers: tax collectors were despised more for national and political than religious reasons; only the Zealots would have regarded the job of tax collecting for the Romans as antithetical *per se* to a life lived in accordance with the law. More relevant is Mark 2.16 pars.: 'sinners' as the antithesis of the 'righteous'. This is precisely the language of sectarianism reviewed above: the sin of the 'sinners' is that they stand outside the boundaries of righteousness as defined by the 'righteous'. We need not assume that the Pharisees were as rigid on this matter as the Essenes: they did not necessarily regard all non-Pharisees as sinners – perhaps only those who made light of Pharisaic concerns.[68] Nevertheless, the conclusion presses upon us: *The more that members of the Jewish community departed from the standards which the Pharisees as a rule saw to be necessary to maintain covenant righteousness, the more likely these Pharisees would be to dub them 'sinners'.*

Pharisees in Galilee?

One other issue cannot be ignored: whether the Gospel's portrayal of Jesus coming under attack from Pharisees *in Galilee* is credible. Sanders questions it, following the conclusion of Smith: 'There is strong evidence that there were practically no Pharisees in Galilee during Jesus' lifetime.'[69] But Smith's reading of the evidence is at least open to question, and may have to be discounted as tendentious.[70]

1. It is certainly the case that the only Pharisees Josephus speaks of in Galilee had been sent from Jerusalem (*War* 2.569; *Life* 189–98). But in these accounts Josephus was not attempting to describe social or religious life in Galilee; he was writing a military history, and the Pharisees in question are mentioned because they served as emissaries from Jerusalem. For the same reason he speaks of synagogues only in the context of narrating factional disputes (*Life* 276–80, 293–303) and mentions the sabbath only when it inhibited military action (*Life* 159, 275–79; *War* 2.634). A more accurate description of Josephus' testimony on this matter, therefore, would be that the only Pharisees Josephus had *cause* to mention in these passages were from Jerusalem. Since the matter of whether there were or were not Pharisees in Galilee is irrelevant to his purpose, his silence on the score means nothing.

2. Smith plays down the significance of the fact that the great Pharisee Yohanan ben Zakkai lived in Galilee – in a village called 'Arav – for eighteen years (probably between 20 and 40 CE), during which time only two cases of *halakah* were brought to him.[71] But as Neusner has noted, the explanation for this may simply be that Yohanan was not yet well known and that the Galileans preferred to seek *halakic* rulings elsewhere.[72] We may note in addition that

Hanina ben Dosa, who is once described as Yohanan's pupil (*b. Ber.* 34b), also came from 'Arav.[73] Yohanan's period of residence in Galilee may not therefore be read as evidence for Pharisaic disengagement from Galilee. On the contrary, it may be evidence of a deliberate Pharisaic strategy to station some of the most promising younger Pharisees in different parts of the country to ensure that *halakic* rulings were readily available.[74] Indeed, if part of Pharisaic motivation in practising temple purity outside the temple was to demonstrate and maintain covenant righteousness throughout Israel, a natural corollary would be for some at least to follow the Pharisaic *halakoth* in different population centres throughout the promised land.

3. Smith has overlooked a further piece of evidence of potential importance. In *Ant.* 20.38–48, Josephus narrates the conversion of Izates, king of Adiabene, who initially had been told that circumcision would not be necessary. But then another Jew arrived, one Eleazar, who came from Galilee and who had a reputation for being very strict (πάνυ ἀκριβής) concerning the ancestral laws (20.43). When he learned of the situation he sternly warned Izates against committing the impiety of offending against the law and thereby against God (20.44) Since ἀκριβής is Josephus' characteristic description of the Pharisees (see above, 'The Pharisees in Josephus'), the most obvious conclusion is that Eleazar was a Pharisee. And even if he was not so designated he clearly shared the typical Pharisaic concern to maintain the law and the traditions with scrupulous care. Either way, Eleazar confirms that at the time of Jesus Galilee was by no means devoid of those who observed the law with Pharisaic strictness. Moreover, the episode provides some confirmation that such a one would also and naturally be concerned that others who yoked themselves to Israel should be properly observant of the law. The issue here, of course, is that of circumcision, but in the perspective of the devout, proper observance of food laws and sabbath were equally obligatory for the member of the covenant people.[75] And the readiness to find fault with others who failed to maintain that observance would likely be equally vocal.

4. Finally, we may simply repeat the point already made: that the evidence of the Gospels themselves cannot *all* be dismissed or postponed to a post-70 context. Passages like Mark 2 and 7 in particular must be allowed as testimony at least for the presence of *some* Pharisees on *some* occasions in Galilee in the period before 70 CE. No more than that is needed.[76] It is not even necessary to argue for many Pharisees having residence in Galilee. As Mark 7.1 indicates, Pharisees may have been sent or have come down from Jerusalem to view the new phenomenon which Jesus represented.[77] In short, the relative lack of reference to Pharisees in Galilee

constitutes very little of a case for rejecting the Gospels' own testimony on the point. There is evidence that some Pharisees, or equally strict devotees to the law and the customs, did live in or come from Galilee. And the likelihood that such a popular movement as the one represented by Jesus would attract attention from the larger grouping of Pharisees in Jerusalem must be considered rather high, and certainly much higher than either Smith or Sanders allows.

We may conclude, therefore, that Pharisees were liable to be critical of conduct and teaching which called into some question the priorities they regarded as covenant imperatives. Those who sat light to this righteousness they would regard as unrighteous, or 'sinners'. If Jesus was seen to encourage such attitudes they would be likely to criticize him too. All the more so if on other points Jesus and the Pharisees shared similar concerns: the closer Jesus was to the Pharisees, the more he would actually constitute a threat to their identity and boundaries, and the more hostile they would be to him. There is no good reason to doubt that Jesus came under such criticism already during his period of success and popularity in Galilee. The Gospel pictures offered in Mark 2 and 7 are at this point wholly plausible and should not be lightly discarded. There is no need to exaggerate Pharisaic influence on religious attitudes and practices of the day,[78] or Pharisaic hostility to non-Pharisees or to 'people of the land' in particular. But neither is it helpful to resort to caricature, as though the Gospels' portrayal depended on the assumption that the Pharisees were 'supersnoopers' who spent their time looking for infringements of sabbath or purity *halakoth*. All that the data require is that there were Pharisees in Galilee at some points during Jesus' ministry who were critical of his conduct, in respect of sabbath, ritual purity, and table-fellowship with those whom the Pharisees regarded as 'sinners'. That portrayal fits too well with all the available data to be set aside.

... AND JESUS

Despite the objection raised most recently by Sanders, the earliest portrayal of Jesus in relation to Pharisees and sinners is remarkably consistent with what we know of his Pharisaic contemporaries. The degree to which the evidence is mutually supportive has not been given sufficient weight.

1. The Pharisees were scrupulous in their interpretation of the law and maintenance of the customs handed down (so Josephus; and Paul and the Gospels agree).

2. One very important aspect of that strictness in relation to law and tradition was a concern to maintain temple purity at the daily meal table (so rabbinic tradition, which is strongly supported by

the Gospels and consistent with a view which Paul had abandoned [contrast Gal. 1.13–14; Rom. 14.14]).

3. Such zeal for the law as expressed not least in ritual was probably one of the chief identity markers of the 'sect' of the Pharisees, which marked them off from other Jews at least in the degree of their devotion. Where any threat to that identity and boundary was perceived, Pharisees were liable to react against that threat; the more zealous they were, the more violent the reaction (as Paul himself confirms; and again the Gospels cohere).

4. As a sect with clear ideas of what character of life and conduct was required to maintain the covenant righteousness of the people of God, Pharisees were highly likely to regard as 'sinners' those who disagreed with them and who lived in open disregard of this righteousness – as had the groups behind the early *Enoch* writings, the *Psalms of Solomon,* and the Dead Sea Scrolls (so again the Gospels).

5. Other scattered evidence refutes the notion that the Pharisees would have avoided Galilee, and suggests rather that at least some Pharisees would have been concerned enough about a movement in Galilee like that around Jesus to inquire more closely into it and to criticize it for failure on sensitive points where they saw their interpretation of Israel's heritage being disregarded or threatened (as, once again, the Gospels narrate).

In short, it is very likely, after all, that the portrayal of Pharisees, sinners, and Jesus in passages like Mark 2 and 7 accords very closely with the historical realities of Jesus' ministry and may not be discounted as a retrojecton of later controversies into the period of Jesus' ministry.

Indeed, far from being left with an uncomfortable wedge between Jesus and Gentile Christianity, the overall perspective we have gained from our study enables us to recognize an important line of continuity between Jesus and his successors. For behind the particular objections and charges levelled against Jesus was the central fact that Jesus was ignoring and abolishing boundaries which more sectarian attitudes had erected *within* Israel. This is in no way an anti-Semitic conclusion, nor should it be regarded as a blanket criticism of all Pharisees. It simply attempts to reckon seriously with what was an *internal* Jewish dispute, a confrontation between Jewish factions. Nor does it necessarily implicate the Pharisees in Jesus' crucifixion: that is a further question requiring further discussion. Nor does it solve all problems regarding the transition from Jesus to Paul: that too requires more careful delineation. But at least it does help us see how a Christianity which broke through the boundaries of Israel's own distinctiveness sprang from a Jesus who posed such a challenge to the boundary between Pharisee and sinner. In other words, the recognition of the Jewishness of Jesus need not separate Jesus from the Christianity he founded, just as the recognition of the Christian significance of Jesus need not separate him from the faith of his own people.

Notes

1. Particularly G. F. Moore, 'Christian Writers on Judaism', *HTR* 14 (1921), 197–254; R. T. Herford, *The Pharisees* (London: George Allen & Unwin, 1924; Boston: Beacon Press, 1962); and J. Parkes *The Conflict of the Church and the Synagogue* (1934; New York: Atheneum, 1969).
2. See especially the debate occasioned by R. Ruether's *Faith and Fratricide: The Theological Roots of Anti-Semitism* (New York: Seabury Press, 1974); A. T. Davies, ed., *AntiSemitism and the Foundations of Christianity* (New York: Paulist Press, 1979); and J. G. Gager, *The Origins of Anti-Semitism* (New York: Oxford University Press, 1983); *Anti-Judaism in Early Christianity, Vol. 1 Paul and the Gospels*, ed. P. Richardson, Vol. 2 *Separation and Polemic*, ed. S. G. Wilson, Studies in Christianity and Judaism (Waterloo, Ontario: Wilfrid Laurier University, 1986). Note also C. Klein, *Anti-Judaism in Christian Theology* (Philadelphia: Fortress Press, 1978); and from the Jewish side S. Sandmel, *Anti-Semitism in the New Testament* (Philadelphia: Fortress Press, 1978).
3. See, e.g., W. D. Davies, *The Setting of the Sermon on the Mount* (New York and Cambridge: Cambridge Univ. Press, 1964), 256–315, esp. 290–2; J. Koenig, *Jews and Christians in Dialogue* (Philadelphia: Westminster Press, 1979), chs 4 and 6; and F. Mussner, *Tractate on the Jews* (London: SPCK, 1984), 164–76.
4. The most recent proponents are H. Maccoby (*The Mythmaker: Paul and the Invention of Christianity* [London: Weidenfeld & Nicolson, 1986], 45–9 [the phrase is used on pp. 208–10]) and E. Rivkin (*What Crucified Jesus?* [Nashville: Abingdon Press, 1984]). For earlier literature, see esp. D. R. Catchpole, *The Trial of Jesus* (Leiden: E. J. Brill, 1971).
5. Most recently by H. Falk (*Jesus the Pharisee* [New York: Paulist Press, 1985]) and Maccoby (*Mythmaker*, 29–44). So also J. T. Pawlikowski (*Christ in the Light of Christian-Jewish Dialogue* [New York: Paulist Press, 102]). The claim is usually firmly denied on the Christian side; see, e.g., S. Westerholm, *Jesus and Scribal Authority*, Coniectanea biblica, New Testament (Lund: C. W. K. Gleerup, 1978), 128.
6. E. P. Sanders, *Jesus and Judaism* (Philadelphia: Fortress Press, 1985).
7. See ibid., expecially ch. 7, 'The Sinners', which is a reworking of 'Jesus and the Sinners', *JSNT* 19 (1983), 5–36.
8. For other literature, see D. A. Hagner, *The Jewish Reclamation of Jesus* (Grand Rapids: Zondervan, 1984), 23–39; and Mussner, *Tractate*, 109–14.
9. Though some Jewish scholars are willing to shift 'blame' for the hostility to Jesus from one group within first-century Judaism to another: from Pharisees to high priests (Rivkin, *What Crucified Jesus?*) or to Pharisees over against charismatics (G. Vermes, *Jesus the Jew* [London: William Collins, 1973], 80–2), or from Pharisees in general to the house of Shammai in particular (A. Finkel, *The Pharisees and the Teacher of Nazareth* [Leiden: E. J. Brill, 1964], 134–43; Falk, *Jesus*). Cf. J. Bowker, *Jesus and the Pharisees* (New York and Cambridge: Cambridge Univ. Press, 1973): Pharisees/*perushim* as a more extreme wing of the Hakamim (sages). For older discussion, see, e.g., J. Jocz, *The Jewish People and Jesus Christ* (London: SPCK, 1954), 17–42.
10. See, e.g., A. Harnack, *What is Christianity?* (London: William & Norgate, 1901); and W. Wrede, *Paul* (London: Green, 1907), 177–80.
11. Sanders, *Jesus*, 210.

12. For questions of methodology, see, e.g., J. Neusner, 'The Use of the Later Rabbinic Evidence for the Study of First-Century Pharisaism', in *Approaches to Ancient Judaism: Theory and Practice*, Brown Judaic Studies 1 (Missoula, Mont.: Scholars Press, 1978), 215–28. But P. S. Alexander's protest ('Rabbinic Judaism and the New Testament', *ZNW* 74 [1983], 237–46) is evidently still necessary.

13. J. Neusner, *The Rabbinic Traditions about the Pharisees before 70*, 3 vols. (Leiden: E. J. Brill, 1971).

14. Ibid., 3:303–4.

15. J. Neusner, *From Politics to Piety: The Emergence of Pharisaic Judaism* (Englewood Cliffs, N. J.: Prentice-Hall, 1973), 81–96.

16. J. Neusner, *Judaism: The Evidence of the Mishnah* (Chicago: Univ. of Chicago Press, 1981, 69–70.

17. Sanders, *Jesus*, 188, n.59.

18. Neusner, *Rabbinic Traditions* 3:279. See also idem, 'The Fellowship (חבורה) in the Second Jewish Commonwealth', *HTR* 53 (1960), 125, 128.

19. Neusner, *From Politics to Piety*, 87–8.

20. See, e.g., Philo *Leg.* 361; Plutarch *Quaest. Conviv.* 4.5; Tacitus *Hist.* 5.4.2

21. Seneca *Ep. Mor.* 108.22: 'Abstinence from certain kinds of animal food was set down as a proof of interest in the strange cult.' Cicero *Pro Flacco* 28.67: 'barbarous superstition'. Tacitus *Ann.* 2.85.4: '. . . Jewish rites . . . that superstition'.

22. Josephus, on the other hand, can give an extensive account of the Essenes (*War* 2.119–261) since he had distinguished them from the Pharisees and since they were no longer a factor within Judaism in the post-70 period.

23. Note also that the very name 'Pharisees' (the 'separated') points to their having a characteristic practice that set them apart from their fellow Jews. See esp. E. Schürer, *The History of the Jewish People in the Age of Jesus Christ*, rev. and ed. G. Vermes et al., vol. 2 (Edinburgh: T. & T. Clark, 1979), 396–8: 'A separation from uncleanness is always a simultaneous separation from unclean persons.' 'The Pharisees must have obtained their name from a separation in which the main body of the people did not participate, in other words, from having set themselves apart, by virtue of their stricter understanding of the concept of purity . . . from that uncleanness which, in their opinion, adhered to a great part of the people itself'. See also nn. 29, 53 below.

24. See again n. 21 above.

25. M. Smith, 'Palestinian Judaism in the First Century', in *Israel: Its Role in Civilization*, ed. M. Davies (New York: Jewish Theological Seminary of America, 1956), 75–6.

26. Neusner, *From Politics to Piety*, 65.

27. cf. Schürer, *History*, 395: 'However indifferent to politics Pharisaism was to begin with, the revolutionary trend which gained increasing ground among the Jews in the first century CE is to be attributed, indirectly at least, to its influence'.

28. According to Neusner (*Judaism in the Beginning of Christianity* [London: SPCK, 1984], 53), the Pharisees 'claimed the right to rule all the Jews by virtue of their possessing the "Oral Torah" of Moses'; so also Schürer, *History*, 389–91; and Rivkin, *What Crucified Jesus?*, 41, 44–7. Sanders (*Jesus*, 188) thinks that Josephus has exaggerated the success of the Pharisees but accepts that 'there is every reason to think that the Pharisees tried to have their views of the law carry the day'.

29. A. I. Baumgarten, 'The Name of the Pharisees', *JBL* 102 (1983), 413–17. Baumgarten goes on to argue that the name 'Pharisees' probably also involved a play on the sense *parosim*, 'specifiers', during our period (pp. 422–8).

30. Regrettably Maccoby chooses to ignore or to discount Paul's own testimony in Rom. 11.1; Gal. 1.13–14; Phil. 3.4–6; and to argue the fanciful thesis that Paul

was a Greek/Gentile on the basis of a reference in Epiphanius (*Pan.* 30.16.6–9), whose tendentiousness is not hard to detect. Since Paul's role as persecutor would require political sanction, it must certainly have enjoyed high priestly backing, and co-operation between high priest and Pharisee on such a matter is entirely plausible (cf. *Ant.* 2.411, 4.159–60; *Life* 21, 191–4).

31. So, e.g., Neusner (*Judaism in the Beginning*, 45–61; and 'Three Pictures of the Pharisees: A Reprise', in *Formative Judaism: Religious, Historical, and Literary Studies*, 5th ser., Brown Judaic Studies 91 [Chico, Calif.: Scholars Press, 1985], 51–77) still confines his discussion of the Pharisees to our other three sources. E. Rivkin (*A Hidden Revolution* [Nashville: Abingdon Press, 1978]) recognizes the importance of Paul's testimony but devotes only a little over two pages to it.

32. See further J. D. G. Dunn, '"Righteousness from the Law" and "Righteousness from Faith": Paul's Interpretation of Scripture in Romans 10:1–10', in *Tradition and Interpretation in the New Testament* (E. E. Ellis Festschrift), ed. G. F. Hawthorne (Grand Rapids: Wm. B. Eerdmans, 1987), 216–28. See also my *Romans*, Word Biblical Commentary 38 (Waco: Word, Inc., 1988), 586–7. In the Mishnah note particularly *Sanh.* 9.6.

33. For the importance of atonement and forgiveness within Judaism, see esp. E. P. Sanders, *Paul and Palestinian Judaism: A Comparison of Patterns of Religion* (Philadelphia: Fortress Press, 1977), index: 'atonement' and 'forgiveness'.

34. See ἴδιος, in *Greek-English Lexicon of the New Testament*, ed. W. Bauer, W. F. Arndt, and F. W. Gingrich. Cf. E. P. Sanders, *Paul, the Law, and the Jewish People* (Philadelphia: Fortress Press, 1983), 38: '"Their own" righteousness, then, is not characterized as being self-righteousness, but rather as being the righteousness which is limited to followers of the law' (further literature in n. 107). See also Dunn, *Romans*, pp. 587–8.

35. Sanders, *Jesus*, 199, 209, 264.

36. Ibid., 178, 265.

37. So Sanders would maintain; for others, see W. G. Kümmel, *Introduction to the New Testament* (London: SCM Press, 1975), 98 n. 65.

38. Kümmel, *Introduction*, 98; and see now esp. M. Hengel, *Studies in the Gospel of Mark* (Philadelphia: Fortress Press, 1985), 1–30, nn.

39. See esp. G. Alon, *The Jews in Their Land in the Talmudic Age*, vol. 1 (Jerusalem: Magnes Press, 1980).

40. See the much fuller tradition-history analysis in J. D. G. Dunn's 'Mark 2:1– 3:6: A Bridge between Jesus and Paul on the Question of the Law', *NTS* 30 (1984), 395–414; reprinted above, ch. 1. See also idem, 'Jesus and Ritual Purity: A Study of the Tradition History of Mark 7:15', in *A cause de l'Evangile*, Festschrift J. Dupont, Lectio Divina 123 (Paris: Editions du Cerf, 1985), 251– 76; reprinted above, ch. 2. Among other literature, see, e.g., H. Merkel, 'Jesus und die Pharisäer', *NTS* 14 (1967–8), 194–208, esp 202–6; H. F. Weiss, φαρισαῖος, in *TDNT* 9:41; Westerholm, *Jesus*, 71–5, 96–103; and Mussner, *Tractate*, 176–9.

41. In his various studies (see nn. 13, 15, 16, 28 above), Neusner notes that in the pre-70 rabbinic traditions, concern for observances of sabbaths and festivals follows rulings on ritual purity and agricultural matters in frequency.

42. C. Thoma (*A Christian Theology of Judaism* [New York: Paulist Press, 1980], 113) summarizes the position fairly: 'Not only the final, redacted parts of the New Testament but even the earlier ones indicate opposition as well as affinity between Jesus and Pharisees'.

43. Sanders questions whether *haberim* and Pharisees were identical but accepts that 'before 70 there was probably an appreciable overlap between Pharisees and *haberim*' (*Jesus*, 187). Bowker (*Jesus*, 35) expresses the point neatly: 'There is no indication that all Pharisees were members of a fellowship, although all members were Pharisees and accepted their views on Jewish law.' See also A. Oppenheimer, *The 'Am Ha-aretz* (Leiden: E. J. Brill, 1977), 118–19; and

Westerholm, *Jesus*, 13–15. It is worth noting that the more one discounts Josephus' picture of the Pharisees as widely influential (as Sanders does; see n. 28 above), the more closely they will tend to approximate to the *haberim*–whereas the less significant the *haberim* were within the important Pharisee sect, the more difficult it is to account for the strong influence they had on subsequent rabbinic ideals. In fact *haberim* and 'Pharisee' are usually regarded as to all intents and purposes synonymous terms (see esp. Schürer, *History*, 398–9). On Pharisees and sages, scribes and Pharisees see Bowker, *Jesus*, esp. 13–15, 21–3. Rivkin (*Hidden Revolution*) sees 'scribes' and 'Pharisees' as synonymous terms; contrast J. Jeremias, *Jerusalem in the Time of Jesus* (Philadelphia: Fortress Press, 1969), 254–6.

44. Sanders, *Jesus*, esp. 177–80; see n. 68 below.
45. Ibid., esp. 180–7.
46. Sanders' criticism is directed particularly against J. Jeremias, *New Testament Theology*, vol. 1, *The Proclamation of Jesus* (London: SCM Press, 1971), 108–13; see Sanders, *Jesus*, esp. 385 n. 14. But see also n. 68 below.
47. See esp. H. Mol, *Identity and the Sacred* (Oxford: Basil Blackwell, 1976), 57–8: 'It is precisely the boundary . . . which provides the sense of identity.'
48. Mol, *Identity*, 233; and M. Douglas, *Purity and Danger* (London: Routledge & Kegan Paul, 1966), 62–5, 128.
49. Douglas, *Purity*, 124. Cf. P. L. Berger and T. Luckman, *The Social Construction of Reality* (Baltimore: Penguin Books, 1967), 126: 'The appearance of an alternative symbolic universe poses a threat because its very existence demonstrates empirically that one's own universe is less than inevitable.'
50. See esp. L. A. Coser, *The Foundations of Social Conflict* (London: Routledge & Kegan Paul, 1956).
51. Coser, *Foundations*, 67–72.
52. See above, n. 23 As J. Neusner ('The Pharisees in the Light of the Historical Sources of Judaism', in *Formative Judaism*, Brown Judaic Studies 37 [Chico, Calif.: Scholars Press, 1982], 71–83) notes, since Pharisees lived among their fellow Jews (contrast the Qumran covenanters), 'this made the actual purity-rules and food-restrictions all the more important, for only they set the Pharisee apart from the people among whom he constantly lived'. Jeremias (*Jerusalem* 259–62), however, makes the surprising assumption that the regulations regarding the Qumran community can be used to build up a picture of 'Pharisaic communities'. But see Oppenheimer, '*Am Ha-aretz*, 147–51.
53. Bowker, *Jesus*, 21: 'In *theory* the extent of the Hakamic movement was coterminous with the Jewish people. . . . The movement was not intended to be a party within Israel. It was intended to be Israel itself.' There is all the difference, however, between such a self-perception or ideal and the social reality of such a movement. Bowker also notes that 'Pharisees/*perushim*' probably first appeared as a description of the Hakamic movement used by *others* (p. 15). See also n. 63 below.
54. Neusner shows keen awareness of the sociological dimensions of his discussion; see, e.g., *Judaism*, 69–75.
55. For the possibility of quite serious conflict among the Pharisees themselves, see above, n. 9. That Pharisees would also differ in their attitudes to Jesus (cf. esp. Luke 13.31) is also inherently probable.
56. Sanders, *Jesus*, 206.
57. In one place, Sanders does define 'sinners' quite properly as 'those beyond the pale and outside the common religion by virtue of their implicit or explicit rejection of the commandments of the God of Israel' (ibid., 210). But the question is, What counted as implicit rejection of the commandments? And in whose eyes?
58. J. A. Goldstein, *I Maccabees*, Anchor Bible 41 (New York: Doubleday & Co., 1976), 123–4.

59. We need not presuppose that a clear rupture had already taken place within Israel at this time such as the establishment of the Qumran community involved (see, e.g., Sanders, *Paul*, 367–74; and J. C. Vanderkam, *Textual and Historical Studies in the Book of Jubilees* [Missoula, Mont.: Scholars Press, 1977], 281–3), but a factional attitude is clearly evident.

60. Sanders, *Paul*, 360; and G. W. E. Nickelsburg, *Jewish Literature between the Bible and the Mishnah* (Philadelphia: Fortress Press, 1981), 48.

61. cf. L. Hartman, *Asking for a Meaning: A Study of I Enoch 1–5*, Coniectanea biblica, New Testament (Lund: C. W. K. Gleerup, 1979), 132.

62. See, e.g., M. Black, *The Scrolls and Christian Origins* (London: Thomas Nelson & Sons, 1961), 23–4; G. Vermes, *The Dead Sea Scrolls* (London: William Collins & Co., 1977), 152; and Nickelsburg, *Jewish Literature*, 131.

63. See further M. Newton, *The Concept of Purity at Qumran and in the Letters of Paul*, SNTSMS 53 (Cambridge: Cambridge Univ. Press, 1985), esp. 15–19. We need not attempt any further clarification on the very difficult question of whether the Qumran covenanters regarded themselves as the people of the covenant *in toto*, and so Pharisees, etc., as those outside the covenant ('sinners'); or as representative of the eschatological people of the covenant whose boundaries at least in principle stretched beyond the membership of the sect (see Sanders, *Paul*, 240–57). Either way the point remains the same: they regarded others as sinners who saw themselves as full, law-abiding members of the covenant people and who were so regarded by the bulk of their fellow Jews.

64. R. B. Wright, 'Psalms of Solomon', in *The Old Testament Pseudepigrapha*, ed. J. Charlesworth, vol. 2 (New York: Doubleday & Co., 1985), 642. Sanders warns against a simple lumping-together of Sadducees with Hasmoneans (*Paul*, 403–4). A straightforward equation of the psalmist(s) with the Pharisees should also be avoided, although of the Jewish sects known to us 'it is the Pharisees whom they most closely approximate' (Nickelsburg, *Jewish Literature*, 212).

65. The accusations of a passage like 8.11–13 should not be read as an impartial and objective testimony. This is factional propaganda and polemic, with a fair degree of exaggeration, reflecting the priority which the 'righteous' placed on the correct observance of rituals laid down in the Torah.

66. Where opponents are identified, the usual assumption is that Pharisees are in view. See, e.g., D. Flusser, *Jesus* (New York: Herder & Herder, 1969), 47; and Jeremias, *Jerusalem*, 250.

67. As Sanders (*Paul*) tends to do – though, of course, he is treating the texts on their own terms.

68. The antagonism between Pharisees (or *haberim*) and the people of the land should not be exaggerated; see Oppenheimer, *'Am Ha-aretz*, 156–69; and Sanders, *Jesus*, esp. 177–80. We should note also the references in Luke 7.36; 11.37; 14.1, which speak of Pharisaic hospitality. But Jeremias has not over-stated the position as much as Sanders claims (see n. 46 above).

69. M. Smith, *Jesus the Magician* (New York: Harper & Row, 1978), 157; cited by Sanders, *Jesus*, 292, 390 n. 90. Josephus (*Ant.* 18.15) does imply that the Pharisees' influence was greatest in the cities, though in the same context he refers to their influence on the people, the multitude (18.15, 17).

70. I owe several observations in what follows to a working paper prepared by my research student Paul Trebilco.

71. Smith, *Jesus*, 157.

72. J. Neusner, *A Life of Rabban Yohanan ben Zakkai*, 2d ed. (Leiden: E. J. Brill, 1970), 47.

73. ibid., 47, 51.

74. ibid., 48; and Sean Freyne, *Galilee from Alexander the Great to Hadrian, 323 B.C.E. to 135 B.C.E.: A Study of Second Temple Judaism* (Wilmington, Del.: Michael Glazier, n.d.), 317, 321–3, 341 n. 78. I. Abrahams (*Studies in Pharisaism and the Gospels*, ser. 1 [1917; New York: Ktav, 1967]) refers to

Büchler's conjecture that Shammai was a Galilean. See further Freyne, *Galilee*, 341 n. 74.
75. Circumcision: esp. Gen. 17.9–14. Food laws: esp. Lev. 11; Deut. 14; 1 Macc. 1:62–3; cf. Acts 10.14; 11.3. Sabbath: esp. Exod. 31.12–17; Isa. 56.6–8.
76. Smith's talk of 'the synoptics' picture of a Galilee swarming with Pharisees' (*Jesus*, 157) is an unnecessary exaggeration.
77. Apart from Josephus' accounts of Pharisees being sent to Galilee (*War* 2.569; *Life* 189–98), there is a rabbinic tradition that one of Johanan's pupils was sent to investigate a *hasid* living at Beth Rama (probably Galilee) who is said to have been strangely ignorant of purity regulations (Freyne, *Galilee*, 316). See also Vermes, *Jesus*, 56–7.
78. See again n. 28 above.

Additional Note

For another critique of Sanders' *Jesus and Judaism*, in some degree complementary with Chapter 3, see B. D. Chilton, 'Jesus and the Repentance of E. P. Sanders', *Tyndale Bulletin* 39 (1988) 1–18.

A. I. Baumgarten, 'The Pharisaic *Paradosis*', HTR 80 (1987) 63–77, argues that 'the terms *paradosis* of the elders and of the fathers were deliberate attempts by the Pharisees to give their tradition a pedigree it might have seemed to lack. As such, they hoped to defend their tradition at a vulnerable point, and raise it from merely that of a school to the patrimony of the nation' (p. 77).

R. A. Wild, 'The Encounter between Pharisaic and Christian Judaism: Some Early Gospel Evidence', *NovT* 27 (1985) 105–24, takes up Neusner's view of Pharisaism at the time of Jesus as a 'sectarian movement rather than the dominant form of Judaism'. From this he deduces the unlikelihood of Pharisees being so concerned about the observance of Jesus' disciples as the Jesus-tradition depicts (referring particularly to Mark 7.1–23 and 2.15–17), unless 'Jesus and his disciples actually did follow the Pharisaic way of life' (p. 118; similarly p. 122). Wild thus shows no awareness of the factionalism or concern to define and defend boundaries evidenced in the talk of 'sinners', as demonstrated above, but he rightly detects something of the 'in-house' nature of such passages – 'in-house' as reflecting debates both between fellow Jews (Christian and non-Christian) and between fellow Christians.

C. Tuckett, 'Q, the Law and Judaism', *Law and Religion. Essays on the Place of the Law in Israel and Early Christianity*, ed. B. Lindars, Cambridge: James Clarke (1988) 90–101, is sympathetic with Wild's suggestion, that

Originally Jesus' disciples had close links with the pharisaic movement, so that other Pharisees apparently expected the disciples to conform to their own mores. Such a picture emerges from both the Markan and Q material examined. However it is only in Q that Jesus himself emerges as one who affirms these links positively ... It would thus appear that the community which preserved the Q material also preserved positive links with the pharisaic movement in a way that most other primitive Christian groups about which we have any evidence did not ... Certainly Q reflects a strongly conservative Jewish-Christian group within primitive Christianity.

He concludes that

at some stage at least, the Q community may have had a close relationship with the small sectarian movement in pre-70 Judaism which we call Pharisaism. No doubt this relationship was a dialectical one in that non-Christian Pharisees were evidently hostile to the Christian group. But the very existence of such hostility may well be evidence that the Christian group was claiming to be a genuine part of the pharisaic movement (p. 100).

Similarly K. Berger, 'Jesus als Pharisäer und frühe Christen als Pharisäer', *NovT 30* (1988) 231–62, maintains that the Jesus-tradition evidences a degree of mutual concern between Pharisees and Jesus, both in matters on which they agreed (Mark 12.19–34) and in matters which they thought worthy of discussion (p. 237). Particularly important was the issue of purity, with its social implications for group identity and boundaries (p. 238). Where Jesus differed from Pharisees was in his understanding of the positive power of purity/holiness ('offensive Reinheit/Heiligkeit'), a power to overcome impurity, through table-fellowship, physical contact, etc. In effect Jesus lived a new kind of Pharisaism, 'an eschatological-pneumatic Pharisaism', where purity and the question of boundaries were still the central problem, but where Jesus' power actually achieved the objectives of the Pharisees (pp. 246–7). So too Jesus did not contest the Pharisees' standing with God. The problem lay not with their lacking righteousness but with their unwillingness to rejoice over the acceptance of sinners (p. 249). 'According to the Synoptics, the Pharisees failed not through their achievements-righteousness, but in that they did not go along with Jesus' openness to the sinners and impure' (p. 250). Although I am not entirely happy with Berger's broad use of 'Pharisaism' ('Jesus is a Pharisee with authority' – p. 247), my main dispute with him would be over his assumption of a 'diaspora-Pharisaism' particularly marked by law-observance (p. 232) – again not giving enough weight to the faction-alism of Palestinian Judaism.

L. W. Countryman, *Dirt, Greed and Sex,* London: SCM (1989) sums up the significance of purity ritual well and in a way which reinforces the argument of the final paragraph of Chapter 3, though without any engagement with Sanders:

For the Hellenistic Jew of the Diaspora, purity continued to function almost entirely as a way of distinguishing Jew from Gentile ... In Palestine, by contrast, the purity code was, to a large extent, simply the way of life of the dominant population group. It served ... as a daily reminder of Israelite identity. Of more importance, however, was that particular interpretations of the purity code, especially those of the Essenes and Pharisees, became ways of distinguishing one Jew from another, both in terms of their understanding of the code and in terms of their devotion to the keeping of it. In both cases, the code was still serving its intrinsic function of establishing and keeping boundaries; the boundaries thus guarded, however – ethnic in one case, sectarian in the other – were significantly different (pp. 64–5).

Similarly A. J. Saldarini, 'The Social Class of the Pharisees in Mark', *The Social World of Formative Christianity and Judaism*, ed. J. Neusner et al., Philadelphia: Fortress (1988) 69–77. He takes up J. Neyrey, 'The Idea of Purity in Mark's Gospel', *Semeia* 35 (1986) 91–128, who shows that the purity rules in Mark function as boundary-setting mechanisms for the community. Saldarini concludes:

Thus the Pharisees were the defenders of a certain kind of community, and Jesus challenged the Pharisees' vision of community by attacking their purity regulations concerning washing and food as well as Sabbath practice. The effect of Jesus' teaching was to widen the community boundaries and loosen the norms for membership in his community (p. 72).

Compare and contrast H. Maccoby, *Judaism in the First Century*, London: Sheldon (1989), who, as usual, drives his own line of argument through the evidence with single-mindedness. The Pharisees were 'a three-tiered movement consisting of Sages, rank-and-file Pharisees, and "people of the land" ... The Pharisees never regarded themselves as a sect, but as the religious leaders of the whole people ... [They were] the religious leaders of the overwhelming majority of the nation' (pp. 12–13). 'Jesus was probably a member of that movement [the Pharisees]' and 'his hostile critics were probably not the Pharisees but the Sadducees', with 'Pharisees' later substituted for 'Sadducees' in the tradition (pp. 42–51). 'Jesus' policy towards tax gatherers ... was perfectly in accord with Pharisee thinking' (pp. 100–2). Despite his knowledge of rabbinic Judaism, Maccoby's grasp of the realities of pre-70 Judaism is exceedingly tenuous.

4

'A Light to the Gentiles', or 'The End of the Law'? The Significance of the Damascus Road Christophany for Paul

I

One of the most striking, and at the same time most puzzling features of Paul's writings is the way he speaks of his conversion. The fact that he thinks of it as his *commissioning* rather than as a conversion has of course often been noted. So, for example, John Knox: for Paul

> its major significance lay in the fact that the experience made him a witness of the Resurrection and thus qualified him to be an apostle (referring to 1 Cor. 9:1, 15:8 and Gal. 1:11–17). But he never cites it as the explanation (although it was undoubtedly the occasion) of his Christian life.[1]

What is even more striking, however, is the fact that he understood his commissioning from the first as having the Gentiles in view. This is not presented as a deduction or a corollary which Paul drew from some *other* conviction given to him in or brought home to him by the encounter on the Damascus road. It belonged to the central conviction itself. The primary purpose of the risen Christ's appearance was to send him to the Gentiles.

The evidence on the point is quite clear. Galatians 1.15–16–ὅτε δὲ εὐδόκησεν (ὁ θεὸς) ... ἀποκαλύψαι τὸν υἱὸν αὐτοῦ ἐν ἐμοί, ἵνα εὐαγγελίζωμαι αὐτὸν ἐν τοῖς ἔθνεσιν ... The force of the ἵνα should not be diluted. So far as Paul was concerned, God's purpose in revealing his Son in Paul (that is, on the Damascus road) was to commission Paul as apostle to the Gentiles. And though it has often been argued that this full significance of the Damascus road Christophany may only have come to him later or grown within Paul's conscious thought over a period,[2] Paul's own claim is that it was there in the beginning, already clear to him before he first met the other apostles, a well-formed conviction which owed nothing to them (1.16–17) and everything to that initial revelation (1.1, 11–12).[3]

Elsewhere Paul speaks in more general terms: Christ appeared to

89

him to make him an apostle (1 Cor. 9.1; 15.8–9). But for Paul that always meant 'apostle to the Gentiles' (Rom. 11.13). It is most unlikely that Paul ever thought of himself as called to be an apostle (without further specification), and only later concluded that his apostleship was to the Gentiles.[4] So far as he was concerned what he received from the risen Christ was grace and apostleship εἰς ὑπακοὴν πίστεως ἐν πᾶσιν τοῖς ἔθνεσιν (Rom. 1.5; so also 15.15–16).

Similarly with Paul's use of the μυστήριον motif. Clearly the mystery for Paul was the divine purpose to bring in the Gentiles into the people of God (Rom. 11.25), the mystery 'made known to all the nations, to bring them to the obedience of faith' (16.25–6: εἰς ὑπακοὴν πίστεως εἰς πάντα τὰ ἔθνη γνωρισθέντος).[5] According to Colossians 1.26–7 it was precisely this ministry which Paul was given (by implication, in the initial commissioning which constituted and shaped the rest of his life): to make known 'the riches of the glory of this mystery among the Gentiles'. The same point is made more explicitly in Ephesians 3: he (Paul) had been given the stewardship of God's grace (compare Rom. 1.5), by means of relevation (κατὰ ἀποκάλυψιν – compare Gal. 1.12, 16), the mystery of the Gentiles being fellow-heirs, members of the same body, partakers of the promise in Christ Jesus through the gospel; it was of this gospel Paul had been made a minister by the gift of God's grace to preach to the Gentiles . . . (3.2–9).

If final confirmation is necessary we need simply refer to the accounts of Paul's conversion in Acts. In each case, though in strikingly different ways, the same point is made. The purpose of the risen Christ in stopping Paul short on the road to Damascus was to send him to the Gentiles. And in each case the statement of this purpose is an integral part of the story itself. To Ananias the Lord says, 'He is a chosen instrument of mine to carry my name before the Gentiles' (9.15). Ananias informs Paul: 'You will be a witness to all men of what you have seen and heard' (22.15). Most striking of all, in the third account it is the Lord himself in the Damascus road encounter itself who tells Paul that he is sending him to the Gentiles (26.17–18).[6] Clearly what is being preserved here is the same conviction to which Paul himself gave expression in his own letters: that his calling to become apostle to the Gentiles was not merely rooted in the Damascus road epiphany but constituted its chief content and its most immediate as well as most lasting impact.[7]

II

In view of the emphasis which Paul (and the earliest Christian traditions) placed upon this point, and the consistency of that emphasis, the treatment of Paul's conversion-commissioning by successive commentators is somewhat surprising. For even where there is a recognition of this Pauline emphasis, the tendency generally has been to place the focus of the Damascus road encounter elsewhere, with the call to the Gentiles understood, implicitly or explicitly, as a secondary corollary, a deduction which Paul may not have drawn for some time. The temptation to attempt to spell out the rationale of the conclusion, 'therefore to the Gentiles', has rarely been resisted, but almost always the reasoning process envisaged seems a good deal more circuitous, even tortuous, than can be easily encompassed by the rather bald statements of Paul and the other traditions.[8]

One possibility has been to depict the main impact of the Damascus road epiphany in *Christological* terms. So, for example, H. G. Wood and Philippe Menoud have argued that the scandal for Paul the persecutor was the earliest Christian claim that the crucified Jesus was the expected Messiah. Consequently the Christological fact of Jesus' Messiahship is the first thing that his Damascus road experience brought home to him, with the soteriological significance seen as secondary, and the call to the Gentiles barely considered.[9] Certainly there must be something of this involved in Paul's radical rethink. As a devout Jew the cross would have been a scandal to him (1 Cor. 1.23), and the fact that 'Christ' has become such an established referent for Jesus, not least in such formulations as 'Christ died' and 'Christ crucified',[10] clearly implies that this was part of the base-rock faith of the first Christians to which Paul was converted. But it is hardly enough to explain the rationale of Paul's commissioning: the conviction 'Jesus is Messiah' hardly leads immediately to the corollary, 'therefore to the Gentiles'. More damaging is the fact that Paul himself never seems to trace out or imply such a progression of thought. The recognition of Jesus' Messiahship is insufficient explanation of Paul's apostolic self-understanding.

In recent years the more popular explanation has focused on the *soteriological* aspects of the Damascus road epiphany. The argument here generally runs as follows: that already before Paul's conversion the first Christians (or at least the Hellenists) had posed the alternatives, salvation through Christ rather than through the law. This was why Saul the Pharisee persecuted them so fiercely – out of zeal for the law (Phil. 3.6). Paul's conversion therefore was conversion to this understanding of salvation. The conviction 'to the Gentiles' then follows as an immediate corollary: since faith in Christ, or the gospel of Christ, is now seen to have replaced the law in God's scheme of salvation, it follows that this gospel must be open to all men and not just Jews.[11] The most forceful and influential exposition along these lines in recent years has been offered by Ulrich Wilckens. Paul's conversion to the gospel of

Christ and his commission to the Gentiles are linked because Christ appeared to him as 'the end of the law' (Rom. 10.4); his appearance to Paul indicates that in Christ there has been a decisive transition in the terms of salvation-history; 'Christ ὑπὲρ ἡμῶν', rather than the law (of the Jews), means 'for us', both Jew and Gentile.[12]

Here too there must be at least some truth in this explanation, as Philippians 3.5–9 surely indicates. But is it so clear that a sharp antinomian antithesis between law and Christ had already been drawn prior to Paul? The testimony of Acts 6—8 indicates more a break with temple and cult rather than with the law as a whole, or the law in principle. And even Paul's zeal for the law probably speaks more of the Pharisee's high evaluation of the law in all its outworking (Gal. 1.14) than of a complete breach with the law on the part of the Hellenists.[13] The difficulty here is this: the more complete we see the breach between law and gospel to be *before* Paul's conversion, the more difficult it is to explain why the sort of confrontation described in Galatians 2.1–10 and 11–14 did not occur sooner; and the more difficult it is to understand why it was Paul who came to be regarded as the chief arch-heretic and apostate in Jewish Christian tradition (*Epistula Petri* 2.3; *Clem. Hom.* 17.18–19).[14] The more obvious line of reasoning is that Paul was so remembered because he was in fact the one who brought the tension between law and gospel (already present in Jesus' own ministry – Mark 7.1–23//Matt. 15.1–20[15] to its sharpest and indeed antithetical expression. At the very least the neat link forged by Wilckens ('the end of the law', therefore 'to the Gentiles') must stand in question. Certainly Paul himself never poses such an argument or justification for his mission to the Gentiles. Rather, the *immediacy* of his conviction, 'to the Gentiles', and the *delay* before Paul's and Gentile Christian practice was seen as a threat to Jewish Christian self-understanding, together suggest that Paul's calling to the Gentiles may have been the *primary* feature of the Damascus road encounter for Paul, with the implications for the law and its bearing on the gospel being more the *corollary*, worked out with increasing sharpness over the early years of his work as a missionary of the church at Antioch.

The variation on this view, that it was the Damascus road experience itself which posed the sharpness of the antithesis to Paul, can also claim some support. Either we could say that Paul's own experience of grace in that encounter (accepted by Christ despite his persecution inspired by zeal for the law) brought home to him 'the bankruptcy of the law and the all-sufficiency of Christ' there and then, and therefore the accessibility of that grace to Gentile as well as Jew (compare 1 Cor. 15.10).[16] Or we could argue that Paul's confrontation with a Jesus crucified and cursed by the

92

more: That the law led him to do the wrong thing — persecute Jesus!

law (Gal. 3.13), but now obviously vindicated by God, convinced him there and then that the law could no longer function as God's instrument of salvation,[17] and that therefore the gospel of this Jesus should go to Gentile as well as to Jew. But the problem remains the same in each case: nowhere does Paul himself develop or even hint at this line of argument. Moreover, Jewish Christians before Paul must surely have been confronted by the same charge, that the crucified Jesus was accursed by God (Deut. 21.23); yet there is no suggestion that their recognition of Christ's vindication caused them to pass a negative judgement on the law.[18] Once again both exegetical base and the necessary rationale seem to be inadequate to sustain the case argued.

III

In recent years the work of Seyoon Kim has brought the question of the importance of Paul's Damascus road experience for the understanding of Paul's faith and theology back to the forefront of discussion.[19] His thorough and well-argued thesis marks a significant step forward in the discussion. His claim is that crucial emphases of Paul's gospel, both soteriological *and* Christological, were derived directly from the Damascus road event. Indeed he is prepared to argue that central features of Paul's Christology and soteriology were formed to a considerable extent in that encounter itself.

So far as its soteriological significance is concerned, Kim adds little to the main thesis already argued by Wilckens and others. 'Rom. 10:2–10 corresponds with Paul's autobiographical statements especially in Phil. 3:4ff.' so that Romans 10.4 can be attributed directly to Paul's conversion: 'in the Christophany on the road to Damascus Paul received the knowledge of Christ as the end of the law'.[20] This affirmation made with minimal argument in the opening pages of the book is already a statement of his conclusion on the point.[21] Its main elaboration comes in his section on 'Paul the Persecutor', in which he ties together the evidence of Philippians 3.5–6 and Galatians 3.13: the former indicating that Christians' criticism of the law was the main reason for Paul's persecuting zeal, the latter that Paul himself must have used Deuteronomy 21.23 when persecuting the Christians. 'The two offences, the criticism of the law and the proclamation of the crucified Jesus as the Messiah, belonged together: the Christians criticized the law in the name of Jesus the Messiah ... So Paul was confronted with the alternative: either the law or the crucified Christ.'[22] Kim's later treatment of 'Justification' in his chapter on 'Soteriology' is simply a restatement of this earlier finding. Paul's own experience of grace on the Damascus road is the basis of his

93

doctrine of justification. 'Paul perceived the revelation of the Son of God on the Damascus road as the revelation of God's righteousness apart from the law (Rom. 3:21) immediately.' 'At the Damascus revelation Paul came to understand that "no man is justified by (works of) the law" and so to see the fundamental problem of the law itself.'[23]

The Christological thesis grows out of 2 Corinthians 3.4—4.6, particularly 4.4 and 6, and again is already stated *in nuce* in the opening pages: 'the risen Christ must have appeared to Paul accompanied by the radiance of light which was perceived by him as the divine glory'.[24] The elaboration of this thesis develops partly out of the preceding argument about Christ and the law. 'This Corinthians passage indicates not only that at the Damascus revelation Paul realized that Christ had superseded the Torah but also that *at the same time* he perceived Christ as the true Wisdom' (since the Torah had previously been identified with divine Wisdom).[25] But the main elaboration and principal contribution of the book focuses on the use of εἰκὼν τοῦ θεοῦ in 2 Corinthians 4.4. The phrase itself carries great weight: 'the conception of Christ as the εἰκὼν τοῦ θεοῦ both in 2 Cor. 4:4 and Col. 1:15 clearly conveys the sense that Christ is the (visible, therefore material) manifestation of (the invisible) God, and therefore his likeness to God is strongly implied in it'.[26] This is filled out by reference to the epiphanic visions in Jewish apocalyptic, particularly Ezekiel 1.26 and Daniel 7.13: what Paul saw (or understood himself to be seeing) was Christ as 'the physical embodiment of divinity';[27] 'Paul's Damascus experience must have led him immediately to Dan. 7:13 because he saw a heavenly figure "like a son of man" just as Daniel did.'[28] Into this already complex pattern Kim weaves a further strand by identifying the concepts Son of God (Gal. 1.16) and image of God (2 Cor. 4.4): 'to see the risen Christ as appearing "like a son of God" is the same as to see him as having the εἰκόνα of God'.[29] This εἰκών-Christology provides a further root for Paul's Wisdom Christology (Wisd. 7.26), and it develops also into his Adam Christology (compare Gen. 1.26f.). 'Thus, both Paul's Wisdom-Christology and Adam-Christology are grounded in the Damascus Christophany.'[30] The latter conclusion in addition allows Kim to elaborate the soteriological significance of the Damascus road encounter for Paul beyond the claims about justification inherited from Wilckens and others. If Christ is the Son and image of God, then God has restored in him the divine image and glory lost by Adam: hence Paul's concepts of believers being adopted as sons of God, being transformed into Christ's image and made a 'new man' in him, the last Adam.[31]

What of Paul's own conclusion, 'therefore to the Gentiles'? Kim fully recognizes that 'for Paul the Christophany on the Damascus road constituted ... his apostolic commission for the Gentile mission'.[32] He is quite clear that the decisive revelation of the 'mystery' of Romans 11.25 f. came to Paul on the Damascus road, and he goes on to argue that Paul was probably decisively influenced on this point by Isaiah 6 and 49. 1–6.[33] But how does this tie in to Kim's main Christological and soteriological thesis? Unfortunately he does not address this question at any length.[34] Such rationale as he does offer lists the conviction of 'universal mission' as a corollary to the 'new creation' corollary of his Adam Christology, itself derived from the Damascus road Christophany.[35] But that 'therefore to the Gentiles' does not seem to have the immediacy it had for Paul, so that the question about the correlation of these different emphases in Paul's response to and understanding of the Damascus road Christophany remains open. How did it all hang together or tie up in Paul's thinking?

IV

As the most recent and most thorough study in the area of our concern, Kim's monograph deserves to be given the main focus of attention. Its central thesis can be questioned at a number of points.

1. 2 Corinthians 4.4, 6 can very properly be taken as a reference to Paul's Damascus road experience, even though Paul expresses himself in more generalized terms. But to what extent can this passage be taken as a description of what Paul *saw?* He certainly uses the language and imagery of light shining, which naturally suggests some correlation with the description in Acts (9.3 – αὐτὸν περιήστραψεν φῶς ἐκ τοῦ οὐρανοῦ; similarly 22.6 and 26.13), but the talk is of the impact of the event on Paul rather than a description of the event itself: God has shone his light ἐν ταῖς καρδίαις ἡμῶν; the light is 'the light of the gospel', 'the light of knowledge' (τὸν φωτισμὸν τοῦ εὐαγγελίου . . ., φωτισμὸν τῆς γνώσεως . . .). And the fact that Paul makes it a generalized description of Christian conversion confirms that he cannot be thinking particularly of the features which *distinguished* his conversion from those which followed (compare 1 Cor. 15.8 – 'last of all'). In fact the whole passage is still influenced by the Midrash on Exodus 34 (2 Cor. 3.7–18),[36] with Moses' entrance unveiled into the presence of God seen as the type of *all* Jewish conversion from old covenant to new; and the theme of divine glory (δόξα) is drawn more from there than anywhere else (2 Cor. 3.7–11, 18; 4.4, 6).[37]

2. Whatever we make of 2 Corinthians 4.4, 6 in particular, the question still stands, What did Paul see on the Damascus road? Christ 'clothed in glory', could be deduced from 2 Corinthians 4.4, 6 (cf. 1 Cor. 15.43; Phil. 3.21).[38] But Kim also deduces from

the important role played in early Christology by Psalm 110:1 that Paul 'saw him exalted by God and enthroned at his right hand',[39] saw him as the εἰκὼν τοῦ θεοῦ, as 'one like a son of man' (Dan. 7.13), 'one like a son of God'.[40] But this is now reading a tremendous amount into the few very allusive references Paul makes to the Damascus road experience itself. Does it follow that because Paul uses the titles 'Lord' and 'Son' in 1 Corinthians 9.1 and Galatians 1.16 we should conclude that Paul *saw* Jesus as enthroned, as 'Son' (however that would be expressed visually)? May these titles not simply be referents rather than descriptions, Paul's way of saying 'The one I encountered then I know (now) as "Lord" and "Son of God"'? Is it even so clear that the ὅς ἐστιν εἰκὼν τοῦ θεοῦ is a description of what Paul saw, rather than a confessional formula attracted by association of ideas to what has gone before, in the style of a liturgical coda?

3. Assuming that Jesus appeared to Paul as a glorious figure, do the parallels cited by Kim support the view that Paul must at once have jumped to the conclusion that this was a divine figure, the figure of hypostatized Wisdom, properly speaking a *theo*phany, as Kim clearly wants to infer?[41] But the same range of evidence indicates that the glorious figures seen in some visions were frequently identified as angels (Dan. 10; *Apoc. Zeph.* 6.11–15; 2 *Enoch* 1.5; *Apoc. Abr.* 11; *Asc. Isa.* 7.2), or as dead heroes of the past now transfigured or exalted in some degree (Samuel – 1 Sam. 18.13–14; the righteous – Wisd. 5.5; Jeremiah – 2 Macc. 15.13–14; Enoch – *Jub.* 4.23; 2 *Enoch* 22.8; Adam and Abel – *Test. Abr.* A 11–13). Kim's assumption that the man-like figure of Daniel 7's vision is a divine figure,[42] is highly questionable, since the man-like figure seems rather to represent the saints of the Most High over against the beast-like figures who represent the enemies of Israel.[43] Even more questionable is Kim's attempt to merge different elements of different visions into a composite form of theophanic vision (in a manner disturbingly similar to the *religionsgeschichtliche* constructs of the 'pre-Christian Gnostic redeemer myth' or the 'divine man') – particularly Ezekiel 1.26, Daniel 7.13, and the identification of the figure seen as Messiah and Son of God.[44] Some partial merging of this sort is evident in the Similitudes of Enoch (1 *Enoch* 46) and 4 Ezra 13; and it has certainly occurred in the vision of Revelation 1.13–14.[45] But can we assume that the whole composite was already in play in Paul's mind at the time of his conversion, simply on the basis of the 'image' language used in 2 Corinthians 4.4? Where the whole point of the argument is to demonstrate that a Christology, which is certainly evident later, actually emerged in Paul's thought following (or even at) the Damascus road encounter, a more carefully delineated exposition is necessary.[46]

4. Kim's thesis is strongest when he is able to argue that Paul

was converted to a view he had previously fought against. But in this case his thesis is that it was Paul who first made the identification of Christ as divine Wisdom.[47] Again we must ask whether the use of εἰκὼν τοῦ θεοῦ in 2 Corinthians 4.4 is strong enough evidence that Paul traced this identification back to the Damascus road Christophany.[48] The fact that the talk of 'wisdom' features so prominently in the Corinthian correspondence suggests more strongly, if anything, that a greater stimulus for Paul was the misuse of 'wisdom' ideas in Corinth itself.[49]

5. Since the argument turns so much on the use of εἰκὼν τοῦ θεοῦ in 2 Corinthians 4.4, it is worth enquiring more closely whether the thought is not more of Adam than of Wisdom.[50] The allusion to creation in 4.6 does not tell either way. More to the point is the fact that in other occurrences of εἰκών in the undisputed Paulines the thought is of Adam not of Wisdom (1 Cor. 11.7; 15.49; compare Rom. 1.23). More significant is the eschatological thrust of the most closely parallel passages – the transformation of believers into the image of Christ or of God as the goal of the whole process of salvation which climaxes in resurrection (2 Cor. 3.18—5.5; compare particularly Rom. 8.29; 1 Cor. 15.49; also Phil. 3.21). In this motif the image which Christ bears (or is) is that of the last Adam, Christ as fulfilling the original purpose God had in making man to be his image (Gen. 1.26).[51]

6. By way of corollary it should be noted that the affirmation of Christ as 'Lord' also ties back into Adam Christology, by virtue of the integration of Psalm 110.1 with Psalm 8.6 – Christ as Lord fulfilling God's original purpose for Adam's domination over 'all things'.[52] This development is too widespread to be attributed solely to Paul, and it could even predate his own contribution to Adam Christology (Mark 12.36; 1 Cor. 15.25–7; Eph. 1.20–2; Heb. 1.13—2.8; 1 Pet. 3.22).[53] If so, it suggests that the thought of the risen Jesus as eschatological man, as the one beginning a new form of humanity in which God's image and glory is fully expressed, was quite a prominent feature of earliest Christian thinking, and that in using the εἰκών language of the exalted Christ in 2 Corinthians 4.4 Paul was more likely to have had that emphasis in mind.

It should not go unnoticed that this shift in emphasis helps to resolve the problem from which we have started. For if indeed the εἰκὼν τοῦ θεοῦ in 2 Corinthians 4.4 speaks primarily of Christ as Adam, then the immediate corollary is that in 2 Corinthians 3—4 Paul deliberately transforms the matrix of salvation-history from Israel and Sinai to man and creation. The rationale of Paul's thought would then have been more direct: if with Christ now raised from the dead God's purpose for man (and not simply Israel) has been realized, it must follow that the object of his concern is mankind as a whole and not merely the Jews; God's purpose (not least in stopping Paul short in his full flight as a persecutor on behalf of Israel's prerogatives and law) must be to realize through Christ his purpose of creation and not simply of election. The puzzling 'therefore to the Gentiles' thus becomes a more immediate deduction from the Damascus road Christophany than even Kim allows. Conversely, since 'to the Gentiles' is so central in Paul's recollection of his conversion, it probably confirms that Paul intended the εἰκών language of 2 Corinthians 4.4 to evoke Adam rather than Wisdom motifs, and that the Wisdom Christological corollary may have taken longer to develop than Kim envisages.[54]

V

Kim's restatement of the soteriological significance of the Damascus road encounter for Paul is open to the same critique offered above of the earlier formulations of the same thesis (part II above). In particular, the more significance one reads back into the Damascus road event (Christ at once seen as the end of the law), the less easy it is to understand why the confrontations of Galatians 2 did not take place earlier. Kim himself recognizes that he may be pushing his thesis too hard. In his final restatement he contents himself with the claim: 'it is probably better to think that Paul saw the full implications of the Damascus revelation and more or less completely formulated the main lines of his theology soon after the Damascus revelation – certainly, at latest by the time of the Apostolic Council ... – than to posit a long period of slow development'.[55] But since the Apostolic Council took place about fifteen years after his conversion, probably more than half-way through his life as a Christian, this qualification only serves to undermine the boldness of the earlier claims and to pose once again the issue of what was the *immediate* impact of the Damascus road Christophany and what was its theological rationale in Paul's mind.

I suspect in fact that the sharpness of the antithesis, *either* Jesus *or* the law, was indeed a later development, at least in the sharpness with which Paul poses it explicitly or implicitly in Galatians 3, Romans 10, and Philippians 3; moreover that the antithesis as antithesis was more the corollary of 'therefore to the Gentiles' than vice-versa.

(a) This would certainly accord best with the sequence of Galatians 1—2. There the commission 'to the Gentiles' is clear from the first (1.16), whereas circumcision only emerges as a clear issue some fourteen or seventeen years later (2.1–10), and 'covenantal nomism' (the food laws and purity standards which regulated daily life and all social intercourse) only emerges as an issue

98

after that (2.11–18). What becomes evident from the latter episode is precisely that the great bulk of Jewish Christians did *not* see an antithesis between faith in Christ and a life regulated by the Torah. So the question cannot be avoided: When and how soon did it become an either-or antithesis in earliest Christian thought (including Paul's)? Certainly the simple assumption that Paul read Romans 10.4 straight off from his experience on the Damascus road does not seem to accord too well with the testimony of Galatians 1—2.[56]

(b) Wherever Paul poses the antithesis in his writings (explicitly or implicitly), he does so within the context of and as part of what amounts to a redefinition of the people of God. In Galatians 3 the question is, Who are Abraham's offspring? The definition is reworked in terms of promise rather than law – the promise which had the Gentiles in view from the first (particularly vv. 8, 14). In Romans 9—10 it is Israel's failure as a nation which is in view (9.31), the assumption of Paul's kinsmen that righteousness is something which is peculiarly theirs and not anybody else's (10.3). In Philippians 3 the contrast is drawn between the before and after of his conversion, where the 'before' all has to do with Paul's previous self-definition of himself as a loyal and devout Jew (3.4–6). In each case the clear implication is that his own conversion involved a shattering of his self-identity as a member of the people of God (Israel). Not any striving for self-achievement, not even the possibility of fulfilling the whole law (compare Gal. 5.14), but his devoutness *as a Jew* was what was called in question. A reassessment of the role of the law was of course bound up with this, but not the law as a revelation of God's will (compare Rom. 13.8–10), rather the law in its function of marking the boundary between the righteous and the sinner, between Jew and Gentile.[57] The clear implication of all this is that the insight, 'therefore to the Gentiles also', was a much more fundamental part of Paul's conversion rethink, and not simply a corollary to some other principle independently arrived at.

(c) The clue for this rationale may lie in Galatians 3.13 with its citation of Deuteronomy 21.23, 'Cursed is everyone who hangs on a tree.' It is now generally agreed that Deuteronomy 21.23 had already been referred to crucifixion at the time of Jesus (4QpNah. 1.7–8; 11QTempleScroll 64.6–13).[58] So the probability must be ranked as high that it had been used in the earliest Jewish polemic against the first expression of Christian faith in Jesus as Messiah – probably by Paul himself. If so, then we may fairly conclude that the line of thought behind Galatians 3.13 was part of the reversal which Paul experienced in the Damascus road Christophany. The point is this: that for Paul the loyal Jew, the curse of Deuteronomy 21.23 was the opposite of the blessings of the covenant (particu-

99

larly Deut. 27—8); to be cursed by God was to have the covenant revoked, to be put out of the covenant (27.58–68) – that is, to be put in the position of the Gentile sinner. The crucifixion of Jesus meant that God had rejected him, numbered him with the Gentiles, reckoned him as outside the covenant. The Damascus road Christophany must obviously have turned such a line of reasoning completely on its head, for it indicated clearly that God had accepted and vindicated this one precisely as the crucified. The *immediate* corollary for Paul would be that God must therefore favour the cursed one, the sinner outside the covenant, the Gentile.[59] And thus it can be easily seen how the conclusion 'therefore to the Gentiles' could follow directly from the Damascus road Christophany and not at some further remove as a corollary to more elaborate Christological and soteriological schemes.

VI

To sum up and conclude.

1. Paul's own testimony, that his commissioning to preach Christ to the Gentiles was given him in his encounter with the risen Christ on the road to Damascus, ought to be accorded greater importance in discussions of Paul's conversion and of the origin of his characteristic and distinctive theological emphases. Paul's conclusion, 'therefore to the Gentiles', seems to lie closer to the root of his theology than has generally been recognized.[60]

2. Although all attempts to 'get inside' the rationale of Paul's thought processes at the time of his conversion are inevitably speculative, Paul's own assertions make most sense when we see the primary Christological significance of the Christophany for Paul in terms of Adam Christology and the primary soteriological significance in terms of a radical redefinition of the boundary marking out membership of the covenant people of God. In other words, he saw Christ as the 'image of God', as the risen embodiment and therefore eschatological fulfilment of God's plan from the beginning to share his glory with the human kind he had created. And he understood this glorious vindication as a reversal of the curse of Deuteronomy 21.23, and therefore as implying God's covenant concern to embrace both outsider and insider, sinner as well as blameless, Gentile as well as Jew.

3. The corollary to this is that other important emphases of Paul's theology as we now have it may have to be regarded as the product of further reflection on Paul's part, rather than as an immediate deduction from the Damascus road Christophany. In particular, Paul's Wisdom Christology seems to owe a good deal to the stimulus of responding to the vigorous wisdom theology which he encountered at Corinth. And the sharpness of his antithesis

between Christ and the law must certainly owe a good deal to the debate about circumcision at Jerusalem (Gal. 2.1–10) and the confrontation about covenant restraints on social intercourse at Antioch (Gal. 2. 11–18).

4. The thesis argued here has the further value of showing how Paul's earliest theological impulses as a Christian may well have been related to and even to some extent dependent on a central feature of the Jesus-tradition. Paul the persecutor would presumably have regarded the cross as the inevitable outworking and consequence of Jesus' disregard for the rules of the covenant during his ministry (particularly his association with 'sinners' – Mark 2. 15–17; Matt. 11.19//Luke 7.34).[61] The reversal of the Damascus road would then carry with it a radical revision in attitude to this feature of Jesus' ministry: God accepts sinners, including 'Gentile sinners', as did Jesus when on earth (an echo of this may be implicit in Gal. 2.17). If this is so we have a further valuable link between Jesus and Paul.

I gladly dedicate this essay to the memory of George Caird. His *The Apostolic Age* was one of the first books I read as a young student of theology. Its careful scholarship provided a model from which I greatly benefited then and since.

Notes

1. J. Knox, *Chapters in a Life of Paul* (London, 1954), 117; see also, e.g., J. Munck, *Paul and the Salvation of Mankind* (London, 1959), 11–35; Wilckens (n. 12 below), 12; M. Hengel, *Between Jesus and Paul* (London, 1983), 53; K. Stendahl, *Paul Among Jews and Gentiles* (London, 1977), 7–12; J. Blank, *Paulus: Vom Jesus zum Christentum* (München, 1982), 20; Kim (n. 19 below), 56; H. Koester, *Introduction to the New Testament* (Philadelphia, 1982), ii. 100. The perennial attraction of speculation on the psychology of Paul's conversion, though renounced regularly in the above, is attested by J. G. Gager, 'Some Notes on Paul's Conversion', *NTS* 27 (1980–1), 697–704, who suggests that Paul's compulsion to engage in Gentile evangelism was part of Paul's attempt to reduce 'post-decision dissonance'; but here as elsewhere Paul's own assertions should be given greater weight than our speculative reconstructions.

2. e.g. Dupont (n. 11 below): 'He did not claim that Christ had given him the command to evangelize the Gentiles and there is nothing to allow us to imagine that this injunction was given him explicitly at this time' (193); even more emphatically, M. S. Enslin, *Reapproaching Paul* (Philadelphia, 1972), 64–5; cf. H. Schlier, *Galater*[4] (Göttingen, 1965), 56; but also F. Mussner, *Galaterbrief*[3] (Freiburg, 1977), 87–8. However, the fact that Paul here clearly evokes the commissioning of Isa. 49. 1–6 ('. . . formed me from the womb . . . a light to the nations . . .') and Jer. 1.4–5 ('Before I formed you in the womb . . . I appointed you a prophet to the nations') should not be so lightly ignored. Paul at least intended it to be understood that his commission came to him directly from and in the Damascus encounter. See further Munck especially, 24–9.

3. On the significance of the verbs used in 1.16 and 18 see my 'The Relationship between Paul and Jerusalem according to Galatians 1 and 2', *NTS* 28 (1982), 462–6, below, ch. 5. The strength of Paul's assertions in Gal. 1.1, 11–12 seems

to tell against the view that Paul inherited the Gentile mission from the Hellenists. How far the Hellenists had already gone in opening the gospel to the Gentiles is not clear either from Galatians or from Acts (Hengel, *Between Jesus and Paul*, 53–4). On the question of whether the universal mission originated further back, with Jesus himself, see now E. Best, 'The Revelation to Evangelize the Gentiles', *JTS* 35 (1984), 1–30; C. H. H. Scobie, 'Jesus or Paul? The Origin of the Universal Mission of the Church', *From Jesus to Paul*, F. W. Beare FS, ed. P. Richardson and J. C. Hurd (Waterloo, Ontario, 1984), 47–60.

4. cf. M. Dibelius and W. G. Kümmel, *Paul* (London, 1953): 'The supposition that Paul was converted a second time – from missionary to the Jews to missionary to the Gentiles – is untenable, for he speaks too clearly of one radical conversion (Phil. 3:7–11). He began the mission to the Gentiles not more than some weeks or months after the occurrence, and his decisive motive for doing so must have lain in the experience of conversion' (50).

5. Although these words were added later to the letter they succeed in summing up a central theme of Romans. See further, J. D. G. Dunn *Romans*, WBC 38, (Dallas, 1988), 916–17.

6. G. B. Caird, *The Apostolic Age* (London, 1955): 'The third account agrees more closely than the other two with Paul's own description, and it is best to follow this version and to assume that the Gentile mission was an integral part of Paul's original call to apostleship' (123); see also Munck (n. 1, above), 27. For more cautious assessments of the Acts evidence see G. Lohfink, *The Conversion of St Paul* (Chicago, 1976); C. W. Hedrick, 'Paul's Conversion/Call. A Comparative Analysis of the Three Reports in Acts', *JBL* 100 (1981), 415–32.

7. The different accounts in Acts and Galatians of Paul's activities following his conversion at least agree to the extent that they show him active in evangelism (Acts 9.19–30; Gal. 1.23).

8. This is not an appeal to an auditory element in the Damascus road encounter, as though it would suffice to say Paul heard the words 'I am sending you to the Gentiles' (Acts 26.17–18). Even were that to have been the case (and an auditory element in visionary experiences can hardly be ruled on *a priori* grounds), the words heard must have spoken to some established understanding or train of thought in Paul. It is the rationale of that movement in Paul's thought, however achieved, which is the subject of investigation.

9. H. G. Wood, 'The Conversion of Paul: Its Nature, Antecedents and Consequences', *NTS* 1 (1954–5), 276–82; P. H. Menoud, 'Revelation and Tradition: The Influence of Paul's Conversion on his Theology', *Interpretation* 7 (1953), 131–41. A link could be made through Isa. 49. 1–6, on the assumption that the first Christians had already attributed Messianic significance to it, except that Paul refers the passage more to *himself* (n. 2 above), or by arguing that the conviction that the Messianic era had already come carried with it a cosmic or world-wide perspective (cf. Blank op. cit. n. 1 above, 21 ff.), except that the typical Jewish eschatological hope was for the Gentiles to come *in* to Israel (Mt. Zion) rather than out of a mission *out to* the Gentiles (Ps. 22.27; Isa. 2.2–3; 56: 6–8; Zech. 14.16; Tob. 13.11; *Ps. Sol.* 17.33–5; Matt. 8.11//Luke 13.29).

10. See, e.g., G. Bornkamm, *Das Ende des Gesetzes: Ges. Aufs. I* (München, 1952), 40; W. Kramer, *Christ, Lord, Son of God* (London, 1966), 26–8; J. D. G. Dunn, *Unity and Diversity in the New Testament* (London, 1977), 42–3.

11. See, e.g., J. Dupont, 'The Conversion of Paul, and its Influence on his Understanding of Salvation by Faith', *Apostolic History and the Gospel*, F. F. Bruce FS, ed. W. W. Gasque and R. P. Martin (Exeter, 1970), 176–94. This has been the dominant view in German scholarship – see, e.g., P. Stuhlmacher, '"Das Ende des Gesetzes": Über Ursprung und Ansatz der paulinischen Theologie', *Versöhnung, Gesetz und Gerechtigkeit* (Göttingen, 1981), 176 and n. 22.

12. U. Wilckens, 'Die Bekehrung des Paulus als religionsgeschichtliches Problem',

Rechtfertigung als Freiheit: Paulusstudien (Neukirchen, 1974), 11–32 (particularly 15, 18, 23–5). So Stuhlmacher 179–86.

13. See Additional Note below.
14. Further details in Dunn, *Unity and Diversity*, 241.
15. See futher ch. 2 above.
16. So F. F. Bruce, *Galatians* (Exeter, 1982), 93–4.
17. See, e.g., those cited by Sanders and Räisänen in n. 18 below.
18. E. P. Sanders, *Paul, the Law, and the Jewish People* (Philadelphia, 1983), 25–6; H. Räisänen, *Paul and the Law* (Tübingen, 1983), 249–50.
19. S. Kim, *The Origin of Paul's Gospel* (Tübingen, 1981).
20. ibid., 3–4.
21. See particularly ibid., 126, 307–8.
22. ibid., 46–8.
23. ibid., 269–311, quotations from pp. 271 and 283.
24. ibid., 8.
25. ibid., 128–36, quotation from 128 (my emphasis).
26. ibid., 219. See also particularly J. Jervell, *Imago Dei* (Göttingen, 1960), 214–8; followed by C. K. Barrett, *2 Corinthians* (London, 1973), 132–5.
27. Kim, 226; the phrase is from C. C. Rowland's thesis, 'The Influence of the First Chapters of Ezekiel on Jewish and Early Christian Literature' (Cambridge, Ph.D., 1974), to which Kim acknowledges his indebtedness. See now Rowland's own publication, *The Open Heaven* (London, 1982).
28. Kim, 251.
29. ibid., 257.
30. ibid., 257–67, quotation from p. 267 (italicized).
31. ibid., 315–29, 332.
32. ibid., 57.
33. ibid., 74–99; note also 10, 23–4. See also n. 2. above.
34. One of the unfinished tasks to which Kim alludes in his closing paragraph (335).
35. ibid., 268. Kim makes a distinction between the commission for the Gentile mission and Paul's conception of a world-wide mission (which took time, 'perhaps more than a decade', for its full development – 60–1). But does Paul make such a distinction? Cf. Gal. 1.16 with Rom. 1.5 – ἐν πᾶσιν τοῖς ἔθνεσιν; also Isa. 49.6 – 'I will give you as a light to the nations, that my salvation may reach to the ends of the earth'. See also nn. 2 and 4 above.
36. See, e.g., my '2 Corinthians 3.17 – "The Lord is the Spirit"', *JTS* 21 (1970), 309–20.
37. Rowland, *Open Heaven*, like Kim, treats Gal. 1.12, 16 as a reference to what Paul saw, but does not draw 2 Cor. 4.4, 6 into the discussion (376–9). Somewhat misleadingly he compares 2 Cor. 3.18 when speaking of ascents to heaven which involve separation from the earthly body (384).
38. Kim, 7, 228.
39. ibid., 108, 111, 225; cf. Rowland, *Open Heaven*, 378.
40. ibid., 193, 224, 251, 257.
41. ibid., 198, 214, 222–3.
42. ibid., 208, 246; but clouds of heaven denote a mode of transport through or to heaven, rather than determine the status of the one so carried as divine (cf. 1 Thess. 4.17; Rev. 11.12).
43. See further M. Casey, *Son of Man* (London, 1979); J. D. G. Dunn, *Christology in the Making* (London, 1980), 67–82; B. Lindars, *Jesus, Son of Man* (London, 1983), 1–16. Kim's complete failure to reckon with any of Casey's work is regrettable, and all the more surprising in his sequel, *'The "Son of Man"' as the Son of God* (Tübingen, 1983). The flimsy possibilities which he draws from 4QpsDan Aᵃ and variant readings of the Greek text of Dan. 7.13 are scarcely sufficient to overthrow the clear indications of the NT writings, that in the

beginnings of Christianity 'son of man' had no titular significance or heavenly referent outside Christian circles. Since both the Similitudes of Enoch and 4 Ezra are to be dated after the time of Jesus and Paul (as Kim accepts – n. 46 below), and since they both present their conception of the heavenly figure (Son of Man, Man) as though it were a fresh interpretation of the Dan. 7 vision (see Casey, *Son of Man* and Dunn, *Christology*, above), they can scarcely be called as evidence for the pre-Christian Jewish understanding of Dan. 7.

44. Kim, *Origin*, 214–15, 246, 248. One should hesitate more than Kim does before taking the phrase 'one like a son of man' out of the context of Dan. 7, where it has a clear function in contrast to creatures like extraordinary beasts, and where it is distinguished from the figure on the throne, and linking it to Ezek. 1.26, where it is the occupant of the throne itself who is referred to and who is described with the greatest tentativeness and reserve as a 'likeness like the appearance of a Man'.

45. See particularly C. Rowland, 'The Vision of the Risen Christ in Rev. 1.13ff.', *JTS* 31 (1980), 1–11.

46. Kim accepts Black's view that the Similitudes of Enoch stem from 'the same period and vintage' as 4 Ezra (*Origin*, 247).

47. Kim, *Origin*, 114–17, 127–36, 258–60.

48. '... grounded *ultimately* in Paul's Damascus experience' (Kim, ibid., 114, my emphasis) leaves more scope for other input.

49. See further my *Christology* § 24, especially 179.

50. See, e.g., M. Black, 'The Pauline Doctrine of the Second Adam', *SJT* 7 (1954), 174; R. Scroggs, *The Last Adam* (Oxford, 1966), 68, 96–9; A. T. Lincoln, *Paradise Now and Not Yet* (SNTSMS 43, Cambridge, 1981), 190. Jervell also regards 2 Cor. 3.18—4.6 as an exposition of Gen. 1.27 (173–6), but is distracted by his belief that Paul's 'image of God' language is influenced by 'the Philonic-gnostic conception of the divine Anthropos' (217) – a thesis which Kim rightly rejects (*Origin*, 162–83).

51. Scroggs: 'Christ as image of God clearly describes eschatological humanity' (99). D. J. A. Clines, 'The Image of God in Man', *Tyndale Bulletin* 19 (1958), 53–103, points out that Gen. 1.26 is better translated 'Let us make man as our image' or 'to be our image' (75–80). On the significance of Adam Christology in Paul see my *Christology*, 105–13, 126–7.

52. See further my 'Was Christianity a Monotheistic Faith from the Beginning?" *SJT* 35 (1982), particularly 327–8.

53. Dunn, *Christology*, 108–9.

54. Dunn, *Christology*, § 24, especially 194–6.

55. Kim, *Origin*, 335; so earlier 102–3.

56. See further Dunn, 'Relationship', below ch. 5; also 'The New Perspective on Paul', *BJRL* 65 (1983), 95–122, below ch. 7.

57. See further my 'Works of the Law and the Curse of the Law (Gal. 3: 10–14)', *NTS* 31 (1985) 523–42, below, ch. 8.

58. See particularly J. A. Fitzmyer, 'Crucifixion in Ancient Palestine, Qumran Literature and the New Testament', *CBQ* 40 (1978), 493–513.

59. See again ch. 8 below, particularly n. 60.

60. cf. Hengel, n. 1 above: 'This calling forms the basis of his whole theology' (53); Stendahl, n. 1 above: 'Again and again we find that there is hardly a thought of Paul's which is not tied up with his mission ... The "I" of his writings is not "the Christian" but "the Apostle to the Gentiles"' (12).

61. See further my "Pharisees, Sinners and Jesus', *The Social World of Formative Christianity and Judaism*, ed. P. Borgen et al. (Philadelphia, 1988), 264–89, above, ch. 3.

Additional Note

In the interval between submitting the above article to the Caird memorial volume and its appearance, another monograph very similar to that of Kim appeared. C. Dietzfelbinger, *Die Berufung des Paulus als Ursprung seiner Theologie*,[1] although its dialogue with Kim is minimal.

Dietzfelbinger's thesis is also quite close to Kim's, at least so far as the question of the impact of Paul's conversion/calling on his understanding of the law and the Gentiles is concerned. The Damascus road event was indeed the origin of his theology (pp. 90, 96f.), and *'from the beginning* the problem of the law must have dominated his theology' (p. 115). Since Paul had been persecuting the law-critical Hellenists 'out of zeal for the law' (p. 23), it was this 'law-critical' version of the gospel to which he would have been converted (p. 144). Dietzfelbinger follows a course similar to the usual line of argument, despite any clear evidence that Paul followed this train of thought: if the law cursed Jesus and yet God made him Lord, then it is the Torah itself which is under a curse; the implication of the Damascus road event for Paul was that Christ was 'the end of the law' (pp. 105–6, 118, 125). Like Kim, he recognizes in the final section that 'the Damascus event' is a commissioning to the Gentiles (pp. 137ff.), but that conclusion was a secondary deduction from the primary conviction about Christ bringing the law to an end (p. 145).

Four more specific points are worth making.

(a) The argument about the significance of the Damascus road event for Paul's understanding of the law depends to a considerable extent on what is believed about the Hellenists' attitude to the law. Dietzfelbinger rightly recognizes that Galatians 1.13f. and Philippians 3.5 must indicate that Paul's persecution of the Hellenist Christians was an expression of his 'zeal for the law'. But does it follow immediately from this that the Hellenists had already developed an expression of the gospel 'critical of the law', as Dietzfelbinger assumes? Dietzfelbinger, like so many before him, has failed to inquire what 'zeal for the law' would mean for a Pharisaic Jew. The answer is clear from even a brief study of the motif of 'zeal for the law' in Jewish tradition up to the time of Paul. Any Jew who spoke of 'zeal for the law' would almost certainly have in mind the principal and classic examples of such zeal – Simeon and Levi (Judith 9.4; Jubilees 30.5–20; both referring to Gen. 34), Phinehas (Num. 25.10–13; Sir. 45.23–4; 1 Macc. 2.54; 4 Macc. 18.12), Elijah (Sir. 48.2; 1 Macc. 2.58) and Mattathias (1 Macc. 2.19–26; Josephus. *Ant.* 12.271).[2] The point is that in each case zeal was kindled by conduct which threatened or breached the boundaries which marked out and preserved Israel's distinctiveness as the people of God. And zeal was expressed by taking the sword against the offenders. It was just the same zeal which motivated Paul in his persecution of the Hellenist Christians. Dietzfelbinger recognizes something of this social function of the law (pp. 24–9, 141–2). But he fails to see the importance of this for Paul's persecution and subsequent conversion. It was not the law as such of which the Hellenists were 'critical'. More precisely we should say that their conduct would seem, to a zealous Jew, to threaten the boundaries marking out Israel as God's people. That is to say, at the heart of the issue for Paul the persecutor was the boundary between

Jew and Gentile and the conviction that the Hellenist-Jewish Christians were disregarding and breaking it down and so threatening the whole identity of the covenant people. This suggests, as argued above, that the Jew/Gentile issue was at the centre of Paul's opposition and so also at the heart of his conversion/commissioning. It also leaves open the question of how quickly the ramifications of this became evident for Paul in such issues as continued Jewish Christian observance of the food laws, a question which provides a *leit-motif* in the following chapters (see further below on Räisänen).

(b) Consequently Dietzfelbinger also misses the significance of Galatians 3.13–14 and its reference to Deuteronomy 21.22f. He recognizes that it probably was already used in polemic against Christians, perhaps by Paul the persecutor himself as well (pp. 36–40). But again he misses the covenant dimension of the passage, set as it is within the classic exposition of Israel's covenant theology (Deuteronomy). However, when we realize that Deuteronomy 21.22f. can also be seen in 'boundary' terms (above pp. 99–100 = *Glory*, pp. 264–5), the argument becomes increasingly persuasive that it was this aspect of Paul's understanding of the law which was transformed in the Damascus road event. Not so much that Christ was 'the end of the law', and then the calling to the Gentiles as a corollary. But Christ 'the end of the law' in its function of excluding Gentiles as Gentiles, and of marking out the grace of God as limited to those within the boundary of the law.[3] The crucified out-law owned by God means that God owns those without-law.

(c) Consequently also Dietzfelbinger falls into the quite traditional mistake of overemphasizing the sharpness and extent of the antithesis Paul draws between the law and Christ or between the law and promise (p. 95). He quite ignores Romans 8.4 and his allusion to passages like Romans 3.31 and 13.8–10 (pp. 113–14) is cursory in the extreme. This issue underlies the following chapters, so I need say no more on it here.

(d) Finally, we might simply note Dietzfelbinger's argument that while Paul's sense of commissioning in all probability emerged from the Damascus road event, his claim to apostolic status was a corollary drawn out by him only later (pp. 145–6). This is certainly put in question by Paul's own account of things in Galatians 1.1, 11–12 and 1 Corinthians 9.1. And the fact that he did not go at once to Jerusalem to gain approval for his sense of commissioning (Gal. 1.16–17)[4] likewise suggests that Paul from the first asserted a degree of independence of authorization by the risen Christ which constituted at least a *de facto* claim to apostolic status. But see further Chapter 5.

H. Räisänen too devotes a paper primarily to a critique of Kim–'Paul's Call Experience and his Later View of the Law',[5] with a brief critique of Dietzfelbinger at pp. 87–90. A briefer and updated version, shorn of its detailed response to Kim, appeared subsequently as 'Paul's Conversion and the Development of his View of the Law', *NTS* 33 (1987) 404–19.

In somewhat similar vein to Chapter 4 above, Räisänen disputes that Paul's theology of justification by faith and not by works of the law emerged immediately from his Damascus road experience. Galatians 1—2 and particularly the Antioch incident indicate at least some degree of development in Paul's perception and statement of what justification by faith involved and in his explicit 'theology of the law' (pp. 66–7). Likewise he notes the direct connection between Paul's call vision and his work among Gentiles (*NTS* 33 [1987] 406–7). On these points I find myself in close agreement with Räisänen. Furthermore, Räisänen strengthens (a) above by drawing attention to the use of the word Ἰουδαισμός in Galatians 1.13. 'The word carries connotations which hint at those *practices* which separated Jew from Gentile ... in 1.13 the emphasis lies on "particularly Jewish" *practices*' (p. 65). This adds further weight to the argument of (a), since 'Ἰουδαισμός first appears in Jewish literature (2 Macc. 2.21; 8.1; 14.38) as a designation for the national religion in its self-conscious distinctiveness and fierce loyalty to the law and the traditional customs which marked Judaism off from the wider syncretistic Hellenism. Räisänen, however, fails to follow through this recognition that it is the social significance of the law and the ethnically restrictive character of 'covenantal nomism' which stands at the heart of Paul's critique of the law, and his response to Dietzfelbinger on the significance of Deuteronomy 21.22f. also misses its relevance to Paul's understanding of his call to the Gentiles (88–90; *NTS* 33 [1987] 412). The rest of his article goes beyond the scope of the above chapter and takes up issues already dealt with in his earlier writings and discussed in the following chapters.

Notes

1. WMANT 58, Neukirchen: Neukirchener (1985).
2. See further my *Romans*, WBC 38, Dallas: Word (1988) 586–7; and *m.Sanh.* 9.6 (I owe this reference to my colleague, C. T. R. Hayward).
3. See my *Romans* 589–91.
4. See ch. 5 below.
5. *The Torah and Christ*, Helsinki: Finnish Exegetical Society 45 (1986) 55–92

5

The Relationship between Paul and Jerusalem according to Galatians 1 and 2*

1. What does Galatians 1—2 tell us about the relationship between Paul and the Jerusalem apostles during the 'tunnel' period between his conversion and his earliest correspondence? That is one of the key questions relating to the beginnings of Christianity which has never achieved a completely satisfactory resolution. It is clear enough that in Galatians itself Paul is striving to assert his independence from Jerusalem – that is hardly to be disputed. But that explanation has always left a number of puzzling loose ends. It is certainly a necessary explanation but has proved insufficient in itself to explain all that Paul says. We may think, for example, of the admission in 2.2 that the decision of the Jerusalem apostles regarding Paul's gospel could have rendered his missionary work useless;[1] and the awkward syntax of 2.3–5 has given rise to various theses at odds with the clear overall thrust of these two chapters.[2]

A fresh approach to our opening question from a sociological perspective in the past decade has succeeded in throwing fuller light on our passage.[3] In particular B. Holmberg's observation that 'the dialectic between being independent of and being acknowledged by Jerusalem is the keynote of this important text'[4] encapsulates a valuable insight into the inner tension of the position being maintained by Paul in Galatians 1—2 and suggests at least one plausible explanation for the awkwardness of Paul's language which could eliminate most of the loose ends. We should note also the recent contributions of H. D. Betz in which he analyses 1.12—2.14 as a 'statement of facts' on the model of a legal defence plea in accordance with recommended practice of various standard authorities on rhetoric.[5] Though the parallel can be pushed too far (would the Galatians have been likely to read Paul's letter in this light?), it does strongly reinforce the probability that Paul's presentation was carefully formulated and does help explain some of the otherwise puzzling omissions and emphases in the narrative.

Unfortunately none of these recent studies has succeeded in

* This paper emerged from the Nottingham New Testament Seminar's study of Galatians during adacemic year 1980–1 and was first delivered to that seminar in January 1981. I wish to record my debt of gratitude to the members of the seminar, since many of the points made here are the fruit of our corporate reflections.

tying up all the loose ends, and a fully coherent presentation of Paul's relations with Jerusalem as presented in Galatians 1—2, which gives proper weight to *all* that Paul says, is still lacking. The problem can be focused most usefully in the *verbs* Paul uses to describe his contacts with Jerusalem during the key period. If we could but feel the weight of these words and hear the overtones Paul intended we would be well on the way to an adequately comprehensive answer to our opening question. A major flaw of earlier studies is that they have not scrutinized all of these words with sufficient care, or taken sufficient pains to relate them to each other. The verbs which require closer scrutiny are προσανέθεμην (1.16), ἱστορῆσαι (1.18), ἀνεθέμην (2.2) and προσανέθεντο (2.6). These we will analyse in turn, taking due account both of their wider usage in ancient Greek literature and of their context in Galatians.

2. προσανατίθημι. 'When he ... was pleased to reveal his Son in me ... immediately I did not confer with flesh and blood (εὐθέως οὐ προσανεθέμην σαρκὶ καὶ αἵματι), nor did I go up to Jerusalem to those who were apostles before me ...' (1.15–17). What is it that Paul denies here? Προσανατίθεσθαί τινι is usually rendered simply 'take counsel with someone'. But the parallels cited by LSJ and BAGD suggest that a more technical meaning may be in view.

(a) Chrysippus (third century BC) speaks of a certain man who having had a dream consulted with the interpreter of dreams (προσαναθέσθαι ὀνειροκρίτῃ).[6]

(b) Philodemus (first century BC) characterizes the self-willed man (αὐθέκαστος) as one who does not consult with anyone (οἷος μηδενὶ προσαναθέμενος) about going abroad, about buying or selling, about starting something or bringing other matters to completion,[7] where the thought is most likely of a consultation with priests or soothsayers about the propitiousness of particular courses of action.

(c) Diodorus Siculus (first century BC) relates an odd incident in the life of Alexander and goes on to tell how he consulted with the seers concerning the portent (τοῖς μάντεσι προσαναθέμενος περὶ τοῦ σημείου – 17.116.4).

In each case it would seem that προσανατίθεσθαί τινι does not simply mean 'consult with someone' in general, but has the more technical sense of consulting with someone who is recognized as a qualified interpreter about the significance of some sign – a dream, or omen, or portent, or whatever. The only other relevant example cited by LSJ and BAGD is from Lucian, *Juppiter Tragoedus* 1, where Hermes invites Zeus to confide in him (ἐμοὶ προσανάθου). Here the sense is more general, but this may simply be a case of a technical term broadening out in usage over the decades (Lucian is second century AD). The other three examples cited above are sufficient at least to raise the possibility that at the time of Paul the phrase still had its more technical sense and was deliberately used by Paul for that reason in Galatians 1.16.

When we turn back to Galatians 1.16 with this possibility in mind Paul's train of thought gains fresh significance. The most obvious sense of verses 15f. is that Paul did not consult with flesh and blood about the significance of the revelation he had received, about his understanding of 'the revelation of Jesus Christ' (v. 12) as a call to preach the gospel to the Gentiles. It was not necessary for him to consult with any man[8] about the meaning of his revelation and commissioning; the meaning came in the revelation itself,[9] it came to him independently without human agency,[10] it came to him direct from God. In particular he did not need to go up to Jerusalem to those who were apostles before him (v. 17), to those, that is, who within the circle of Jesus' followers would be regarded as most qualified to give an authoritative interpretation of what he (Paul) had seen and heard on the Damascus road.[11]

This understanding of verse 16 makes excellent sense in the context of Galatians 1. It fits well with Paul's repeated insistence that his apostleship and his gospel came neither from man, nor through man, but through Jesus Christ, through a revelation of Jesus Christ (1.1, 11f.). Had Paul gone immediately to Jerusalem following his conversion it would have been difficult to contest the claim that his understanding of this revelation had been given him when he consulted with the Jerusalem apostles. But precisely such a consultation is what Paul emphatically denies: he did *not* immediately consult with (mere) human beings or hasten to the apostles in Jerusalem ($εὐθέως$ has the place of emphasis[12] and probably governs both phrases[13]). By the time he did first visit Jerusalem three years had elapsed and the meaning of 'the revelation of Jesus Christ' at Damascus had been clearly established 'in' Paul without any reference to outside human agency, including the Jerusalem apostles.[14]

A technical sense for $προσανεθέμην$ therefore becomes quite probable — 'consult in order to be given a skilled or authoritative interpretation'. Indeed we may put the case more strongly: only by recognizing such a sense in $οὐ$ $προσανεθέμην$ can we give sufficient weight to the $εὐθέως$ of 1.16 and the ready admission that seventeen years later he did discuss ($ἀνεθέμην$) his gospel with the Jerusalem apostles (2.2 – see 4 below).

3. $ἱστορέω$. 'Then after three years I went up to Jerusalem $ἱστορῆσαι$ $Κηφᾶν$, and remained with him fifteen days. But I saw ($εἶδον$) none of the other apostles, except James the brother of the Lord' (Gal. 1.18f.). '$Ἱστορῆσαι$ $Κηφᾶν$ today is regularly translated 'to visit Cephas',[15] an interpretation which goes back to Chrysostom –

110

ἱστορῆσαι Πέτρον, ὅπερ οἱ τὰς μεγάλας πόλεις καὶ λαμπρὰς καταμανθά-
νοντες λέγουσιν (PG 61.651). Chrysostom has been regularly followed likewise in his two other assertions: that ἱστορῆσαι could not
mean 'to get information, knowledge from Peter' (οὐκ ὡς μαθησόμε-
νός τι παρ' αὐτοῦ οὐδὲ ὡς διόρθωσίν τινα δεξόμενος);[16] and that
ἱστορῆσαι is to be distinguished from ἰδεῖν as meaning to see and
honour Peter (ἰδεῖν αὐτὸν καὶ τιμῆσαι τῇ παρουσίᾳ).[17] However, a
closer examination of lexical parallels suggests that Chrysostom
and those who have followed him have been misled.

The basic meaning of ἱστορεῖν is to inquire into, or about, or
from' (LSJ). For example, Polybius 3.48.12 – 'On these points I
can speak with some confidence as I have inquired about the
circumstances from the men present (περὶ τῶν πράξεων παρ' αὐτῶν
ἱστορηκέναι τῶν παρατετευχότων τοῖς καιροῖς) and have personally
inspected the country . . .' With impersonal objects the sense of
inquiry is still strong: for example, Plutarch, *Moralia* 516C –
'Finally he (Aristippus) sailed for Athens and slaked his burning
thirst with draughts from the fountainhead (Socrates), and engaged in a study of the man and his words and his philosophy (καὶ
τὸν ἄνδρα καὶ τοὺς λόγους αὐτοῦ καὶ τὴν φιλοσοφίαν ἱστόρησεν) . . .'; and
Epictetus 3.7.1 –

It is proper for us laymen to make enquiry (πυνθάνεσθαι) of you
philosophers what the best thing in the world is – just as those who have
come to a strange town make enquiry of the citizens and people who are
familiar with the place – so that having learned what it is (ἱστορήσαντες),
we may go in quest of it ourselves and behold it (θεώμεθα) as do strangers
with the sights in the cities.

This sense of inquiry for the sake of information can be eroded in
the direction of a traveller's or tourist's 'sight-seeing', as the
examples in MM suggest. But there too in the fuller inscriptions
quoted the thought of inspection or examination or careful scrutiny of the famous sight is probably still in the background,[18] as
indeed explicitly in Chrysostom himself (καταμανθάνουντες).[19] In
particular in the passage usually cited from Josephus, *Ant.* 1.203,
the thought of a visit in order to examine or ascertain is difficult to
exclude:

'Lot's wife . . . was changed into a pillar of salt. I have seen (ἱστόρησα)
this pillar which remains to this day.'

However in Galatians 1.18 we have a personal object (ἱστορῆσαι
Κηφᾶν), where the thought of inquiry can be present in a more
direct way than an impersonal object allows.[20] Thus in Herodotus:

2.19 – Concerning this [the flooding of the Nile] none of the Egyptians
could tell me anything when I asked them what power the Nile has
(ἱστορέων αὐτοὺς ἥντινα δύναμιν ἔχει ὁ Νεῖλος) to be contrary in nature to
all other rivers;

111

3.77 – [The seven Persians coming into court] met there the eunuchs who carry messages to the king; who asked the seven with what intent they had come (οἳ σφεας ἱστόρεον ὅ τι θέλοντες ἥκοιεν) . . .

In two other passages from Josephus the sense of inquiry is less strong, but the verb still denotes an encounter which provides information thus enabling an informed judgement or report concerning the individual in view.

War 6.81 – Julianus, a centurion in the Bithynian contingent, a man of some mark, and distinguished above all whose acquaintance I made (ἱστόρησα) during that war in the science of arms, strength of body and intrepidity of soul, . . .

Ant. 8.46 – I have seen (ἱστόρησα) a certain Eleazar . . . free men possessed by demons, and this was the manner of the cure . . .

It is difficult to avoid the conclusion that in our period the thought of 'gaining information' is always present in ἱστορῆσαι, whether in the foreground or background of the meaning, and that even when it approaches ἰδεῖν in usage it is precisely the sense of 'finding out about or from' which distinguishes ἱστορῆσαι from ἰδεῖν. The lexical parallels therefore strongly support LSJ's rendering of ἱστορῆσαι Κηφᾶν as 'visit Peter for the purpose of inquiry', or G. D. Kilpatrick's stronger alternative, 'to get information from Cephas'.[21]

This rendering makes better sense of Galatians 1.18 in its context than has usually been realized. The main difficulty has been that at first sight it seems to run counter to Paul's defence (n. 16 above): if Paul was so concerned to assert his independence from Jerusalem he would hardly have used a word which explicitly acknowledged his indebtedness to Peter.[22] But now we have seen good reason to conclude that Paul's attempt to distance himself from Jerusalem had a much more specific issue in view – viz. his interpretation of the revelation given him on the Damascus road (above p. 110). He was not trying to stand aloof from Jerusalem in respect of everything to do with the new movement. What he wanted to safeguard was quite simply the claim that his basic understanding of the gospel to the Gentiles came direct from God (vv. 11–12; note also 2.2).[23] It was precisely his understanding of his apostleship to the Gentiles which he refused so resolutely to attribute to any human authority (v. 1). That defence had been successfully and emphatically made in 16 and 17 – the revelation of Christ for the proclamation of Christ to the Gentiles was complete, its significance firmly established in Paul a full three years before his first encounter with Peter or any of the other apostles. That point being made, Paul was quite ready to acknowledge his indebtedness to Peter for further information – no doubt primarily background information about the ministry of Jesus while on earth

112

as well perhaps as the very beginnings of the new movement centred on the risen Christ.

That Paul would have had a natural curiosity about this Jesus who had appeared to him outside Damascus is *prima facie* obvious, and we can hardly doubt that the fortnight with Peter was largely spent in passing on such information[24] – it is only the misunderstanding of Paul's defence in Galatians 1 and a dogmatically imposed distinction between the historical Jesus and the Christ of faith which has enabled commentators and translators to ignore this most probable meaning of ἱστορῆσαι in the first place. It also makes best sense of the distinction between ἱστορῆσαι Κηφᾶν and ἰδεῖν Ἰάκωβον (vv. 18f.): he paid a courtesy call on James, but he used his time with Peter, the one who had been closest to Jesus,[25] to make inquiry, to draw out the sort of information which had not come to him with the apostle-making gospel-giving revelation three years earlier.

4. ἀνατίθημι. 'Then after fourteen years I went up again to Jerusalem ... I went up in accordance with a revelation. And I laid before them (ἀνεθέμην αὐτοῖς) the gospel which I preach among the Gentiles, but privately before those of repute, lest somehow I was running or had run in vain' (2.1–2). Here there is less dispute over the meaning of ἀνατίθεσθαι. BAGD define it well: 'declare, communicate, refer with the added idea that the person to whom a thing is referred is asked for his opinion, lay something before someone for consideration'. But does the word tell anything about the relationship between the two parties involved? In particular, does it have any overtone of submitting to a higher authority an issue which the one making the submission was incompetent to resolve on his own? Does Paul's use of the word amount to an acknowledgement on his part that the authority of his gospel depended on Jerusalem's approval?[26]

Here again the parallels elsewhere are instructive, for they make it sufficiently clear that there is no indication in the word itself of the relative competence or status of the parties involved. For example, Plutarch, *Moralia* 772D, and Alciphron 3.23.2, use it to signify a communication between friends. Even in Polybius 21.46.11, speaking of a disputed territorial issue being referred to the Senate, it is the proconsul (Manlius) and the ten legates who do so, having already disposed of Antiochus' empire. Most striking for us are two other passages – 2 Maccabees 3.9, and the one nearest home, Acts 25.14. In the former, Heliodorus, king Seleucus' plenipotentiary, informed (ἀνέθετο) Onias the high priest about the report of the temple's wealth that had been given to the king and inquired (ἐπυνθάνετο) whether it was really so. Here the role of the one to whom reference was made was simply that of confirming the information communicated – whether he confirmed or denied it the authority to evaluate and act upon the report lay wholly in Heliodorus' hands at that point. In Acts 25.14 it was Festus, the Roman procurator, who laid Paul's case before king Agrippa (ἀνέθετο). The speech which follows is simply a report of the case, but implicit is Festus' request for Agrippa's opinion on the affair. But this is no consultation between equals: Festus' request is partly a matter of courtesy, and partly a matter of the chief representative of Roman power in the area seeking advice from that one of Rome's client kings best able to advise on Jewish affairs.

It is clear from these examples that ἀνατίθεσθαι τινι τι tells us nothing about the relative status of the parties involved. In the closest parallels the one to whom reference was made did not have an integral part to play in the decision to be taken concerning the information communicated. His role was essentially secondary – a matter of advising the one who had to make the judgement, or of confirming a judgement already reached. Nor is there any implication in the word itself that the party to whom reference was made had the right to demand or claim that it should be so; in every case reference depended on whether the referring body thought it necessary or useful. Such findings point to an obvious conclusion: that Paul chose this word in Galatians 2.2 to *avoid* giving the impression that he went to Jerusalem 'cap in hand' to gain an authoritative ruling on a matter (the validity of his gospel) on which he had insufficient competence to decide.

When we set this finding in the context of Galatians 2.2 it becomes evident that Paul is striving to hold a delicate balance in defining his relations with Jerusalem. On the one hand he makes it clear that this visit took place (probably) seventeen years after the revelation which had determined and defined for him his gospel and apostleship to the Gentiles – nothing that happened at such a distance in time from that decisive event could undermine or call in question the direction or significance of his commissioning by God through Jesus Christ. Moreover, he goes out of his way to point out that he went up in accordance with (a further) revelation (κατὰ ἀποκάλυψιν) – thus presumably excluding any suggestion that his visit to Jerusalem was in response to a summons from the mother church.[27] Furthermore, he calls the Jerusalem leadership οἱ δοκοῦντες, 'men of repute', a phrase which acknowledges the high standing in which the pillar apostles[28] were held (by others), without constituting an endorsement by Paul himself (cf. 2.6, 9).[29] The use of this last expression in particular reinforces the impression that Paul's choice of ἀνάθεσθαι was similarly designed to characterize the balance between Paul's recognition of the Jerusalem apostles' eminence and authority and his even firmer assertion of independence in the authority of his gospel and apostleship.

On the other hand he adds, 'lest somehow ($\mu\acute{\eta}$ $\pi\omega\varsigma$) I should be running or had run in vain' (2.2c). The clause certainly indicates a genuine concern on Paul's part for the success or failure of his missionary work among the Gentiles; as elsewhere in Paul the $\mu\acute{\eta}$ $\pi\omega\varsigma$ denotes a real, not merely hypothetical possibility (1 Cor. 8.9; 9.27; 2 Cor. 2.7; 9.4; 11.3; 12.20; Gal. 4.11; 1 Thess. 3.5).[30] The judgement of the Jerusalem apostles mattered to Paul; an adverse judgement concerning his gospel would have rendered his work past and present ineffective and useless ($\epsilon\grave{\iota}\varsigma$ $\kappa\epsilon\nu\acute{o}\nu$ – cf. 2 Cor. 6.1; Phil. 2.16; 1 Thess. 3.5).

How is it that Paul in the same breath can both assert his independence of the Jerusalem apostles and yet also acknowledge that the effectiveness of his work depended on their approval of his gospel? We cannot put this seeming contradiction less strongly without lessening the force of Paul's own language. What was it that was at stake here? Not, it would appear, Paul's conviction as to the *truth* of his gospel; such an admission would run too sharply counter to the firm assertions of Galatians 1.[31] Nor does it seem to meet the force of 2.2c to argue that Paul's concern was simply for the future unity of the whole church,[32] or that he feared the future depredations of Judaizers;[33] 2.2c seems rather to envisage the possibility of a decision made by the Jerusalem apostles which would at a stroke nullify the effectiveness of his past and current missionary work. It was this *effectiveness* of his gospel which Paul was concerned for.[34] Presumably he had been preaching that acceptance of the good news of Jesus Christ without circumcision brought Gentiles into the people of God, made them heirs of God's promise to Abraham together with believing Jews (it is hardly likely that the main thesis of Galatians was completely new to the Galatians).[35] But Jerusalem's refusal to acknowledge the validity of this proclamation would render it ineffective (not false), because as a result, whether Paul liked it or not, the churches he had already founded would be distinct from believing Israel; and adverse decision by the Jerusalem apostles would make it impossible for Gentile churches to be seen in their true continuity with the religion of Israel, of the prophets, of Jesus' first disciples.[36]

Paul's understanding of the mutual relations involved in the process of laying his gospel before the Jerusalem apostles is probably further illuminated by his understanding of prophecy and its evaluation. Elsewhere I have drawn attention to Paul's insistence that the inspired utterance of the prophet is not self-authenticating for the rest of the church but has to be evaluated by the other prophets or the rest of the church at large (1 Cor. 2.13; 12.10; 14.29; 1 Thess. 5.19–22).[37] So seriously did he take this necessity of spiritual authority being recognized (and not simply blindly followed) that he regularly circumscribed his own authority by the freedom of his converts, asking for acknowledgement of his authority and not simply obedience to it (1 Cor. 5.3–5; 7.40; 14.37f.; 2 Cor. 2.6–8; 8.10; 1 Thess. 4.2–8; Philem. 14).[38] The point of the parallels is that such evaluation and acknowledgement in Paul's view did not *give* authority to the prophecy or instruction – they *recognized* the authority of a true word of the Spirit (distinguishing it from false prophecy), and by so recognizing it ensured its greater effectiveness within the community of the Spirit. Paul evidently was thinking along the same lines in Galatians 2.2 – striving to maintain a balance between the authority of his own apostolic commissioning and gospel and that of the wider community of faith.

In short, in laying his gospel before the Jerusalem apostles what he sought was not so much their approval (without which his gospel would have no validity) as their recognition of his gospel's validity (without which his gospel would lose its effectiveness).

5. προσανατίθημι. 'But from those reputed to be something – what they once were matters nothng to me; God shows no partiality – the men of repute added nothing to me (προσανέθεντο) . . .' (2.6). It is difficult to catch the precise force of (προσανέθεντο) here since we lack any close parallels. The use of the same verb in 1.16 does not help since the context seems to exclude any thought of the Jerusalem apostles submitting something to Paul for his judgement. The weaker sense of 'submit for consideration' would fit with verse 10, but still seems too weak for the immediate context, where it is the authoritative ruling and backing of the Jerusalem apostles which Paul seems to have in mind. Such a sense could have been achieved by using ἀνάθεσθαι as in 2.2; whereas the choice of the unusual προσανατίθεσθαι once again must have been deliberate, as more appropriate to the exercise of authoritative ruling.[39] The closest parallel is probably Xenophon, *Memorabilia* 2.1.8, where it has the sense of 'take an additional burden on oneself' (LSJ). Commentators generally agree that with the ἐμοί an active equivalent of Xenophon's usage is most probable. This could be given a weaker rendering, 'give further teaching, instruction about the new faith'.[40] But this too does not fit well with the context, where it is the question of specific requests or authoritative rulings on disputed issues which seems to be in view (contrast 1.18). A much stronger rendering, 'laid no further requirement on me',[41] is probably too strong in view of Paul's careful use of ἀνάθεσθαι in 2.2; he would not have admitted to accepting any requirements as such from Jerusalem. But the intended meaning most probably lies somewhere between these last two alternatives, and we would perhaps best be advised to settle for the ambiguity of JB, 'had

116

nothing to add to the Good News as I preach it', or of NIV, 'added nothing to my message'.[42]

The choice of this unusual, perhaps deliberately obscure word reflects the fact that Paul here was caught on the horns of a somewhat awkward dilemma. To acknowledge the Jerusalem apostles' overall authority to determine the terms on which the gospel could be received and Gentiles accepted into Israel's new covenant would have jeopardized the Gentile mission if the 'Judaizers' in Galatia could have claimed Jerusalem's authority. Yet, at the same time, the pillar apostles' authoritative ruling in 2.6 was one he had to appeal to if his gospel was to be effective and his vision of Gentile converts being brought into the people of God to be fully realized. It was this attempt to hold on to Jerusalem's authority and yet at the same time to hold it at arm's length which explains the contortions of syntax in this section of Galatians. Above all else Paul wanted to make it clear that the pillar apostles acknowledged the validity of his circumcision-free gospel to the Gentiles. That was where he wanted his readers to recognize the significance and force of Jerusalem's authority: Titus was not circumcised despite strong advocacy on the part of some that he should be (2.3–5);[43] the pillars recognized and welcomed the effectiveness of Paul's missionary work among the Gentiles, acknowledging its circumcision-free message to be directed by God and used by God, the second prong of a two-pronged strategy to win both Jew and Gentile to faith in the Christ of Israel, the Son of God (2.7–9).[44] They added nothing, no further content, request, instruction or requirement to the circumcision-free gospel (2.6), except the encouragement to remember the importance of almsgiving (2.10). At this point Jerusalem's backing was absolutely crucial to Paul's whole understanding of the gospel and its outworking in his missionary strategy.

On the other hand he had no desire to lean on Jerusalem's authority more heavily than was absolutely necessary. Hence once again the distancing phrase, 'those reputed to be of some account' ($\tau\hat{\omega}\nu$ $\delta o\kappa o\acute{\upsilon}\nu\tau\omega\nu$ $\epsilon\hat{\iota}\nu a\iota$ $\tau\iota$ – 2.6),[45] and its slightly querulous echo three verses later, 'those regarded as pillars' ($o\acute{\iota}$ $\delta o\kappa o\hat{\upsilon}\nu\tau\epsilon\varsigma$ $\sigma\tau\hat{\upsilon}\lambda o\iota$ $\epsilon\hat{\iota}\nu a\iota$ – 2.9).[46] Hence too the highly revealing parenthesis, 'what they once were makes no difference to me; God shows no partiality'. Here Paul's language indicates clearly enough both that at that time the Jerusalem apostles were accorded a status and authority (what they once[47] were – $\acute{o}\pi o\hat{\iota}o\acute{\iota}$ $\pi o\tau\epsilon$ $\mathring{\eta}\sigma a\nu$ – note the imperfect tense)[48] which is (now) a matter of indifference to him ($o\mathring{\upsilon}\delta\acute{\epsilon}\nu$ $\mu o\iota$ $\delta\iota a\phi\acute{\epsilon}\rho\epsilon\iota$ – note the change of tense);[49] and also that in his view the Jerusalem apostles are (still) accorded too high a status and authority by some – but not by God ($\pi\rho\acute{o}\sigma\omega\pi o\nu$ $\acute{o}$ $\theta\epsilon\grave{o}\varsigma$ $\acute{a}\nu\theta\rho\acute{\omega}\pi o\upsilon$ $o\mathring{\upsilon}$ $\lambda a\mu\beta\acute{a}\nu\epsilon\iota$).[50] Hence too the

117

presumably deliberate avoidance of a verb in the final clause of 2.9 and first clause of 2.10, since as the syntax stands almost any verb would suggest that the pillars had the same authority to send out Paul as they had to send out Peter,[51] and since it would be hard to avoid the impression that almsgiving was an obligation which Paul accepted from the pillars.[52] Paul does not seem too concerned to deny such impressions – probably because he had made sufficiently clear the point that really mattered: his gospel for the Gentiles given him by God had been fully acknowledged by the Jerusalem leadership.

6. What then was Paul's relationship with the Jerusalem apostles as reflected in Galatians 1—2? The answer which emerges from our detailed examination of the four key words is somewhat confusing, for different elements seem to point in different directions: at some points Paul vehemently protests his independence of Jerusalem, at others he seems readily to acknowledge some sort of dependence. In order to make sense of the whole picture it is necessary to postulate a three-fold distinction.

(a) *Paul maintains the independence of his gospel and apostleship as to its validity and authority.* To be more precise, Paul maintains the God-givenness and divine authority of his interpretation of the gospel as open to the Gentiles without the requirement of circumcision. This was certainly his attitude at the time he wrote his letter to the Galatians (1.1, 12). But he also maintains that this was the case from the beginning: having been given his gospel (1.11), that is, his understanding of the gospel in its reference to the Gentiles (1.16), through the Damascus road 'revelation of Jesus Christ' (1.12), he did not immediately check it out with any human authority including those who had been apostles before him (1.17). It was only after a period of three years that he went up to Jerusalem and stayed with Peter, and that was for the purpose not of validating his gospel, but of finding out information other than the gospel itself (1.18). He is quite adamant on this point and insists with a solemn oath that he did not see any other of the apostles, except James the Lord's brother (1.19–20) – denying so fiercely what presumably had been asserted by others,[53] that is, presumably that on that visit he had taken counsel with all the Jerusalem apostles, thereby promoting the further implication that they had at that time commissioned him or validated his gospel. No doubt for the same reason he denies any personal contact with any of the Judean churches, the most ancient assemblies of the new movement[54] – his gospel was fully independent of all those who might claim and no doubt were claiming precedence in the faith, and so a more authoritative understanding of the faith (1.22–3);

118

from the beginning his missionary endeavour had been independent of Jerusalem and the Judean churches.[55]

A further fourteen years elapsed before he went once again to Jerusalem to lay his gospel before the recognized leaders – not because they had summoned him, but because God had commanded him (κατὰ ἀποκάλυψιν); not because he doubted the truth of his gospel, but because it could not be effective without their support (2.2). Despite strenuous attempts of those Paul calls 'false brothers' to maintain the necessity of circumcision in order to become one of Abraham's seed, Paul did not give way (2.3–5). And in the end the Jerusalem leadership gave their backing to Paul: they did not ask him to change his gospel at all (2.6); on the contrary they acknowledged publicly that his gospel was indeed the gospel, or at least the gospel so far as the uncircumcised were concerned (2.7), and the effectiveness of God's grace through Paul and his gospel (2.8–9).

It was this *divine authority* for his ministry and gospel, and its *acknowledgement* by the Jerusalem leadership that Paul regarded as of *first* importance. That is clearly the main point of his defence in Galatians 1—2; that was clearly what he wanted to impress on the 'foolish Galatians' above all else.

(b) *Paul acknowledges his earlier dependence on the Jerusalem leadership*. His use of προσανατίθεσθαι in 1.16 is probably an implicit acknowledgement that the Jerusalem apostles were the appropriate authorities to consult for an interpretation of an important revelation. And while he did not require such validation of his message or ministry from Jerusalem, he did find it necessary after his initial spell in Arabia and Damascus to have more information regarding his new faith. His visit to Peter for this purpose strongly suggests that it was information about Jesus' pre-Easter ministry which he had in mind, from the one who had been Jesus' most prominent disciple. He freely acknowledges his indebtedness to Peter at this point (1.18), though his encounter with James during that fortnight had been much more casual – either a 'seeing' in passing or a courtesy call (1.19).

Paul's second visit to Jerusalem was particularly significant. The purpose was evidently to secure the backing of the accepted leadership in Jerusalem for his circumcision-free gospel to the Gentiles. The very fact that he and Barnabas went in the first place was itself an acknowledgement that Jerusalem was where such issues should be determined, and that the opinion of the Jerusalem apostles mattered to Paul.[56] Indeed Paul explicitly states that Jerusalem's judgement on the issue could make all the difference to the effectiveness of his work (2.2): without their acknowledgement of his gospel to the Gentiles the outcome of his mission would be what Paul himself could not count as success – presumably because for him the gospel was the gospel of God's promise to Abraham, and receiving the gospel meant receiving that promise and becoming part of Abraham's people.

It is not so surprising, then, when Paul continues, 'But Titus, though a Greek, was not compelled to be circumcised' (2.3) – the implication being that Titus *could* have been compelled, that is, had the Jerusalem apostles insisted, Paul would have had to go along with them. Whether Paul would actually have 'fallen in line' had the decision in Jerusalem gone against him is a moot point (cf. 2.14);[57] Paul is happy to admit the weight of the Jerusalem apostles' authority at this point simply because in the event they decided in his favour. The next two verses strongly suggest that the Jerusalem apostles *advised* Paul to conform or concede the point on account of, or for the sake of the 'false brothers', but evidently they did not insist.[58] Paul denies emphatically that he gave ground to these 'false brothers' – that would have been an unacceptable act of subjection, partly because of the position they maintained, but partly also because they were not apostles – but he does not say anything about refusing to obey the Jerusalem apostles. Evidently, however, the strength of Paul's opposition to the policy of the 'false brothers' was enough to convince the Jerusalem leadership that Paul's view and policy should be supported, rather than that of the 'false brothers'.

2.6 is again significant here: those of repute added nothing to Paul or his gospel – but again the implication is clear that they had the authority to do so had they chosen to exercise it. As in 2.3, the point where Paul is most uninhibited in his acknowledgement of the Jerusalem leadership's authority is, quite understandably, the point at which they threw that authority behind him. The wording of this whole paragraph (vv. 6–10) in fact reads not so much as a conference decision reached by equals but more as a ruling made by the pillar apostles – *theirs* was the decision to recognize Paul's gospel and its effectiveness, it was theirs to proffer the hand of fellowship which symbolized their acceptance of Paul's call to the Gentiles on equal terms with Peter's mission to the circumcised. Paul's was the decisive plea, but theirs was the judgement on whether or not to accept Paul's plea.[59]

At the same time there are probably some indications in verses 7–10 that his victory over the 'false brothers' was not total. If verses 7–8 echo some agreed statement which emerged from the consultation,[60] then it is perhaps significant that only Peter's mission is entitled an 'apostleship', and that Paul and Barnabas are given no title in verse 9.[61] Was there a certain unwillingness on the part of the Jerusalem leadership to give completely unqualified recognition to Paul? – once again because of the 'false brothers'? At all events verse 10 should probably be understood as something more than a good neighbourly suggestion – more in the nature of a policy recommendation backed with the authority of the Jerusalem apostles. Paul, having gained the point that really mattered, was very happy to accede to something already close to his own heart.[62]

In short, there is sufficient indication that during his second visit to Jerusalem Paul still acknowledged the authority of the Jerusalem leadership in the making of policy decisions which affected the whole Christian mission.

(c) *By the time Paul wrote Galatians he was no longer prepared to acknowledge the authority of Jerusalem to the same extent.*[63] This is clearest in 2.6, where the change in tense in the parenthesis is best understood as indicating precisely such a change in Paul's attitude to the Jerusalem leadership – 'what they once were is (now) a matter of indifference to me; God takes no account of such evaluations of status and importance'. But it is also implicit in the repeated use of οἱ δοκοῦντες and its variations (2.2, 6, 9), which enable Paul to refer to the Jerusalem leadership's recognized authority without necessarily acknowledging it himself. Here too the careful use of ἀνατίθεσθαι in 2.2 is probably significant in the same way, and the formulation of 2.6–10 does enable Paul to extract the maximum force from the Jerusalem agreement for his purposes in this letter without compromising the independent authority he claims in relation to the Galatians. The awkwardness of these verses is almost entirely to be explained by the fact that Paul was citing the backing of apostles whose authority in relation to his own missionary work he no longer acknowledged, or no longer acknowledged to the same extent.[64]

We may further note that a change in Paul's relationship with Barnabas is also probably bound up with the altered relationship with Jerusalem. The only points at which Barnabas is mentioned are 2.1 and 2.9. In the former the implication is that Paul and Barnabas were equal partners, whereas Titus was taken along as a kind of assistant (συμπαραλαβών – LSJ). Evidently they went up to Jerusalem not simply on their own account, but as representatives, delegates from the church in Antioch[65] – the practice of a circumcision-free gospel for the Gentiles was after all not exclusively Paul's (the church at Antioch must have been following the practice in large measure for some time at least),[66] so the outcome of the meeting in Jerusalem would affect the whole missionary enterprise associated with Antioch. But later in Galatians 2 Barnabas is mentioned only at the point (v. 9) where Paul speaks of the pillar apostles' formal ratification of the circumcision-free gospel for the Gentiles preached by Paul and Barnabas (representing Antioch). For the rest he speaks only in personal terms, with reference to his own missionary work, even at the cost of switching awkwardly from singular to plural and back again in the same sentence (2.9f.).[67] The probable implication is that at the time of writing Galatians Barnabas was no longer associated with Paul, so that when Paul wrote to the Galatians it was the bearing of the Jerusalem agreement on his own continuing missionary endeavour which filled his mind. The suggestion naturally commends itself that the parting of the ways between Paul and Barnabas, reflected also in Acts 15.39, had already taken place, and that this splitting of such an important and successful partnership was bound up with or part and parcel of the change in Paul's relationship with Jerusalem.

What was it that brought about Paul's change in attitude to the Jerusalem leadership and breach with Barnabas? The answer is almost certainly the incident at Antioch (Gal. 2.11ff.). But that is another subject in itself which requires a separate treatment.[68]

Notes

1. cf., e.g., J. B. Lightfoot, *Galatians* (Macmillan, 1865, [10]1890), pp. 103f.: 'the *prima facie* sense of the passage . . . would be so entirely alien to the spirit of the passage, so destructive of St. Paul's whole argument, and so unlikely under the circumstances, that (it) must be abandoned'.
2. cf., e.g., the famous comment of F. C. Burkitt, *Christian Beginnings* (London, 1924), p. 118: 'Who can doubt that it was the knife which really did circumcise Titus that has cut the syntax of Gal. 2.3–5 to pieces?'
3. See especially the studies of J. H. Schütz, *Paul and the Anatomy of Apostolic Authority* (Cambridge, 1975), pp. 136–50, and B. Holmberg, *Paul and Power: the Structure of Authority in the Primitive Church as reflected in the Pauline Epistles* (Lund, 1977), pp. 14–34.
4. Holmberg, *Paul*, p. 15.
5. H. D. Betz, 'The Literary Composition and Function of Paul's Letter to the Galatians', *NTS* 21 (1974–5), pp. 353–79; also *Galatians* (Hermeneia, 1979), here particularly pp. 58–62, 83. Similarly G. Lüdemann, *Paulus der Heidenapostel. Band I: Studien zur Chronologie* (Göttingen, 1980), pp. 74–7.
6. Cited in both J. von Arnim, *Stoicorum Veterum Fragmenta*, 1922, II.1202 (p. 344), and F. Wehrli, *Klearchos* (Basel, 1948), frag. 76b (p. 30).
7. C. Jensen, περὶ κακιῶν ί (Leipzig, 1911), XVII.25–29 (p. 31).
8. For 'flesh and blood' = 'mere man', cf. Sir. 14.18; Matt. 16.17; 1 Cor. 15.50; Eph. 6.12; *m. Sotah* 8.1; further Strack-Billerbeck I pp. 730f.; see also F. Mussner, *Galater* (Herder, 1974, [3]1977), p. 89 n. 58.
9. This is perhaps part of the reason why Paul says ἀποκαλύψαι ἐν ἐμοί instead of the normal ἀποκαλύπτειν + dative which he regularly uses elsewhere (1 Cor. 2.10; 14.30; Phil. 3.15; also Eph. 3.5): it was a revelation whose import was experienced as an inward compulsion he could not gainsay.
10. cf. Philodemus, who continues: κἄν προσερωτήσῃ τις, (τί) μέλλει ποιεῖν. 'οἶδ ἐγώ' λέγειν . . . (XVII.29ff.). Also Lucian, where Hermes's exhortation ἐμοὶ προσανάθου, λάβε με σύμβουλον πόνων is set in contrast to the preceding καταμόνας σαυτῷ λαλεῖς.
11. cf. T. Zahn (cited in Mussner, *Galater*, p. 90 n. 59); P. Bonnard, *Galates* (CNT 1953): 'προσανατίθημαι signifie probablement prendre conseil, demander un avis autorisé et officiel' (p. 31).
12. Mussner, *Galater*: 'Der Ton liegt auf εὐθέως, wie die auffällige Stellung des Adverbs beweist' (p. 89).

13. M. J. Lagrange, *Galates* (EB 1925) p. 15; and those cited by Betz, *Galatians,* p. 72 n. 165.

14. 'Die Zeitangabe ist nicht in erster Linie in chronologischen Interesse hervorgehoben, sondern um auch durch sie die Unabhängigkeit des Apostels und seines Evangeliums zu betonen' (H. Schlier, *Galater* (KEK ¹³1965), pp. 59f.).

15. e.g., BAGD 'visit for the purpose of coming to know someone'; RSV 'visit Cephas'; NEB 'to get to know Cephas'; JB 'to visit Cephas'; NIV 'to get acquainted with Peter'; 'The sole purpose of this fortnight's visit was to "make the acquaintance" of Peter' (G. Bornkamm, *Paul,* 1969, ET Hodder & Stoughton 1971, p. 28); Mussner follows BAGD; Betz 'pay Cephas a visit'.

16. e.g. G. S. Duncan, *Galatians,* Moffatt 1934: 'he went to *visit* Peter, not to receive instruction from him' (p. 31); Betz, *Galatians*: 'though possible philologically, it runs counter to Paul's defence' (p. 76).

17. e.g. Lagrange, *Galates,* p. 17; O. Cullmann, *Peter: Disciple, Apostle, Martyr* (²1960, ET² SCM Press 1962), p. 40; Schlier, *Galater,* p. 60.

18. *OGIS* 694 (Rom.) – Ἑρμογένης Ἀμασ[εὺ]ς [τὰς] μὲν ἄλλας σύριγγας ἰδὼν ἐθαύμασα, τὴν δὲ τοῦ Μέμνονος ταύτην εἰστορήσας ὑπερεθαύμασα; a Theban inscription, *Kaibel* 1020—Τατιανὸς ἡγεμὼν Θηβάιδος ἱστορήσα[ς] ἐθαύμασεν τὸ θαῦ[μα ξ]υνὸν τῶν σοφῶν Αἰγυπ[τί]ων.

19. 'It denotes visits paid to places of interest with a view to getting information about them on the spot' (F. Rendall, 'Galatians', *The Expositor's Greek Testament* (Hodder & Stoughton, 1917), III p. 155).

20. BAGD examples hardly bear out the sense 'visit for the purpose of coming to know someone', since all but one (*War* 6.81) have impersonal objects. The revised edition (BAGD 197) makes an improvement by adding '... someone or something', but adds no new data to strengthen the case for taking Gal. 1.18 in this sense.

21. G. D. Kilpatrick, 'Galatians 1.18 ΙΣΤΟΡΗΣΑΙ ΚΗΦΑΝ', *New Testament Essays: Studies in Memory of T. W. Manson,* ed. A. J. B. Higgins (Manchester, 1959), pp. 144–9. So earlier Rendall (n. 19 above).

22. G. Howard, *Paul: Crisis in Galatia* (Cambridge, 1979), pp. 36f. uses this point to argue that what Paul was denying in 1.18 was that the visit to Peter had the purpose of *Paul* informing *Peter* about Paul's 'revelation'.

23. 'Nor did he then expound "his gospel" to Peter and James, securing their approval of it (*pace* Ramsay). Otherwise there would have been no need for him, on the second visit, to apprise "those of repute" of "the gospel" he "preached among the Gentiles ..."' (E. Haenchen, *Acts* (KEK ¹⁴1965, ET Blackwell 1971), p. 464).

24. cf. E. Haenchen, 'Petrus-Probleme', *NTS* 7 (1960–1), pp. 187–9; B. Gerhardsson, *Memory and Manuscript* (Lund, 1961), pp. 297–9; F. F. Bruce, *Paul: Apostle of the Free Spirit* (Paternoster, 1977), p. 84; Holmberg, *Paul,* p. 16. On the tension between Gal. 1.12 and 1 Cor. 15.3 see further R. Bring, *Galater* (Berlin and Hamburg, 1968), pp. 54–8; J. D. G. Dunn, *Unity and Diversity in the New Testament* (SCM Press 1977), pp. 66f.

25. Kilpatrick, 'Gal. 1.18', p. 148.

26. cf. Gerhardsson, *Memory:* he 'presented his gospel for the approval of the highest doctrinal court ...' (pp. 276f.).

27. Haenchen, *Acts,* p. 464. Howard argues that the 'revelation' of 2.2 was Paul's initial revelation of 1.12 (*Paul,* p. 38), despite the lack of the definite article with 'revelation' in 2.2, in pursuit of his improbable thesis that Paul's circumcision-free gospel was news to the Jerusalem apostles, even though the gospel had been open to the Gentiles for many years, and preached by Hellenists before Paul, and evidently without requiring circumcision (we can hardly assume that all Gentile converts during that period had already been proselytes).

28. For the different opinions as to whether 'the pillar apostles' = 'those of repute'

or are an inner group within the Jerusalem leadership see Holmberg, *Paul*, p. 22 n. 57.

29. See particularly C. K. Barrett, 'Paul and the "Pillar" Apostles', *Studia Paulina in honorem J. de Zwaan* (Haarlem, 1953), pp. 1–4; Betz, *Galatians*, pp. 86f.

30. See particularly Holmberg, *Paul*, p. 22.

31. See particularly the vigorous exposition of Mussner, *Galater*, pp. 102f.

32. As argued, e.g., by Duncan, *Galatians*, p. 41; A. Oepke, *Galater* (THNT ²1957), p. 45; Schütz, *Paul*, pp. 139f. Bring states it better – 'the unity of the church based on the truth of the gospel' (*Galater*, p. 63). But it is not clear how a breach as such with Jerusalem would have nullified his whole missionary endeavour. Nor is it at all certain that Paul at this stage had a concept of 'the (world-wide) church' (singular) (see J. D. G. Dunn, *Jesus and the Spirit* (SCM Press, 1975), pp. 262f.). Schlier forces the text when he argues that thought of 'the unity of the apostolic office' was also involved for Paul (*Galater*, p. 68; see also Betz's critique of Schlier – *Galatians*, p. 99 n. 399). On the other hand Schütz presses too far the assertion that for Paul apostolic authority is subordinate to the authority of the gospel (*Paul*, particularly p. 145). J. Roloff is better: 'Man kommt darum nicht an der Erkenntnis vorbei, dass Paulus Gal. 2.2 neben 1.1 stellt, *weil sein Apostolat beide Gesichtspunkte erfordert*: er ist Apostel, weil ihn der Auferstandene berufen und gesandt hat, aber er ist es nur, indem er das Evangelium gemeinsam mit den übrigen Aposteln bezeugt ...' (*Apostolat-Verkündigung-Kirche*, Gütersloh 1965, p. 73).

33. So Betz, *Galatians*, p. 88 – '"To run in vain" must reflect the present concern of the Galatians'; cf. Lightfoot, *Galatians*, p. 104 – 'fear lest the Judaic Christians ... might thwart his past and present endeavours to establish a Church on a liberal basis'.

34. cf. T Holtz, 'Die Bedeutung des Apostelkonzils für Paulus', *Nov T* 16 (1974). pp. 121–7.

35. Note in this connection the theological significance of the collection for Paul (J. Munck, *Paul and the Salvation of Mankind* (1954, ET SCM Press 1959), pp. 303 f.; K. F. Nickle, *The Collection* (SCM Press 1966), pp. 129–43; J. D. G. Dunn, *Romans*, WBC 38 (Word 1988) pp. 873–6), which probably accounts for his readiness to embrace the pillar apostles' exhortation to remember the poor in 2.10.

36. cf. particularly P. Stuhlmacher's exposition in terms of the *heilsgeschichtlich* character of Paul's gospel (*Das paulinische Evangelium I. Vorgeschichte* (Göttingen, 1968), pp. 87f.). In Galatians Paul 'was essentially concerned with establishing who constitute the true people of God' (W. D. Davies, 'Paul and the People of Israel', *NTS* 24 (1977–8), p. 10).

37. Dunn, *Jesus*, pp. 233–6; also 'Prophetic "I"-Sayings and the Jesus Tradition', *NTS* 24 (1977–8), pp. 175–98.

38. Dunn, *Jesus*, pp. 278f. Paul, of course, is as certain in Gal. 2.2 of the truth of his gospel as he is in 1 Cor. 14.37f. and 1 Thess. 4.2–8 of the rightness of his judgement.

39. cf. E. D. Burton, *Galatians*, ICC 1921, p. 90; against NEB 'prolong the consultation'. Would ἀνατίθημι (active) have served as well (Schlier, *Galater*, p. 74; Betz, *Galatians*, p. 95)? LSJ renders it more in the sense of 'entrust', and Paul is hardly saying that they 'entrusted nothing to me'. The double prefix should be given weight.

40. Burton, *Galatians*, pp. 89–91; cf. LSJ 'contribute of oneself to another'.

41. e.g. Bonnard, 'prescrire' (*Galates*, p. 40); Holmberg, 'impose something on someone' (*Paul*, p. 23); see particularly the useful discussion in Oepke, *Galater*, pp. 48f.

42. The demand for circumcision both at Jerusalem (2.3) and in Galatia is probably primarily in view (cf. Schlier, *Galater*, pp. 74f.), but he may have had the wider

obligations which the 'men from James' in effect laid upon the Gentile believers in Antioch (2.11ff.); see ch. 6 below.

43. So most commentators; against Burkitt (n. 2 above). How Paul could have 'preserved the truth of the gospel' preached to the Galatians by allowing Titus to be circumcised, when it was precisely the demand for circumcision which threatened the Galatians' freedom (in Paul's view), is an unresolved mystery on Burkitt's interpretation. See also n. 58 below.

44. 2.7–9 hardly constitute a protest by Paul that he had not at that time recognized the authority of the Jerusalem apostles (against Betz, *Galatians*, p. 96); the contrast between 2.6 and 2.7–9 is clear – 'they added nothing to me, but on the contrary recognized the authenticity of the gospel with which I was entrusted both as to its origin and as to its effectiveness as a word of God'.

45. Betz, *Galatians*, p. 92.

46. cf. Barrett, '"Pillar" Apostles', pp. 17f.; J. Bligh, *Galatians* (St Paul 1969), pp. 157–9.

47. On ποτέ see particularly Burton, *Galatians*, pp. 87f.

48. A reference to the Jerusalem apostles' reputation as being a consequence of their relation with Christ during his pre-Easter ministry is less likely – some qualification of ἱστορῆσαι Κηφᾶν would have been probable in that case (against Lightfoot, *Galatians*, p. 108; Duncan, *Galatians*, p. 49; Barrett, '"Pillar" Apostles', pp. 18f.; Schlier, *Galater*, pp. 75f.; see particularly the critique of these and other alternatives in G. Klein, 'Galater 2.6–9 und die Geschichte der Jerusalem Urgemeinde', *ZTK* 57 (1960), pp. 275–82, reprinted in *Rekonstruktion und Interpretation: Gesammelte Aufsätze zum Neuen Testament* (München, 1969), pp. 99–105; Betz, *Galatians*, pp. 93–5). Despite Klein (p. 103) a change in Paul's own attitude to the Jerusalem apostles is most probably implied (D. M. Hay, 'Paul's Indifference to Authority', *JBL* 88 (1969), pp. 37f. with nn. 6, 7). In its context the statement reads too much like Paul's current reaction against the authoritative status which at that time all (himself not excluded) accorded to the Jerusalem apostles (see further below). The Antioch incident in itself is sufficient explanation of his change of attitude (see ch. 6 below).

49. Betz, *Galatians*, p. 94.

50. It is probably no accident that the phrase echoes Deut. 10.17, since it is precisely this reason which Deuteronomy gives when calling for the circumcision of the *heart* (10.16).

51. Barnabas would probably have regarded it more as an authorization by Jerusalem than Paul did; this is probably the chief reason why Paul speaks for himself in 2.7f. when insisting again that it was God who entrusted him with his gospel and blessed it so richly.

52. K. Berger, 'Almosen für Israel: zum historischen Kontext der paulinischen Kollekte', *NTS* 23 (1976–7), pp. 180–204, makes the plausible and valuable suggestion that the Jerusalem apostles may have regarded alms for Israel as the appropriate expression of conversion to the God of Israel for God-fearers who were not willing to be circumcised (= become full proselytes).

53. On the striking parallels between the version of events contested by Paul in Gal. 1–2 and the account in Acts see O. Linton, 'The Third Aspect: A Neglected Point of View: A Study in Gal. 1–2 and Acts 9 and 15', *ST* 3 (1949), pp. 79–95.

54. See references in Betz, *Galatians*, p. 80 and n. 230.

55. Holmberg, *Paul*, p. 17.

56. 'Paulus geht nach Jerusalem und nicht kommen die Jerusalemer Apostel zu ihm' (Schlier, *Galater*, p. 68). 'So war Jerusalem der Ort, an dem die Identität des Evangeliums, zu dem sich Paulus berufen wusste, mit dem, zu dem er sich berufen glaubte, festgestellt werden konnte und musste' (Holtz, 'Bedeutung', p. 145). Does the κατὰ ἀποκάλυψιν imply that Paul would not have gone to

Jerusalem unless commanded by God? If so, this second revelation in effect counterbalanced the independence of his first revelation (1.12), since it reinforced the status of the Jerusalem church in Paul's eyes.

57. cf. Hay, 'Paul's Indifference', pp. 36–44.
58. Lightfoot's note at this point is superior to Burkitt's n. 2 above): 'The counsels of the Apostles of the Circumcision are the hidden rock on which the grammar of the sentence is wrecked' (*Galatians*, p. 106).
59. cf. particularly Holmberg, *Paul*, pp. 23f.; Howard, Paul, pp. 28f.
60. See particularly E. Dinkler, 'Der Brief an die Galater', *VF* 1–3 (1953/5), pp. 175–83, reprinted in *Signum Crucis: Aufsätze zum Neuen Testament und zur christlichen Archäologie* (Tübingen, 1967), pp. 270–82; discussion in Klein, 'Galater 2.6–9', pp. 106f., 118f.; Betz, *Galatians*, pp. 96–8; Lüdemann, *Heidenapostel I*, pp. 86–101. The most significant features are the unusual Pauline talk of the 'gospel of the uncircumcision' and 'gospel of the circumcision', and the use of the name 'Peter' whereas elsewhere in Gal. 1–2 Paul consistently calls him 'Cephas'. Note also how Barnabas is associated with Paul in what seems a formal agreement in 2.9, whereas for the rest of the encounter Paul refers only to himself (see below pp. 473–4).
61. See Betz, *Galatians*, pp. 98, 100.
62. It is less likely that the collection was an issue between Paul and the Galatians, being misinterpreted (by some) as evidence of Paul's inferiority and subserviency to Jerusalem (so L. Hurtado, 'The Jerusalem Collection in Galatians', *JSNT* 5 (1979), pp. 46–62), in which case we would have expected something more than the almost casual mention of it in 2.10. That does not exclude the likelihood that the pillar apostles understood their exhortation as a 'policy recommendation' backed by their authority; whereas Paul understood it simply as the corollary to his understanding of the gospel and of the Gentiles' participation in the inheritance of Israel (see above p. 115 and nn. 35, 36).
63. Against Holmberg, who argues implausibly that the relation between Paul and Jerusalem in his last visit to Jerusalem (56–8 AD) was still the same as during his second visit (Gal. 2.1–10) (*Paul*, p. 56). But see ch. 6 below.
64. cf. Bruce, *Paul*, p. 154.
65. As Holmberg notes (*Paul*, p. 18 n. 37), this is a common opinion today – he cites Haenchen, Georgi, Stuhlmacher, Kasting, Holtz and Schütz.
66. This is one of the points at which we can confidently supplement the evidence of Galatians with the information provided by Acts. Even if the relevance of Acts 15.1f. is disputed by those who equate Paul's second journey to Jerusalem with Acts 11.30, the testimony of 11.20–24 is clear enough.
67. Note also the switch from first person plural in 1.8 to singular in 1.9 – see further particularly R. Bauckham, 'Barnabas in Galatians', *JSNT* 2 (1979), pp. 61–70.
68. See ch. 6 below.

Additional Note

O. Hofius, 'Gal. 1.18: ἱστορῆσαι Κηφᾶν', *ZNW* 75 (1984) 73–85, seeks to refute the claim that ἱστορεῖν can mean 'to get information from'. He cites a range of post-classical Greek usage to conclude that for ἱστορεῖν τινα the meaning 'to get to know someone (personally)' is clearly demonstrated, with the accusative of the person designating the *immediate* object of the verb (84).

In private correspondence H. Riesenfeld warmly encouraged me to sustain my earlier conclusion. The following is the reply I offered in *ZNW* 76 (1985) 138–9.

ONCE MORE – GAL. 1.18: ἱστορῆσαι Κηφᾶν IN REPLY TO OTFRIED HOFIUS

Hofius is right to raise a cautionary voice on the translation of ἱστορῆσαι Κηφᾶν. The translation 'to get information from Cephas' does push the sense rather hard, and I would accept that the better translation is 'to get to know Cephas'. However, I would still want to insist that the process of 'getting to know' includes the idea of 'finding out about', which in Peter's case must surely have included his experience as a disciple of Jesus and his memories of Jesus' ministry.

Hofius fails to give enough weight to the following facts.

(a) The degree to which the idea of 'gaining information' is an integral part of the sense 'getting to know'. This element is present again and again in the passages Hofius himself cites, as I demonstrated in my earlier article – 'getting to know' in the full sense of the informed knowledge of personal encounter (above, pp. 111–12). In other words, 'getting to know' something or someone includes a considerable element of getting to know *about* that something or someone.

(b) Hofius recognizes that a distinction between ἱστορῆσαι and ἰδεῖν (Gal. 1.19) is intended (p. 84). Despite that he continues to translate them both by the same word (*kennenlernen*), allowing the arguably broader usage elsewhere (p. 84, n. 48) to determine the more clearly delimited contrast here. Thus once again the clear implication of the contrast is missed: that Paul got to know Peter at a depth and to a degree that made his time with Peter more than simply a 'visit'; he got to know Peter – he only made James' acquaintance (in passing).

(c) Hofius ignores the fact that Paul spent two weeks with Cephas. The oft-quoted observation of C. H. Dodd still has point: 'At that time he stayed with Peter for a fortnight, and we may presume they did not spend all the time talking about the weather.'[1]

(d) Hofius also overlooks the implied contrast with the οὐ προσανεθέμην of Gal. 1.16, to which I also drew attention in my previous article (above, p. 112). All that Paul seeks to safeguard in recounting his first visit to Jerusalem is any suggestion that his understanding of the gospel (as to the Gentiles) was validated at that time by the Jerusalem leadership. To admit to a two-week visit spent getting to know Peter (and about Peter, but only seeing James) constituted no threat on that front.

In short, even if the emphasis of the actual translation should be changed from 'finding out from Cephas' to 'getting to know Cephas', the implication of Paul's language and the final picture is not so very different. 'Getting to know Cephas' must, by the force of the word and the circumstances of the occasion, have included gaining information about (and indeed from) Peter. An informed knowledge of Peter, through two weeks in his company getting to know him, must have included a good deal of information about Peter's time with Jesus.[2]

In the same year N. Walter included a brief excursus on the interpretation of ἱστορῆσαι Κηφᾶν (Gal 1.18) in his 'Paulus und die urchristliche

Jesustradition', *NTS* 31 (1985) 498–522 (Excursus 506–7).[3] Walter takes up Hofius' critique, but argues that the force of the phrase must be rendered something like 'to take counsel with Cephas', 'to consult with Cephas'. The main difference with my exposition above is that, on Walter's view, we do not need to guess from general considerations or from the phrase itself what the subject of the consultation would have been. If Paul's purpose had been simply to gain background information about Jesus why should Paul regard it as important that he suppressed this 'natural curiosity' for three years? Any why should James not have counted as an equally acceptable source of such 'background information about the ministry of Jesus'? The context however provides a much more precise answer: the subject matter of 1.18 would have been the same as that of 1.16 and 2.2. 'Paul wished "to discover the view of Cephas", "to take counsel with Cephas on the question ", whether in his preaching of the gospel to the Gentiles he was on a course that was also an acceptable one in the view of Peter.' Information on the work and ministry of Jesus would have been important, but as a secondary concern.

This is an attractive reformulation. My only question is whether it gives enough weight to the distinction between the three verbs in 1.16, 1.18 and 2.2. If I am right, Paul goes out of the way in 1.16 to *deny* that he consulted with Peter and the other earlier apostles as to the significance of the revelation given to him on the Damascus road ('whether he had rightly understood the call to apostleship as an apostleship to the Gentiles'). Nor is there 'uncertainty' on that significance implied in 2.2 (*pace* Walter), but only uncertainty as to its outworking. Is Walter's interpretation in danger of conceding in 1.18 what Paul seems to have taken some pains to safeguard in 1.16 and 2.2? Perhaps we would all be best advised to hold to the translation 'get to know Peter' and leave the implications to speak for themselves.

Notes

1. C. H. Dodd, *The Apostolic Preaching and its Developments* (London: Hodder & Stoughton, 1936,[16] 1963). See also R. Y. K Fung, *Galatians*, NICNT (Grand Rapids: Wm B. Eerdmans, 1988), pp. 74–5.
2. cf. C. K. Barrett, *Freedom and Obligation: A Study of the Epistle to the Galatians* (London: SPCK, 1985), p. 52.
3. The essay has now been translated with one or two modifications or additions by A. J. M. Wedderburn, *Paul and Jesus: Collected Essays*, *JSNT Supp*. 37, Sheffield Academic Press 1989, 51–80 (Excursus 64–6).

6

The Incident at Antioch
(Gal. 2.11–18)*

§1 INTRODUCTION

The incident at Antioch, briefly described by Paul in Galatians 2, has long been a source of some perplexity to students of the New Testament. In the patristic period the embarrassment of an account where Paul openly condemned Peter for hypocrisy was avoided by such devious exegesis as that of Clement of Alexandria who maintained that a *different* Cephas was in view, or that of Origen who argued that the whole dispute between Peter and Paul was simulated.[1] On the whole, however, this ceased to be a problem when churchmen found they could cope with the incident within the framework of Petrine and papal supremacy by presenting it as a noble example of Peter's humility. Inevitably it was this aspect which also caught attention in Reformation exegesis, with Paul's rebuke of Peter giving those wishing to protest against the authority of the Papacy just the precedent they needed.[2]

In more recent decades the issues have become more historical than ecclesiastical, with the earlier exegetical assumptions being regularly and sharply questioned. In particular, can we assume that Peter accepted Paul's rebuke and amended his conduct? If he did not, what does that tell us about the development of Paul's missionary work, about his subsequent relations with Jerusalem and Peter, about factions within first-century Christianity (Peter and Paul parties, etc.)?[3] Again, where does the Antioch incident fit within the history of that period? Can we assume that it formed the sequel to the Jerusalem council recounted by Luke in Acts 15? Or is the issue more complex, with the historicity of Acts being called in question in part at least by Paul's account?[4]

For all that the significance of the Antioch incident has been recognized in such discussions, there has been remarkably little detailed work done on the incident itself. The question of whether or not Acts 15 = Galatians 2.1–10 often seems largely to have exhausted the debate. And when commentators or historians have moved on to the Antioch incident they have not paused long over

* This paper was delivered in briefer form at the New Testament Conference in the University of Glasgow, September 1980, and to a seminar at the University of Aarhus, Denmark, in March 1981.

129

what must on any reckoning be a crucial question: *What was the nature of the table-fellowship that Peter enjoyed with the Gentile believers? What was involved in it? What precisely did he withdraw from when the men from James arrived?* The ready assumption lay close to hand that it was all simply a matter of the Jewish food laws and little more need be said.[5] But was it quite so simple? Is this not another exegetical assumption which ought to be examined more closely? Without some clearer idea of what table-fellowship at Antioch involved prior to Peter's withdrawal, our grasp of what was at stake is seriously defective, and consequently also our ability to assess the significance of Peter's and Paul's conduct.

It is on this area and aspect that I wish to focus in what follows. My belief that such an investigation is necessary is the product of reflection on several overlapping and wider issues, a reflection stimulated by various items of recent scholarship. The overlapping and wider issues inform us of the broader historical context within which we must attempt to assess the Antioch incident and will engage our attention in §§ 2 and 3. In the light of our findings there we will attempt some exegesis of Galatians 2.11–18 in the hope of clarifying the incident itself, including the reasons for Peter's conduct and the force of Paul's response (§ 4). Finally we shall consider possible implications for some of the more familiar questions connected with this passage (§ 5).

§2 THE HISTORICAL CONTEXT

The Antioch incident is usually dated in the late 40s of the first century, depending of course on such questions as the date of the Jerusalem council (Acts 15) and the relation between Galatians 2 and Acts 15.[6] Since the crisis at Antioch was provoked by the arrival of 'certain individuals from James' (Gal. 2.12), that is, from Jerusalem, it is important to clarify the relationship between the church in Jerusalem and the church in Antioch at that time, and to examine possible influences on these churches from the broader social and political situation within Palestine and within Palestinian and Diaspora Judaism.

§2.1 *The relationship between the church in Jerusalem and the church in Antioch.* One of the major weaknesses in many reconstructions of Christian origins and New Testament theology has been the failure to grasp the full racial and nationalistic dimensions of the early disputes within Christianity. As K. Stendahl pointed out in a famous essay,[7] Paul's teaching on justification through faith was not intended as an answer to a Luther-like agonizing after personal assurance of salvation. Paul's concern was rather with the relation between Jew and Gentile. His question was not, How can I be saved?, but, How can Gentiles be included within the messianic community of Israel?[8] This essentially racial or nationalistic concept of righteousness as a consequence of God's election of and covenant with Israel has received fresh illumination from the major study by E. P. Sanders with his characterization of Palestinian Judaism in terms of 'covenantal nomism'.[9]

The point is that earliest Christianity was not yet seen as something separate and distinct from Judaism. It was a sect, like other sects within first-century Judaism. The first Christians had some distinct and peculiar beliefs about Jesus; but their religion was the religion of the Jews.[10] So that when Gentiles began to embrace these particular beliefs about Jesus the question raised was still only in terms of what requirements were necessary for Gentiles to join themselves to the people who worshipped the one God and to whom God had sent his Messiah, Jesus. The fact that Paul's main argument in Galatians is about how one becomes Abraham's offspring, heir of his blessing (Gal. 3—4) is sufficient indication of the limits within which both sides had carried on the earlier debate.[11] As we shall see below, circumcision was only one aspect of that debate, and it was probably the incident at Antioch which helped sharpen the issues for Paul.

This nationalistic dimension to the earliest development of Christianity within Judaism also helps us to recognize that the church at Antioch would not have seen itself as an entity independent of the Jews or of the Jewish believers in Palestine. It was simply the believing Jewish community at Antioch embracing more and more God-fearing Gentiles.[12] Almost certainly the majority at heart would simply think of themselves as part of the Diaspora, with Jerusalem still serving as a source of pride and inspiration and a focus for faith and aspiration[13] – despite the persecution which had forced many of the founding members to flee from the capital city (Acts 11.19–20).[14] This would also involve the church at Antioch recognizing the church at Jerusalem as the fountainhead of their distinctive faith (cf. Rom. 15.27) and probably also as the authoritative interpreter of it.

Most significant here is the degree to which Paul's treatment of his own relations with Jerusalem prior to the Antioch incident reinforces the impression that *up until that time he too had taken it for granted that Jerusalem had this primacy and authority.* I refer to the character of Paul's self-defence in Galatians 1—2. As has been recently pointed out, 'the dialectic between being independent of and being acknowledged by Jerusalem is the keynote of this important text and must not be forgotten'.[15] In Galatians Paul is writing *after* the incident at Antioch, and his exposition is heavily coloured by that later viewpoint. But in trying to assert his independence from Jerusalem, and the directness of his apostleship and gospel from Christ, he cannot escape the fact that previously he had readily acknowledged the authority of the Jerusalem apostles.[16] His use of προσανατίθεσθαι ('to consult in order to be given an authoritative interpretation') in 1.16 is probably an implicit acknowledgement that the Jerusalem apostles were recognized by him at that time as the appropriate authorities to consult on the interpretation of the revelation given him at Damascus – the point (as he *now* insists) being that he had *not* consulted them (1.16–17). He does not disguise the fact that his first visit to Jerusalem had been 'to get information from Cephas' (ἱστορῆσαι Κηφᾶν – 1.18),[17] though the information was evidently something different from the gospel already received three years earlier through the revelation of Christ (1.12). The purpose of his second visit to Jerusalem was to consult (ἀνεθέμην) the Jerusalem leadership about his gospel, but he does not hide the fact that what they thought or decided about his gospel would make all the difference to the success or failure of his mission to the Gentiles.[18] The language he uses in 2.2, 6 indicates a certain embarrassment at this admission. He calls the Jerusalem apostles 'the men of repute', a phrase familiar in political rhetoric, where it was used both positively and negatively (derogatively or ironically).[19] The parenthesis of verse 6, with its noticeable change of tense – 'what they were (then) is (now) a matter of indifference to me; God shows no partiality' – is all aimed at *relativizing* the authority of the Jerusalem apostles in the *current* situation in Galatia and at reducing the significance of his *earlier* acceptance of that authority.[20] Likewise when he says 'those of repute added (προσανέθεντο) nothing to me' (2.6),[21] where again the language probably indicates an acknowledgement on his part at that time of Jerusalem's 'right' to instruct or give directives to its daughter churches. So too, it can plausibly be argued that Paul's convoluted statement in verses 7–10 is a further attempt to obscure the degree to which Paul had been willing to accept Jerusalem's authority at that time – the authority clearly expressed in the pillar apostles' recognition of Paul's and Barnabas's missionary success and their approval of a future division of labour.[22] All this points strongly to the conclusion that while Paul *defended a position* at Jerusalem, the three 'pillar' apostles *delivered a verdict*.

Moreover, there is a growing agreement on the view that when Paul went up to Jerusalem this second time it was not as an independent missionary or apostle, but as a delegate from the church at Antioch (so Acts 15.2; cf. 14.4, 14 – 'apostles', that is, of the church at Antioch, 13.2–3).[23] The question discussed at the meeting in Jerusalem was not primarily whether Paul (and Barnabas) were apostles, but whether as apostles of Antioch their practice of not circumcising their converts should continue – that

132

is, whether the church at Antioch's practice of according full acceptance to uncircumcised Gentile believers should continue without modification. The victory or rather concession won by the Antioch delegation did not call in question the authority of the Jerusalem apostles to make this concession. The point is that the church at Antioch could not make this decision by themselves, and readily referred it to Jerusalem. And when subsequently the delegation came from James, the majority of believers in Antioch just as readily accepted the authority of this further ruling regarding the practice of table-fellowship at Antioch.

This nationalistic dimension to the Antioch incident becomes still more significant in the light of the second feature of the broader historical context to which we now turn.

§2.2 *The socio-political situation confronting Judaism in the middle of the first century.* During the period which concerns us, many Jews, no doubt a growing proportion within the Jewish territories, must have believed their distinctive religious and national prerogatives were under increasing threat. The long, drawn out crisis provoked by Caligula's insistence that a statue of himself be set up in the Jerusalem temple is well known (AD 40).[24] And latterly, after the death of Agrippa in AD 44, the situation deteriorated rapidly under a succession of weak Roman procurators.[25] Cuspius Fadus (AD 44–?46) demanded that the vestments of the High Priest be returned to the Romans for safe-keeping (Josephus, *Antiquities* 20.1.1 §6) and had to act against the threatened rebellion led by the self-styled prophet Theudas (*Antiquities* 20.5.1 §§97–9). Tiberius Iulius Alexander (AD ?46–48) crucified James and Simon, the sons of Judas the Galilean, presumably because like their father they were engaged in fomenting unrest against Roman rule on account of its threat to their faith (*Antiquities* 20.5.2 §102).[26] Under Cumanus (AD 48–52) things went from bad to worse, with a near riot in Jerusalem resulting in thousands of deaths (20,000 or 30,000 according to Josephus – *Jewish War* 2.12.1 §§223–7; *Antiquities* 20.5.3 §§105–12), and a succession of disorders involving zealot bands in Samaria and elsewhere (*Jewish War* 2.12.2–5 §§228–38; *Antiquities* 20.5.4–6 §§113–24). Josephus reports that 'from that time the whole of Judea was infested with bands of brigands' (*Antiquities* 20.6.1 §124) – 'brigands' ($\lambda\eta\sigma\tau\alpha\acute{\iota}$) being Josephus' way of describing the Zealots.[27]

The followers of Jesus within Palestine would not have been unaffected by these mounting pressures. The death of Stephen and the subsequent persecution (early or middle 30s) presumably had the effect of ensuring that those followers of the Nazarene who had been exempted from the persecution, or who had returned to Jerusalem thereafter, would take care to show themselves good

Jews, loyal to their religious and national heritage.[28] Agrippa's execution of James (brother of John) in or before AD 44 is presumably also to be explained against this background; Luke notes that 'it pleased the Jews' and encouraged Agrippa to move against Peter (Acts 12.1–3).

Furthermore, we should bear in mind that such pressures towards conformity with the mainstream of nationalistic Judaism were experienced as much *within* the infant Christian communities as from without. It is not simply a matter of coincidence that in the preceding episode involving Peter prior to his arrest, Peter had been criticized by 'the circumcision party' for eating with an uncircumcised Gentile (Acts 11.2–3). The subsequent controversy over the necessity of circumcision clearly indicates that many Jewish believers took it as axiomatic that Gentiles must be circumcised if they were to have a share in the Jewish heritage, and were prepared to exercise considerable advocacy and missionary endeavour to ensure that that heritage was neither diluted nor endangered (Gal. 2.4–5; 5.2–12; Acts 15.1–5; Phil. 3.2). Here too, we may note the evidence of history of traditions analysis of Matthew, which seems to indicate that an earlier re-shaping of the Jesus-tradition took place in a conservative direction vis-à-vis the law and Israel (Matt. 5.17–20; 15.17–20; 23.3, 23; 10.5–6, 23; 15.24; 28.18–20)[29] – a tendency which no doubt reflects the same sort of pressures within the Palestinian churches. Wholly consistent with all this, and not at all surprising in view of it, is Luke's account of Paul's last visit to Jerusalem (probably in AD 57), where James describes the church in Jerusalem (and Palestine?) as consisting of 'many thousands . . . who are all zealous for the law' and who know of Paul only that he is a renegade and menace to their Jewish faith and inheritance (Acts 21.20–1).

The threat to Jewish prerogatives was, of course, not confined to Palestine, nor were Jewish exertions to defend them. Philo gives a clear account of the riots in Alexandria in AD 38, provoked by deliberate attacks on the religious and civic rights of the considerable Jewish population resident there (*Flaccus* particularly 41–54; also *Embassy to Gaius* 132–7).[30] Delegations to the Emperor, the first led by Philo himself, resulted in a reassertion of these rights by Claudius in AD 41. In the same year, according to Dio Cassius, Claudius deprived the Jews resident in Rome of their right of assembly (Dio 60.6.6), and eight years later, according to Suetonius, he expelled the Jews altogether because they were 'constantly rioting at the instigation of Chrestus' (Suetonius, *Claudius* 25.4; cf. Acts 18.2).[31] Since all the other Jewish unrest of this period largely centred on Jewish response to what they perceived as threats to their unique racial and religious status, it may well be that the trouble in Rome was caused by similar Jewish reaction to the success of evangelism in the name of Jesus, like that against Stephen and that against Paul (Acts 6.9–14; 21.27–36; cf. 13.50; 14.2–5, 19; 17.5–7, 13; 18.12–15).[32]

The Jewish *politeuma* in Antioch, the third largest city in the Empire, was not exempt from such unrest. The Byzantine chronicler Malalas (sixth century) reports an anti-Jewish riot there in AD 39–40 (Johannes Malalas, *Chronographia* 10.315). And although Josephus does not mention it, the fact that in 41 Claudius sent to Syria an edict identical to that which secured Jewish rights in Alexandria, strongly suggests that Jewish rights in Syria had been similarly threatened – one of the repercussions, no doubt, either of the Alexandria riots in 38, or of Caligula's threatened desecration of the Jerusalem temple in 40.[33] Josephus does, however, tell us of trouble in Antioch in 67 when Antiochus, an apostate Jew, denounced his father and 'the other (Jews)' for plotting to set fire to the city. These unfortunates were burned to death on the spot. Antiochus then attempted to compel other Jews to offer pagan sacrifice 'since the (remaining) conspirators would be exposed by their refusal'. A few submitted and the rest were massacred (*Jewish War* 7.3.3 §§50–1). Smallwood justifiably argues that only a section of the large Jewish community would have been involved, since a considerable number of 'orthodox' Jews would surely have refused such sacrifice.[34] The charge of arson, she notes, is similar to that laid against the Christians in Rome less than three years earlier, and may well suggest that it was the Christian Jews who were the object of Antiochus' attack. 'The mainspring of Antiochus' malice against the Christians', she concludes not implausibly, 'may have been resentment, possibly even heightened by his own apostasy, against his father's conversion from orthodox Judaism to a despised schismatic sect.'[35]

Whatever the precise details of these various incidents the overall picture is clear enough. During the period in which the Antioch incident took place Jews had to be on their guard against what were or were seen to be repeated threats to their national and religious rights. Whenever such a threat was perceived their reaction was immediate and vigorous. In Palestine itself more and more were resorting to open violence and guerrilla warfare. The infant Christian sect was not exempt from this unrest. Indeed we may generalize a fairly firm conclusion from the above review of evidence: *wherever this new Jewish sect's belief or practice was perceived to be a threat to Jewish institutions and traditions its members would almost certainly come under pressure from their fellow Jews to remain loyal to their unique Jewish heritage.*

The question which such a conclusion leaves us is obvious: To what extent was the Antioch incident the result of such pressures operating upon the infant communities in Palestine and Syria, pressures from Jews loyal to their heritage both without *and* within the sect itself? Against this background the hypothesis becomes rather compelling that the open table-fellowship practised at Antioch was perceived by the Jerusalem church (and perhaps by other Jews) as such a threat. The mission of the men from James would then have been their reaction to that threat.[36] And the danger of diluting or abandoning Israel's heritage with its converse and powerful appeal to national and religious loyalty would have weighed heavily with Peter, Barnabas and the rest.

§2.3 Thus already a fair amount of light has been shed on the Antioch incident from the broader background. We may summarize these preliminary observations thus.

1. At this stage of its growth, the new movement of Jesus' followers would almost certainly still think of themselves as a development *of* and *within* the religion of the Jews (a form of eschatological, messianic Judaism) – not yet a distinct faith or separate religion.

2. Within this movement, the primacy and authority of the Jerusalem apostles in matters of dispute, specifically over what requirements should be laid on Gentiles who wished to associate with the new movement, would be generally acknowledged, and in fact had already been acknowledged by the church at Antioch and by Paul, the delegate/apostle of the Antioch church.

3. The increasing threat to Judaism, especially from the deteriorating political situation in Palestine, and the increasingly polemical response of the Jews themselves, would increase the pressures on those involved in the new movement to show themselves as faithful and loyal Jews. In short, the probability is strong that all the main participants in the Antioch incident would naturally think of themselves as first and foremost Jews (a probability confirmed by Gal. 2.15); as such they would naturally look to Jerusalem for direction; and as such they would inevitably feel themselves moved by the mounting groundswell of Jewish nationalistic and religious sentiment.

With the broader background thus clarified we can now dig more deeply into that which most concerns us – the table-fellowship at Antioch. What was at stake in the Antioch church's practice of table-fellowship? Within the context of Palestinian and Diaspora Judaism in the middle of the first century AD, how would the table-fellowship at Antioch have appeared? – as something unexceptional, as something very unusual, as a breach of Jewish practice and covenantal loyalty which posed a threat, or what? We are accustomed to seeing the issue through the eyes of Paul (Gal. 2.11–18). But how was it seen through the eyes of 'the men from James'? This brings us to the next stage of our analysis.

§3 THE LIMITS OF TABLE-FELLOWSHIP IN THE JUDAISM OF THE LATE SECOND TEMPLE PERIOD

The significance of table-fellowship in the east is well known. In Judaism particularly the *religious* significance of a shared meal was central. 'In Judaism', as Jeremias notes, 'table-fellowship means fellowship before God, for the eating of a piece of broken bread by everyone who shares in the meal brings out the fact that they all have a share in the blessing which the master of the house has spoken over the unbroken bread.'[37] The added significance for the rabbis and their pupils is well characterized in a saying of R. Simeon (c. 100–160 or 170):

> If three have eaten at one table and have not spoken over it words of the Law, it is as though they had eaten of the sacrifices of the dead (Ps. 106.28), for it is written, 'For all tables are full of vomit and filthiness without God' (Isa. 28.8 – 'place' taken as a designation for God). But if three have eaten at one table and have spoken over it words of the Law, it is as if they had eaten from the table of God, for it is written, 'And he said unto me, This is the table that is before the Lord' (Ezek. 41.22). (*m. Abot* 3.3)[38]

No devout Jew could engage in an act of such religious significance casually, and the question of who was and who was not an acceptable table companion must have greatly exercised the minds of such Jews during the period which concerns us, as the Antioch incident itself demonstrates (cf. Acts 11.2–3; 1 Cor. 8—10). To put it another way, part of the pressure on a devout Jew in the 40s and 50s of the first century AD would have been the constraint to observe the limits of acceptable table-fellowship. These limits would be determined partly by the explicit laws in the Torah, particularly concerning unclean foods (Lev. 11.1–23; Deut. 14.3–21), and in differing degrees by the multiplying *halakoth* of the oral tradition concerning tithes and ritual purity.

§3.1 Obedience to *the law on unclean foods* had been one of the make or break issues in the Maccabean rebellion. 'Many in Israel stood firm and were resolved in their hearts not to eat unclean food. They chose to die rather than to be defiled by food or to profane the holy covenant; and they did die' (1 Macc. 1.62–3).[39] No one who cherished the memory of the Maccabees would even dream of eating unclean food. The typical Jewish attitude at the time with which we are concerned is probably well caught by Luke's account of Peter's reaction to the vision given him in Joppa: 'I have never eaten anything that is common or unclean' (Acts 10.14). Jewish devotion on this point was particularly expressed in their abhorrence of pigs and of *pork*. The height of Antiochus Epiphanes' abomination had been his sacrifice of swine on the altar(s) of the temple.[40] Continuing Jewish antipathy to the pig is illustrated by the Mishna's refusal to allow Jews(?) to rear swine *anywhere* (in Israel) (*m. Baba Qamma* 7.7). And Jewish rejection of pork was well known and often commented on in Greek and Roman society. For example, Philo reports Caligula as interrupting his hearing of the Alexandrian delegations with the abrupt question, 'Why do you refuse to eat pork?' (*Embassy to Gaius* 361), and Plutarch devotes one of his *Quaestiones Convivales* to discussion of why Jews abstain from pork (4.5).[41] Clearly abstention from pork was thoroughly characteristic, we may even say universally characteristic, of Jewish conduct both in Palestine and in the Diaspora.

Equally abhorrent to the devout Jew was food tainted by the abomination of *idolatry*, although the extra-biblical documentation is thinner in this case. In addition to 1 Corinthians 8—10 and Acts 15.20, 29, we may mention Josephus' report of how in 64 he sought to aid certain priests of his acquaintance who had been taken prisoner in Rome and who 'even in affliction had not forgotten the pious practices of religion, and supported themselves on figs and nuts' (*Life* 3 §§13–14), presumably in part at least to avoid meat left over from pagan sacrifices (see also 4 Macc. 5.2).[42]

Likewise with meat (of clean animals) from which the *blood* had not been drained, in accordance with the clear and repeated commandments of Moses (Lev. 3.17; 7.26–7; 17.10–14; Deut. 12.16, 23–4; 15.23) – note again Acts 15.20, 29. What constituted a proper slaughtering of a clean animal for food is well defined in rabbinic Judaism by the time of the Mishna (tractate *Ḥullin*; also *Keritot* 5.1), but we can gain some idea of how far the *halakoth* had developed by the middle of the first century from *Ḥullin* 1.2, which reports the debate between the school of Shammai and the school of Hillel on what precisely was allowed by the (presumably) earlier ruling that slaughter with a handsickle was valid.[43]

Obedience to these commands so clearly set out in the Torah was obviously fundamental to devout Jews in our period; it belonged to the distinctiveness of their race and religion and marked them out as Yahweh's chosen people. Such fundamental laws were a limiting factor of considerable consequence for the devout Jew's practice of table-fellowship. They did not, we should note, inhibit his own entertainment of others, where he was responsible for what was served up and for the manner of its preparation. But they would largely prevent him from accepting with an easy conscience invitations from others who might ignore them in whole or in part – hence it is the case of an invitation to someone else's house which Paul discusses in 1 Corinthians 10.27–9.

§3.2 *Ritual purity.* One of the most striking features about the Pharisees in Palestine prior to the Jewish revolt was their preoccupation with defining the limits of table-fellowship more scrupulously. J. Neusner has concluded from his meticulously detailed study of rabbinical traditions about the Pharisees that of the 341 individual rulings from our period 'no fewer than 229 directly or indirectly pertain to table-fellowship, approximately 67% of the whole'.[44] Within these the major concerns were quite clearly ritual purity and tithing.

As to *ritual purity*, the Pharisees quite simply sought to apply the purity laws governing the temple ritual to their everyday lives. Others might quite properly conclude that these laws referred only to the priests when performing their temple service and to themselves only when they went to the temple; outside the temple the laws of ritual purity need not be observed.

> But the Pharisees held that even outside the temple, in one's own home, the laws of ritual purity were to be followed in the only circumstances in which they might apply, namely, at the table. Therefore, one must eat secular food (ordinary, everyday meals) in a state of ritual purity *as if one were a temple priest.*[45]

The detail with which the schools' debates were already concerned, as to the precise circumstances in which foods and food containers would be rendered unclean, indicates clearly the importance of such matters for the Pharisees and their conscientiousness in trying to maintain their purity (cf. Matt. 23.25–6).[46] Particularly important here was the cleansing of the hands which were always liable to uncleanness through an unintentional touching. A complete tractate of the Mishna was to be devoted to the purity of hands (*Yadayim*), and the ramifications must already have been the subject of debate at our time, as our own Gospel traditions also testify (Mark 7.2–5//Matt. 15.2; Luke 11.38).[47]

Tithing was important according to the same logic, since only food which had been properly tithed was ritually acceptable. That is to say, tithing was as much concerned with table-fellowship as ritual washing.[48] Here too it is significant that a whole tractate of the Mishna was to be devoted to rulings about produce not certainly tithed (*Demai*), that is to guidance for the devout Jew in his dealings with Jews whose devotion to the law could not be presumed (particularly the *am ha-aretz*). And again there can be little doubt that scrupulous tithing must have formed an important element in the Pharisaic *halakoth* of pre-AD 70 Palestine, as our own Gospel traditions again confirm (Matt. 23.23; Luke 18.12).[49]

We should not confine the influence of such Pharisaic rulings and practice to their own ranks (the *haberim*). For the well-attested Pharisaic criticisms of Jesus' table-fellowship as an eating with 'tax collectors and sinners' (Mark 2.16 pars.; Matt. 11.19//Luke 7.34; Luke 15.2) and of his eating with unwashed hands (Mark 7.2–5//

139

Matt. 15.2; Luke 11.38) were precisely criticisms of a devout Jew *outside* the Pharisaic circle for not observing the Pharisaic *halakoth* – 'Why do your disciples not live according to the tradition of the elders . . .?' (Mark 7.5//Matt. 15.2).[50]

Nor can we assume that such influence was limited to Palestine. It is true that some *halakic* sources ruled that the law of tithes did not apply 'outside the Land' (e.g. *m. Ḥalla* 2.2; *m. Qiddušin* 1.9). But already in Tobit we read of tithes being scrupulously observed from a home in Nineveh (Tob. 1.6–8).[51] Josephus mentions an edict issued by the pro-consul of Asia Minor to the people of Miletus in the days of Caesar permitting the Jews to 'perform their native rites and manage their produce (τοὺς καρποὺς μεταχειρίζεσθαι) in accordance with their customs' (*Antiquities* 14.10.21 §245), which presumably indicates that the practice of tithing was well established among the Jews of Asia Minor in the first century BC. And Philo tells us that tithing was observed by the Jewish community in Rome (*Embassy to Gaius* 156) and implies that the Alexandrian Jews did the same (*Special Laws* 1.153).[52] As to the purity ritual we may simply note that the practice of Jewish ritual cleansing outside Palestine is presumed by the Epistle of Aristeas 305–6, and that such purifications are described as characteristic of Jews as a people by the Sibylline Oracles 3.592–3 and Josephus, *Against Apion* 2.23, 24 §§198, 203. Philo also testifies to a more general concern in Diaspora Judaism for a punctilious observance of the law (*Migration of Abraham* 89–93). Here too we should note Paul's own testimony, that though he came from the Diaspora, nevertheless he 'advanced in Judaism beyond many of my own age among my people, so extremely zealous was I for the traditions of my fathers' (Gal. 1.14; cf. Phil. 3.6). It is this Pharisaic striving for a rectitude beyond what was written which is probably in view in the fierce condemnation of Matthew 23.15 – a proselytizing zeal on the part of the Pharisees is elsewhere unattested, but they may indeed have been more than willing to 'traverse sea and land' to ensure that those who became proselytes properly understood the full extent of their obligations under the law ('when he becomes a proselyte, you make him twice as much a child of hell as yourselves').

We may justifiably infer, then, that *wherever Pharisaic influence was strong during the middle decades of the first century of our era*, both within Palestine and among strong concentrations of Jews in the Diaspora, *there would be pressure on those who thought of themselves as good Jews to observe the halakic clarifications of the laws on tithes and purity* – that is to say, *pressure on devout Jews (including proselytes) to observe strict limits in their practice of table-fellowship.*

On the other hand we should not assume that this pressure

140

would be constant and consistent. The Pharisees were not the only ones with views on these matters. For a start, the Sadducees denied that the laws of purity were applicable outside the temple.[53] At the other end of the spectrum, the Essenes observed rules of ritual purity even stricter than those of the Pharisees (1QS 3.4–5, 8–9; 5.13; 6.16–17, 25; 7.3, 16; 1QSa 2.3–9; CD 10.10–13; Josephus, *Jewish War* 2.8.5, 9–10 §§129, 149–50).[54] And we know that within the ranks of the Pharisees there were many debates between the schools of Shammai and Hillel about particular details, where the concern in effect was to define the precise limits of table-fellowship.[55] We also know that the Pharisees of our period already distinguished several degrees of purity. Thus the ancient mishna, *Ḥagiga* 2.7 –

> The garments of an am ha-aretz are a source of midras-impurity to Pharisees; the garments of Pharisees are a source of midras-impurity to those who eat terumah (i.e. priests); the garments of those who eat terumah are a source of midras-impurity to those who eat holy things; the garments of those who eat holy things are a source of midras-impurity to those who attend to the water of purification (Num. 19.17–18). Jose b. Joezer was the most pious of the priests and (yet) his apron was a source of midras-impurity to those who ate holy things. All his life Johanan b. Gudgada ate secular food at the degree of ritual purity required for holy things, and (yet) his apron was a source of midras-impurity to those who attended to the water of purification.[56]

Similarly with the Essenes: according to Josephus the novice had to pass through several stages of purification before participating in the common food (*Jewish War* 2.8.7 §§137–9), and a senior member could be rendered impure by the touch of a junior member of the community (*Jewish War* 2.8.10 §150). Once the concept of differing degrees of purity within the temple ritual was translated into rules governing everyday table-fellowship it inevitably meant that different degrees of association were possible – he who lived at a stricter level of purity could not eat with one who observed a less strict discipline.

We may conclude that in the Palestine of our period there was a wide spectrum of teaching and practice on this precise issue – from the *am-ha-aretz* who knew not the law (cf. John 7.49) and Jesus who flouted it at one end, to the stricter Pharisees and 'the many' of the Essenes at the other, with varying degrees of scrupulousness and disagreement about particular details in between.[57] *Insofar as the new sect of followers of Jesus was to any extent influenced by Pharisaic views, its members were bound to be caught up in these debates and cross-currents about the acceptable limits of table-fellowship.* We need simply note here that it is precisely an issue of this sort, and the disagreements between Christians concerning it, which is reflected in the different emphases drawn by Mark and Matthew from Jesus' words about true cleanliness (Mark 7.19; Matt. 15.17, 20).[58]

§3.3 Of particular interest for us is what all this would have meant for the *devout Jew* (including the devout Nazarene) *in his social intercourse with Gentiles*. The dominant tendency within Judaism in the century or so around our period seems to have been to avoid such intercourse as much as possible. The stories of Daniel, of Tobit and of Judith were all held forth as examples of the faithfulness and success of Jews who refused to eat 'the food of Gentiles' (Dan. 1.8–16; Tob. 1.10–13; Jdt. 10.5; 12.1–20; see also 3 Macc. 3.4; *Joseph and Asenath* 7.1). The fear of idolatry and of impurity was a considerable limiting factor, since by definition a Gentile was an idolater and certainly ritual impurity had to be assumed rather than the reverse.[59] Thus the Mishnaic tractate on idolatry is mainly concerned with defining the permissible relationships with Gentiles (*Aboda Zara*). And in several rabbinic sayings the uncleanness of the Gentile is axiomatic: Gentiles are simply 'unclean persons' (*Makkot.* 2.3); 'the dwelling-places of Gentiles are unclean' (*Oholot* 18.7);[60] 'a Gentile is in every respect like to a man who suffers a flux' (*Eliyahu Rabba* 10).[61] Such sayings cannot be dismissed as the later utterances of rabbinic Judaism subsequent to our period. The prohibition on Gentiles entering the temple sanctuary was already well established by our time (cf., e.g., *Antiquities* 12.3.4 §§145–6), and must have been based on the belief that Gentiles were unclean.[62] Already in Jubilees the same attitude is clearly expressed and the line firmly drawn:

> Separate yourself from the nations,
> And eat not with them,
> . . . .
> For their works are unclean,
> And all their ways are a pollution and an abomination and an uncleanness . . . (22.16)

According to the Epistle of Aristeas, Moses

> fenced us round with impregnable ramparts and walls of iron, that we might not mingle at all with any of the other nations, but remain pure in body and soul . . . he hedged us round on all sides by rules of purity, affecting alike what we eat, or drink, or touch, or hear, or see. (139, 142; cf. 106)

And Tacitus scornfully describes the Jewish hatred for the rest of the world: 'they eat separately, they sleep separately . . .' (*separati epulis, discreti cubilibus*) (*Histories* 5.5).

If such views were consistently and rigorously applied, no devout Jew could even have considered participating in table-

142

fellowship with a Gentile.[63] But that is by no means the whole story. For there were Gentiles towards whom even the rabbis could maintain a very positive and welcoming attitude – Gentile converts to Judaism and Gentiles who showed themselves sympathetic to the religion of the Jews. How were they affected by the limits observed by the devout Jew in his table-fellowship? Discussion in this area usually works with a three-fold distinction – the proselyte, the resident alien and the God-fearer (sometimes misleadingly called the 'half-proselyte').[64]

(a) *The proselyte*, or full convert. Israelite religion had always inculcated a positive attitude towards the non-Jewish stranger (*gēr*) who lived within the borders of Israel (Exod. 20.10; 22.21; 23.9, 12; Deut. 1.16; 5.14; etc.). However, by the first century AD these commands concerning the *gēr* had been referred almost completely to the proselyte: already in the LXX the regular translation of *gēr* is προσήλυτος; and in rabbinic Judaism *gēr* always means a Gentile won over to Judaism.[65] A positive approach to proselytization is likewise indicated by such stories as those of Ruth finding shelter under Yahweh's wings (Ruth 2.12) and Achior in Judith 14.10, by Isaiah 56.1–8 addressed to 'the foreigners who join themselves to the Lord' and Matthew 23.15, by the accounts in Josephus of the forcible conversion of the Idumeans by Hyrcanus and of the Itureans by Aristobulus (*Antiquities* 13.9.1 §§257–8; 13.11.3 §§318–19), and by various other accounts and references in both Jewish and non-Jewish sources (e.g. Josephus, *Life* 23 §§112–13; *Antiquities* 18.3.5 §82; Horace, *Satires* 1.4.142–3 – 'we, like the Jews, will compel you to make one of our throng').[66]

As a proselyte the Gentile had undertaken to observe the law, including circumcision, and was more or less a full Israelite (see e.g. Exod. 12.49; Philo, *Special Laws* 1.51–2; *b. Yebamot* 47b).[67] Despite the stigma of being a proselyte (cf. *m. Qiddušin* 4.1), and the suspicion harboured by some rabbis that he was always liable to fall back into his old ways (e.g. *m. Niddah* 7.3; *b. Baba Meṣia* 59b),[68] the proselyte once his initiation was complete came within the same limits of table-fellowship that applied to the native born Jew.[69] Of particular interest to us, however, is the fact that there seems to have been some debate among the rabbis at our period over the degree of uncleanness attaching to the Gentile proselyte at his conversion and over the length of time it took before his uncleanness could be washed away by ritual purification (*m. Pesaḥim* 8.8; *m. Eduyyot* 5.2).[70]

(b) *The resident alien.* Although it understood the biblical *gēr* to refer to the proselyte, rabbinic Judaism also recognized a different category of Gentile, the *gēr tôšāb*, the resident alien. He too lived within the borders of Israel, but unlike the proselyte he accepted only some of the commandments of the Torah.

Just how much he had to accept before being recognized as a *gēr tôšāb* was a subject of dispute among the rabbis. According to R. Meir (c. 150) a sufficient requirement was that the Gentile in question undertook in the presence of three *haberim* to renounce idolatry.[71] Others defined a *gēr tôšāb* as 'a *gēr* who eats of animals not ritually slaughtered, that is, he took upon himself to observe all the precepts mentioned in the Torah apart from the prohibition of (eating the flesh of) animals not ritually slaughtered' (*b. Aboda Zara* 64b). This exemption of the *gēr tôšāb* from the prohibition against animals not ritually slaughtered was determined by Deuteronomy 14.21 – 'You shall not eat of anything that dies of itself; you may give it to the alien (*gēr*) who is within your towns, that he may eat it . . .' – a law which could properly be held to exempt the *gēr tôšāb* from at least some of the restrictions governing the eating of meat, and which thus provided sanction for slackening one of the limits of acceptable table-fellowship. But the *halakah* which gained greatest support and decided the matter was that a *gēr tôšāb* was any Gentile who takes upon himself the seven Noahic laws – that is, he holds himself subject to the established courts of justice, and refrains from blasphemy, idolatry, adultery, bloodshed, robbery, and eating flesh cut from living animals (*b. Aboda Zara* 64b; cf. *b. Sanhedrin* 56a).[72]

Clearly, then, there was some debate among the rabbis in the period before the consensus view was established regarding the definition of a *gēr tôšāb*, a debate in effect as to the terms on which social intercourse with Gentiles living locally might be acceptable. This strongly suggests that there were already during the first-century period diverse views among the rabbis regarding the limits of table-fellowship as they applied to the resident alien.[73] Here we should note also that, despite such rabbinic characterizations of Gentile uncleanness as were cited above (*m. Makkot* 2.3; *m. Oholot* 18.7), the Mishna contains at least two rulings which *presuppose* situations at the meal table where a Gentile (not a *gēr*) was present (*m. Berakot* 7.1; *m. Aboda Zara* 5.5), and the Babylonian Talmud contains discussion of the conditions on which Jews might accept invitations to and participate in Gentile banquets (*b. Aboda Zara* 8a–b). We can only conclude that, in all probability, in the Palestine of our period there was also a diversity among devout Jews in their practice of table-fellowship so far as Gentiles were involved – a diversity similar in extent to or indeed continuous with the spectrum of permissible table-fellowship as determined by the various grades of purity among Jews themselves.

(c) *The God-fearer.* A third group of more acceptable Gentiles were those usually called 'God-fearers' or 'pious Gentiles' – those who showed themselves sympathetic towards Judaism – though whether 'God-fearers' (οἱ φοβούμενοι τὸν θεόν, οἱ σεβόμενοι τὸν θεόν) was a technical term for such may be doubted.[74] However they should be designated, there were certainly many Gentiles (we are talking here particularly of the Diaspora) who were attracted to Judaism and who signified their interest by attaching themselves to Jewish practices in differing degrees. How diverse such attachments were is a question more easily posed than answered. We know from Acts that such Gentiles attended the synagogue or Jewish meetings for worship (Acts 13.16, 26, 50; 16.14; 17.4, 17). Cornelius, in one of the passages in which the phrase φοβούμενος τὸν θεόν most nearly approaches a technical sense (the other is the description of Titius Justus as σεβόμενος τὸν θεόν in 18.7), is described as 'a devout man who feared God, gave alms liberally to the people, and prayed constantly to God' (10.2). We should also recall that pious Gentiles were welcome to worship in the temple (John 12.20; Acts 8.27; also Josephus, *Jewish War* 4.4.4 §275), within, of course, well-defined limits (namely, the court of the Gentiles).[75]

The central question for us, however, is the extent to which such God-fearing Gentiles were expected to keep the law (including the oral traditions) concerning tithing and ritual purity. Josephus' claims in *Against Apion* confirm the attractiveness of Judaism for many Gentiles: many Greeks 'have agreed to adopt (εἰσελθεῖν) our laws' (2.10 §123); our laws 'have to an ever increasing extent excited the emulation of the world at large' (2.38 §280; cf. 2.28 §§209–10). Philo speaks in similar and similarly vague terms in *Life of Moses* 2.17–20.[76] But Josephus becomes more helpfully explicit a little further on in *Against Apion* –

The masses have long since shown a keen desire to adopt our religious observances (εὐσεβείας); and there is not one city, Greek or barbarian, not a single nation, to which our custom of abstaining from work on the sabbath day has not spread, and where the fasts and the lighting of lamps and many of our prohibitions in the matter of food (πολλὰ τῶν εἰς βρῶσιν ἡμῖν οὐ νενομισμένων) are not observed. (*Against Apion* 2.38 §282)

Equally interesting is the succession of notices which demonstrate how attractive the Jewish way of life was for many Gentiles in Rome itself and how alarmed the authorities were in consequence. Plutarch (in a passage which relates to the middle of the first century BC) speaks of a freedman named Caecilius 'who was accused of Jewish practices (ἔνοχος τῷ ἰουδαΐζειν) (*Life of Cicero* 7.6). Seneca mentions autobiographically that in his youth he began to abstain from animal food, but that he abandoned the practice because 'some foreign rites were at that time being inaugurated, and abstinence from certain kinds of animal food was set down as proof of interest in the strange cult' (*Letters* 108.22).

He refers most probably to the persecution of Jewish and Egyptian rites under Tiberius in AD 19 (Tacitus, *Annals* 2.85).[77] Perhaps significant here too is the report of Dio Cassius already cited, that in 41 Claudius forbade the Jews in Rome to hold meetings because they had increased so greatly in number (60.6.6).[78] Better known is the persecution by Domitian of 'those who followed the Jewish way of life (*vitam*) without formally professing Judaism' (Suetonius, *Domitian* 12.2); Dio Cassius, also writing of the late first century AD, speaks of 'many who were drifting into Jewish ways' (τὰ τῶν Ἰουδαίων ἔθη) being condemned for atheism (67.14.1–3).[79] And Juvenal confirms the attractiveness which Judaism obviously exercised for many at this period when he attacks contemporaries who 'learn and practise and revere the Jewish law' and who get themselves circumcised, under the influence of a Sabbath-reverencing, pork-abstaining father (*Satires* 14.96–106). As evidence of Judaism's continuing influence at the other end of the second century AD we may simply note Tertullian's report that many Gentiles in his day observed Jewish feasts and ceremonies and Jewish practice in prayers (*Ad Nationes* 1.13). It would not be unjust to deduce from all this that *many God-fearers attracted by the Jewish law quite naturally would have observed the law in the way native born Jews did – that is, in the way that the developed customs and developing tradition dictated.*

Still more interesting for us, not least because the incident described took place within a few years of the Antioch incident, is the well-known story of the conversion of Izates, king of Adiabene, recounted by Josephus (*Antiquities* 20.2.4 §§38–48). Izates was initially told that he need not be circumcised – 'he could worship God, even without circumcision, if he had fully decided to emulate the hereditary customs of the Jews' (ζηλοῦν τὰ πάτρια τῶν Ἰουδαίων) (*Antiquities* 20.2.4 §41). Since the sticking point was circumcision, we may take it that Izates was prepared to go the whole way apart from that, and 'zeal for hereditary customs' suggests that his devotion would have embraced much at least of the oral law as well as the written Torah (cf. 20.2.3,4 §§34, 38).[80] This may well be confirmed by the fact that when Eleazar came upon the scene from Galilee, described by Josephus as a Jew 'who had a reputation for being extremely strict concerning the hereditary customs' (τὰ πάτρια), the only further step he required of Izates was circumcision (*Antiquities* 20.2.4 §§43–5).

Most interesting of all, however, is Josephus' description of the Jewish *politeuma* in Antioch in the period prior to the Jewish revolt: 'they grew in numbers . . . and were constantly attracting to their religious ceremonies multitudes of the Greeks, and these they had in some measure incorporated with themselves' (κἀκείνους τρόπῳ τινὶ μοῖραν αὐτῶν πεποίηντο) (*Jewish War* 7.3.3 §45).[81] Whatever degree of devotion to the Torah, written and unwritten, on the part of the God-fearing Greeks is implied by this statement, it must denote a considerable measure of acceptance by the Antiochene Jews of these Greeks,[82] and so also a considerable measure of social intercourse between circumcised Jew and uncircumcised Gentile.[83]

We may conclude from all this that there was a broad range of attachments to Judaism and Jewish ways wherever Diaspora settlements had made any impact on the surrounding community – from occasional visits to the synagogue, to total commitment apart from circumcision, with such matters as the sabbath and dietary laws being observed in varying degrees in between. *Pari passu there would be a broad range of social intercourse between faithful Jew and God-fearing Gentile, with strict Jews avoiding table-fellowship as far as possible, and those less scrupulous in matters of tithing and purity willingly extending and accepting invitations to meals where such Gentiles would be present.*

We can also see that the attitude and practice of openness to the Gentile would not have been static. It would depend upon the influence of particular rabbis and of particular rulings in matters of dispute. We may compare, for example, the famous pericope contrasting the response of Shammai and that of Hillel to the Gentile who asked both to teach him the whole Torah while he stood on one foot (*b. Šabbat* 31a). It would depend on the mood of the surrounding populace and local authorities at the time – particularly in Rome, Alexandria and Antioch, where the Jews were strong in numbers and undue influence on their part could be construed as a threat to the state. And at the period which concerns us it would depend not least on the Jews' sense of the mounting threat to their religion and nation which we sketched out earlier (§2.2) and which must have expressed itself in an increasingly hostile attitude to the Gentiles. This last is illustrated by the sequence of events described in Acts 21, which depicts Jerusalem Jews in the late 50s giving ready credence to the rumour that Paul had taken a Gentile into the temple (Acts 21.27–36). Another instance is the report of Josephus that at the beginning of the revolt in 66 Eleazar 'persuaded those who officiated in the temple services to accept no gift or sacrifice from a foreigner' (*Jewish War* 2.17.2 §409). Here too we may mention again the episode of Izates' conversion, which among other things shows that the attitude of the Palestinian Jew was stricter than that of the Diaspora Jew on the question of how far a Gentile had to go to be acceptable (Josephus, *Antiquities* 20.2.4 §§38–48), and which thus provides an interesting parallel to the Antioch incident.

Before moving on, it is worth noting once more, if it is not already clear, that the issues in all this would have been issues for the earliest Christians too, particularly as the circle of Jesus' discipleship began to embrace more and more Gentiles. The extent to which the spectrum of attitude and practice mirrored that within the rest of Judaism is indicated by Paul's advice to the believers in Corinth (including Jews) at one end (1 Cor. 8—10), and at the other by the reaction of the Judean brothers to Peter's eating with a Gentile, even though he was a pious God-fearer and presumably already observed the dietary laws (Acts 11.2–3). At the latter end of the same spectrum we should note also the untypical saying of Jesus preserved for us not surprisingly only by Matthew – 'if he (the brother at fault) refuses to listen even to the church, let him be to you as a Gentile and a tax-collector' (Matt. 18.17).[84] The question for us, of course, is where the Antioch incident, not to mention Acts 15.20, 29, fits into this spectrum. It is to this question that we can now at last turn.

§4 THE ISSUE AT ANTIOCH

Against the background sketched out in the preceding sections, the exegetical alternatives in Galatians 2.11–18 become clearer. The leading question can be posed thus: What did the table-fellowship at Antioch involve *prior* to the coming of the men from James? And what would have been required of the Gentile believers if the table-fellowship was to be resumed after the initial disruption caused by the withdrawal of Peter and the others? To put it another way, What was it that the men from James objected to or found fault with in the table-fellowship at Antioch? And how could that defect be remedied, if at all?

§4.1 *Key phrases.* The exegetical alternatives focus particularly on the key phrases of Paul's challenge, '"If you, a Jew *live like a Gentile and not like a Jew* (ἐθνικῶς καὶ οὐχὶ ἰουδαϊκῶς ζῆς), how can you compel the Gentiles to *judaize* (ἰουδαΐζειν)?" We are Jews by birth and not *Gentile sinners* (οὐκ ἐξ ἐθνῶν ἁμαρτωλοί) ...' (Gal. 2.14–15).[85]

(a) The antithesis ἐθνικῶς/ἰουδαϊκῶς is not precise enough to give us much help, since it could embrace a wide range of contrasts between practices typically Gentile and those typically Jewish. 'To live like a Gentile' must exclude any detailed observance of the law; but need it exclude a more limited observance, such as many Gentiles attracted by Judaism obviously maintained? In particular, since the Noahic rules were thought by many Jews to apply to all mankind, we cannot exclude the possibility that the ἐθνικῶς/ἰουδαϊκῶς antithesis here is the antithesis between what we may call a Noahic lifestyle and a Sinaitic lifestyle, the one being character-istic of God-fearing Gentiles, the other of loyal Jews.[86] The one

148

instance from our other sources which might shed some light comes from Eusebius, where he describes Symmachus as an Ebionite, that is, as one who strongly maintained 'that the law ought to be kept in a more strictly Jewish fashion' (ἰουδαϊκώτερον) (*Ecclesiastical History* 6.17). What 'a more strictly Jewish fashion' means is presumably indicated by Eusebius' earlier description of the Ebionites as those who 'insisted on the complete observation of the law', and who 'were zealous to insist on the literal observance of the law' (*Ecclesiastical History* 3.27.2, 3). This simply serves to confirm that 'to live in a Jewish fashion' was a relative term and did not imply a pattern of behaviour precisely defined or widely agreed among Jews.

(b) Ἰουδαΐζειν is for us the most intriguing word. What was it that Paul accused Peter of requiring from the Gentile believers? Some of the usages elsewhere are as unspecific as the ἐθνικῶς/ἰουδαϊκῶς antithesis – including the reference in Plutarch already cited (*Life of Cicero* 7.6; cf. also Ignatius, *Magnesians* 10.3; *Acts of Pilate* (A) 2.1). But four others offer some illumination. In the LXX of Esther we read that 'many of the Gentiles were circumcised and judaized (καὶ ἰουδάϊζον) for fear of the Jews' (8.17 LXX). So also Theodotus: Jacob would not give Dinah to the son of Hamor 'until all the inhabitants of Shechem were circumcised and judaized (περιτεμνομένους ἰουδάϊσαι)' (Eusebius, *Praep. Evang.* 9.22.5). In Josephus we read a similar characterization of one Metilius, the commander of the Roman garrison in Jerusalem, who 'saved his life by entreaties and promises to judaize and even to be circumcised' (καὶ μέχρι περιτομῆς ἰουδαΐσειν) (*Jewish War* 2.17.10 §454). In each instance 'judaizing' is obviously not the same as being circumcised: it denotes rather the range of possible degrees of assimilation to Jewish customs, with circumcision as the end-point of judaizing; but evidently one could 'judaize' without going the whole way (circumcision).[87] It must therefore describe that range of conduct covered by the term God-fearer (or within Palestine also the term 'resident alien') and signify an embracing of much that characterized the Jewish way of life, enough at any rate for the judaizing individual to be acceptable to devout Jews.

Still more interesting is the passage a little later in *The Jewish War*, not least because it describes the situation in Syria in the mid-60s –

The whole of Syria was a scene of frightful disorder; every city was divided into two camps, and the safety of one party lay in their anticipating the other ... For, though believing that they had rid themselves of the Jews, still each city had its Judaizers (τοὺς ἰουδαΐζον-τας), who aroused suspicion; and while they shrank from killing offhand this equivocal element in their midst, they feared these neutrals (μεμιγ-

149

μένον) as much as pronounced aliens. (*Jewish War* 2.18.2 §§462–3 – Thackeray translation in Loeb)

Here we have confirmation that a considerable number of Gentiles in Syrian cities (including of course Antioch) were attracted sufficiently to Judaism as to have identified or associated themselves in some marked degree with it. Moreover, these Gentiles are further described as μεμίγμενοι, which we might colloquially translate as 'those who had become mixed up with the Jews', and which elsewhere in such a context denotes social intercourse including guest friendship, living with, and sexual intercourse.[88] This strongly suggests that ἰουδαΐζειν can denote a degree of affiliation to Judaism which made possible a high level of social intercourse between Jew and Gentile, including not least unrestricted table-fellowship. Moreover, when taken together with Josephus' testimony in *Jewish War* 7.3.3 §45 (discussed above in §2.2), it clearly implies that the Jewish community at Antioch in the 50s and early 60s had attracted large numbers of Gentiles and that many of these Gentiles were sufficiently ready to conform to Jewish practices as to make possible regular social intercourse including at least guest friendship and table-fellowship.[89]

(c) Ἁμαρτωλοί is not a surprising word to find at this point (Gal. 2.15) in view of the context so far outlined. Ἁμαρτωλός was a word which had by this time in Jewish circles developed a particularly Jewish flavour. It denoted not just a 'sinner' in general terms, but a sinner determined as such precisely by his relation to the law. 'Sinner' was becoming more and more a technical term for someone who either broke the law or did not know the law – the two criticisms of course often amounting to the same thing. Thus already in the LXX of the Psalms the link between 'sinner' and 'lawlessness' (ἀνομία) is well established (Ps. 27.3; 54.3; 91.7; 100.8; 124.3; 128.3 – LXX); the sinner is defined as one who forsakes the law, who does not seek God's statutes (Ps. 118.53, 155 – LXX). And in 1 Maccabees 'sinners' and 'lawless men' are parallel terms (1 Macc. 1.34; 2.44). More striking is the way in which 'sinner' becomes synonymous with 'Gentile' – already in Psalm 9.17, and again in 1 Maccabees 2.48; also *Psalms of Solomon* 1.1; 2.1–2 (cf. Tob. 13.8; Jub. 23.23–4; 4 Ezra 4.23). It was evidently a well-established usage by the time of the first Christians: 'sinners' and 'Gentiles' stand as variant versions of the same Q saying (Luke 6.33 – 'even sinners do the same'; Matt. 5.47 – 'even Gentiles do the same'); and the same equivalence is probably implied in the saying of Jesus, 'the Son of Man is betrayed into the hands of sinners' (Mark 14.41//Matt. 26.45; Luke 24.7), as the parallel with Mark 10.33 also suggests. Gentiles are 'sinners' by reason of the fact that they do not have the law and are disqualified by the law from covenant righteousness (cf. *Clementine Homilies* 11.16).[90]

Still more striking for us is the evidence of how the word was used in relation to Jesus' ministry, as a description of those within Israel whose way of life should have debarred them from the table-fellowship of the devout Jew. It applied not just to those who had abused the written Torah (Luke 7.37, 39 – a prostitute?; cf. Matt 21.32), but to tax collectors (Luke 19.7; cf. Matt. 5.46 with Luke 6.32), and it would seem also to other trades which put the practitioner beyond the pale of what was deemed acceptable (Mark 2.15–17 pars.; Matt. 11.19//Luke 7.34; Luke 15.1–2). Here we are evidently once again back in an area where the limits of acceptability were being determined by the multiplying *halakoth* of the Pharisaic rabbis.[91] That is to say, not just disobedience to the Torah but disregard for the rabbinic rulings on what obedience to the Torah entailed, that was what showed a person to be a sinner. This has become more explicit in the Mishna: a sinner (*rāsā*) is one who treats *halakic* rulings lightly (*m. Eduyyot* 5.6; *m. Abot* 4.7; 5.14).[92]

Given that so much of the Pharisaic teaching of our period was concerned with the limits of acceptable table-fellowship (above §3), and given that the context of Galatians 2.15 is a dispute precisely about whether and under what circumstances a devout Jew could have table-fellowship with Gentiles, the presumption becomes compellingly strong that ἁμαρτωλός in verse 15 belongs to the same range of usage. That is, *it was probably a word used of the Gentile believers by the men from James to express their disagreement or dismay at the table-fellowship being practised by Peter and the other Jewish believers.* And it probably had the connotation of 'unclean' (= Gentile = sinner), one who by his very race was legally disqualified from participating in the table-fellowship of a faithful Jew: 'How could you Peter, a true-born Jew, have table-fellowship with a Gentile sinner?'[93]

§4.2 *Exegetical alternatives.* Our examination of these key phrases in Galatians 2.14–15 against the background outlined earlier thus clarifies the exegetical alternatives open to us. What was involved in the table-fellowship at Antioch before the men from James appeared? How strict was the discipline of diet or ritual purity into which Peter and the others withdrew? On what terms could the table-fellowship have been resumed thereafter?[94] There are basically three alternatives open to us.

(a) The table-fellowship at Antioch practised by the whole community, including Peter and the other Jewish believers, had completely abandoned the laws governing table-fellowship. They no longer observed even the laws of unclean foods; they did not insist on animals being properly killed; they did not hold back over idol food. What the men from James insisted on was a greater observance of the law, perhaps no more than the laws explicitly set out in the Torah. Indeed it can be argued with plausibility that what the men from James brought was the decree of Acts 15.29, which had been agreed in Jerusalem following the Jerusalem conference (Paul's first missionary journey having intervened): 'the demands laid down in Antioch are none other than the demands of the Decree'.[95]

This alternative would give the most obvious sense to two of the phrases examined above – they were living like Gentiles, like Gentile sinners, showing no knowledge of or regard for the principal gift of God to the Jew, the Torah. We may note also that it would fit with Luke's account in Acts 10—11 of Peter's vision at Joppa and his subsequent encounter with Cornelius at Caesarea, where the lesson could have been drawn that the law of clean and unclean no longer applied to the Jewish believer. It could also fit with the hypothesis that the Antioch incident preceded the Jerusalem council (Gal. 2.1–10 = Acts 11.30), and that the Jerusalem council was called to resolve the problem posed by the Antioch incident.[96]

The weakness of this alternative is that it does not fit well into the background illuminated above. (1) It is unlikely that the Jewish believers at Antioch had abandoned the law so completely. So far as we know, such a complete abandoning of the law without protest from within the ranks of the local Jewish Christians themselves is without parallel. Both in Corinth and at Rome a substantial proportion of the Jewish believers clearly felt unable to go so far (Rom. 14.1–2; 1 Cor. 8). We should not, of course, assume a regularity of practice throughout the Diaspora churches over this period. Nevertheless, it must be doubted whether so many Jewish believers at Antioch would have given up the law so unreservedly without it becoming an issue among themselves even before Peter and the men from James arrived. (2) We know from Josephus that the Jewish *politeuma* at Antioch had attracted many Gentiles who evidently showed themselves willing to adopt Jewish customs, at least in some measure. It is likely that the Gentile converts to faith in the Christ Jesus came initially, perhaps even almost exclusively, from the ranks of these God-fearers (cf. Acts 6.5). That would mean that the Gentile believers were already accustomed to observe the Jewish dietary laws in some measure and the table-fellowship of the new sect probably continued in the same fashion. (3) It must be doubted whether Paul would have reacted quite so sharply as he did to a requirement from the Jerusalem delegation merely that the Gentiles should observe the most basic laws of the Torah – the Noahic laws. Later on, he saw such scruples as a threat to Christian liberty, but nevertheless advised his fellow 'liberals' to observe them for the sake of 'the weaker brother' (Rom. 14.13—15.3; 1 Cor. 8.7–13), so he did not regard them as a threat to the gospel in these circumstances. We must allow of course that Paul 'cooled down' somewhat after the Antioch incident and the Galatian letter, but even at the earlier period, would he have seen an acceptance of the Noahic rules as a building up once again of the edifice of Torah righteousness over which he had laboured as a Pharisee (Gal. 2.18)? I think it unlikely: the Noahic requirements were hardly the same as 'the traditions of his fathers' for which he had previously been so zealous (1.14).[97]

(b) At the other end of the scale of possibilities, it is possible that the table-fellowship at Antioch had involved a fair degree of observance of the dietary laws, including even some of the *halakic* elaborations concerning tithes and ritual purity. In such a case the men from James were in effect insisting that these God-fearing Gentile believers go the whole way and become proselytes by being circumcised, and Peter and the other Jewish believers who followed him were giving their demand added force by their actions.[98]

This interpretation would certainly fit with the background of considerable numbers of Gentiles at Antioch showing themselves willing to 'judaize'. It would also provide an even closer match with the story of Izates' conversion, in the contrast there between the Diaspora Jews with a laxer view of what conversion required, and the Jews from Palestine with their insistence on circumcision (cf. *Antiquities* 20.2.4 §§38–46). And again it would fit with the hypothesis that the Jerusalem council was called to resolve the issue raised by the Antioch incident, with an exact match being provided between Galatians 2.12 ('certain men came from James ...') and Acts 15.1 ('And certain men came down from Judea and were teaching the brethren, "Unless you are circumcised according to the custom of Moses you cannot be saved"').

The weaknesses of this second alternative are, however, even more compelling. (1) It does not square with the language used by Paul. Peter's conduct in such a case could hardly be called 'living like a Gentile' (Gal. 2.14). Ἰουδαΐζειν denotes a Gentile's adopting the Jewish customs which made social intercourse possible and is elsewhere distinguished from circumcision, with the latter seen as the crucial final step by which the 'judaizer' became a proselyte. It would be somewhat surprising then if Paul used ἰουδαΐζειν to denote that final step, if they had already been judaizing to such an extent.[99] And ἁμαρτωλός would also be a surprising word to use of Gentiles who were already judaizing to such a degree – that is, showing their knowledge of and regard for the law. (2) Even more difficult is it to see the Antioch incident thus interpreted as the sequel to the Jerusalem agreement recorded in Galatians 2.1–10.[100] According to Paul, the pillar apostles, including James and Peter,

153

had agreed that Gentile believers need not be circumcised. It is not inconceivable that James subsequently succumbed to the growing pressures within Palestine for a more clear-cut loyalty to the religion of Israel (cf. n. 97 above). But it is doubtful whether Peter would have abandoned in Antioch an agreement made in Jerusalem, an agreement reached in the face of already strong pressure from those Paul calls 'false brothers', 'sham believers' (2.4). It is doubtful too that the Jewish believers, particularly the Hellenists, should succumb so completely to pressure of this sort from the Jerusalem which had expelled them.

(c) The third alternative is the intermediate interpretation. The Gentile believers were already observing the basic food laws prescribed by the Torah; in their table-fellowship with the Jewish believers, in particular pork was not used, and when meat was served care had been taken to ensure the beast had been properly slaughtered.[101] In this case what the men from James would have called for was a much more scrupulous observance of the rulings on what the dietary laws involved, especially with regard to ritual purity and tithing (see §3.2 above).

This interpretation fits well with the language of Galatians 2.14–15. It certainly makes sense of Paul's charge that Peter by his action was compelling the Gentile believers to judaize.[102] For as we have seen, $\iota o\upsilon\delta\alpha\dot{\iota}\zeta\epsilon\iota\nu$ elsewhere denotes the adoption of Jewish customs in full measure, though not necessarily circumcision itself: men and women could be said to have 'judaized' without the former having been circumcised (see above §4.1b). Paul's charge against Peter, then, is most likely that by his action he had raised the ritual barriers surrounding their table-fellowship, thereby excluding the Gentile believers unless they 'judaized', that is, embraced a far more demanding discipline of ritual purity than hitherto. The reason why Peter had withdrawn ($\dot{\alpha}\phi\dot{\omega}\rho\iota\zeta\epsilon\nu$) from the table-fellowship in the first place was because the purity status of the Gentile believers had been called in question (Gal. 2.12; cf. 2 Cor. 6.17 with its reference to Isa. 52.11).[103] So too, Paul's description of Peter as previously having lived 'like a Gentile and not as a Jew' could describe a practice of table-fellowship which fell within the limits of the Noahic laws, since already no doubt the view was current that the commandments given to Noah (Gen. 9) applied to all the nations (descendants of Noah) and not just the Jews (cf. *Jub.* 7.20).[104] Probably this was the level of table-fellowship which Peter had previously learned to practise in his encounter with the God-fearing Cornelius (Acts 10—11), and which the 'circumcision party' had criticized on that earlier occasion (Acts 11.2–3; though see also below n. 111). Moreover, in the phrase 'Gentile sinners', $\dot{\alpha}\mu\alpha\rho\tau\omega\lambda o\dot{\iota}$ will not here be simply a synonym for 'Gentiles' who know not the law, but could have more

154

the connotation of its use within Palestine for Jews who disregarded the law by their mode of life (see above §4.1c). That is to say, 'Gentile sinners' could mean Gentiles who knew the law but whose regard for it was seriously defective in practice.

This interpretation also fits into the background of Palestine at that time – particularly the increasing nationalism as Israel's position and religious prerogatives were seen to be under a mounting threat. The pressure would be on the good Jew to withdraw more and more into a stricter definition and practice of his national religion. Here we may recall the debate between the schools of Shammai and Hillel as to the seriousness of the Gentile proselyte's uncleanness (*m. Pesaḥim* 8.8; *m. Eduyyot* 5.2); also the probability that the stricter school of Shammai gained the ascendancy in the pre-70 period.[105] Palestinian Jews who believed in Jesus would experience the same pressures, as the Gospel of Matthew in particular confirms. Not only do the Gospels testify that Christians too were caught up in a debate about true cleanliness, where the meaning of Jesus' definition of cleanliness was at issue, and where Matthew's emphasis is distinctly more conservative than Mark's (Mark 7.19; Matt. 15.17, 20). But Matthew also gives evidence of an even more conservative *Christian* tradition behind Matthew 5.19 and 23.3, 23, where the *Christian* respect for the Pharisaic *halakoth* cannot have been very different from (and may have been very close to) the views postulated here for the men from James.[106] Against this background the third alternative for our interpretation of the Antioch incident makes excellent sense. As Eleazar coming from Palestine made a higher demand on the would-be proselyte Izates than the Diaspora Jew Ananias (Josephus, *Antiquities* 20.2.4 §§41–5), so the men from James made a higher demand on the God-fearing Gentile believers than the Jewish believers in Antioch itself.

Finally, we can say that this interpretation of Galatians 2.11–18 also fits well into the preceding context in Galatians. When the pillar apostles in Jerusalem accepted Paul's gospel (2.5–7) and agreed to the division of missionary labour (2.7–9), what had been at dispute and what was agreed were the requirements laid by the gospel *upon the Gentiles*. The requirements laid upon the Jews had not been at issue. What about table-fellowship? Nothing seems to have been said (Gal. 2.6d, 10).[107] Why so? Possibly because the parties to the agreement did not think about table-fellowship or consider whether it would be affected by the agreement. Or possibly because they assumed that Gentile believer and Jewish believer would avoid social intercourse. Yet neither of these possibilities can be rated very highly, since social intercourse including table-fellowship was evidently quite normal, though carefully regulated, both within Palestine between the devout Jew and the *gēr tôšāb* and in the Diaspora between the devout Jew and the God-fearer, and since the issue must have arisen for the new sect as soon as Gentiles began to believe in Jesus without undergoing circumcision, as again the Cornelius episode confirms. It would be hardly likely, for example, that Titus ate his meals in splendid isolation when he visited Jerusalem with Paul and Barnabas (Gal. 2.3). On the contrary, the fact that table-fellowship was not at issue on that occasion strongly suggests that Titus observed a high standard of ritual purity during that visit.[108]

Much the greater probability lies with the further suggestion that the pillar apostles simply assumed that the devout Jewish believer would continue to observe the hereditary customs already surrounding the meal table (even if not all the refinements currently under debate among the Pharisees). In which case they would have assumed also that the table-fellowship between believing Jew and believing Gentile in Antioch involved a considerable regard for the religious scruples of the devout Jew and so was maintained at a fairly high level of ritual purity.[109] This would be in line with the degree of scrupulosity earlier attributed to the Jerusalem brothers in Acts 11.2–3, where an uncircumcised Gentile *per se* was an improper table companion, because of his Gentile uncleanness (cf. Acts 10.14–15; 11.8–9). It would fit with the probability that Titus observed a high standard of table purity while in Jerusalem with Paul and Barnabas: many of the local Jewish believers would then be more likely to assume that this was the accepted practice in the more mixed communities of the Diaspora. And it would certainly explain the reaction of the men from James when they arrived from Jerusalem: they were surprised and shocked by the minimal level of law observance in Antioch; to them it would appear as though the whole heritage distinctive of Israel and most prized by Judaism, the law of Moses, was being abandoned.[110] In the same way Paul's language probably echoes the surprise he felt that the Jerusalem believers were still thinking of the Gentile believers as 'sinners' (Gal. 2.15, 17), still categorizing them in terms of their relation to the law.

The reasoning behind Peter's withdrawal from table-fellowship is still harder to elucidate. But given the fuller context we have now reconstructed, the most likely interpretation is along these lines. (1) He could not deny the logic of Jerusalem's demand, that a Jew live like a Jew. Nothing in the Jerusalem agreement had altered that, whatever freedom it had given to the Gentile believers.[111] (2) As a native of Palestine, indeed a Galilean, he could feel the pressure of the steadily mounting threat against Judaism, and so the strong attractiveness of the call to hold loyal to the hereditary customs (see above §2.2). (3) In particular he would appreciate the counter-threat felt by the Palestine believers from the more rigorous and more fanatically loyal of their fellow religionists. For Jewish believers to appear to be abandoning their national and religious heritage, or for a rumour to that effect to get about, was to invite retribution and even death (cf. again Acts 6.11–14; 8.1–3; 21.20–1, 27–36; 23.12–15).[112] Not only so, but many of his fellow Jewish believers evidently shared these more rigorist views, and Peter may indeed have 'feared the circumcision party' (Gal. 2.12) – that is, feared if not for his life, at least for his authority and effectiveness within the Jewish Christian communities of Palestine.[113] (4) Moreover, as one who had been specifically designated as a missionary to his fellow Jews (Gal. 2.7–9), Peter would recognize the importance of retaining a good standing in Jewish eyes, or at least of not needlessly offending those who were formulating Jewish attitudes and reactions in such threatening times. To become known himself as a 'sinner' would at once cut him off from the bulk of faithful Jews.[114] (5) Again a delegation from James, if that is a correct designation, was not to be lightly ignored. As we have seen, the church at Antioch, including Paul and not unnaturally Barnabas, had in effect already acknowledged Jerusalem's authority in judging matters of controversy, when they submitted the issue of circumcising Gentile believers to the pillar apostles (Gal. 2.2, 9). Moreover, of the pillar apostles, James had already established himself as the leading figure in Jerusalem (Gal. 2.9). Consequently a group who came from Jerusalem with the explicit (or claimed) backing of James could expect the church at Antioch to fall in line with their judgement. And Peter acted accordingly. (6) At least one other consideration may well have influenced Peter. Since so many Gentiles outside the new sect, in Antioch and elsewhere, seemed very ready to declare their attraction to Judaism by judaizing as far as circumcision (above §4.1b), it was not unreasonable to expect that the Gentile believers in Antioch would be willing to subject themselves to a similar degree of *halakic* observance for the sake of their Jewish brothers. The issue of whether the Gentile believers need be circumcised had been settled in favour of Gentile liberty of action. The issue was now of Jewish believers remaining loyal to their ancestral faith, and in return they might expect the Gentile believers to conform to the sensibilities of their Jewish brothers, in much the same way as they had been willing to 'judaize' when they were 'God-fearers'.[115] Some such pragmatic considerations, acted out as they would see it within the spirit of the Jerusalem agreement, must presumably lie behind the actions of Peter, Barnabas and the other Jewish Christians – actions, however, which Paul could only see and denounce as an unprincipled compromise of the gospel (2.13–14).[116]

To conclude, the third alternative seems to provide the best

157

solution. The table-fellowship at Antioch had not totally disregarded the law but probably had paid due heed to the basic dietary laws of the Torah. Peter, having already become less tied to the more elaborate scruples of the brothers in Judea (Acts 10—11), found no difficulty in joining in such table-fellowship, as Barnabas, more used to Diaspora ways, was already doing. The men from James, however, were shocked at what seemed to them a minimal level of Torah observance and a far too casual and unacceptable attitude to the Torah. They would no doubt point out that the earlier agreement made in Jerusalem had in no way changed the obligations to Torah obedience resting on the Jewish believer, and must have insisted that the Jewish believers in Antioch conduct themselves with greater discipline and greater loyalty to the Torah, more like their fellow believers in Palestine and with a similar regard for the heritage of Jewish tradition and custom. Peter, persuaded by this charge of disloyalty and out of concern for the future of the Jewish Christian assemblies and 'the mission to the circumcised', withdrew into a more disciplined ritual and 'the rest of the Jews' followed suit – swayed no doubt by Peter's example and authority (Gal. 2.13), but also hoping, we may presume, that the Gentile believers would adapt their own lifestyle to this more rigorous code of conduct.

§4.3 It was at this point that Paul intervened and confronted Peter. The vividness with which he recalls the scene indicates the importance of the stand which he felt he must make. Indeed it is likely that in verses 14–18 he lives again through the line of reasoning which had forced him to the conclusion that Peter was wrong and which he had used against Peter.[117] In particular it was the use of 'sinner' by the Jerusalem delegation in reference to the Gentile believers and the table-fellowship at Antioch which probably brought home to him the incompatibility of such language with the gospel agreed earlier in Jerusalem ('that a man is justified not by works of law but through faith in Jesus Christ' – 2.16).[118] If Gentiles are 'in Christ' (v. 17) and yet still 'sinners', then we who are with them 'in Christ' are thereby found to be sinners too, and Christ has become an 'agent of sin' ($\dot{\alpha}\mu\alpha\rho\tau\dot{\iota}\alpha\varsigma$ $\delta\iota\dot{\alpha}\kappa\text{ovo}\varsigma$).[119] But that cannot be right (v. 17). I cannot live my life 'in Christ' and at the same time give the law the significance it had when I was a Pharisee (Gal. 2.14; cf. Phil. 3.5–6), for the law neither gives nor expresses life in Christ (Gal. 3.10–11, 21–2) but simply shows me up as a transgressor (2.18; 3.19; cf. Rom. 3.20; 4.15; 5.13, 20; 7.7–11).[120]

The significance of Paul's stand should not be underestimated. For the first time, probably, he had come to see that the principle of 'justification through faith' applied not simply to the acceptance of the gospel in conversion, but also to the whole of the believer's life. That is to say, he saw that justification through faith was not simply a statement of how the believer entered into God's covenanted promises (the understanding of the gospel agreed at Jerusalem); it must also regulate his life as a believer. The covenantal nomism of Judaism and of the Jewish believers (life in accordance with the law within the covenant given by grace – see above n. 9) was in fact a contradiction of that agreed understanding of justification through faith.[121] To live life 'in Christ' *and* 'in accordance with the law' was not possible; it involved a basic contradiction in terms and in the understanding of what made someone acceptable to God. Thus Paul began to see, as probably he had never seen before, that the principle of justification through faith meant a redefining of the relation between the believer and Israel – *not* an abandoning of that link (a flight into an individualism untouched by Jewish claims of a monopoly in the election and covenant grace of God), but a redefining of it – a redefining of how the inheritance of Abraham could embrace Gentiles apart from the law.[122] To begin with the Spirit and through faith rules out not just justification by works of law, but life lived by law (covenantal nomism) also – the very argument which he develops in the rest of Galatians.[123]

§5 CONCLUSIONS AND COROLLARIES

If this exegesis is on the right lines, it sheds light on some of the other major issues relating to Galatians 2, and the incident itself has to be seen as an important watershed in Paul's personal development and in the development of Christian self-understanding and of the missionary endeavour of the new movement. At this stage all I can do is outline these corollaries briefly.

§5.1 We do not receive much help in resolving the problem of how to relate Acts 15 to Paul's autobiographical account in Galatians 1—2. Our understanding of the Antioch incident does, however, clarify what remains the single most difficult feature in Acts 15 when compared to Galatians 2: in Acts 15 the Jerusalem council pronounces explicitly *both* on the issue of circumcision as though the issue had hitherto been unresolved, *and* on the minimal requirements necessary before table-fellowship can take place (15.20, 29); whereas Paul's account in Galatians 2 shows that the circumcision issue had *already* been resolved *before* the issue of table-fellowship became the subject of controversy. If Galatians 2 preceded Acts 15, the fact that circumcision seems still to have been an issue at the council remains a puzzle.[124] And if Galatians 2.1–10 is Paul's account of the Jerusalem council (= Acts 15), the ruling of Acts 15.20, 29 that Gentiles should have nothing more

159

than the Noahic requirements laid upon them renders the Antioch incident scarcely credible (particularly in the light of Gal. 2.6d).

The most plausible solution to this dilemma is that the 'Jerusalem council' settled only the circumcision issue, and that the so-called 'apostolic decree' stipulating the limits of table-fellowship reflects a later agreement, an accommodation between Jewish and Gentile believers once the Gentile mission had become well established. The date when the 'decree' was first formulated remains uncertain. Observance of the Noahic laws had probably been the practice in Antioch before the incident, as we have seen. And certainly such observance had Paul's approval subsequently in the mixed churches of the Gentile mission (1 Cor. 8.7–13; Rom. 14.13—15.3). At some stage it became the rule also within the sphere of Jerusalem's continuing influence (Antioch, Syria and Cilicia), possibly not till the late 50s (cf. Acts 21.25), but quite probably even earlier as part of Jerusalem's response to the success of the Gentile mission.[125] Since Luke recounts only one major discussion on such issues (the Jerusalem council), and since the practice behind the 'decree' was so long established in the Gentile mission (more or less from the start), Luke presumably felt at liberty to trace the agreement formally back to that crucial debate about the Gentile mission.

§5.2 Our findings strengthen the probability that Paul's rebuke of Peter at Antioch was unsuccessful. The most frequently adduced consideration here is that Paul would have mentioned it if Peter had given way (as he was careful to do in relating the earlier encounter in Jerusalem – Gal. 2.1–10). And this is almost sufficient in itself to make the case.[126] But in addition we can now note the fuller light we have been able to shed on the reasons which probably weighed with Peter in his original decision to withdraw from the table-fellowship in Antioch. The more understandable and reasonable his decision to withdraw, the less likely was he to go back on it. Despite the fierceness of Paul's attack ('acted insincerely', etc.), Peter is unlikely to have agreed that their common belief in justification through faith (Gal. 2.16) was endangered. To observe the law as a principle regulating conduct did not undermine justification through faith. Covenantal nomism was not at odds with the election of grace. Consequently Jewish believers could still remain true to their heritage, and it was not unfair to ask Gentile believers to respect that degree of discipline in their social intercourse, particularly since 'judaizing' was nothing strange to God-fearers in Antioch.[127]

§5.3 It follows also that the Antioch incident had a decisive effect in shaping Paul's future. Hitherto an apostle/missionary of Antioch, he could no longer act as the Antioch church's delegate –

160

the consequence, a breach with the church at Antioch. Hitherto a partner of Barnabas, he could no longer work easily with one whose lifestyle was at such odds with his own – the consequence, a breach with Barnabas (cf. Acts 15.39–40). In short, as a result of the Antioch incident, Paul became an independent missionary. Confirmation of this comes from Acts itself. Only on his first outreach are he and Barnabas called 'apostles' (Acts 14.4, 14) – that is, apostles of Antioch. And whereas Paul's first recorded missionary endeavour can properly be designated a 'missionary journey' (starting from and returning to Antioch), his subsequent work can hardly be classified as 'second and third missionary journeys', since he clearly settles for lengthy periods, first at Corinth and then at Ephesus as his base of operations (Acts 18.11; 19.8–10). The Antioch incident therefore had incalculable consequences on the development of the Gentile mission, as a mission which was to a decisive degree independent of Jewish Christianity, and which from the outset was challenging and beginning to break away from the self-understanding of Jewish Christianity.[128]

§5.4 In particular, a plausible occasion for the writing of Galatians becomes increasingly attractive. If the Galatians in question are the churches of south Galatia,[129] then we are talking about churches established by Paul and Barnabas while they were still missionaries of the church at Antioch. That is to say, we are talking of Antioch's daughter churches. In which case the decision of the church at Antioch to fall in line with the ruling or wishes of the men from James would be thought by many to apply by extension to these daughter churches. Not unnaturally, then, shortly after Paul's own disgruntled departure from Antioch, a delegation probably set out from Jerusalem or from Antioch itself to visit these churches, including the churches of Galatia. Whether the more conservative members of the delegation gained control or had the control from the beginning is not clear. Either way, the demands evidently made by the delegation seem to have capitalized on the victory won at Antioch and to have pressed home the usual question of the Jewish missionary to the God-fearing Gentile: If you have come so far, why not go the whole way and become a proselyte (cf. *Antiquities* 20.2.4 §§43–5; Juvenal, *Satires* 14.96–9)?[130] By this time Paul would probably already have crossed into Europe, and the news may not have reached him till he had established himself at Corinth. But when it did, his anger exploded. Precisely what he had feared would happen had happened: the failure to see the incompatibility of justification through faith and covenantal nomism was now threatening the heart of the gospel; as he had tried to point out to Peter at the time of the incident itself . . .[131]

161

§5.5 A further element in Paul's concern would be that he saw his sphere of operations being threatened and eroded. The agreement that he should go to the uncircumcised and Peter to the circumcised (Gal. 2.9) was being put in jeopardy. Hence the violence of his response (Gal.). Hence too the violence of his later response in 2 Corinthians 10—13 and Philippians 3.2, when he saw unscrupulous apostles encroaching even more deeply on his area of responsibility (2 Cor. 10.13–16). And though he lost at Antioch (lost both influence and backing), he probably managed to hold the line elsewhere. In particular, the fact that the churches of Galatia took part in the collection (1 Cor. 16.1; cf. Acts 20.4) presumably means that the Galatian churches remained faithful to Paul – thus explaining why it was that Paul's letter to the Galatians was preserved for posterity.

We may perhaps speculate further that it was this victory of Paul in Galatia and the tremendous growth of Diaspora churches modelled on Pauline lines which showed James that a more moderate policy on table-fellowship in the mixed communities of the Diaspora was being called for by the Spirit (Acts 15.13–21, 23–9), and which in turn made possible the renewal of a more harmonious relationship between Paul and Barnabas (1 Cor. 9.5–6; cf. Col. 4.10–11). In other words, though Paul lost the debate at Antioch his subsequent success as missionary to the Gentiles ensured the victory of his views in the longer term.

§5.6 Finally, we might simply note that this exegesis of the Antioch incident helps to explain the problem posed for our understanding of Paul's theology by Sanders' exposition of Judaism's 'covenantal nomism' (above n. 9). Was not Judaism firmly rooted in God's electing and forgiving grace, so that justification through faith was a phrase which could describe the basis for Judaism as well as for the particular expression of faith in the Messiah Jesus? What was this Judaism that Paul was so polemical against? Why was he so polemical? The Antioch incident is probably the key to the solution. The Antioch incident convinced Paul that justification through faith and covenantal nomism were not two complementary emphases, but were in direct antithesis to each other. Justification through faith must determine the *whole* of life and not only the starting-point of discovering (or being discovered) by God's grace. Consequently, it is precisely in Galatians that we find the strongest assertion that righteousness is a hope still to be realized (Gal. 5.5).[132]

In short, the Antioch incident was probably one of the most significant events in the development of earliest Christianity. It shaped the future of Paul's missionary work, it sparked off a crucial insight which became one of the central emphases in Paul's subsequent teaching, and consequently it determined the whole character and future of that young movement which we now call Christianity.

Notes

1. See further J. B. Lightfoot, *Galatians* (London/New York: Macmillan, 1865; 10th ed. 1890) 128–32; F. Overbeck, *Über die Auffassung des Streits des Paulus mit Petrus in Antiochien (Gal. 2.11ff.) bei den Kirchenvatern* (1877; reprinted Darmstadt: Wissenschaftliche Buchgesellschaft, 1968); F. Mussner, *Galaterbrief* (Freiburg/Basel/Wien: Herder; 1974, 3rd ed. 1977) 146–54.
2. See, e.g., commentaries by Luther and Calvin.
3. These issues were first raised in their present sharp form by the work of F. C. Baur, *Paul: his Life and Works* (1845; ET 2 vols; London/Edinburgh: Williams & Norgate, 1873) 1.133–6; also *Church History* (1853; ET 2 vols; London/Edinburgh: Williams & Norgate, 1878) 1.54–5.
4. See, e.g., the history of discussion reviewed by W. W. Gasque, *A History of the Criticism of the Acts of the Apostles* (Tubingen: J. C. B. Mohr/Grand Rapids: Eerdmans, 1975), Index 'Gal. 2' and 'Gal. 2.1–10'. The most recent attempt to reconstruct a Pauline chronology solely on the basis of the Pauline correspondence, with consequent considerable manipulation of the Acts data, is that of G. Lüdemann, *Paulus, der Heidenapostel. Band I: Studien zur Chronologie* (Göttingen: Vandenhoeck & Ruprecht, 1980), who also argues unnecessarily and implausibly that the Antioch incident preceded the second Jerusalem visit of Gal. 2.1–10 (pp. 77–9, 101–5; for earlier bibliography see J. Eckert, *Die urchristliche Verkündigung im Streit zwischen Paulus und seinen Gegnern nach dem Galaterbrief* [Regensburg: Friedrich Pustet, 1971] p. 193 n. 3). But see already J. Dupont, 'Pierre et Paul à Antioche et à Jerusalem', *RSR* 45 (1957) 42–60, 225–39; reprinted *Etudes sur les Actes des Apôtres* (Paris: Editions du Cerf, 1967) 185–215. See also n. 6 below.
5. See, e.g., E. D. Burton, *Galatians* (ICC; Edinburgh: T. & T. Clark, 1921) 104; P. Bonnard, *Galates* (CNT; Neuchatel/Paris: Delachaux & Niestle, 1953) 51; A. Oepke, *Galater* (THNT; 2nd ed.; Berlin: Evangelische, 1957) 56; F. V. Filson, *A New Testament History* (London: SCM, 1965) 224–5; F. F. Bruce, *Paul: Apostle of the Free Spirit* (Exeter: Paternoster, 1977) 176; H. D. Betz, *Galatians* (Hermeneia; Philadelphia: Fortress, 1979) p. 107 and n. 448.
6. The Jerusalem council has been dated as early as AD 43 (e.g. F. Hahn, *Mission in the New Testament* [1963; ET London: SCM, 1965] 91), and as late as AD 51 (e.g. J. Knox, *Chapters in a Life of Paul* [1950; New York: Abingdon-Cokesbury/London A. & C. Black, 1954] ch. V), but the majority prefer 48 or 49 as most probable in view of other chronological data available to us (see the brief summary in R. Jewett, *Dating Paul's Life* [Philadelphia: Fortress/ London: SCM, 1979] 1–2). For the various alternative correlations of Gal. 2 with the Jerusalem visits recorded in Acts (Acts 11.30; 15; 18.22) see also Jewett, ch. IV, and further below n. 96 and §5.1. The Antioch incident is usually thought to have taken place a few months after the second Jerusalem visit. A. Suhl however argues for an interval of four years between the two, the first missionary journey intervening (*Paulus und seine Briefe* [Gütersloh: Gütersloher, 1975] 70, 322–3, 340; cf. Hahn, *Mission* 82; E. Haenchen, *Acts* [KEK; 14th ed., 1965; ET Oxford: Blackwell, 1971] 439; A. J. M. Wedderburn, 'Some Recent Pauline Chronologies', *ExpT* 92 [1980–81] 103–8), and B. Reicke for an interval of five years, the 'second missionary journey' intervening ('Der geschichtliche Hintergrund des Apostelkonzils und der Antiochia-Episode, Gal. 2.1–14', *Studia Paulina in honorem J. de Zwaan* [Haarlem: De

Erven F. Bohn N.V., 1953] 175–6, 183; also *The New Testament Era* [1964; ET Philadelphia: Fortress, 1968; London: A. & C. Black, 1969] 214). But since Paul takes such care to itemize the intervals between his contacts with the Jerusalem leadership he would hardly have passed over such an interval with a mere ὅτε δέ (Gal. 2.11); contrast the use of the same linking phrase in Gal. 1.15, 2.12 and 4.4.

7. K. Stendahl, 'The Apostle Paul and the Introspective Conscience of the West', *HTR* 56 (1963) 199–215.

8. K. Stendahl, *Paul Among Jews and Gentiles and Other Essays* (Philadelphia: Fortress/London: SCM, 1976), including a reprint of his earlier essay (n. 7 above): 'The doctrine of justification by faith was hammered out by Paul for the very specific and limited purpose of defending the rights of Gentile converts to be full and genuine heirs to the promises of God to Israel.'

9. E. P. Sanders, *Paul and Palestinian Judaism: A Comparison of Patterns of Religion* (London: SCM, 1977). Sanders defines 'covenantal nomism' as 'the view that one's place in God's plan is established on the basis of the covenant and that the covenant requires as the proper response of man his obedience to its commandments, while providing means of atonement for transgression' (p. 75). 'The overall pattern of Rabbinic religion as it applied to Israelites ... is this: God has chosen Israel and Israel has accepted the election ... As long as he (the Israelite) maintains his desire to stay in the covenant, he has a share in God's covenantal promises, including life in the world to come. The intention and effort to be obedient constitutes the *condition for remaining in the covenant*, but they do not *earn* it' (p. 180).

10. See further my *Unity and Diversity in the New Testament* (London: SCM/Philadelphia: Westminster, 1977) §54.1; L. H. Schiffman, 'At the Crossroads: Tannaitic Perspectives on the Jewish-Christian Schism', *Jewish and Christian Self-Definition*, Vol. II, *Aspects of Judaism in the Graeco-Roman Period* (ed. E. P. Sanders; London: SCM Press, 1981) 115–56.

11. The debate continues after Galatians in the same terms, particularly in Romans; see, e.g., J. Munck, *Christ and Israel: An Interpretation of Romans 9–11* (1956; ET Philadelphia: Fortress, 1967); W. D. Davies, 'Paul and the People of Israel', *NTS* 24 (1977–8) 4–39; J. D. G. Dunn, *Romans* (WBC 38; Word, 1988).

12. The fact that the new movement was first given a distinctive name in Antioch ('Christians' – Acts 11.26) need not imply a distinction between the new movement and the synagogue, but only a distinction *within* Judaism (like Josephus' three sects – *Jewish War* 2.8.2 §119 etc.). The absence of any mention of hostility from synagogue authorities in Antioch against the 'Christians' in any of our sources may well be significant here (see further below).

13. Note, e.g., how Paul takes up and adapts the Jewish theme of the heavenly Jerusalem (Gal. 4.25–6), as also Heb. 12.22 and Rev. 3.12; 21.2, 10. Apocalyptic and rabbinic references in Str-B 3.573, 796.

14. Stephen's views as represented in Acts 7 should not be understood as calling for an abandoning of Judaism. On the contrary they can be readily understood as a recall to a more primitive and purified form of Judaism (see particularly M. Simon, *St. Stephen and the Hellenists in the Primitive Church* [London/New York/Toronto: Longmans Green, 1958]). Paul of course presses still further back behind Moses the lawgiver to Abraham the man of faith.

15. B. Holmberg, *Paul and Power: the Structure of Authority in the Primitive Church as Reflected in the Pauline Epistles* (ConBNT 11; Lund: C. W. K. Gleerup, 1978) 15.

16. For what follows see more fully J. D. G. Dunn, 'The Relationship between Paul and Jerusalem according to Gal. 1 and 2', *NTS* 28 (1982) 461–78 = ch. 5 above.

17. G. D. Kilpatrick, 'Galatians 1.18 ΙΣΤΟΡΗΣΑΙ ΚΗΦΑΝ', *New Testament Essays: Studies in Memory of T. W. Manson* (ed. A. J. B. Higgins; Manchester: Manchester University, 1959) 144–9. But see the more careful statement in the reply to Hofius, above p. 127.

18. The point is not that Paul's gospel might be judged invalid, but that its effect among Gentiles might be nullified (see further my 'Gal. 1 and 2', ch. 5 above).

19. See particularly C. K. Barrett, 'Paul and the "pillar" Apostles', *Studia Paulina in honorem J. de Zwaan* (Haarlem: De Erven F. Bohn N.V., 1953) 1–4, 17–18; Betz, *Galatians* 86–7, 92.

20. cf. D. M. Hay, 'Paul's Indifference to Authority', *JBL* 88 (1969) 37–8; Betz, *Galatians* 94–5.

21. cf. Burton, *Galatians* 89–91; Oepke, *Galater* 48–9.

22. cf. Bruce, *Paul* 154, and the fuller discussion in Betz, *Galatians* 96–103.

23. See Holmberg, *Paul* 18 and those cited by him in n. 37; also M. Hengel, 'Die Ursprünge der christlichen Mission', *NTS* 18 (1971–2) 18; Betz, *Galatians* 84.

24. Philo, *Embassy to Gaius* 184–338; Josephus, *Jewish War* 2.10.1–5 §§184–203; *Antiquities* 18.8.2–9 §§261–309; Tacitus, *Histories* 5.9.

25. 'It might be thought, from the record of the Roman procurators . . . that they all, as if by secret arrangement, systematically and deliberately set out to drive the people to revolt. Even the best of them . . . had no idea that a nation like the Jews required above all consideration for their religious customs . . .' (E. Schürer, *History of the Jewish People* [revised ed. G. Vermes and F. Millar; Edinburgh: T. & T. Clark; Vol. 1, 1973] 455).

26. The cause of Judas' rebellion had been the census ordered by Quirinius in AD 6 (*Antiquities* 18.1.1 §§4–6).

27. See the discussion in M. Hengel, *Die Zeloten* (Leiden/Köln: E. J. Brill, 1961) 42–7.

28. It may not be without significance that Paul describes himself as ζηλωτής (Acts 22.3; Gal. 1.14) when speaking of his persecution of the followers of Jesus (Reicke, 'Hintergrund' 178). See further documentation in my *Romans* 586–7.

29. cf. the essays of Bornkamm and Barth in G. Bornkamm, G. Barth and H. J. Held, *Tradition and Interpretation in Matthew* (1960; ET London: SCM, 1963); Hahn, *Mission* 54–9, 63–8, 120–8; D. Hill, *Matthew* (NCB; London: Oliphants, 1972) 66–72; B. J. Hubbard, *The Matthean Redaction of a Primitive Apostolic Commissioning: an Exegesis of Matthew 28.16–20* (SBLDS 19; Missoula: Scholars, 1974); R. A. Guelich, *The Sermon on the Mount: a Foundation for Understanding* (Waco: Word Commentary, 1982) 161–74.

30. Philo describes it as an 'attack against our laws by seizing the meeting houses (synagogues) . . . (and) the destruction of our citizenship . . .' (*Flaccus* 53).

31. However there is much dispute as to whether there were in fact two separate incidents in AD 41 and 49 (see below n. 78).

32. Acts 6.13 – 'This man never ceases to speak words against this holy place and the law . . . will change the customs which Moses delivered to us'; Acts 21.28 – 'This is the man who is teaching men everywhere *against the people* and the law and this place.'

33. cf. C. H. Kraeling, 'The Jewish Community at Antioch', *JBL* 51 (1932) 148–50. See further W. A. Meeks and R. H. Wilken, *Jews and Christians in Antioch in the First Four Centuries of the Common Era* (SBLSBS; Missoula: Scholars, 1978) 4.

34. Kraeling reckoned a Jewish population of at least 45,000 Jews out of a total population of roughly 300,000 in Antioch in the days of Augustine ('Antioch' 136); but see also Meeks and Wilken, *Antioch* 8.

35. E. M. Smallwood, *The Jews Under Roman Rule* (Leiden: E. J. Brill, 1976) 362. Other details in Meeks and Wilken, *Antioch* 4–5, who also refer (p. 18) to the suggestion of W. Farmer, 'Jesus and the Gospels', *Perkins Journal* 28/2 (1975)

31–6, that the decisive break between Jews and Christians in Antioch came in the aftermath of the Jewish revolt (AD 66–70).

36. So particularly Reicke, 'Hintergrund' 172–87; R. Jewett, 'The Agitators and the Galatian Congregation', *NTS* 17 (1970–1) 204–6 – 'My hypothesis therefore is that Jewish Christians in Judea were stimulated by Zealotic pressure into a nomistic campaign among their fellow Christians in the late forties and early fifties' (p. 205); F. F. Bruce, *Galatians* (NIGTC; Exeter: Paternoster, 1982) 130–1.

37. J. Jeremias, *New Testament Theology. Vol. 1: The Proclamation of Jesus* (1971; ET London: SCM, 1971) 115.

38. I. Abrahams records the report that at the feast held on the circumcision of Elisha b. Abuyah (c. 65 AD), while the other guests were partaking of meat and wine, Eleazar b. Hyrkanos and Joshua b. Hananiah sat 'stringing together' the words of the scriptures like pearls on a cord (*Studies in Pharisaism and the Gospels* [First Series 1917; reproduced New York: Ktav, 1967] 56).

39. cf. Josephus' characterization of the situation following Alexander's death: 'Whenever anyone was accused by the people of Jerusalem of eating unclean food or violating the Sabbath or committing any other such sin, he would flee to the Shechemites . . .' (*Antiquities* 11.8.7 §346).

40. Josephus, *Antiquities* 13.8.2 §243; cf. Diodorus, *Bibliotheca Historica* 34–35.1.4. See also 1 Macc. 1.47; 2 Macc. 6.18–23.

41. See also Petronius, *Fragments* 37; Seneca, *Letters* 108.22; Epictetus in Arrian, *Dissertations* 1.22.4; Tacitus, *Histories* 5.4; Juvenal, *Satires* 14.98; Sextus Empiricus 3.223.

42. For Jewish abhorrence of idolatry see Schürer, *History* (revised ed. Vol. 2; Edinburgh: T. & T. Clark, 1979) 81–3. See further G. F. Moore, *Judaism* (Vol. 1; Cambridge: Harvard, 1927) 325; Str-B 3.54–5; 4.366–72. The *halakah* forbidding meat from pagan temples is attributed to Akiba (*m. Aboda Zara* 2.3); see also *b. Aboda Zara* 8a–b.

43. See J. Neusner, *The Rabbinic Traditions about the Pharisees before 70* (3 vols; Leiden: E. J. Brill, 1971) 2.242. For rabbinic Judaism's further rulings on the command against the eating of blood see Str-B 2.734–9.

44. Neusner, *Rabbinic Traditions* 3.297 (the rulings itemized on pp. 291–4); also *From Politics to Piety: the Emergence of Pharisaic Judaism* (Englewood Cliffs: Prentice-Hall, 1973) 86. For the broader background see Neusner, *The Idea of Purity in Ancient Judaism* (Leiden: E. J. Brill, 1973) particularly ch. 2; 'nearly 25% of Mishnaic law in quantity concerns purity' (p. 8).

45. Neusner, *Politics to Piety* 83; also 'The Fellowship (חבורה) in the Second Jewish Commonwealth', *HTR* 53 (1960) 125–42; R. Meyer, θαρισαῖος, *TDNT* 9 (1974) 15, 18; though G. Alon argues that one of the disputes among the Pharisees was over the question of how far the laws of purity extended – to the sphere of the temple and priests or to the whole of Israel ('The Bounds of the Laws of Levitical Cleanness', *Jews, Judaism and the Classical World* [Jerusalem: Magnes, 1977] 190–234).

46. J. Neusner, 'First Cleanse the Inside', *NTS* 22 (1975–6) 486–95, sees in Matt. 23.25–6 evidence of a stage in Pharisaic thinking at which the purity of the inside of a vessel was not determinative for cleanness ('the Shammaite rule'). But see H. Maccoby, 'The Washing of Cups', *JSNT* 14 (1982) 3–15, who however ignores the implication of the saying that the practice of cleansing cups and plates has particular reference to the Pharisees (Matt. 23.16–26 – '. . . you say . . . you tithe . . . you cleanse . . .').

47. See Schürer, *History* 2.475–8; A. Oppenheimer, *The Am Ha-aretz: a Study in the Social History of the Jewish People in the Hellenistic-Roman Period* (Leiden: E. J. Brill, 1977) 121–4; S. Safrai and M. Stern, eds, *The Jewish People in the First Century* (2 vols; Assen/Amsterdam: Van Gorcum, 1974, 1976) 2.802, 829–31; J. Bowker, *Jesus and the Pharisees* (London: Cambridge University,

1973) 70–1; J. Parkes, *The Foundations of Judaism and Christianity* (Vallentine Mitchell, 1960) 134, 141–3. See further Str-B 1.695–704; and the analysis of *Yadayim* in J. Neusner, *A History of the Mishnaic Law of Purities* XIX (Leiden: E. J. Brill, 1977). For a fuller and more careful discussion of 'Pharisees' at the time of Jesus and Paul, see ch. 3 above.

48. 'Tithing was a dietary law' (Neusner, *Politics to Piety* 80, 83).
49. See particularly Oppenheimer, *Am Ha-aretz* 69–79. See further Safrai and Stern, *Jewish People* 818–25. Examples of rabbinic references have been cited by Bowker, *Jesus and Pharisees* index 'tithe'.
50. See also the discussion in Alon, *Jews* 205–11 (and below n. 55), and again in the fuller treatment in ch. 3 above.
51. Parkes, *Foundations* 141–2.
52. See further Oppenheimer, *Am Ha-aretz* 49–51.
53. Safrai, *Jewish People* 828, and Alon, *Jews* 233–4, both referring to A. Geiger, *Urschrift und Übersetzungen der Bibel* (Frankfurt-am-Main: 1928) 223; Schürer, *History* 2.409–10.
54. See further Schürer, *History* 2.569, 582, and J. Riches, *Jesus and the Transformation of Judaism* (London: DLT, 1980) 117–28, with further bibliography in their notes; now also M. Newton, 'The Concept of Purity at Qumran and in the Letters of Paul' (SNTSMS; Cambridge University, 1985), ch. 2. Cf. the sabbath *halakoth* at Qumran (L. H. Schiffmann, *The Halakhah at Qumran* [Leiden: E. J. Brill, 1975]; P. Sigal, *The Emergence of Contemporary Judaism*. Vol. 1, *The Foundations of Judaism: Part 1, From the Origins to the Separation of Christianity* [PTMS 29; Pittsburgh: Pickwick, 1980] 297–302), whose comparative severity confirms the Synoptics' picture of the extent to which the Torah was already being elaborated in the pre-AD 70 period. See also Hengel, *Zeloten* ch. 4, and ch. 1 above.
55. Neusner, *Rabbinic Traditions* 2.
56. See Neusner, *Rabbinic Traditions* 1.63–4; Oppenheimer, *Am Ha-aretz* p. 60 n. 119. I follow Oppenheimer's translation. Those mentioned came from the period before the destruction of the second temple. Midras-impurity = 'impurity contracted by an object on which one with a discharge (see Lev. 12.2; 15.2, 25) sits, treads, lies or leans . . . The impurity is conveyed to anyone who carries, or is carried on, the object' (Oppenheimer 60).
57. See further Oppenheimer, *Am Ha-aretz* 61–2; S. Freyne, *Galilee from Alexander the Great to Hadrian 323 BCE to 135 CE* (Wilmington: Glazier/Notre Dame: University of Notre Dame, 1980) 306–7, and ch. 3 above.
58. See further ch. 2 above.
59. Alon, *Jews* 170–4; Schürer, *History* 2.81–4. See also n. 68 below.
60. Similar rabbinic material is collected by Neusner, *History* IV (Leiden: E. J. Brill, 1974) 340–5.
61. Cited by Danby, *The Mishnah* (London: Oxford University, 1933) Appendix IV. Other references in Str-B 1.449–50; Alon, *Jews* 149–59.
62. Alon, *Jews* 165–7. See the whole chapter, 'The Levitical Uncleanness of Gentiles', *Jews* 146–89; against A. Büchler, 'The Levitical Impurity of the Gentiles in Palestine before the year 70', *JQR* 17 (1927) 1–81.
63. See further Str-B 4.374–8.
64. Str-B 2.715–23; R. Meyer, πάροικος, *TDNT* 5 (1967) 850; E. Lerle, *Proselytenwerbung und Christentum* (Berlin: 1960) 24–39. On the inappropriateness of the title 'half-proselyte' see Moore, *Judaism* 1.326–7, 339; K. G. Kuhn, προσήλυτος, *TDNT* 6 (1968) 731 n. 31. See also below n. 74.
65. See K. Lake, *The Beginnings of Christianity. Part I: The Acts of the Apostles* (Vol. V; London: Macmillan, 1933) 82–4; Kuhn, *TDNT* 6.736–7.
66. See B. J. Bamberger, *Proselytism in the Talmudic Period* (1939; New York: Ktav, 1968) 15–16, 267ff.; Stern in Safrai and Stern, *Jewish People* 622–3.

Here again I would wish to make a more careful statement of the point; see my *Romans* xlvii–xlviii.

67. Josephus, *Antiquities* 20.2.4 §39 describes the would-be proselyte Izates as 'a Jew'. See further Kuhn, *TDNT* 6.732–3; Schiffman, 'Tannaitic Perspectives' (above n. 10) 124–5.

68. Other references in Moore, *Judaism* 1.341 and notes; Kuhn, *TDNT* 6.737; *EncJud* 13.1185.

69. See further Moore, *Judaism* 1.329–35, 342–5; Bamberger, *Proselytism*; J. Jeremias, *Jerusalem in the Time of Jesus* (3rd ed., 1962; ET London: SCM, 1969) 320–34; Kuhn, *TDNT* 6.736–40, who deduces from CD 14.3–6 and 1QS 2.19–23; 6.8–9 that *gērim* existed in branch establishments of the Essene order, but not at Qumran itself (p. 735).

70. See particularly Alon, *Jews* 172–4. The modern debate has concentrated on the origin of proselyte baptism. Most now agree that proselyte baptism had already become an accepted practice by the middle of the first century AD. In addition to Alon see, e.g., Str-B 1.102–8; H. H. Rowley, 'Jewish Proselyte Baptism and the Baptism of John', *HUCA* 15 (1940) 313–34; J. Jeremias, *Infant Baptism in the First Four Centuries* (1958; ET London: SCM, 1960) 24–9; Schiffman, 'Tannaitic Perspectives' 127–36; against Lerle, *Proselytenwerbung* 52–60; S. Zeitlin, 'Proselytes and Proselytism during the Second Commonwealth and the Early Tannaitic Period' (1965), *Studies in the Early History of Judaism* II (New York: Ktav, 1974) 413; Bamberger (1968) XXI–XXII.

71. See also Moore, *Judaism* 1.325 and n. 1.

72. See further Moore, *Judaism* 1.339; Str-B 2.729–39; 3.37–8; Kuhn, *TDNT* 6.740–1.

73. cf. Str-B 2.722–3.

74. See particularly Lake, *Beginnings* 5.84–8; F. Siegert, 'Gottesfürchtige und Sympathisanten', *JSJ* 4 (1973) 109–64; N. J. McEleney, 'Conversion, Circumcision and the Law', *NTS* 20 (1973–4) 325–8; Smallwood, *Jews* 206 n. 15; M. Wilcox, 'The "God-fearers" in Acts – A Reconsideration', *JSNT* 13 (1981) 102–22; though see also M. Stern, *Greek and Latin Authors on Jews and Judaism* Vol. II (Jerusalem: Israel Academy of Sciences and Humanities, 1980) 103–6. On the significance of Josephus' description of Poppaea, wife of Nero, as θεοσεβής see Siegert 151–61, particularly 160–1; Smallwood 278 n. 79 and 281 n. 84. Rabbinic references in Str-B 2.719–20; H. Balz, θοβέω, *TDNT* 9 (1974) 207. See also my *Romans* xlvii–xlviii.

75. On the much-quoted *Antiquities* 14.7.2 §110 see however Lake, *Beginnings* 5.85.

76. cf. one of the occasional rabbinic sayings which recognize that non-Jews can be righteous and acceptable to God, attributed again to R. Meier – 'A goy who keeps the Torah is of much greater value in God's sight than even the high-priest himself' (*Sipra Lev.* 18.5 – cited by Kuhn, *TDNT* 6.741) – though we have already noted how liberal R. Meir was in his definition of a *gēr tōšāb*.

77. For more detail see Smallwood, *Jews* 201–10.

78. On the relations of Dio's note to Suetonius' report of Claudius' expulsion of the Jews in 49 (*Claudius* 25.4) see Smallwood, *Jews* 210–16, and cf. Stern, *Greek and Latin Authors II* 114–16. See also my *Romans* xlviii–xlix.

79. Dio refers particularly to Flavius Clemens, cousin of Domitian and consul, and father of the nominated heirs to the throne; see the discussion in Smallwood, *Jews* 376–83; Stern, *Greek and Latin Authors II*, 380–4; on *Deut. Rabbah* 2.24 see also Siegert, 'Gottesfürchtige' 110–11.

80. τὰ πάτρια (ἔθη) (or τὰ πατρῷα ἔδη) is regularly used of hereditary customs stretching beyond those written down or codified, and sometimes of the unwritten tradition in distinction from the written – as in Philo, *Drunkenness* 193; *Dreams* 2.78; *Life of Moses* 1.31; *Rewards and Punishments* 106; *Flaccus*

52; cf. 3 Macc. 1.3; Gal. 1.14. Note particularly Philo, *Special Laws* 4.150 – 'Children ought to inherit from their parents ... ancestral customs (ἔθη πάτρια) which they were reared in and have lived with even from the cradle, and not despise them because they have been handed down without written record. Praise cannot be given to one who obeys the written laws ... But he who faithfully observes the unwritten deserves commendation ...' Josephus, *Antiquities* 13.16.2 §408 speaks of the 'regulations introduced by the Pharisees in accordance with the tradition of their fathers' (κατὰ τὴν πατρῴαν παράδοσιν). See further LSJ, πάτριος.

81. Note also his earlier description of the people of Damascus 'whose wives with a few exceptions had become captivated (ὑπηγμένας) by the Jewish religion' (*Jewish War* 2.20.2 §560).

82. We may recall also that the proselyte, Nicolaus, one of the seven in Acts 6.5, came from Antioch.

83. In the violence which marked relations between Jews and non-Jews in Syria in AD 66, Antioch was one of only three cities which spared their Jewish inhabitants (*Jewish War* 2.18.5 §479).

84. The verse probably reflects the attitude of Jewish Christian churches rather than that of Jesus during his ministry in Palestine (see, e.g., A. H. McNeile, *Matthew* [London: Macmillan, 1915] 266–7; M. Goguel, *The Primitive Church* [1947; ET London: George Allen & Unwin, 1964] 39 n. 1, 526; P. Gaechter, *Matthäus* [Innsbruck/Wien/München: Tyrolia, 1963] 600–1; W. Grundmann, *Matthäus* [THNT; Berlin: Evangelische, 1968] 419).

85. There is no break in thought between v. 14 and v. 15 – see below n. 117.

86. S. Schechter, *Aspects of Rabbinic Theology* (1909; New York: Schocken, 1961) 206–7; Str-B 3.37–8; Sanders, *Paul* 210–11. See also nn. 90, 93 below.

87. Note also Origen, *Fragment* 8, on John 1.13 – οὗτοι προτίθενται τὴν σάρκα περιτεμνόμενοι καὶ ἐν τῷ προφανεῖ ἰουδαΐζειν θέλουτες.

88. See LSJ, μείγνυμι B.

89. 'What Paul brands "judaizing" – circumcision and dietary laws for Gentiles – was not a barrier to Christianity but quite attractive to Gentiles, who were enamoured of what was Oriental' (Stendahl, *Paul* 70) – true of dietary laws; not so of circumcision. On the question of whether circumcision was always required of the would-be proselyte see also McEleney, 'Conversion' 328–33; and n. 109 below.

90. cf. Str-B 3.36, 41–3, 126–8; K. H. Rengstorf, ἁμαρτωλός, *TDNT* 1 (1964) 324– 6; H. Schlier, *Galater* (KEK, 1949; 4th ed.; Göttingen: Vandenhoeck & Ruprecht, 1965) 89; W. G. Kümmel, '"Individualgeschichte" und "Weltgeschichte" in Gal. 2.15–21', *Christ and Spirit in the New Testament: Studies in Honour of C. F. D. Moule* (ed. B. Lindars and S. S. Smalley; London: Cambridge University, 1973) 159–60; also n. 93 below.

91. See particularly Rengstorf, *TDNT* 1.327–8; Jeremias, *Jerusalem* 303–12; cf. H. Braun, *Spätjüdisch-häretischer und frühchristlicher Radikalismus* (BHT 24; 2 vols; Tübingen: J. C. B. Mohr, 1957; 2nd ed. 1969) 2.38 n. 1.

92. Rengstorf, *TDNT* 1.322–3. See further the more careful treatment in ch. 3 above.

93. cf. Betz, *Galatians* 115; and above n. 90.

94. It is not necessary to argue that the Lord's Supper was specifically in Paul's mind at this point (see particularly H. Lietzmann, *Galater* [HNT; Tübingen: J. C. B. Mohr; 3rd ed. 1932] 14, and Schlier, *Galater* 83–4), in view of the importance we have now seen was attached to *all* table-fellowship (cf. Acts 11.3). In any case the bread and the wine had probably not yet been distinguished from the meal itself at this stage (see my *Unity and Diversity* §40). Commentators usually note that the imperfect συνήσθιεν (Gal. 2.12) implies a regular rather than occasional pattern of table-fellowship.

95. D. R. Catchpole, 'Paul, James and the Apostolic Decree', *NTS* 23 (1976–77)

428–44. Cf. earlier A. C. McGiffert, *A History of Christianity in the Apostolic Age* (Edinburgh: T. & T. Clark, 1897) 211–17, who notes that Ritschl suggested that the decree stemmed from the church of Jerusalem at a time other than that designated by Acts, in the first edition of his *Entstehung der altkatholischen Kirche*, but that he abandoned the view in the second edition of *Entstehung* (p. 213 and n. 4); D. W. B. Robinson, 'The Circumcision of Titus and Paul's "Liberty"', *ABR* 12 (1964) 40–1.

96. So, e.g., W. M. Ramsay, *St. Paul the Traveller and the Roman Citizen* (London: Hodder & Stoughton, 1895; 14th ed. 1920) 48–60; A. S. Geyser, 'Paul, the Apostolic Decree and the Liberals in Corinth', *Studia Paulina in honorem J. de Zwaan* (Haarlem: De Erven F. Bohn N.V., 1953) 124–38; F. F. Bruce, *New Testament History* (New York: Doubleday Anchor Book, 1972) ch. 22; Suhl, *Paulus* 46–70; other references in Jewett, *Dating* 69–75 and 144 n. 36. Others argue more plausibly that the accounts of a second and third visit to Jerusalem in Acts 11 and Acts 15 stem from different traditions of the same event – i.e. Acts 11.27–30 = Gal. 2.1–10 = Acts 15 – see, e.g., Lake, *Beginnings* 5.203–4, who follows Weizsäcker, McGiffert and Schwarz (pp. 201–2); J. Jeremias, 'Zum Quellenproblem der Apostelgeschichte' (1937), reprinted *Abba* (Göttingen: Vandenhoeck & Ruprecht, 1966) 238–55; P. Benoit, 'La deuxieme visite de Saint Paul à Jerusalem', *Bib* 40 (1959) 778–92; Catchpole, 'Apostolic Decree' 432–8.

97. Catchpole argues that the decree was something of a *volte-face* on the part of the Jerusalem leaders ('a thorough-going, not a mediating, proposal' – 'Apostolic Decree' 431, also pp. 441–3); but he does not allow for the possibility that Paul's own position vis-à-vis Jerusalem was also undergoing change in the period prior to the Antioch incident (see §2.1 above) and that the Antioch incident itself was a significant crisis in Paul's own theological development (see §§4.3, 5.3 below). See further ch. 5 above, and the Additional Note to this chapter.

98. So Suhl, *Paulus* 71; G. Howard, *Paul: Crisis in Galatia* (SNTSMS 35; Cambridge: Cambridge University, 1979) 25; Betz, *Galatians* 112; cf. Schlier, *Galater* 86.

99. cf. Mussner, *Galater* 145 n. 53: 'In das ἰουδαΐζειν ist zwar bei den antiochenischen Heidenchristen nicht die Beschneidung eingeschlossen, aber das Leben nach den jüdischen Speisegesetzen'. Note also the distinction between adopting Jewish customs and circumcision in Juvenal and Josephus (§3.3c above).

100. For the view that the Antioch incident *preceded* the second Jerusalem visit see n. 4 above.

101. cf. J. Weiss, *Earliest Christianity* (1914; ET 1937; New York: Harper Torchbook, 1959) 264 – 'Hitherto the converted Gentiles in Antioch . . . had been treated in the same way as the so-called "God-fearing" Gentiles in the Jewish communities of the Dispersion: they were admitted to the religious services without being circumcised and observed only a part of the ceremonial commands'.

102. That 'compel' here (2.14) denotes indirect pressure rather than an explicit demand is generally recognized by commentators. It is supported by the imperfect tenses of ὑπέστελλεν and ἀφώριζεν, which imply a somewhat drawn out process rather than a clean and sharp break.

103. Betz, *Galatians* 108.

104. Lake, *Beginnings* 5.209 cites *Sib. Or.* 4.24–34 (probably late first century AD) as a parallel. I disagree with Catchpole when he argues that 'it would be quite impossible to describe existence under the Decree as living ἐθνικῶς' ('Decree' 441).

105. See Neusner, *Rabbinic Traditions*, particularly 3.315, 318; also 'First Cleanse the Inside', *NTS* 22 (1975–6) 494–5; cf. W. D. Davies, *Paul and Rabbinic*

Judaism (London: SPCK, ²1955) 9; Meyer, *TDNT* 9.27–8, 31; A. Finkel, *The Pharisees and the Teacher of Nazareth* (Leiden: E. J. Brill, 1974) 134–43.

106. cf. E. Haenchen, 'Mätthaus 23', *Gott und Mensch* (Tübingen: J. C. B. Mohr, 1965) 30–1, 39–40; E. Schweizer, *Matthäus* (NTD; Göttingen: Vandenhoeck & Ruprecht, 1973) 281, 283, 285; Guelich, *Sermon on Mount* 169.

107. 'The right hand of fellowship' (2.9) did not of itself specify what kind of fellowship (cf. Betz, *Galatians* 100).

108. The 'false brothers' were evidently suspicious of the freedom claimed by Paul (2.4), but in this instance their suspicions and opposition focused only on the question of circumcision.

109. It may well be significant here that the Jerusalem leadership thought it necessary to urge only the importance of almsgiving on the mission to the uncircumcised (Gal. 2.10), since there is some evidence that 'alms for Israel' were regarded as the appropriate expression of conversion to the God of Israel for God-fearers who were not willing to be circumcised (see K. Berger, 'Almosen für Israel: zum historischen Kontext der paulinischen Kollekte', *NTS* 23 [1976–7] 180–204). In the case of such a convert a high level of judaizing could be taken for granted.

110. cf. particularly W. Bousset, 'Galater', *Die Schriften des Neuen Testaments* (4 vols; Göttingen: Vandenhoeck & Ruprecht, 1917) 2.46.

111. What significance would the Cornelius episode have had for Peter? If Cornelius was a 'judaizing' God-fearer before he met Peter, he may even have been already maintaining a fairly high level of ritual purity. In which case the clear signs of God's acceptance of him (Acts 10.10–16, 34–5, 44–6) would have counted only towards a resolution of the circumcision issue itself (cf. Acts 11.3 and Peter's response). That is to say, Cornelius would have been a precedent on Paul's side in the Jerusalem debate (Gal. 2.1–10; cf. Acts 15.7–11), but may not have provided a sufficiently close parallel to guide Peter in the incident at Antioch. In any case the agreement at Jerusalem (Gal. 2.9) could be regarded as the agreed resolution of such anomalies as Cornelius.

112. See §2.2 and n. 36 above, and n. 116 below; also F. F. Bruce, *Men and Movements in the Primitive Church* (Exeter: Paternoster, 1979) 35–6.

113. The point would gain greater force if οἱ ἐκ περιτομῆς denoted Jews rather than Jewish Christians; so G. Dix, *Jew and Greek: a Study in the Primitive Church* (London: A. & C. Black, 1953) 43–4; Reicke, 'Hintergrund' 176–83; J. Munck, *Paul and the Salvation of Mankind* (1954; ET London: SCM, 1959) 107; W. Schmithals, *Paul and James* (1963; ET London: SCM, 1965) 66–7; K. F. Nickle, *The Collection: A Study in Paul's Strategy* (London: SCM, 1966) 65; J. H. Schütz, *Paul and the Anatomy of Apostolic Authority* (SNTSMS 26; Cambridge: Cambridge University, 1975) 153–4; Suhl, *Paulus* 72. The phrase is not sufficiently explicit in itself (cf. Acts 10.45; 11.2; Rom. 4.12; Col. 4.11; Tit. 1.10) and equally permits the thesis that a faction of Jewish Christians is indicated thereby (so E. E. Ellis, 'The Circumcision Party and the Early Christian Mission' [1968], *Prophecy and Hermeneutic in Early Christianity* [WUNT 18; Tübingen: J. C. B. Mohr/Grand Rapids: Eerdmans, 1978] 116–28).

114. cf., e.g., McGiffert, *History* 206–7; Weiss, *Earliest Christianity* 265; T. W. Manson, 'The Problem of the Epistle to the Galatians' (1940), *Studies in the Gospels and Epistles* (Manchester: Manchester University, 1962) 180–1.

115. cf. Bruce, *Paul* 177; H. Köster, *Einführung in das Neuen Testament* (Berlin/New York: Walter de Gruyter, 1980) 540. See now also J. McHugh, 'Galatians 2.11–14: Was Peter Right?', *Paulus als Missionar und Theologe und das antike Judentum*, hrsg. M. Hengel (Tübingen: Mohr, 1990).

116. 'In Paul's opinion, Cephas' action must be understood in terms of political compromise . . .' (Betz, *Galatians* 109ff).

171

117. Most scholars agree that the thought runs on from v. 14 to vv. 15ff. (see, e.g., Lightfoot, *Galatians* 113–14; Bousset, *Schriften* 2.46–8; M. J. Lagrange, *Galates* [EB; Paris: Gabalda; 2nd ed. 1925] 45–6; R. Bultmann, 'Zur Auslegung von Galater 2.15–18' [1952], *Exegetica* [Tübingen: J. C. B. Mohr, 1967] 394–9; O. Bauernfeind, 'Der Schluss der antiochenischen Paulusrede' [1954], reprinted *Kommentar und Studien zur Apostelgeschichte* [Tübingen: J. C. B. Mohr, 1980] 449–63; Munck, *Paul* 125–7; and in the past twenty years, Schmithals, *Paul and James* 72–6; K. Kertelge, 'Zur Deutung des Rechtfertigungsbegriffs im Galaterbrief', *BZ* 12 [1968] 212; G. Bornkamm, *Paul* [1969; ET London: Hodder & Stoughton, 1971] 46; D. Guthrie, *Galatians* [NCB; London: Oliphants, 1969] 89; J. Bligh, *Galatians* [London: St. Paul, 1969] 235; H. Feld, '"Christus Diener der Sünde"', *TQ* 153 [1973] 119–31; Mussner, *Galater* 135; Schütz, *Paul* 150–3; W. H. Ollrog, *Paulus und seine Mitarbeiter* [WMANT 50; Neukirchen: Neukirchener, 1979] 206–8; G. Bouwman, '"Christus Diener der Sunde"'; Auslegung von Galater 2.14b–18', *Bijdragen* 40 [1979] 44–54), a probability greatly strengthened when the appropriateness of the word ἁμαρτωλός (vv. 15, 17) to the context of the Antioch incident is appreciated (see §4.1c above). Whether vv. 14–18 (or 21) represent what Paul actually said on the occasion, or would have liked to say with the benefit of hindsight, does not affect the point. That Paul turned his back abruptly on the Antioch incident at the end of v. 14 and addressed himself solely to the Galatian situation is correspondingly less likely (against, e.g., Kümmel, 'Individualgeschichte' 161–2; Betz, *Galatians* 114; U. Wilckens even questions whether the ἀναγκάζειν ἰουδαΐζειν of 2.14 can refer to the Antioch incident – 'Was heisst bei Paulus: "Aus Werken des Gesetzes wird kein Mensch gerecht"?' [1969], reprinted *Rechtfertigung als Freiheit: Paulusstudien* [Neukirchen: Neukirchener, 1974] 86–7 – but see §4.1 above). The Gentile Galatian readership could hardly have understood the ἡμεῖς of v. 15 as other than a reference to Peter and Paul.

118. That Paul is citing an agreed position is probable, whether Paul was deliberately following classical rhetorical practice or not (as argued by Betz, *Galatians* 114–17). In fact vv. 15–21 fit the form of the *propositio* at best awkwardly: vv. 17–18 rings oddly as a statement of the point to be discussed, and the attempt to divide vv. 19–20 into four theses to be elaborated in the rest of the letter is overscrupulous and artificial.

119. See particularly Burton, *Galatians* 124–30; Mussner, *Galater* 176–7. One can recognize that Paul is echoing the language used by the men from James ('seeking to be justified', cf. Rom. 10.3; 'sinner', see §4.1c above) without having to conclude that Paul is actually quoting his opponents (Feld, 'Christus') or debating with an imaginary opponent diatribe style (Bouwman, 'Christus'); cf. Ollrog, *Paulus* 209 n. 20. J. Lambrecht, 'The Line of Thought in Gal. 2.14b–21', *NTS* 24 (1977–8) 484–95, argues oddly that 'a reference to the Antioch incident is not present in vv. 15–16 nor is that incident directly alluded to by the terms ἁμαρτωλοί and ἁμαρτία of v. 17', but also that 'it can hardly be doubted that with the phrase "building up again" Paul is alluding to Peter's conduct at Antioch . . .' (p. 493).

120. With v. 18 we probably hear the last echo of Paul's rebuke of Peter. Betz is correct to the extent that with vv. 19–21 we move into formulations which were probably forged by his maturer reflections on the issues involved and more directly stimulated by and oriented towards the challenge confronting him in Galatia. Cf. Schlier, *Galater* 87–8. Since there are at least some indications that Paul's view of the law developed still further after Galatians (cf. J. W. Drane, *Paul: Libertine or Legalist?* [London: SPCK, 1975]; H. Hübner, *Das Gesetz bei Paulus* [Göttingen: Vandenhoeck & Ruprecht, 1978; 2nd ed. 1980], we should beware of exegetical conclusions with regard to Galatians which depend too heavily on parallels in Romans.

121. cf. and contrast H. Räisänen, 'Legalism and Salvation by the Law', *Die Paulinische Literatur und Theologie* (Hrsg S. Pedersen; Aarhus: Forlaget Aros/ Göttingen: Vandenhoeck & Ruprecht, 1980) 63–83.
122. cf. Davies, 'Paul and the People of Israel' 9–10.
123. See further ch. 9 below.
124. It was this consideration which caused Lake to abandon his earlier advocacy of Ramsay's view (above n. 96; Lake, *Earlier Epistles of St. Paul* [London: Rivingtons, 1911] 274–93) – see *Beginnings* 5.201. The puzzle cannot be resolved by arguing that Gal. 2.1–10 was only a private meeting (2.2) (see n. 96 above). Verses 3–10 show that however the consultation began it soon involved a running debate with a wider circle than 'those of repute'. The argument that vv. 4–5 form a parenthesis, which refers to the situation in Galatia at the time of writing (Geyser, 'Apostolic Decree' 132–4; Bruce, 'Galatian Problems I. Autobiographical Data', *BJRL* 51 [1968–69] 302, 306; also *Paul* 159), only complicates rather than clarifies the difficulty of the grammar at that point (see ch. 5 above, p. 120 and n. 58) and the formal character of the agreement in 2.7–10 (see my ch. 5 above, p. 126 n. 60) implies a setting which involved a wider circle of the Jerusalem believers. See also Catchpole, 'Apostolic Decree' 435.
125. The specification of Antioch, Syria and Cilicia in Acts 15.23 does not necessarily require a date for the 'decree' prior to the first missionary journey (as Catchpole argues – 'Apostolic Decree' 438–9, 442). The Galatian churches seem to have sided with Paul (see §5.5 below), so that Jerusalem's sphere of influence (in the north and north-west), where her authority would have been unquestioned, was limited to Antioch, Syria and Cilicia (contrast 2 Cor. 10.13–16). Nor is it necessary to deny that Jerusalem itself was behind the final decree (as does Haenchen, *Acts* 470–1), since the success of the Gentile mission would have made many Gentile Christians within Jerusalem's area of authority restive under their tighter discipline (cf. Weiss, *Earliest Christianity* 311–15; L. Goppelt, *Apostolic and Post-Apostolic Times* [1962; ET London: A. & C. Black, 1970] 78), and a table-fellowship between Jew and Gentile on the basis of the Noahic rules could after all be defended as properly lawful according to the Torah (had Paul made his defence at Antioch on that basis he would probably have stood a better chance of winning). On the earliest form of the 'decree' see particularly W. G. Kümmel, 'Die älteste Form des Aposteldekrets' (1953), *Heilsgesehen und Geschichte, Ges. Aufs. 1933–64* (Marburg: N. G. Elwert, 1965) 278–88. See also Additional Note point 3 below.
126. This is probably the dominant view today. See, e.g., McGiffert, *History* 208; Weiss, *Earliest Christianity* 275–6; B. W. Bacon, 'Paul's Triumph at Antioch', *JR* 9 (1929) 204–23; Haenchen, *Acts* 476; P. Gaechter, *Petrus und seine Zeit* (Innsbruck/Wien/Munchen: Tyrolia, 1958) 251–4; Bornkamm, *Paul* 47; H. Conzelmann, *History of Primitive Christianity* (1969; ET Nashville/New York: Abingdon/London: DLT, 1973) 68, 90; Bligh, *Galatians* 233–4; R. Bauckham, 'Barnabas in Galatians', *JSNT* 2 (1979) 64–5; Köster, *Einführung* 540; other references in Holmberg, *Paul* 34 n. 117.
127. Josephus' report of the attractiveness of Judaism to the Greeks in Antioch in the period prior to the Jewish rebellion (*Jewish War* 7.3.3 §45 – quoted above, §2.2; and *Jewish War* 2.18.5 §479, referred to above in n. 83) may reflect the situation in Antioch following Paul's defeat and the degree of assimilation between Jews, Jewish-Christians and judaizing Greeks (cf. Smallwood's assessment of *Jewish War* 7.3.3 §§46–53 also cited in §2.2).
128. cf. P. Stuhlmacher, *Das paulinische Evangelium 1. Vorgeschichte* (Göttingen: Vandenhoeck & Ruprecht, 1968) 106–7; Hengel, 'Ursprünge' 18; also *Acts and the History of Earliest Christianity* (1979; ET London: SCM Press, 1979) 122–3; T. Holtz, 'Die Bedeutung des Apostelkonzils für Paulus', *NovT* 16 (1974)

110–48; Schütz, *Paul* 151–2; Bauckham, 'Barnabas' 67; Ollrog, *Paulus* 16–17, 206, 213–14.

129. As I believe to be most probable – see particularly F. F. Bruce, 'Galatian Problems 2. North or South Galatia', *BJRL* 52 (1969–70) 243–66; Ollrog, *Paulus* 55–6; others listed by W. G. Kümmel, *Introduction to the New Testament* (1973; revised ET Nashville/New York: Abingdon/London: SCM, 1975) 296 n. 3. See now C. J. Hemer, *The Book of Acts in the Setting of Hellenistic History* (Tübingen: Mohr, 1989) ch. 7.

130. Gal. 5.11 makes plausible sense as a reference to Paul's circumcision of Timothy (as reported by Acts 16.3) – the point being that Paul's Galatian opponents would have failed to see the distinction between Titus and Timothy which would have made all the difference in Paul's eyes. For an alternative interpretation of Gal. 5.11 see P. Borgen, 'Paul Preaches Circumcision and Pleases Men', *Paul and Paulinism: Essays in Honour of C. K. Barrett* (ed. M. D. Hooker & S. G. Wilson; London: SPCK, 1982) 37–46.

131. cf. A. Wainwright, 'Where did Silas Go? (and what was his connection with *Galatians?*)', *JSNT* 8 (1980) 66–70. See also ch. 9 below.

132. See further my 'The New Perspective on Paul', *BJRL* 65 (1983) 95–122, and ch. 7 below.

Additional Note

In the issue of *JSNT* in which the above article first appeared the editor also published two invited responses. The first was by J. L. Houlden, *JSNT* 18 (1983) 58–67, the second by D. Cohn-Sherbok, *JSNT* 18 (1983) 68–74.

Houlden offers the following critique.

1. AI ('The Incident at Antioch') argues in effect 'that the intimate connections between justification by faith and the place of the Law were only arrived at later, an addition to an earlier structure' (p. 59). Whereas in Galatians and Romans the two seem to be integrated 'as if from scratch'. So far as acceptance by God is concerned, Christ and the law are radical alternatives. Paul does not treat the law as a sliding scale, and the question one of more obedience or less. His previous opposition to Christianity included dismissal of Christ as one accursed by the law. The reversal of that opinion 'necessitated a negative verdict upon the Law, and compromise was excluded by the very nature of the dilemma ... The alternatives, Christ or the Law, ... go back to the very root of Paul's Christian life' (pp. 59–60).

2. The thesis of AI is implausible in relation to the teaching of Jesus. Mark's portrayal of Jesus' attitude to the law is to be trusted in preference to Matthew's. In which case it was Jesus' radicalism in relation to the law which Paul recaptured, and in Paul's view the men from James were 'apostates' (p. 63). A developmental hypothesis is again undermined.

3. Preferable to the attempt to fit some of Acts into a historical reconstruction at the cost of discounting other elements (particularly 'the Apostolic Decree'), it is better to recognize more of Acts as 'a theological story', with key features of it as 'largely a Lucan creation' (pp. 65–6).

4. It is unjustifiable to take it for granted that in 1 Corinthians 8 (as in

Rom. 14) 'Paul's discussion is concerned with the limits of the acceptance of Jewish food laws' (p. 66).

5. Did the Antioch incident permanently alter Paul's relationship with the Jerusalem church? Romans 15.26f. seems to indicate a continuing willingness to accord 'a certain primacy to Jerusalem' (p. 67).

Houlden sums up: 'It is hard to make sense of the Antioch incident, in the light of the probabilities of early Christian history, in any way which exonerates the Jerusalem church leaders from apostasy from the teaching of Jesus on the matter of the Law' (p. 67).

1. *What was Paul's view of the law, and how quickly did it develop?* Houlden's first point goes to the heart of the matter. Can we properly speak of development in Paul's understanding of justification by faith, or were the statements of Galatians and Romans simply restatements (= repetitions) of what he had held from the beginning of his apostleship? Behind that lies a question Houlden does not ask: What was the fault which Paul found with the law? Until the latter question is clarified it is not possible to deal with the former. In the studies which followed this one it was in effect this latter question which I tried most of all to clarify. My findings, in summary, are that Paul does not think in terms of *quantitative* obedience of the law, as though Christians needed to obey a smaller quantity of commandments (Gal. 5.14 – 'the *whole* law'). Paul is not thinking simply in terms of initial acceptance by Christ, nor does he make a clear distinction between 'getting in' and 'staying in' (to use Sanders' terminology in *Paul, the Law, and the Jewish People*). On the contrary, the Antioch incident was precisely about what 'staying in' meant for Jewish Christians, and Galatians itself addresses not the question of initial acceptance, but the question of *continuation* (Gal. 3.3; see further ch. 9 below). Rather the function of the law (the whole law) to which Paul objects is its social function, the law as marking out the area within which God's saving power may be experienced, the law as marking off Israel in its distinctive privilege from 'Gentile sinners'. This is what began to emerge for me first in 'New Perspective' (ch. 7 below) and with more careful statement in 'Works of the Law' (ch. 8 below).

As to the issue of development in Paul's understanding at this point: no doubt the point was implicit from the beginning; Paul would certainly have claimed so, in his own terms. My conclusion, however, is that its full ramifications only became explicit and clear to Paul over a period. Thus in 'A Light to the Gentiles' (ch. 4 above) I have attempted to clarify what Paul's Damascus road conversion/commissioning would have meant for his attitude to the law. In 'The Relationship' (ch. 5 above) I have shown how Galatians 1 and 2 give evidence of a developing and changing relationship of Paul with the Jerusalem church, which presumably carried with it some implications for a clarification in his own understanding of the law's significance for Gentile converts. And in the above essay I had already drawn attention sufficiently to the surprising fact that the Jerusalem church took such a long time to object to what was happening in Antioch. Since communication between the two centres cannot have been non-existent during that period, the implication again is of some change over the period, at least in perception of what was happening and its significance. Part of that, I have argued above, must have been the

175

growing religious and national tensions caused within Jerusalem by the deteriorating political situation. Part of it must also have been the surprising increase of Gentile converts (surprising even for synagogues accustomed to entertaining a fair number of God-fearers). The breaking-point would presumably come when the number of Gentile converts was seen to threaten and change the hitherto prevailing balance of the new congregations, introducing complications not foreseen even at the earlier agreement in Jerusalem. Alternatively, the Jewish Christians at Antioch may have been gradually slackening their practice of the law over this period – a suggestion going back to Chrysostom.[1]

When matters came to a head at Antioch they focused in effect on the issue of the continuing covenantal loyalty of Jewish Christians: Jewish Christians surely needed to maintain their observance of these key obligations laid on members of the covenant people. The clear implication, both of the incident itself and of Galatians 2.16 (see 'New Perspective' = ch. 7 below) is that Jewish Christians assumed that such loyalty was in no way at odds with justification by faith. It was *they* who were making a distinction between 'getting in' and 'staying in', *not* Paul. Paul's point was precisely the opposite: that a consistent expression of justification by faith made it impossible to require such works of the law as an essential mark and condition of maintaining status as heirs of the promise. My suggestion is that it was the Antioch incident which brought the either-or character of the issue to a head and caused Paul to formulate his teaching more explicitly on this issue than he had before, or had cause to before (for a fuller overview see ch. 9 below).

2. *The teaching of Jesus.* On Houlden's second point, which is obviously crucial to him, I may refer particularly to the essays on Mark 2.1—3.6 and 7.15 (chs 1 and 2 above). There is sufficient evidence in the tradition-history behind these passages to make it extremely doubtful whether we can reduce the issue to a simple choice between Mark's and Matthew's versions of Jesus' teaching – as though one is unvarnished truth and the other some kind of distortion of that truth. And if Jesus' teaching was more ambiguous, or at least capable of the divergent interpretations of Matthew and Mark, it makes much more sense of a developmental hypothesis, according to which the Jerusalem church took Jesus' teaching in a more conservative way, and it was only in the context of the burgeoning Gentile mission that the same teaching was seen to have a more radical edge or potential. In short, Houlden takes much too lightly the whole question of how Jesus' teaching would have been heard within Palestinian Judaism – and how it would have been heard as transmitted in contexts outside Palestine.

3. *The Apostolic Decree.* I accept that a weakness of my overall hypothesis is the inevitably speculative attempt to make historical sense of 'the apostolic decree' (Acts 15.20, 29); though my suggested solution is hardly original.[2] The answer is not, I think, to discount the historical value of Acts even more, as Houlden does. And I would be interested to explore a variation of a thesis recently put forward by P. Borgen,[3] in which he argues that the earliest form of the agreement in 15.20, 29 would have been non-controversial, a list of minimal requirements for proselytes which had long been part of regular Jewish teaching given to proselytes. Paul himself

would have used such lists in his missionary preaching; this is implied in Galatians 5.19–21 (note the προεῖπον, 'as I told you before'). And such teaching could well have been part of his report to the Jerusalem leadership in Galatians 2.2. In which case such teaching would have been taken for granted before, during and after the Jerusalem meeting, and the reaffirmation of such basic restrictions would not have been regarded as anything 'added' in Galatians 2.6.[4]

Such a thesis would help explain why Luke inserts the 'decree' where he does – an agreement seen to be more significant in hindsight than it had been at the time (somewhat like Peter's acceptance of Cornelius). The problem remains about the inclusion of some food restrictions, or more precisely, *only* some food restrictions in the 'decree'. This could be resolved in one of two ways. Either the earlier form of the agreement did not refer to any food restrictions as such, with 'blood' denoting 'bloodshed' (Borgen's preferred solution). Or it did in fact refer only to some food restrictions – requiring a level of observance of Jewish food traditions which the Gentile Christians in Antioch honoured and had been honouring. In which case the 'men from James' would have attempted to 'tighten the screw', somewhat as suggested in Chapter 6 above. Either way, the absence from Acts 15 of any mention of eating unclean foods, which must have been at the heart of the Antioch incident, is a fact whose significance has been given too little weight in attempts to relate the 'apostolic decree' to the incident in Antioch.

4. *The relevance of 1 Corinthians 8 and Romans 14.* Houlden is one of a number who question whether the issue at 1 Corinthians 8 and Romans 14 focused on or included Jewish food laws. I believe strongly that they did, and have presented the reasons for this conclusion in my *Romans*, pp. 795, 799–802 and 818–19.[5]

5. *Paul and Jerusalem.* On the relationship between Paul and Jerusalem I should refer simply to Chapter 5 above. Meier likewise questions the conclusion of Meeks and Wilken that 'Paul made himself independent of Antioch as well as of Jerusalem' by adding, 'Antioch, yes; Jerusalem, no'.[6] However, while Romans 15.26f. does, of course, acknowledge 'a certain primacy to Jerusalem', it does not alter the picture significantly. Paul's objection was to that primacy misunderstood and overstated. The theological objections of Galatians, 2 Corinthians 10—13 and Philippians 3 have to be set alongside the (also) theological principle outlined in Romans 9—11.

The response by Cohn-Sherbok makes three points.

6. There is insufficient evidence to sustain the view that there was mounting pressure from within Judaism on Jews/Jewish Christians to observe the law faithfully in the period prior to the Jewish revolt in 66 (the criticism is echoed by R. Y. K. Fung).[7] Cohn-Sherbok continues:

Concerning those Jews who put pressure on other Jews to conform to the legal requirements of the Jewish faith, in all likelihood they would have done this not necessarily because of any external threat, but simply because it is what Judaism as a religion requires. And it should not surprise us that within the new Christian sect the same attitude was manifest. (p. 70)

I am grateful for Cohn-Sherbok's confirmation on the latter point. In my view he has spelt out precisely what would have been the logic of the 'men from James' – 'what Judaism as a religion requires'. Part of my argument, however, is that within the diversity of pre-70 Judaism there was greater flexibility, so that 'the men from James' would have been pressing for a more rigorous (they would no doubt say 'more consistent') practice. The parallel with Eleazar and Izates[8] is close, except that Eleazar wanted an already strongly 'judaizing' Izates to follow the same logic to its ultimate conclusion (circumcision). As no doubt did Paul's opponents in Galatia.

On the former point I freely acknowledge that my evidence for an increasing pressure to observe the law more faithfully is circumstantial. The nearest parallel would be the mounting political pressure which resulted in the Maccabean revolt two hundred years earlier. The fact that the practices at Antioch drew no adverse comment from Jerusalem for such a long time is sufficiently surprising to demand some explanation. The hypothesis of a changing and developing situation provides at least part of such an explanation. And Peter's fear of 'those of the circumcision' certainly suggests some sort of pressure.[9]

7. Cohn-Sherbok's second point mistakes my thesis in some measure: my suggestion is that at Antioch prior to the coming of the 'men from James' there was a modest or 'Noahic' level of law observance, not a more elaborate observance on the part of the Gentile Christians. But the main weight of his discussion turns on the significance of the Cornelius episode: in brief, whereas Peter had resisted criticism for eating with the Gentile Cornelius in Acts 11.1ff., at Antioch he gave way to similar pressures; hence Paul's criticism.

The question here, though, is whether the Cornelius episode can be regarded as a complete precedent. Given that Cornelius was already a 'devout God-fearer' (Acts 10.2), he had presumably 'judaized' to a considerable degree, evidently stopping some way short of circumcision. In which case Peter's eating with him would not have posed such strains as the table-fellowship at Antioch evidently did. The difference in Peter's response (Acts 11.1ff. compared with Gal. 2.12) would then be explained by the fact that at Antioch the table-fellowship was much slacker in observing 'the traditional customs'. Fung also ignores such considerations.

8. Cohn-Sherbok's final criticism is that in 'The Incident at Antioch' the Conclusions and Corollaries of §5 are far too speculative. 'Speculative' I accept; but such hypotheses are necessary if we are to make the best sense, including theological sense, of several key features of earliest Christian faith and life – features whose repercussions are of potential significance for our understanding of Christianity today. Luke presents one synthesis, one which at certain points we can see puts a gloss over less pleasant historical events. If we are to do as much justice as possible to these first fathers of Christianity (and to the Christianity they nurtured) we do need to attempt a reconstruction of the whole skull out of such fragments of bone and teeth left to us.

In a subsequent article some further criticism was offered by T. Holtz, 'Der antiochenische Zwischenfall (Galater 2.11–14)', NTS 32 (1986) 344–61.

9. Holtz's criticism focuses on my §4.2 and my advocacy of the third alternative – that Gentile believers at Antioch had already been observing the basic food laws, and that the men from James required a much more scrupulous observance.[10] His principal objection centres on the meaning of ἐθνικῶς in verse 14. Even though its use is polemic, it can hardly denote a lifestyle somewhat on the pattern of the Noahic commandments, but only a non-Jewish pattern of table-fellowship which was restricted by no particular Jewish prescription. The contrast ἐθνικῶς ζῆν – ἰουδαΐζειν is not a matter of relative less-or-more adherence to food laws, but describes a basic transformation of lifestyle. Only so can we make sense of Paul's insistence that the offer of salvation is for *all* who believe, apart from the law, by faith alone (pp. 351–2). In consequence Holtz advocates the first alternative:[11] the requirements brought by the James' people were 'thoroughly moderate', in effect only the requirements which Gentiles living in the land of Israel were expected to observe (pp. 354–5).[12]

Holtz's advocacy makes the view even more attractive than when I first examined it in writing 'The Incident at Antioch'. But I am still not persuaded that it is to be adopted. (a) Unfortunately Holtz does not attempt to respond to the three considerations which seemed to me to count against it[13] and which still seem to me to carry considerable weight as soon as we set the text of Galatians 2.11–14 within what we know of the historical context of Jews, God-fearers and Christians in Antioch in the middle decades of the first century. (b) Holtz's argument certainly makes it easier to see why Peter, Barnabas and the rest would have abandoned the shared table-fellowship; on his view, the people from James were asking so little! The consequence, however, is to portray Paul as highly doctrinaire and wholly inflexible, in marked contrast to his own later practice (1 Cor. 8—10; Rom. 14). (c) And there is another factor to be considered. The milder and more minimalist the demands of the men from James, the more astonishing the demand now confronting the Galatians (in effect, for a judaizing all the way to circumcision). The smaller the gap between the 'men from James' and a complete disregard for the law, the wider the gap between the 'men from James' and those who subsequently demanded circumcision of Gentile converts. The solution I found myself pushed to at least has the virtue of explaining how a heightened demand for observance of Jewish distinctives ('judaize') could readily be escalated to a demand to go the whole way (become proselytes). (d) So the question still stands: whether ἐθνικῶς ζῆν cannot mean other than 'live in complete disregard for all Jewish laws', or whether it could still denote a lifestyle appropriate to and characteristic of *Gentiles* who consort in some degree with Jews while retaining their identity as Gentiles (including resident aliens),[14] but *not* appropriate to *Jews* who seek to remain faithful to the ancestral traditions in order to maintain their identity as Jews. If that is a possible reference for the phrase 'live as Gentiles', and Holtz himself notes that the phrase here is 'a polemical generalisation' (p. 345), then the main force of his objection is critically weakened, and the other considerations just noted gain added significance.

A more recent critique is offered by P. F. Esler, *Community and Gospel in Luke-Acts. The Social and Political Motivation of Lucan Theology*.[15]

10. Esler questions my view that in the first century CE less scrupulous

179

Jews willingly extended and accepted invitations to meals at which Gentiles would be present (p. 76),[16] and goes on to cite a sequence of Greco-Roman and Jewish texts to demonstrate 'that as a general rule Jews did refrain from eating with Gentiles and that this was a feature which was perceived to characterize their life-style from as early as the late fourth century BCE until far into the classical period . . .' (p. 77). 'The antipathy of Jews towards table-fellowship with Gentiles, in the full sense of sitting around a table with them and sharing the same food, wine and vessels, was an intrinsic feature of Jewish life for centuries before and after our period' (p. 84). Since Gentiles were thought to be actually impure 'it is difficult to imagine how it would be possible for any genuine table-fellowship to occur even between Jew and Gentile in a Jewish home' (p. 86). Consequently, so far as the AI is concerned, Esler thinks that what the men from James must have required, and Peter accepted, in order to rehabilitate table-fellowship between Gentiles and Jews was for the Gentiles to become Jews through circumcision. This is what 'judaize' in Galatians 2.14 must mean – 'to become Jews through circumcision'.[17] My alternative suggestion, that the demand was 'to tighten up' the practice of table-fellowship 'by the adoption of the Pharisaical features of hand-washing and of tithing of the produce used at these meals' represents 'a serious trivialization of the issues in dispute' (p. 88).

Regrettably Esler's discussion is vitiated by the fact that he views the whole issue in terms of two monolithic and undifferentiated blocks – Jews and Gentiles. I do not dispute the broad lines of his argument. In the same article (AI, pp. 17–18, above pp. 142–3) I drew attention to the same range of evidence which he marshalls and subsequently developed the point that food laws in particular functioned as a boundary between Jew and Gentile, widely perceived as such both from within and from without the Judaism of the period (see chs 7 and 8 below). But Esler fails completely to note that the discussion of the above chapter was directed towards the fact that 'Gentiles' were not an undifferentiated mass; and the investigation of Chapter 3 above has also demonstrated that the same was true of the first-century 'Jews'.

(a) Esler ignores the fact of God-fearers and the significance of the verb ἰουδαΐζειν discussed above (pp. 144–7, 149–50 = AI, pp. 21–3, 26–7), although he himself had discussed the question of 'God-fearers in Luke-Acts' earlier (pp. 36–45). The point is that there were Gentiles, evidently a significant number, who showed themselves attracted by the beliefs and practices of Judaism and who began to 'judaize', that is, to live like Jews, to follow a Jewish way of life, including observance of the food laws (above pp. 145–6, 149 = AI, pp. 22–3, 26). Why would God-fearing Gentiles live like Jews, except in order to associate with Jews, at synagogue and festival? And no doubt also in guest friendship (above p. 150 = AI, p. 27).[18] The boundary between Jew and Gentile was there, for all to see. But not a few Gentiles evidently wished to cross that boundary, and did so, and were counted as acceptable in Diaspora synagogue circles because of their worship of God and their readiness to judaize. Regrettably in his near quotation from p. 147 above[19] Esler has blurred the point by missing out a key word. In talking of table-fellowship between Jew and Gentile what I have had in mind is table-fellowship between 'less scrupulous Jews' and '*such* Gentiles', that is, 'God-fearing Gentiles'. The Gentiles whom Esler quotes were content to describe Jews and Judaism from outside, or from an actively hostile position. It was the sympathetic and actually judaizing Gentiles to whom I referred.[20]

(b) Nor has Esler really taken on board the significance of my talk of '*less scrupulous* Jews'. The 'Jews' too were not an undifferentiated mass living in uniform life-patterns. The evidence collected above (ch. 3) confirms that there was a spectrum of law observance regarding table-fellowship *within* Judaism. That is to say, there were those who observed the dietary, tithing and purity rulings with a greater degree of scrupulosity. And there were (many) others who were less scrupulous. Moreover, the ideal of eating separately held forth by Daniel, Tobit, Judith, etc., depicted a Judaism under threat, having to maintain its covenant distinctiveness in the face of Gentile hostility and pressure to eliminate such distinctiveness. But with proselytes, resident aliens and God-fearers, the position was quite different. Judaism was no missionary religion, but where Gentiles showed themselves ready to judaize and convert, the indications are that most Jews welcomed them warmly. And within the spectrum of Jewish praxis in the matter of table-fellowship, no doubt the less scrupulous would have been much more ready as a rule to mingle with God-fearers than the more scrupulous.

(c) The sharpness of the polarization between 'Jews' and 'Gentiles' which Esler assumes makes the practice at Antioch prior to the arrival of the men from James very hard to credit. Had *all* Jewish Christians so immediately and totally abandoned a hitherto strict and unyielding separation from all Gentiles? Had *all* Jewish Christians in consequence separated themselves so totally and completely from their fellow Jews in Antioch (as such a breach with hitherto uniform Jewish practice would have necessitated)? And did nothing of this get back to the Jews or Jewish Christians in Jerusalem prior to the delegation from James? All this does not seem very likely or very credible.[21] Even less that Peter should go back so quickly on the agreement made by all the main parties (James, Peter and Paul) at Jerusalem (Gal. 2.1–10) by insisting that the Gentile Christians in Antioch should now, after all, be circumcised.[22] Moreover, Esler's characterization of my suggested solution[23] as 'a serious trivialization of the issues in dispute' is a serious misjudgement. It was over such 'trivialization' that the factions within Judaism discounted other Jews as 'sinners' and apostates (see again ch. 3 above). What might seem to us trivial matters were issues which went to the heart of Jewish identity and covenant faithfulness for many Jews of the time. It is precisely because the Antioch incident was a boundary situation, where some Jews were pushing back or redefining the boundaries (not wholly abandoning them) and others were fearful that such conduct constituted a threat to these boundaries and thus to the identity and religious security of those whom the boundary protected, that the Antioch incident became an incident in the first place.

Notes

1. *Homilies* Vol. 3, 430ff.; I owe the reference to my colleague John McHugh.
2. See, e.g., Meier in R. E. Brown and J. P. Meier, *Antioch and Rome*, London: Chapman (1983) 38, 42–3.
3. 'Catalogues of Vices, The Apostolic Decree, and the Jerusalem Meeting', *The Social World of Formative Christianity and Judaism*, H. C. Kee Festschrift, ed. J. Neusner et al., Philadelphia: Fortress (1988) 126–41; also delivered to the Durham NT Seminar in January 1989 under the title 'No Apostolic Decree'.
4. cf. also the discussion in P. J. Achtemeier, *The Quest for Unity in the New Testament Church*, Philadelphia: Fortress (1987) 83–5.
5. WBC 38, Dallas: Word (1988).
6. Meier and Brown, *Antioch and Rome* 39–40.
7. R. Y. K. Fung, *Galatians*, NICNT, Grand Rapids: Eerdmans (1988) 7, n. 23.
8. See above p. 146 = AI, p. 23.
9. Bruce, *Galatians* 131. See also ch. 4 above.
10. Above p. 146 = AI, p. 31.
11. Above p. 154 = AI, p. 29.
12. On the resident alien see above pp. 143–4 = AI, pp. 20–1. Holtz is followed by Fung, *Galatians* 107.
13. Above pp. 152–3 = AI, pp. 29–30.
14. cf. Holtz 355.
15. SNTSMS 57, Cambridge University (1987).
16. Referring to AI, p. 23, above p. 147.
17. Compare and contrast Holtz above. The full range of options reviewed above (§4.2) is still in play.
18. According to Esler, 'Dunn offers not a shred of evidence for Jews eating with Gentiles in this period' (p. 77) – an ungenerous and unsympathetic assessment of the evidence offered. He must also assume that the table-fellowship at Antioch between Jew(ish Christian) and Gentile (Christian) was a complete departure from Jew/Gentile relations in Syria, despite the evidence from Josephus, cited above pp. 149–50 = AI, pp. 26–7. F. Watson, *Paul, Judaism and the Gentiles. A Sociological Approach*, SNTSMS 56, Cambridge University (1986), likewise ignores the fact of God-fearers in assuming that there was nothing between '(Gentile) acceptance of individual (Jewish) customs' and 'conversion to Judaism' (189 n. 69).
19. AI, p. 23; on Esler 76.
20. See also A. T. Kraabel, 'The Roman Diaspora: Six Questionable Assumptions', *Essays in Honour of Yigael Yadin*, ed. G. Vermes & J. Neusner, *JJS* 33 (1982) 445–64.
21. Against Watson, *Paul* 36–8, who assumes what his thesis needs to prove: viz. that the Gentile mission 'involved the complete separation of the church from the synagogue' in effect from the start (*Paul* 38).
22. Esler makes no attempt to respond to the considerations marshalled above (pp. 151–3 = AI, pp. 29–30).
23. That the men from James insisted on a clear reassertion of the boundary lines around the covenant people by demanding a more scrupulous maintenance of food laws and purity rules than those currently observed in the Christian congregation at Antioch.

7

The New Perspective on Paul*

I

When chatting with other New Testament specialists I occasionally mention the fact that I am engaged in writing a commentary on Paul's letter to the Christians in Rome. The most frequent response is one of surprise, sometimes even amazement – 'Not *another* commentary on Romans!' The underlying implication is that we have had quite sufficient commentaries on Romans, that surely there can be nothing new or novel to say on such a well-worked document, that a new commentator is bound to spend most of his time simply repeating the thoughts of his predecessors. I cannot say that I am particularly taken aback by such responses, because when I was first invited to write the commentary my own reaction was more or less the same – a rather stultifying sense that it had all been said before, that interpretation of Pauline theology had lost a lot of steam, and that the really interesting and challenging frontiers in New Testament studies were to be found elsewhere.

I do not for a moment want to suggest that a commentator should refrain from re-expressing the old truths and rich insights of former days and previous commentators on Paul. Mere novelty is not of itself a mark of merit, and novelty for its own sake should certainly not be encouraged in an interpreter or expositor of any text. As students of Paul we all would be the poorer if scholars like F. F. Bruce or Otto Kuss or Heinrich Schlier had refused to distil their lifetime's study of Paul into single volumes, simply because they did not have some revolutionary new theories to put forward.[1] Nor do I wish to imply that fresh thought on particular points of Pauline theology or lively debate on particular passages within the Pauline corpus has been lacking. If we think only in terms of the last few years, for example, there has been more than one controversial reconstruction of Pauline chronology.[2] Older emphases on the significance of Paul's conversion for his subsequent theology, and on the importance of the apocalyptic aspect of his teaching, have been strongly and fruitfully revived.[3] There has been a challenging reappraisal of the way in which Paul was regarded in

* The Manson Memorial Lecture delivered in the University of Manchester on 4 November 1982. Subsequently delivered in modified form as one of the Wilkinson Lectures in the Northern Baptist Theological Seminary, Illinois, under the title 'Let Paul be Paul'.

the ancient church.[4] Interesting new hypotheses on the development of Paul's thought between his writing of Galatians and his writing of Romans have been formulated,[5] and the posing of sociologically inspired questions has thrown up some important new insights.[6] The old introductory questions as to the occasion for and situation addressed by particular letters still provokes heated controversy,[7] and we can even say that a new subdivision of the literary criticism of the letters has recently been opened up – rhetorical criticism.[8] As a final example, perhaps I could be forgiven for hoping that one or two useful comments on Paul's religious experience, ecclesiology and Christology have flowed from my own pen.[9]

In none of these cases, however, could I confidently say that I have been given (I speak personally) what amounts to a new perspective on Paul. In some cases the old pattern has been shaken up somewhat and the pieces have fallen a little differently. In other cases particular aspects of Paul's writing and thought have received fuller illumination or previous conclusions have had a question mark appended to them. In others I strongly suspect red herrings have been drawn in and wild geese chased. But none have succeeded in, to use a contemporary phrase, 'breaking the mould' of Pauline studies, the mould into which descriptions of Paul's work and thought have regularly been poured for many decades now. There is, in my judgement, only one work written during the past decade or two which deserves that accolade. I refer to the volume entitled *Paul and Palestinian Judaism* by E. P. Sanders [formerly] of McMaster University in Canada.[10]

Sanders' basic claim is not so much that Paul has been misunderstood as that the picture of Judaism drawn from Paul's writings is historically false, not simply inaccurate in part but fundamentally mistaken. What is usually taken to be the Jewish alternative to Paul's gospel would have been hardly recognized as an expression of Judaism by Paul's kinsmen according to the flesh. Sanders notes that Jewish scholars and experts in early Judaism have for long enough been registering a protest at this point, contrasting rabbinic Judaism as they understand it with the parody of Judaism which Paul seems to have rejected. Thus, for example, Solomon Schechter: 'Either the theology of the Rabbis must be wrong, its conception of God debasing, its leading motives materialistic and coarse, and its teachers lacking in enthusiasm and spirituality, or the Apostle to the Gentiles is quite unintelligible'; or a few lines later, James Parkes: '. . . if Paul was really attacking "Rabbinic Judaism", then much of his argument is irrelevant, his abuse unmerited, and his conception of that which he was attacking inaccurate'.[11] But such protests seem to have fallen for the most part on deaf ears. For a hundred years now, as Sanders observes, the majority of New Testament scholars have maintained a fundamental antithesis between Paul and Judaism, especially rabbinic Judaism, and have seen this antithesis as a central factor, usually the central factor, in understanding Paul the Jew-become-Christian.[12]

The problem focuses on the character of Judaism as a religion of salvation. For rabbinic specialists the emphasis in rabbinic Judaism on God's goodness and generosity, his encouragement of repentance and offer of forgiveness is plain. Whereas Paul seems to depict Judaism as coldly and calculatingly legalistic, a system of 'works' righteousness, where salvation is *earned* by the *merit* of good *works*. Looked at from another angle, the problem is the way in which Paul has been understood as the great exponent of the central Reformation doctrine of *justification by faith*. As Krister Stendahl warned twenty years ago, it is deceptively easy to read Paul in the light of Luther's agonized search for relief from a troubled conscience.[13] Since Paul's teaching on justification by faith seems to speak so directly to Luther's subjective wrestlings, it was a natural corollary to see Paul's opponents in terms of the unreformed Catholicism which opposed Luther, with first-century Judaism read through the 'grid' of the early sixteenth-century Catholic system of merit. To a remarkable and indeed alarming degree, throughout this century the standard depiction of the Judaism which Paul rejected has been the reflex of Lutheran hermeneutic. How serious this is for New Testament scholarship may be seen when we recall that the two most influential New Testament scholars of the past two generations, Rudolf Bultmann and Ernst Käsemann, both read Paul through Lutheran spectacles and both made this understanding of justification by faith their central theological principle.[14] And the most recent full-scale treatment of this area of Pauline theology, on Paul and the law, still continues to work with the picture of Paul as one who rejected the perverted attempt to use the law as a means of earning righteousness by good works.[15]

Sanders, however, has built up a different presentation of Palestinian Judaism at the time of Paul. From a massive treatment of much of the relevant Jewish literature for that period, a rather different picture emerges. In particular, he has shown with sufficient weight of evidence that for the first-century Jew, Israel's covenant relation with God was basic, basic to the Jew's sense of national identity and to his understanding of his religion. So far as we can tell now, for first-century Judaism everything was an elaboration of the fundamental axiom that the one God had chosen Israel to be his peculiar people, to enjoy a special relationship under his rule. The law had been given as an expression of this covenant, to regulate and maintain the relationship established by the covenant. So, too, righteousness must be seen in terms of this relationship, as referring to conduct appropriate to this relationship, conduct in accord with the law. That is to say, obedience to the law in Judaism was never thought of as a means of *entering* the covenant, of *attaining* that special relationship with God; it was more a matter of *maintaining* the covenant relationship with God. From this Sanders draws out his key phrase to characterize first-century Palestinian Judaism – 'covenantal nomism'. He defines it thus:

> covenantal nomism is the view that one's place in God's plan is established on the basis of the covenant and that the covenant requires as the proper response of man his obedience to its commandments, while providing means of atonement for transgression ... *Obedience maintains one's position in the covenant, but it does not earn God's grace as such* ... Righteousness in Judaism is a term which implies the *maintenance of status* among the group of the elect.[16]

If Stendahl cracked the mould of twentieth-century reconstructions of Paul's theological context, by showing how much it had been determined by Luther's quest for a gracious God, Sanders has broken it altogether by showing how different these reconstructions are from what we know of first-century Judaism from other sources. We have all in greater or less degree been guilty of modernizing Paul. But now Sanders has given us an unrivalled opportunity to look at Paul afresh, to shift our perspective back from the sixteenth century to the first century, to do what all true exegetes want to do – that is, to see Paul properly within his own context, to hear Paul in terms of his own time, to let Paul be himself.

The most surprising feature of Sanders' writing, however, is that he himself has failed to take the opportunity his own mould-breaking work offered. Instead of trying to explore how far Paul's theology could be explicated in relation to Judaism's 'covenantal nomism', he remained more impressed by the *difference* between Paul's pattern of religious thought and that of first-century Judaism. He quickly – too quickly in my view – concluded that Paul's religion could be understood only as a basically different system from that of his fellow Jews. In Christianity a quite different mode of righteousness operated from that in Judaism, righteousness which is through faith in Christ, 'from God' and not 'from the law' (Phil. 3.9). Paul had broken with the law for the simple reason that following the law did not result in his being 'in Christ'. Christ was the end of the law (Rom. 10.4). It was this change of 'entire systems' which made it unnecessary for Paul to speak about repentance or the grace of God shown in the giving of the covenant.[17]

But this presentation of Paul is only a little better than the one rejected. There remains something very odd in Paul's attitude to his ancestral faith. The Lutheran Paul has been replaced by an idiosyncratic Paul who in arbitrary and irrational manner turns his face against the glory and greatness of Judaism's covenant theology and abandons Judaism simply because it is not Christianity. It may be, of course, that Paul was totally bowled over by his encounter with the risen Christ outside Damascus, and this experience gave him a jaundiced and unfairly prejudiced view of his erstwhile faith from that time on. But Paul was by no means the only Jew who became a Christian, and it is difficult to see such an arbitrary jump from one 'system' to another commending itself quite as much as it in the event obviously did to so many of his fellow Jews.

The critiques of Sanders which inevitably followed have also failed in greater or less measure to capitalize on the new perspective opened up by Sanders, either because they dispute the main thrust of Sanders' thesis, or because they do not know quite what to make of Paul when viewed from that perspective. Hans Hübner, for example, continues to operate largely within the classic Reformation categories, criticizing Sanders for failing to see Paul's attack on 'legalistic works-righteousness' as central for Paul's theology.[18] On the other hand, Heikki Räisänen accepts Sanders' strictures on Paul: Paul *does* misrepresent and distort the Judaism of his own day. He has separated law from covenant and adopted a Gentile point of view. Having 'become internally alienated from the ritual aspects of the law' over the years, he has branded 'the covenantal theology of his Jewish-Christian opponents as salvation by works of the law', thus attributing to the law a different role than the Jewish Christians themselves did.[19] And Morna Hooker points out the oddity of Sanders' conclusion, that the 'pattern of religion' which emerges from Sanders' study of Palestinian Judaism bears a striking similarity to what is commonly believed to be the religion of Paul, but then struggles with only little more success than Sanders to explain why it was in that case that Paul felt the need to distance himself from that Judaism.[20]

Sanders himself has returned to the subject in a monograph entitled *Paul, the Law, and the Jewish People*, the manuscript of which he kindly permitted me to read. In it he broadens out the perspective on Paul from the narrower question of 'getting in and staying in' the covenant, which was the preoccupation of *Paul and Palestinian Judaism*, and restates his position in more detail. The picture of Judaism which emerges from this fuller study of Paul does correspond to Judaism as revealed in its own literature. Paul attacks covenantal nomism, the view that accepting and living by the law is a sign and condition of favoured status. It was never God's intention, so Paul argues, that one should accept the law in order to become one of the elect. 'His real attack on Judaism is against the idea of the covenant ... What is wrong with the law, and thus with Judaism, is that it does not provide for God's ultimate purpose, that of saving the entire world through faith in Christ ...'[21] But he still speaks of Paul breaking with the law, he still has Paul making an arbitrary jump from one system to another and posing an antithesis between faith in Christ and his Jewish heritage in such sharp, black-and-white terms, that Paul's occasional defence of Jewish prerogative (as in Rom. 9.4–6) seems equally arbitrary and bewildering, his treatment of the law and of its place in God's purpose becomes inconsistent and illogical, and we are left with an abrupt discontinuity between the new movement centred in Jesus and the religion of Israel which makes little sense in particular of Paul's olive tree allegory in Romans 11.[22]

I must confess that I find Sanders' Paul little more convincing (and much less attractive) than the Lutheran Paul. I am not convinced that we have yet been given the proper reading of Paul from the new perspective of first-century Palestinian Judaism opened up so helpfully by Sanders himself. On the contrary, I believe that the new perspective on Paul does make better sense of Paul than either Sanders or his critics have so far realized. And, if I may, I would like in what follows to make a beginning to an exegesis and description of Paul's theology from this perspective.

II

Let me attempt to demonstrate my case by focusing particularly on one verse and attempting to set it as fully as possible into its historical context. I refer to Galatians 2.16. This is the most obvious place to start any attempt to take a fresh look at Paul from our new perspective. It is probably the first time in the letters of Paul that his major theme of justification by faith is sounded. As such, the way in which it is formulated may well tell us much, not only about the theme itself, but about why it meant so much to Paul. We are encouraged in this hope by the fact that this first statement seems to grow out of Paul's attempt to define and defend his own understanding of justification, over against whatever view was held by his fellow Jewish Christians from Jerusalem and Antioch; and also that it seems to form the basic statement of his gospel on which he builds his plea to his Galatian converts to hold steadfast to the gospel as he first proclaimed it to them.

It will perhaps be helpful if I sketch out the immediate preceding context of this important verse more fully. Paul has been recalling the unhappy incident at Antioch some time previously. At Antioch Gentiles had been accepted fully into the circle of those Jews who believed that Jesus was God's Anointed and that, though rejected by the leaders of his own people, God had raised him from the dead. The leading apostles at Jerusalem had already agreed that such Gentiles need not be circumcised in order to be counted as fellow believers (Gal. 2.1–10). At Antioch the custom was for all those who had been baptized in this faith in Jesus the Christ to share a meal in common when they met – Jews together with Gentiles. But then 'certain individuals' had arrived from James in Jerusalem (2.11), and evidently they had found it unacceptable that the Jewish Christians should act in such disregard for the food laws laid down by Moses – the laws on clean and unclean foods, the laws on the proper slaughter of animals for meat, and probably also the various regulations governing tithing, ritual purity and avoidance of idol food already current among the more devout Jews. Whatever the men from James said or however they acted, it had an effect. Peter and all the other Jewish believers, including even Paul's associate Barnabas, withdrew from the fellowship meals, presumably in order to demonstrate their continuing loyalty to their ancestral faith – to demonstrate that believing in Jesus did not make them any the less devout Jews (2.12–13). But Paul had confronted Peter and accused him of hypocrisy, of not following the straight path of the gospel. In front of the whole community of believers he appealed to Peter: 'If you, a Jew, live like a Gentile and not like a Jew, how can you compel the Gentiles to judaize?' – that is, to observe the food laws and table regulations drawn out from the law by the devout Jews (2.14).[23] Then Paul goes on, probably not repeating the precise words he used to Peter at Antioch, but probably echoing the line of argument which he tried to develop on that occasion,[24] 'We who are Jews by nature and not Gentile sinners, know that a man is not justified by works of law except through faith in Christ Jesus. And we have believed in Christ Jesus, in order that we might be justified by faith in Christ and not by works of law, because by works of law shall no flesh be justified' (2.15–16) – the last clause echoing Psalm 143.2.

What precisely was Paul arguing here? What were the nuances and overtones which his fellow Jewish Christians would have recognized and appreciated? A careful analysis may well yield fruitful results.

(a) First, then, how did Paul mean to be understood by his sudden and repeated talk of *being justified*'? – 'Knowing that a man is not justified by works of law ... in order that we might be justified by faith in Christ ... by works of law shall no flesh be justified'. The format of his words shows that he is appealing to an accepted view of Jewish Christians: 'we who are Jews ... know ...'[25] Indeed, as already noted, Paul is probably at this point still recalling (if not actually repeating) what it was he said to Peter at Antioch. Not only so, but his wording shows that he is actually appealing to Jewish sensibilities, we may say even to Jewish prejudices – 'we are Jews by nature and not sinners of the Gentiles'. This understanding of 'being justified' is thus, evidently, something Jewish, something which belongs to Jews 'by nature', something which distinguishes them from 'Gentile sinners'.[26] But this is covenant language, the language of those conscious that they have been chosen as a people by God, and separated from the surrounding nations. Moreover, those from whom the covenant people are thus separated are described not only as Gentiles, but as 'sinners'. Here, too, we have the language which stems from Israel's consciousness of election. The Gentiles are 'sinners' precisely in so far as they neither know nor keep the law given by God to Israel.[27] Paul therefore prefaces his first mention of 'being justified' with a deliberate appeal to the standard Jewish belief, shared also by his fellow Jewish Christians, that the Jews as a race are God's covenant people. Almost certainly, then, his concept of righteousness, both noun and verb (to be made or counted righteous, to be justified), is thoroughly Jewish too, with the same strong covenant overtones – the sort of usage we find particularly in the Psalms and Second Isaiah, where God's righteousness is precisely God's covenant faithfulness, his saving power and love for his people Israel.[28] God's justification is God's recognition of Israel as his people, his verdict in favour of Israel on grounds of his covenant with Israel.

Two clarificatory corollaries immediately follow.

1. In talking of 'being justified' here Paul is not thinking of a distinctively *initiatory* act of God. God's justification is not his act in first *making* his covenant with Israel, or in initially accepting someone into the covenant people. God's justification is rather God's acknowledgement that someone is in the covenant – whether that is an *initial* acknowledgement, or a *repeated* action of God (God's saving acts), or his *final* vindication of his people. So in Galatians 2.16 we are not surprised when the second reference to being justified has a future implication ('we have believed in Christ Jesus in order that we might be justified ...'), and the third reference is in the future tense ('by works of law no flesh shall be justified'). We might mention also Galatians 5.5, where Paul speaks of 'awaiting the hope of righteousness'. 'To be justified' in Paul cannot, therefore, be treated simply as an entry or initiation formula;[29] nor is it possible to draw a clear line of distinction between Paul's usage and the typically Jewish covenant usage. Already, we may observe, Paul appears a good deal less idiosyncratic and arbitrary than Sanders alleges.

2. Perhaps even more striking is the fact which also begins to emerge, that at this point Paul is wholly at one with his fellow Jews in asserting that justification is *by faith*. That is to say, integral to

190

the idea of the covenant itself, and of God's continued action to maintain it, is the profound recognition of God's initiative and grace in first establishing and then maintaining the covenant. Justification by faith, it would appear, is not a distinctively Christian teaching. Paul's appeal here is not to *Christians* who happen also to be Jews, but to *Jews* whose Christian faith is but an extension of their Jewish faith in a graciously electing and sustaining God. We must return to this point shortly, but for the moment we may simply note that to ignore this fundamental feature of Israel's understanding of its covenant status is to put in jeopardy the possibility of a properly historical exegesis. Far worse, to start our exegesis here from the Reformation presupposition that Paul was attacking the idea of *earning* God's acquittal, the idea of meritorious works, is to set the whole exegetical endeavour off on the wrong track. If Paul was not an idiosyncratic Jew, neither was he a straightforward prototype of Luther.

(b) What then is Paul attacking when he dismisses the idea of being justified '*by works of the law*'? – as he does, again, no less than three times in this one verse: '. . . not by works of law . . . not by works of law . . . not by works of law . . .' The answer which suggests itself from what has already been said is that he was thinking of *covenant* works, works related to the covenant, works done in obedience to the law of the covenant. This is both confirmed and clarified by both the immediate and the broader contexts.

As to the immediate context, the most relevant factor is that Galatians 2.16 follows immediately upon the debates, indeed the crises, at Jerusalem and at Antioch which focused on two issues – at Jerusalem, circumcision; at Antioch, the Jewish food laws with the whole question of ritual purity unstated but clearly implied. Paul's forceful denial of justification by works of law is his response to these two issues. His denial that justification is from works of law is, more precisely, a denial that justification depends on circumcision or on observation of the Jewish purity and food taboos. We may justifiably deduce, therefore, that by 'works of law' Paul intended his readers to think of *particular observances of the law like circumcision and the food laws*. His Galatian readership might well think also of the one other area of law observance to which Paul refers disapprovingly later in the same letter – their observance of special days and feasts (Gal. 4.10). But why these particular 'works of the law'? The broader context suggests a reason.

From the broader context, provided for us by Greco-Roman literature of the period, we know that *just these observances were widely regarded as characteristically and distinctively Jewish*. Writers like Petronius, Plutarch, Tacitus and Juvenal took it for granted that, in particular, circumcision, abstention from pork, and the sabbath, were observances which marked out the practitioners as Jews, or as people who were very attracted to Jewish ways.[30] These, of course, were not all exclusively Jewish practices – for example, not only Jews practised circumcision. But this makes it all the more striking that these practices were nevertheless widely regarded as both characteristic and distinctive of the Jews as a race – a fact which tells us much about the influence of Diaspora Judaism in the Greco-Roman world. It is clear, in other words, that just these observances in particular functioned as identity markers, they served to identify their practitioners as Jewish in the eyes of the wider public, they were the peculiar rites which marked out the Jews as that peculiar people.

When we set this alongside the Palestinian Judaism illuminated by Sanders, the reason for this becomes clearer, we can see why just these observances were regarded as so distinctively Jewish. The Jews regarded them in the same way! This strong impression of Greco-Roman authors, as to what religious practices characterize the Jews, was simply a reflection of the typical, the dominant, attitude of the Jews themselves. These identity markers identified Jewishness because they were seen by the Jews themselves as fundamental observances of the covenant. They functioned as badges of covenant membership. A member of the covenant people was, by definition, one who observed these practices in particular. How could it be otherwise, since precisely these practices belong so clearly to the basic ground rules of the covenant?

If we think of circumcision, no loyal Jew could ignore the explicit stipulations of Genesis 17:

And God said to Abraham, 'As for you, you shall keep my covenant, you and your descendants after you throughout their generations. This is my covenant, which you shall keep, between me and you and your descendants after you: Every male among you shall be circumcised. You shall be circumcised in the flesh of your foreskins, and it shall be a sign of the covenant between me and you ... So shall my covenant be in your flesh an everlasting covenant. Any uncircumcised male who is not circumcised in the flesh of his foreskin shall be cut off from his people; he has broken my covenant.' (Gen. 17.9–14)

What could be clearer than that? There are some indications that a few Diaspora Jews avoided the literal force of this command by spiritualizing it,[31] but they are noteworthy precisely as being so exceptional. Circumcision remained an identification marker of Jewishness, of membership of the Jewish people, in the eyes both of the Gentiles and of the Jews themselves.

The laws on clean and unclean foods do not hold such a central place in the Torah (Lev. 11.1–23; Deut. 14.3–21). But we know that at least from the time of the Maccabees they had assumed increasing importance in Jewish folklore and Jewish self-understanding. The Maccabean martyrs were remembered precisely as those who 'stood firm and were resolved in their hearts not to eat unclean food' and who 'chose to die rather than to be defiled by food or to profane the holy covenant' (1 Macc. 1.62–3). And the heroes of the popular tales beloved by several generations of Jews, Daniel, Tobit and Judith, had all shown their faithfulness to God precisely by their refusal to eat 'the food of Gentiles' (Dan. 1.8–16; Tob. 1.10–13; Judith 10.5; 12.1–20). Without question, then, the devout Jew of Paul's day would regard observance of the laws on clean and unclean foods as a basic expression of covenant loyalty. Moreover, from what we now know of the Pharisees at the time of Paul, not to mention also the Essenes at Qumran, the maintenance of ritual purity, particularly the ritual purity of the meal table, was a primary concern and major preoccupation.[32] No wonder then that the men from James were so upset by the slackness of Peter and the other Jewish Christians at Antioch on these matters. And no wonder that Peter and Barnabas could not resist this strong appeal to national identity and covenant faithfulness precisely with regard to these items of the law, these practices of the covenant.

As to the observance of special days, particularly the sabbath, we need only recall that the Jewish Scriptures treat the sabbath as a fundamental law of creation (Gen. 2.3), that the sabbath was the only feast day to be stipulated in the decalogue (Exod. 20.8–11; Deut. 5.12–15), and that it was explicitly linked by Isaiah with the covenant as a determinative expression of covenant loyalty which would provide the basis on which Gentiles would unite with Jews in the last days in a common worship of the one God (Isa. 56.6–8). Here, too, was a work of the law which had the same basic character of defining the boundaries of the covenant people, one of these minimal observances without which one could hardly claim to be a good Jew, loyal to the covenant given by God's grace to Israel.

Given this almost axiomatic tie-up between these particular regulations of the law and covenant membership, it is no exaggeration to say that for the typical Jew of the first century AD, particularly the Palestinian Jew, *it would be virtually impossible to conceive of participation in God's covenant, and so in God's covenant righteousness, apart from these observances, these works of the law.* If it helps, some may like to compare the role of the sacraments (baptism and the Lord's Supper) in Christianity today. These have very much the same fundamental role in Christian self-understanding as circumcision, table regulation and sabbath had in the Jewish self-understanding of Paul's day. Even though we acknowledge the Quakers and the Salvation Army as Christian bodies, even so any attempt to define the boundary markers which identify and distinguish Christians as Christians will almost certainly give a primary place to baptism and the Lord's Supper. If an unbaptized Christian is for most of us a contradiction in terms, even more so was a Jew who did not practise the works of the law, circumcision, table regulations and sabbath.

The conclusion follows very strongly that when Paul denied the possibility of 'being justified by works of the law' it is precisely this basic Jewish self-understanding which Paul is attacking[33] – the idea that God's acknowledgement of covenant status is bound up with, even dependent upon, observance of these particular regulations – the idea that God's verdict of acquittal hangs to any extent on the individual's having declared his membership of the covenant people by embracing these distinctively Jewish rites.

Two clarificatory corollaries again follow.

1. 'Works of law', 'works of the law' are nowhere understood here, either by his Jewish interlocutors or by Paul himself, as works which *earn* God's favour, as merit-amassing observances. They are rather seen as *badges*: they are simply what membership of the covenant people involves, what mark out the Jews as God's people; given by God for precisely that reason, they serve to demonstrate covenant status. They are the proper response to God's covenant grace, the minimal commitment for members of God's people. In other words, Paul has in view precisely what Sanders calls 'covenantal nomism'. And what he denies is that God's justification depends on 'covenantal nomism', that God's grace extends only to those who wear the badge of the covenant. This is a historical conclusion of some importance, since it begins to clarify with more precision what were the continuities and discontinuities between Paul, his fellow Jewish Christians and his own Pharisaic past, so far as justification and grace, covenant and law are concerned.

2. More important for Reformation exegesis is the corollary that 'works of the law' do *not* mean 'good works' in general, 'good works' in the sense disparaged by the heirs of Luther, works in the sense of self-achievement, 'man's self-powered striving to undergird his own existence in forgetfulness of his creaturely existence' (to quote a famous definition from Bultmann).[34] The phrase 'works of the law' in Galatians 2.16 is, in fact, a fairly restricted one: it refers precisely to these same identity markers described above, *covenant* works – those regulations prescribed by the law which any good Jew would simply take for granted to describe what a good Jew did. To be a Jew was to be a member of the covenant, was to observe circumcision, food laws and sabbath. In short, once again Paul seems much less a man of sixteenth-century Europe and

much more firmly in touch with the reality of first-century Judaism than many have thought.

(c) In contrast to righteousness understood in terms of works of the law, Paul speaks of righteousness *through faith in Jesus Christ* – not just faith as such, but faith in Jesus Christ, Jesus Messiah. We are at once reminded that this is an internal Christian debate – between Paul and Peter, two Jews, but Jews who are also believers in Jesus. Paul appeals to what was obviously the common foundation belief of the new movement. What distinguishes Peter, Paul and the others from their fellow Jews is their belief in Jesus as Messiah.

But here we must be sure of what we are saying. Is it in fact this faith in *Jesus* (as) Messiah which marks them off from their fellow Jews, or is it their belief in justification by *faith*, as has so often been assumed? In the light of Sanders' findings, as we have already noted, it is much less obvious than once appeared that the typical first-century Jew would have denied justification by faith. The emphasis on God's electing grace, his covenantal mercy and loving-kindness, the very fact that one of Paul's key terms, 'the righteousness of God', is drawn directly from the Old Testament in form and content – all this raises the question, *What is the point at issue here?* If not 'justification by faith' as God's initiative in declaring in favour of men, if not 'works of law' as merit-earning good works, then what? What precisely is involved in Paul's contrast between being justified by works of law and being justified by faith in Jesus Messiah?

Our verse suggests one answer: Paul's point is precisely that these two *are* alternatives – justification by works of law and justification by faith in Jesus are *antithetical opposites*. To say that God's favourable action towards anyone is dependent in any degree on works of the law is to *contradict* the claim that God's favour depends on faith, faith in Jesus Christ. Indeed it is quite likely that Galatians 2.16 reflects the step by which Paul's thinking hardened these two propositions into a clear-cut antithesis. Let me try to explain how I reach this conclusion.

According to verse 16a the common ground (between Peter and Paul) is that 'a man is not justified by works of law *except* through faith in Jesus Christ'. Notice how he expresses the last phrase – 'except through faith in Jesus Messiah'. According to the most obvious grammatical sense, in this clause faith in Jesus is described as a *qualification* to justification by works of law, not (yet) as an antithetical alternative. Seen from the perspective of Jewish Christianity at that time, the most obvious meaning is that *the only restriction on justification by works of law is faith in Jesus as Messiah.* The only restriction, that is, to covenantal nomism is faith in Christ. *But*, in this first clause, covenantal nomism itself is not

195

challenged or called in question – restricted, qualified, more precisely defined in relation to Jesus as Messiah, but not denied. Given that in Jewish self-understanding covenantal nomism is *not* antithetical to faith,[35] then at this point the only change which the new movement calls for is that the traditional Jewish faith be more precisely defined as faith in Jesus Messiah. This is evidently the accepted view of Jewish Christians to which Paul appeals.

The point, then, is that the common ground from which Paul's argument moves out need not be understood as setting covenantal nomism and faith in Christ in antithesis. As Peter's conduct and the conduct of the rest of the Jewish believers at Antioch made abundantly clear, so far as the Jewish Christian was concerned, belief in Jesus as Messiah did not require him to abandon his Jewishness, to give up the badges of his national religion, to call in question works of the law as the still necessary response of the Jew to God's covenant grace. And why not? Why should a Jewish belief in a Jewish Messiah make any difference to these long-established Jewish distinctives?

But Paul followed a different logic – the logic of justification by faith: what is of grace through faith cannot depend in any sense, in any degree, on a particular ritual response. If God's verdict in favour of an individual comes to effect through his faith, then it is dependent on nothing more than that. So, in repeating the contrast between justification by works of law and justification through faith in Jesus Christ, Paul alters it significantly: what were initially juxtaposed as complementary, are now posed as straight alternatives – '. . . knowing that a man is not justified from works of law *except* through faith in Jesus Christ, we have believed in Christ Jesus in order that we might be justified from faith in Christ, and *not* from works of law . . .' Moreover, in describing justification by faith in Christ, Paul varies the formula slightly: we are justified not only *through* faith in Christ but also *from* faith in Christ – the implication quite probably being that in Paul's view faith in Christ is the only necessary and sufficient response that God looks for in justifying anyone.

In other words, in verse 16 Paul pushes what began as a qualification of covenantal nomism into an outright antithesis. If we have been accepted by God on the basis of faith, then it is on the basis of faith that we are acceptable, and *not* on the basis of works. Perhaps, then, for the first time, in this verse faith in Jesus Messiah begins to emerge not simply as a *narrower* definition of the elect of God, but as an *alternative* definition of the elect of God. From being *one* identity marker for the Jewish Christian alongside the other identity markers (circumcision, food laws, sabbath), faith in Jesus as Christ becomes the primary identity marker which renders the others superfluous.

196

This line of exposition can be re-expressed in a slightly different way, with more emphasis on the salvation-history significance of Christ. The question Paul was in effect grappling with at this point is this: How do we Jewish believers relate our covenantal nomism, our works of law, our obligations under the covenant, to our new faith in Jesus as the Christ? Or, in slightly broader terms: What difference does the coming of Jesus the Messiah make to our traditional understanding of the covenant? The answer of many Jerusalem believers seems to have been, None; no difference; it is still God's covenant with Israel into which Gentiles can be received on the recognized and well-established conditions. Others, including the leading apostles, were willing to dispense Gentile believers from the need to be circumcised as an entry requirement, but when it came to the 'crunch' they still in effect expected the Gentile believers to live as those within the covenant in traditional terms, to maintain covenant status by, in particular, conforming with the food and purity regulations which governed the meal table – even Peter and Barnabas (2.12–14). Their answer to the question was in effect: Christ's coming has made some difference, but in the day-to-day event not much; the people of God are still to be defined in essentially and distinctively Jewish terms. But at precisely this point Paul begins to develop a different answer.

In brief, Paul's new answer is that the advent of Christ had introduced the time of fulfilment, including the fulfilment of his purpose regarding the covenant. From the beginning, God's eschatological purpose in making the covenant had been the blessing of the nations: the gospel was already proclaimed when God promised Abraham, 'In you shall all the nations be blessed' (Gal. 3.8; Gen. 12.3; 18.18). So, now that the time of fulfilment had come, the covenant should no longer be conceived in nationalistic or racial terms. No longer is it an exclusively Jewish *qua* Jewish privilege. The covenant is not thereby abandoned. Rather it is broadened out as God had originally intended – with the grace of God which it expressed separated from its national restriction and freely bestowed without respect to race or work, as it had been bestowed in the beginning. This is roughly the argument of Galatians 3—4, as also developed later in Romans 3—4.

The decisive corollary which Paul saw, and which he did not hesitate to draw, was that the covenant is no longer to be identified or characterized by such distinctively Jewish observances as circumcision, food laws and sabbath. *Covenant* works had become too closely identified as *Jewish* observances, *covenant* righteousness as *national* righteousness.[36] But to maintain such identifications was to ignore both the way the covenant began and the purpose it had been intended to fulfil in the end. To continue to insist on such works of the law was to ignore the central fact for Christians, that with Christ's coming God's covenant purpose had reached its intended final stage in which the more fundamental identity marker (Abraham's faith) reasserts its primacy over against the too narrowly nationalistic identity markers of circumcision, food laws and sabbath.

If this understanding of Galatians 2.16 is correct, then we are in fact being given the unique privilege in this verse of witnessing a very crucial development for the history of Christianity taking place, before our very eyes, as it were. For in this verse we are seeing the transition from a basically Jewish self-understanding of Christ's significance to a distinctively different understanding, the transition indeed from a form of Jewish Messianism to a faith which sooner or later must break away from Judaism to exist in its own terms.

Once again two clarificatory corollaries.

1. We should not let our grasp of Paul's reasoning slip back into the old distinction between faith and works in general, between faith and 'good works'. Paul is not arguing here for a concept of faith which is totally passive because it fears to become a 'work'. It is the demand for a *particular* work as the necessary expression of faith which he denies. As he puts it later in the same letter, 'In Christ Jesus neither circumcision nor uncircumcision is of any avail, but faith working through love' (5.6).

2. Nor should we press Paul's distinction between faith and works into a dichotomy between faith and ritual, simply because the works of the law which he has in mind belong to what has often been called the ritual or ceremonial law. There *is* a distinction between outward and inward, between ritual and spiritual, but no necessary antithesis. Paul has no intention here of denying a ritual expression of faith, as in baptism or the Lord's Supper. Here again we should keep the precise limitations of Paul's distinction between faith in Christ and works of law before us. What he is concerned to exclude is the *racial* not the *ritual* expression of faith; it is *nationalism* which he denies not *activism*. Whatever their basis in the Scriptures, these works of the law had become identified as indices of Jewishness, as badges betokening race and nation – inevitably so when race and religion are so inextricably intertwined as they were, and are, in Judaism. What Jesus has done by his death and resurrection, in Paul's understanding, is to free the grace of God in justifying from its nationalistically restrictive clamps for a broader experience (beyond the circumcised Jew) and a fuller expression (beyond concern for ritual purity).

(d) Finally, we should take note of the last clause of our verse, where Paul probably alludes to Psalm 143.2.[37] Our thesis also helps explain why Paul should use the Psalm in the way he does, why he

both modifies and adds to the Psalmist's words. In Psalm 143.2 we
read the plea:

> Enter not into judgement with your servant;
> for no man living is righteous before you.

Paul does two things to the second half of the Psalm verse: he adds
'from works of law', and he substitutes 'all flesh' for 'all living'.
Where the Psalmist said

> no living (being) will be justified before you,

Paul rephrases thus,

> by *works of law* no *flesh* will be justified.[38]

How can he justify restricting the more general statement by
adding 'from works of law'? The simplest answer is probably given
in the substitution of 'all flesh' for 'all living'. 'All flesh' is a quite
acceptable synonym for 'all living'. But it has the merit, for Paul, of
focusing the unacceptability of man in his fleshliness. By that, of
course, Paul will not intend a dualism between spirit and matter,
however dualistic his antithesis between spirit and flesh may seem
later on in Galatians 5. He certainly has in mind man's weakness,
his corruptibility, his dependence on the satisfaction of merely
human appetites (4.13–14; 5.16–17; 6.8). But the word 'flesh' also
embraces the thought of a merely human relationship, of a heritage
determined by physical descent, as in the allegory of Galatians 4
(4.23, 29).[39] That is to say, in speaking of 'all flesh' Paul has in view
primarily and precisely those who think their acceptability to God
and standing before God *does* depend on their physical descent
from Abraham, their national identity as Jews. It is precisely this
attitude, which puts too much stress on fleshly relationships and
fleshly rites, precisely this attitude which Paul excoriates in his
parting shot in 6.12–13 – 'they want to make a good showing in the
flesh ... they want to glory in your flesh'.

With the Psalm reference thus more sharply defined in terms of
physical and national identity, the addition of 'from works of law'
becomes merely clarificatory. It does not narrow the Psalmist's
assertion any further; rather it ties into and emphasizes more
clearly the 'all flesh'. For works of the law, epitomized in this letter
by circumcision, are precisely acts of the flesh. To insist on
circumcision is to give a primacy to the physical level of relationship which Paul can no longer accept. 'Works of the *law*', because
they put such an emphasis on such marks of racial identity, are,
ironically, no different from 'works of the flesh' (5.19), so far as
acceptability before God is concerned – precisely because these
works of the law in effect imprison God's righteousness within a
racial and national, that is, fleshly framework. Whereas those who

belong to Christ, from Paul's perspective, have passed through a different starting-point (the gift of the Spirit – 3.3), have crucified the flesh (5.24), and the life they now lead in the flesh they live not in terms of fleshly rites or fleshly relationships but by faith in the Son of God (2.20). God's purposes and God's people have now expanded beyond Israel according to the flesh, and so God's righteousness can no longer be restricted in terms of works of the law which emphasize kinship at the level of the flesh.

Two final corollaries by way of clarification.

1. Yet once more we must note that it is *works* of the law that Paul disparages, not the law itself or law-keeping in general. In his latest contribution to the discussion Sanders recognizes the nationalistic significance of circumcision, food laws and sabbath,[40] but he keeps taking the phrase 'works of the law' as though it was simply a fuller synonym for 'law'. So far as Sanders is concerned, 'no man shall be justified by works of law' is just the same as saying, 'no man shall be justified by the law'.[41] But Paul is as little opposed to the law *per se* as he is to good works *per se*. It is the law understood in terms of *works*, as a Jewish prerogative and national monopoly, to which he takes exception. The law understood in terms of the command to 'love your neighbour as yourself' is another matter (Gal. 5.14).

2. So, too, lest the point still be confused, I repeat, Paul here is not disparaging works in general or pressing a dichotomy between outward ritual done in the flesh and inward grace operative in the spirit. Once again we must observe the limited target he has in his sights. It is works which betoken racial prerogative to which he objects, acts done in the flesh because faith in Christ is reckoned insufficient as the badge of covenant membership which he denounces. Over against Peter and the other Jewish Christians Paul insists that God's verdict in favour of believers comes to realization through faith, from start to finish, and in no way depends on observing the works of law which hitherto had characterized and distinguished the Jews as God's people.

III

So much for Galatians 2.16. Time does not permit me to follow the development of the same line of argument through the rest of the letter, though I believe that it helps resolve more than one crux in subsequent chapters. Likewise, Paul's later letter to the Roman Christians gains considerably in coherence when viewed from the same perspective. For example, when in Romans 3.27 Paul affirms that boasting is excluded, he is not thinking of boasting in self-achievement or boasting at one's good deeds.[42] It is the boasting of the Jew which he has in mind – the boasting in Israel's special relationship with God through election, the boasting in the law as the mark of God's favour, in circumcision as the badge of belonging to God (Rom. 2.17–29). Among other things, this means that there is no significant development in Paul's thought on this particular point, at least, between Galatians and Romans. However, further exposition will have to await the commentary on Romans which I mentioned at the beginning, and which, as you may appreciate, I am now a good deal more enthusiastic about writing than I was when first asked.

It would also be premature, of course, to build extensive conclusions on the basis of just one verse. Nevertheless, there is some obligation at the end of a lecture like this to attempt some summing up, and at least to sketch out the preliminary results which seem to follow so far from this new perspective on Paul, but which must naturally be subjected to further testing.

(a) In Galatians 2.16 Paul actually addresses Judaism as we know it to have been in the first century – a system of religion conscious of its special relationship with God and sensitive to its peculiar obligations within that relationship. The criticisms of Paul for his misunderstanding of Judaism therefore involve a double failure of perspective. What Jewish scholars rejected as *Paul's* misunderstanding of Judaism is *itself* a misunderstanding of Paul, based on the standard Protestant (mis)reading of Paul through Reformation spectacles. When we take these Reformation spectacles off, Paul does not appear to be so out of touch with his first-century context as even Sanders thinks. Sanders in effect freed Pauline exegesis from its sixteenth-century blinkers, but he has still left us with a Paul who could have made little sense to his fellow Jews and whose stated willingness to observe the law elsewhere (1 Cor. 9.19–23) must have sounded like the most blatant self-contradiction.

(b) The major exegetical flaw of Sanders' reconstruction of Paul's view of the law (and of course not only his)[43] is his failure to perceive the significance of the little phrase 'works of the law'. He recognizes rightly that in disparaging 'works of the law' Paul is not disparaging good works in general, far less is he thinking of good works as earning merit. But by taking 'works of law' as equivalent to 'doing the law' in general (the normal exegesis), he is led to the false conclusion that in disparaging 'works of the law' Paul is disparaging law as such, has broken with Judaism as a whole. To be fair, the mistake is a natural one, since Judaism had itself invested so much significance in these particular works, so that the test of loyalty to covenant and law was precisely the observance of circumcision, food laws and sabbath.[44] But it is these works in particular which Paul has in mind, and he has them in mind precisely because they had become the expression of a too narrowly

201

nationalistic and racial conception of the covenant, because they had become a badge not of Abraham's faith but of Israel's boast.[45] Although Sanders has seen this point quite clearly,[46] he does not follow it through, and his failure to distinguish 'works of the law' from 'doing the law' prevents him from developing the insight properly.[47]

This failure has had serious consequences for Sanders' larger thesis. For had he delimited more precisely the force of Paul's negative thrust against works of the law, he would have been able to give a more adequate account of Paul's more positive attitude to the law elsewhere. In particular, he would not have had to press so hard the distinction between 'getting in' (not by doing the law) and 'staying in' (by keeping the law), a distinction which seems very odd precisely at Galatians 2.16, where the issue at Antioch was the day-to-day conduct of those who had already believed (2.14), and where Paul's concern regarding the Galatians is over their ending rather than their beginning (3.3).[48] In consequence also he would not have had to argue for such an arbitrary and abrupt discontinuity between Paul's gospel and his Jewish past, according to which Sanders' Paul hardly seems to be addressing Sanders' Judaism. Whereas, if Paul was really speaking against the too narrow understanding of God's covenant promise and of the law in nationalist and racial terms, as I have argued, a much more coherent and consistent reconstruction of the continuities and discontinuities between Paul and Palestinian Judaism becomes possible.

(c) All this confirms the earlier important thesis of Stendahl, that Paul's doctrine of justification by faith should not be understood primarily as an exposition of the individual's relation to God, but primarily in the context of Paul the Jew wrestling with the question of how Jews and Gentiles stand in relation to each other within the covenant purpose of God now that it has reached its climax in Jesus Christ.[49] It is precisely the degree to which Israel had come to regard the covenant and the law as coterminous with Israel, as Israel's special prerogative, wherein the problem lay. Paul's solution does not require him to deny the covenant, or indeed the law as God's law, but only the covenant and the law as 'taken over' by Israel. The models of the man of faith are for Paul the founding fathers, Abraham, Isaac and Jacob, where covenant membership was neither determined by physical descent (racial consanguinity) nor dependent on works of law (Rom. 4; 9.6–13). This certainly involved something of an arbitrary hermeneutical procedure, whereby the example of Abraham in particular was treated not only as typical and normative, but also as relativizing those subsequent Scriptures which emphasize Israel's special place within God's affections. But it is a procedure which Paul is more than willing to argue for and defend rather than simply to state in a take-it-or-leave-it, black-and-white way.

Once again, however, we are beginning to push too far beyond the proper limits of the present essay, and I must desist. But hopefully I have said enough to show how valuable the new perspective on Paul may be in giving us a clearer insight into and appreciation of him and his theology.

Notes

1. F. F. Bruce, *Paul: Apostle of the Free Spirit* (Exeter, 1977); O. Kuss, *Paulus: die Rolle des Apostels in der theologischen Entwicklung der Urkirche* (Regensburg, 1971); H. Schlier, *Grundzüge einer paulinischen Theologie* (Freiburg/Basel/Wien, 1978).
2. A. Suhl, *Paulus und seine Briefe: ein Beitrag zur paulinischen Chronologie* (Gütersloh, 1975); R. Jewett, *Dating Paul's Life* (London, 1979); G. Lüdemann, *Paulus, der Heidenapostel Band I: Studien zur Chronologie* (Göttingen, 1980).
3. S. Kim, *The Origin of Paul's Gospel* (Tübingen, 1981); J. C. Beker, *Paul the Apostle: the Triumph of God in Life and Thought* (Philadelphia, 1980).
4. A. Lindemann, *Paulus im ältesten Christentum* (Tübingen, 1979).
5. J. W. Drane, *Paul: Libertine or Legalist?* (London, 1975); H. Hübner, *Das Gesetz bei Paulus* (Göttingen, 1978, ²1980).
6. See particularly the work of G. Theissen, *Studien zur Soziologie des Urchristentums* (Tübingen, 1979), partial ET, *The Social Setting of Pauline Christianity* (Edinburgh, 1982).
7. See, e.g., K. P. Donfried, ed., *The Romans Debate* (Minneapolis, 1977); R. McL. Wilson, 'Gnosis in Corinth', *Paul and Paulinism: Essays in Honour of C. K. Barrett*, ed. M. D. Hooker and S. G. Wilson (London, 1982), pp. 102–14; G. Howard, *Paul: Crisis in Galatia* (Cambridge, 1979).
8. See particularly H. D. Betz, 'The Literary Composition and Function of Paul's Letter to the Galatians', *NTS*, 21 (1974–5), pp. 353–79; also *Galatians* (Hermeneia: Philadelphia, 1979); W. Wuellner, 'Paul's Rhetoric of Argumentation in Romans', *CBQ*, 38 (1976), pp. 330–51, reprinted in *The Romans Debate* (n. 7 above), pp. 152–74; also 'Greek Rhetoric and Pauline Argumentation', *Early Christian Literature and the Classical Intellectual Tradition: in honorem R. M. Grant*, ed. W. R. Schoedel and R. L. Wilken (Paris, 1979), pp. 177–88; R. Jewett, 'Romans as an Ambassadorial Letter', *Interpretation*, 36 (1982), pp. 5–20.
9. I refer particularly to *Jesus and the Spirit* (London, 1975) and *Christology in the Making* (London, 1980).
10. E. P. Sanders, *Paul and Palestinian Judaism: a Comparison of Patterns of Religion* (London, 1977). Cf. the estimate of W. D. Davies in the Preface to the fourth edition of his *Paul and Rabbinic Judaism* (Philadelphia, 1981): 'a work of immense learning and penetration, a major milestone in Pauline scholarship . . . of potentially immense significance for the interpretation of Paul' (pp. xxix–xxx).
11. Sanders, *Paul*, p. 6. See the fuller survey 'Paul and Judaism in New Testament scholarship' on pp. 1–12.
12. Sanders traces the dominance of this very negative evaluation of the Judaism of Paul's time back to F. Weber, *System der altsynagogalen palästinischen Theologie aus Targum, Midrasch und Talmud* (1880), revised as *Jüdische Theologie auf Grund des Talmud und verwandter Schriften* (Leipzig, 1897). For the following

paragraph see also Sanders on 'The persistence of the view of Rabbinic religion as one of legalistic works-righteousness' (*Paul*, pp. 33–59).

13. K. Stendahl, 'The Apostle Paul and the Introspective Conscience of the West', *HTR*, 56 (1963), pp. 199–215, reprinted in his *Paul Among Jews and Gentiles* (London, 1977), pp. 78–96. See also the several recent contributions by W. D. Davies in this area – 'Paul and the People of Israel', *NTS*, 24 (1977–8), pp. 4–39; also *Paul and Rabbinic Judaism*⁴, pp. xxvii f.; also 'Paul and the Law: Reflection on Pitfalls in Interpretation', *Paul and Paulinism* (n. 7 above), pp. 4–16.

14. e.g. R. Bultmann, *Jesus Christ and Mythology* (London, 1960); 'Demythologizing is the radical application of the doctrine of justification by faith to the sphere of knowledge and thought' (p. 84); E. Käsemann, *Das Neue Testament als Kanon* (Göttingen, 1970): 'Die Rechtfertigung des Gottlosen ... muss als Kanon im Kanon betrachtet werden ...' (p. 405).

15. Hübner (n. 5 above).

16. Sanders, *Paul*, pp. 75, 420, 544. Worth noting is the fact that J. Neusner, though fiercely critical of Sanders' methodology, nevertheless accepts Sanders' understanding of Judaism in terms of 'covenantal nomism' as valid. That rabbinic discussions *presupposed* the covenant and 'were largely directed toward the question of how to fulfil the covenantal obligations' is to Neusner a 'wholly sound and ... self-evident proposition'. 'So far as Sanders proposes to demonstrate the importance to all the kinds of ancient Judaism of covenantal nomism, election, atonement, and the like, his work must be pronounced a complete success' – 'Comparing Judaisms', *History of Religions*, 18 (1978–9), pp. 177–91 (here pp. 177, 180).

17. See particularly Sanders, *Paul*, pp. 550–2.

18. H. Hübner, 'Pauli Theologiae Proprium', *NTS*, 26 (1979–80), pp. 445–73.

19. H. Räisänen, 'Legalism and Salvation by the Law', in *Die Paulinische Literatur und Theologie*, hrsg. S. Pedersen (Göttingen, 1980), pp. 63–83.

20. M. Hooker, 'Paul and Covenantal Nomism', *Paul and Paulinism* (n. 7 above), pp. 47–56.

21. Sanders, *Paul, the Law, and the Jewish People*, p. 47.

22. cf. H. Räisänen, 'Paul's Theological Difficulties with the Law', *Studia Biblica 1978*, vol. III, ed. E. A. Livingstone (*JSNTSupp.* 3: Sheffield, 1980), pp. 301–20.

23. See J. D. G. Dunn, 'The Incident at Antioch (Gal. 2.11–18)', reprinted above, ch. 6.

24. 'Incident at Antioch', ch. 6 above, p. 172, n. 117.

25. It is unlikely that Paul wrote εἰδότες δέ. (1) δέ is omitted by P⁴⁶ as well as by other important manuscripts, and was probably introduced by a scribe who misread the flow of Paul's thought and assumed that an adversative particle should be added. (2) Had Paul wished to give adversative force he would have more probably written ἡμεῖς ἐσμέν φύσει Ἰουδαῖοι ... οἴδαμεν δὲ ... (contrast Rom. 6.9 and 2 Cor. 4.14 with Rom. 8.28). In fact what he wrote is 'We Jews by nature ... knowing that ...' (cf. H. Schlier, *Galater* [Göttingen, ⁴1965], p. 89). If he did not follow the construction through consistently, that is hardly untypical of Paul. (3) The ἐὰν μή confirms that v. 16a is intended to express the *Jewish* (Christian) understanding of justification through faith (see p. 195 above).

26. Clem. Hom. 11.16 – 'The Jew believes God and keeps the law ... But he who keeps not the law is manifestly a deserter through not believing God; and thus is no Jew, but a sinner ...' Cf. K. Kertelge, 'Zur Deutung des Rechtfertigungsbegriffs im Galaterbrief', *BZ*, 12 (1968), p. 213; U. Wilckens, 'Was heisst bei Paulus: "Aus Werken des Gezetzes wird kein Mensch gerecht"?', (1969), *Rechtfertigung als Freiheit: Paulusstudien* (Neukirchen, 1974), pp. 87–8; F. Mussner, *Galaterbrief* (Freiburg/Basel/Wien, ³1977), pp. 167–9.

27. See Dunn, 'Incident at Antioch', ch. 6 above, §4.1c; also J. D. G. Dunn, *Romans* (Dallas, 1988), pp. lxix–lxx.
28. See particularly S. K. Williams, 'The "Righteousness of God" in Romans', *JBL*, 99 (1980), pp. 260f.; Dunn, *Romans*, pp. 40–2. For references to the Dead Sea scrolls see also Mussner, *Galaterbrief*, pp. 168f.
29. Sanders repeatedly emphasizes that 'to be righteoused' (*sic*) in Paul is 'transfer terminology'. See further, Dunn, *Romans*, p. 97.
30. Full details in M. Stern, ed., *Greek and Latin Authors on Jews and Judaism* (Israel Academy of Sciences and Humanities: Jerusalem, Vol I, 1976, Vol. II, 1980), §§ 194, 195, 258, 281, 301.
31. See Philo, *Migr.*, 89–93; cf. *Qu. Ex.*, II, 2.
32. See particularly J. Neusner, *From Politics to Piety* (Englewood Cliffs, 1973), pp. 80, 83–90.
33. Kertelge (n. 26 above): 'Die *erga nomou* in v. 16 sind also der Ausdruck des jüdischen Selbstbewusstseins von v. 15' (p. 215).
34. R. Bultmann, *Theology of the New Testament*, I (ET, London, 1952), p. 254. Cf., e.g., H. Ridderbos, *Paul: an Outline of his Theology* (1966; ET, London, 1977), p. 139; E. Käsemann, *Romans* (HNT, 1973; ET, London, 1980), pp. 93, 102, 284; Hübner, *Gesetz*, p. 102; Beker, *Paul*, p. 247.
35. Mussner, *Galaterbrief*: 'Der Jude lässt die pln. Antithetik "Glaube" – "Werke des Gesetzes" – nicht gelten, ja sie ist ihm unverständlich' (p. 170).
36. A phrase I owe to N. T. Wright; see his Oxford D. Phil. thesis: *The Messiah and the People of God: a study in Pauline Theology with particular reference to the argument of the Epistle to the Romans* (1980), pp. 89f.
37. Despite Mussner's misgivings (*Galaterbrief*, pp. 174f.), Paul probably did intend an allusion to the Psalm, as the parallel with Rom. 3.20 confirms, since the allusion is clearer there.
38. The omission of 'before you' from Ps. 143.2 in Gal. 2.16 has no significance, as the *retention* of the phrase in the Rom. 3.20 allusion to the same passage makes clear.
39. See J. D. G. Dunn, 'Jesus – Flesh and Spirit: an Exposition of Romans 1.3–4', *JTS*, 24 (1973), pp. 43–9.
40. See n. 46 below.
41. See also E. P. Sanders, 'On the Question of Fulfilling the Law in Paul and Rabbinic Judaism', *Donum Gentilicum: New Testament Studies in Honour of David Daube*, ed. C. K. Barrett, E. Bammel and W. D. Davies (Oxford, 1978), pp. 103–26.
42. Contrast those cited in n. 34 above.
43. It is unfair to pick out Sanders, since this is the common view of the matter, usually the result of basing exegesis primarily on Gal. 3.11 and of reading 3.10 in the light of it without sufficient reference to the initial emphatic statement of 2.16. See, e.g., N. A. Dahl, *Studies in Paul* (Minneapolis, 1977), pp. 106, 170; U. Wilckens, 'Zur Entwicklung des paulinischen Gesetzverständnis', *NTS*, 28 (1982), pp. 166–9; Mussner, *Galaterbrief*: 'Nur eine naive Exegese könnte ... "die Werke des Gesetzes" auf die rituellen Vorschriften des Judentums beschranken' (p. 170). But see n. 45 below.
44. We may compare the way in which in fundamentalist circles doctrines of substitutionary atonement and inerrancy of Scripture have been regarded as touchstones of orthodoxy, even when several other doctrines are acknowledged to be of equal or greater importance.
45. The same point applies to the distinction between the ritual and the moral law frequently attributed to Paul. The point is that Paul does not presuppose or develop that distinction as such. His more negative attitude to the ritual prescriptions of the law arises from the fact that it is precisely in and by these rituals as such that his Jewish kinsmen had most clearly marked themselves out

as God's people the Jews – and been identified by others as 'that peculiar people' (see n. 30 above).

46. See, e.g., his *Paul, the Law, and the Jewish People*, p. 33 – 'Boasting' in Rom. 3.27 refers to 'the assumption of special status on the part of the Jews' (also p. 35); his recognition of the significance of circumcision, sabbath and food laws (pp. 101–2) – 'the most obvious common denominator to these laws is the fact that they distinguish Jews from Gentiles' (p. 114); and his quotation from Gaston ('Israel as a whole interpreted the righteousness of God as establishing the status of righteousness for Israel alone, excluding the Gentiles') and Howard ('Their own righteousness' is their 'collective righteousness to the exclusion of the Gentiles') in his notes (p. 61, n. 107). The earlier article by J. B. Tyson, '"Works of Law" in Galatians', *JBL*, 92 (1973), pp. 423–31, shares similar strengths and weaknesses.

47. e.g. 'The explanation of "not by faith but by works"', then, is "they did not believe in Christ" . . . Israel's failure is not that they do not obey the law in the correct way, but that they do not have faith in Christ' (p. 37) – where I would rather say, 'they relied on their covenant status, as attested by the works of the law, rather than on Christ'; 'His criticism of his own former life is not that he was guilty of the attitudinal sin of self-righteousness, but that he put confidence in something other than faith in Jesus Christ' (p. 44) – *Tertium datur!*, . . . guilty of putting his confidence in his being a Jew and in his zeal as a devout Jew; 'The only thing that is wrong with the old righteousness seems to be that it is not the new one' (p. 140) – No! that it was too narrowly and nationalistically 'Jewish'; 'In Pauline theory, Jews who enter the Christian movement renounce nothing' (p. 176) – except their claim to a Jewish monopoly of divine righteousness.

48. Sanders tries to grapple with this point in his first main section of *Paul, the Law, and the Jewish People* (p. 52, n. 20), and in effect acknowledges that the issue is 'being in' (what covenant membership involves) rather than a distinction between getting in and staying in as such. The Jewish Christians and Judaizers wanted not simply a one-off action from the Gentile believers, but a continuing lifestyle in accordance with the Torah.

49. cf. Stendahl, *Paul among Jews and Gentiles, passim* – e.g. '. . . a doctrine of faith was hammered out by Paul for the very specific and limited purpose of defending the rights of Gentile converts to be full and genuine heirs to the promises of God to Israel' (p. 2).

Additional Note

'The New Perspective' brought a number of responses – particularly rejoinders from H. Räisänen and H. Hübner, the former delivered at the Basel SNTS Seminar at which I also delivered the first version of my 'Works of the Law' paper (ch. 8 below), and in which Hübner also participated. Räisänen's paper was published as 'Galatians 2.16 and Paul's Break with Judaism', *NTS* 31 (1985) 543–53, reprinted in *The Torah and Christ*, Helsinki: Finnish Exegetical Society 45 (1986) 168–84. And in the same year Hübner's response also appeared, '*Was heisst bei Paulus "Werke des Gesetzes"?*', *Glaube und Eschatologie*, W. G. Kümmel Festschrift, ed. E. Grasser and O. Merk, Tübingen: Mohr (1985) 123–33.

Räisänen's criticism is the most sustained. He makes four principal points.

1. The noun phrase δικαιοσύνη θεοῦ and the verb διακαιοῦσθαι must be carefully distinguished. Galatians 2.16 *does* have in view *entry* into the community; δικαιοῦσθαι there is 'transfer terminology' and is different from pre-Christian Jewish usage.[1]

2. The continuity between Judaism and Paul is overstressed. The faith of which Galatians 2.16 speaks is not faith in the sense of (Jewish) recognition of God's covenant grace. It is faith *in Jesus Christ*, and *this* is something novel in Judaism.[2] And even if 'justification by faith' could be described as a Jewish theologoumenon, Dunn does acknowledge that Paul's further emphasis on justification by faith in Christ as an antithetical alternative to covenantal nomism was bound to result in a break away from Judaism.[3]

3. The suggestion of a movement in thought within Galatians 2.16 does not square with the text. 'The flow of thought in verse 16 is quite smooth. There is no formal indication of a contrast between the beginning and the end ... Justification by works of the law is denied throughout verse 16, as it is in the rest of the letter.'[4] Stuhlmacher (see below) also made the same point: can Galatians 2.16a and 16b be read in the sense of a 'radicalizing gradation'?

4. The attack Paul mounts is not simply on a particular *attitude* to the law,[5] but on the law itself. Jews as well as Gentiles must *enter* the new community. Paul's positive comments on the law are not to be explained away: they reflect Paul's attempt to maintain and emphasize continuity with Judaism ('Dunn comes close to describing Paul's position as *Paul himself* wished it to be understood'). But his actual teaching on the law was inconsistent with that objective; his position amounted to a *de facto* break with Judaism (as Sanders has so clearly seen).[6] In short, 'Paul's critique of the law is much more radical than Dunn allows and we should not shrink from speaking of his "break" with Judaism.'[7]

In response:

1. I am not impressed by attempts to pull δικαιοσύνη θεοῦ and δικαιοῦσθαι too far apart. Of course the terms δικαιοσύνη, δικαιοσύνη θεοῦ and δικαιοῦσθαι have different functions and different ranges of reference. But these functions and ranges also overlap. In particular, it is 'the righteousness of God' which 'makes righteous', as is surely clear in Romans 3.21–4, 26; and 'righteousness' is the effect of God 'making righteous', as is clear in Romans 4.2–3, 5, Galatians 3.6, 8 and 5.4–5. My point is that this degree of overlap prevents a neat dichotomy of reference, whereby the verb can be limited to 'transfer terminology'.

(a) 'Righteousness' is not only a status granted at conversion (by 'transfer'), but can also be used in reference to an ongoing status, or living relationship (as in Rom. 5.21), and to describe the end-point of the whole process (as in Rom. 6.16 and Gal. 5.5). 'The righteousness of God' is to be seen, therefore, as the outgoing power of grace which grants, sustains and finally secures that 'righteousness', not just a once-for-all act of transfer.

(b) The verb certainly does denote 'transfer' on several occasions; nearly half the relevant Pauline uses are aorist and perfect tenses. But more than half are present and future tenses. To be sure, the present tenses could be taken as 'timeless' presents, but most of the future tenses are best taken as referring to future (= final) justification (on the day of judgement) (Rom. 2.1; 3.20; Gal. 2.16; 5.4). Moreover, the aorists in Romans 8.30 appear to cover (in retrospect) the whole salvation process that lies between 'being called' and 'being glorified'; that is to say, they probably embrace the whole process from initial acceptance by God ('transfer') to the final vindication at the seat of judgement.[8] So too in Galatians 2.17 the aorist includes the seeking of justification as an ongoing goal. When these two sets of considerations are taken together (a and b), it becomes clearer that by 'the righteousness of God' Paul means the power of divine grace which is effective 'for salvation' (Rom. 1.16–17), from first to last.[9]

(c) The crucial fact remains that in the Antioch incident, and in Galatians, Paul was confronted by a view which insisted that covenant status could not be sustained without 'works of the law'. In Jewish covenant theology, that also meant final vindication could not be assured without 'works of the law'. And in the Jewish-Christian adaptation of that, covenant status and final vindication depended on justification by faith completed by 'works of the law' (the clear implication of Gal. 3.2–5; cf. Jas. 2.22–4). Paul's point is to insist precisely that the ongoing process of salvation is wholly of a piece with its beginning; that as their initial acceptance by God was through faith, so is their continuation (Gal. 3.2–5) and their final acceptance (Gal. 5.5).[10] Consequently the range of tenses in Galatians 2.16 probably denotes a richer theology of justification than Räisänen allows. To paraphrase the verse: 'Since man is justified through faith in Jesus Christ (the present tense can cover the whole process), we have believed in Christ Jesus (aorist = 'transfer') in order that we might be justified from faith in Christ and not from works of law (the aorist tense can refer to the goal of the whole process, as in 2.17 – the point being that justification is by *faith* from start to finish) because (as will become apparent at the last judgement) "no flesh will be justified by works of the law".' This seems a superior solution to Räisänen's, who can only maintain his attempt to limit the verb to 'transfer terminology' by allowing that 'in effect one has to "enter" *twice*: first here and then at the final judgment'.[11] With this admission my point has been largely conceded: Galatians 2.16 has in view *not only* the *initial* act of acceptance, but the question of what then is necessary to ensure *final* acceptance.

2. Of course Paul has in mind not just justification by faith, but justification by faith in Christ. Justification by faith *in Christ* is, if you like, the Jewish-*Christian* refinement of Jewish election theology, which I characterized as 'justification by faith' to underscore the presupposition of divine grace which is central to that theology. It is that Jewish-Christian understanding which provides Paul with sufficient common ground for his dialogue with his fellow Jewish believers in Christ, and out of that Paul develops his own more characteristic emphasis (Gal. 2.15–16). I do not dispute that the end result of this development was a breach between (rabbinic) Judaism and Christianity. I *do* dispute that this was ever Paul's intention or that it was inevitable within the context of the much broader stream of pre-70 Judaism. Within that broader stream Paul's interpretation of covenant and promise was a legitimate option for Jews (and Judaism) within a wider range of options.

3. I recognize that the lack of a clear adversative at the start of the

second clause of Galatians 2.16 makes for a distinct weakness in my exegesis. However, there is an equal or more serious weakness in the more normal exegesis, which can be posed thus. What is it that 'we Jews know' (Gal. 2.15–16)? That 'justification is by faith in Jesus Christ' – Yes! So clearly Paul has *Christian* Jews in mind, and almost certainly his rebuke to Peter at Antioch, or at least that situation.[12] But the problem is that these same Christian Jews (at Antioch) had also evidenced their belief that Christian Jews must still practise 'the works of the law' (in this case the Jewish food laws). So they evidently did not accept, in practice at any rate, that justification is by faith in Christ and *not* by works of law. In Galatians 2.16 Paul therefore attempts to press this antithesis as an 'either-or' (against the Jewish-Christian 'both-and'). As initial justification was by faith in Christ, and not by works of the law, so the outworking of that initial 'transfer' should be consistent with it – justification by faith in Christ and not by works of the law, for that will be the basis of the final judgement (Ps. 143.2). In short, Räisänen has grounds for his objection when Galatians 2.16 is read on its own, but when the context is taken into consideration the logic of the verse seems to favour the exegesis offered in Chapter 7 above.[13]

4. I am not particularly happy with Räisänen's characterization of my understanding of Paul as attacking 'a particular attitude to the law', though I do use the phrase as one of a number of possible ways of distinguishing my view of the matter from that of Räisänen. What I am more clear on is that Räisänen's own characterization of Paul as critiquing the law itself is much too blunt. Paul does seem to critique the law in a passage like Galatians 2.19. But he also defends the law in Romans 7.7–25 and affirms the law in passages like Romans 3.31, 8.4 and Galatians 5.14. And his critique is regularly more nuanced – law as 'letter' (Rom. 2.27; 7.6; 2 Cor. 3.6), 'works of the law' (Gal. 2.16; etc.), law as used by sin (Rom. 7.7–14), law understood as defining the scope of God's righteousness (Rom. 10.3–4), law as keeping Israel in a state of immaturity (Gal. 3.23—4.5), and so on. Whether this is better described as an 'attitude to the law' or the law perceived as operating in a certain way, defining the people of God, making specific demands on that people ('works of the law'), is perhaps a merely semantic quibble. What I am more certain of is that Räisänen has missed (as have many writing in this area) both such nuances and what I go on to describe in the next chapter as 'the social function of the law'.[14] Consequently I find Paul's treatment of the law a good deal more consistent than either Sanders or Räisänen. And talk of a 'break' with the law or with Judaism becomes less justified. To assume that baptism in the name of Jesus meant not just *entry* into the community (sect?) of believers in Jesus, but also in effect an *exit* from Judaism is a serious misperception of the self-understanding of both Jewish Christians and Paul. The 'new covenant' did not mean a new religion, but the eschatological fulfilment of the old in Messiah Jesus, not a *third* olive tree!,[15] but the full flourishing of the one olive tree cultured by God's electing grace (Rom. 11.16–24).

5. Besides Räisänen's sharp critique of 'The New Perspective', Hübner seems to have been content largely to describe 'The New Perspective' and

to echo the classic treatments of such as Bultmann and Käsemann that by 'works of the law' Paul has in mind the human attempt to lay claim on God, the thought of self-boasting before God, the law perverted as a means to self-justification.[16] He has therefore not really recognized or addressed the challenge posed to that view by 'the new perspective'. And since I have continued to elaborate that perspective and to show how deep are its foundations in the Pauline texts and the historical context, it may be sufficient to refer to the following chapter and to my *Romans*.[17]

In contrast to both the above, one may simply note the much more positive acceptance of the basic thesis of Chapter 7, from the Catholic side, by K. Kertelge, 'Gesetz und Freiheit im Galaterbrief', *NTS* 30 (1984) 382–94, particularly 391 and n. 24.

'The New Perspective' also drew some private correspondence with P. Stuhlmacher (24.9.83, my reply 3.10.83), who was then presumably working on his own response to Sanders and Räisänen;[18] and with E. P. Sanders (12.9.84, my reply 1.10.84), the principal debate partner in 'The New Perspective'.

The correspondence with Stuhlmacher clarified some points, and he lodged two further objections. (6) 'Works of the law' cannot be reduced to circumcision, food commandments and sabbath observance, as Romans 2.17ff. and 3.9–20 show. (7) Philippians 3.4–11 shows that the justification issue is as old as his calling; it is from here that his 'teaching' is to be determined, and not just from the Antioch controversy.

6. On the first point, I fully agree that Paul's critique does not reduce to questions of circumcision, food laws and sabbath, and I acknowledge that my formulation of the issue in 'The New Perspective' could be read too easily as though that is all that Paul had in mind when he spoke of 'works of the law'. This was one of the reasons why I returned to the subject in the following essay (ch. 8). There I make the point that the law had become too closely identified with Israel, as marking out Israel and marking off Israel from other nations, so that Gentiles by definition were 'outside the law', 'sinners' = outlaws. For those 'within the law', 'works of the law' are what the law requires; the two phrases are co-ordinate; 'works of the law' are what Sanders refers to in his phrase 'covenantal nomism'. But Israel's history had reinforced the reality of the law as a boundary dividing Israel from the (other) nations, and the Maccabean crisis in particular had focused that boundary function on two or three key 'make or break' issues – especially circumcision and food laws. They remained prominent at the time of Paul, for the same reason. In short, that is why it is precisely circumcision and food laws which are so much to the fore when Paul speaks of 'works of the law' in Galatians – *not* because they are the only 'works' which the law requires, but because they had become the crucial test cases for covenant loyalty and for maintaining Jewish identity as the people chosen by God for himself alone.

7. The second charge had in effect already been made by Houlden in his response to 'The Incident at Antioch' (ch. 6), and I may refer simply to the Additional Note 1 there. Paul's insight does go back to his call on the Damascus road, but I do think it took the circumcision issue at Jerusalem and the food laws controversy at Antioch to bring out for Paul the full

significance of his initiatory revelation and of the agreement that justification is by faith (alone!).

8. The letters exchanged with Sanders were lengthy and served to clarify the areas of our agreement and disagreement. I hope it is sufficiently clear from the above chapter how great is my indebtedness to Sanders. 'The New Perspective' is the one which he has made possible. I did attempt to document that indebtedness,[19] and could have noted further examples of agreement. Moreover, I was probably unfair in the original text at n. 46, in which I speak of Sanders only 'glimpsing' the point, and which I therefore have modified for this reprint. In view of the extent of our agreement it became important to understand the 'why' and to clarify the 'what' of our *dis*agreement. In my letter of 1.10.84 I suggested two main reasons.

(a) In his earlier book Sanders posed Paul's Christianity and Judaism as two different 'systems'.[20] It is probably this which heightens the impression for Sanders that Paul's 'conversion' was a 'transfer', involving a complete 'break' with the law and rejection of the law.[21] In my opinion, however, the break was not as radical as Sanders maintains and Paul was not so out of tune with the rest of first-century Judaism as Sanders believes. So, for example, when Sanders says, 'Israel's failure is not that they do not obey the law in the correct way, but that they do not have faith in Christ',[22] I disagree. Paul *does* criticize his fellow Jews for 'not obeying the law in the correct way' (Rom. 3.27, 31; 9.30–2; Gal. 3.10–11). Nor do I agree that Paul 'cast off, denied ... the election and the law',[23] only an abuse and misunderstanding in particularist (Sanders' term) and nationalist terms (my word).[24] In all these cases I would argue that my distinction between 'works of the law' and 'the law' is important, because 'works of law' denotes that way of regarding the law (as an identity and boundary marker defining the people of God) which Paul rejects – but not the law itself, the law seen from a different perspective and in different terms. But I have already said enough on this in response to Räisänen (point 4 above).

(b) The mistake of posing too radical an antithesis between Paul and Judaism/the law is compounded by the distinction between 'getting in' and 'staying in'. The debate in Galatians cannot be subsumed under the head of 'entry', not at least under 'entry' in sharp distinction from 'staying in'.[25] The disagreement is pointed up by Sanders' assertion that 'Paul's statement "not by works of law" has to do with entry into the body of Christ'.[26] 'Works of law' are what good Jews do to enact and demonstrate their loyalty to the covenant as given to Israel as Israel's special prerogative; entry requirements are only part of it, as again the Antioch incident shows. It is because Sanders seems to focus so much of Paul's critique of Judaism on questions of *entry* that Sanders' Paul does not seem to be addressing Sanders' Palestinian Judaism.

(c) It is this double, and in this context doubly false, distinction (Judaism and Christianity as two quite different 'systems'; 'getting in' and 'staying in') which, I believe, causes Sanders' to criticize Paul's view as not making a logical whole, as inconsistent, as not harmonizable, etc.[27] The awkwardness in *Paul* results from *Sanders'* distinctions. In particular, he tries to resolve the tension between Paul's negative and positive statements regarding the law by confining the negative to the 'getting in' question and the positive to the issue of 'staying in'.[28] In other words, the illogicality Sanders finds in Paul is as much or more of his own making, the result of his pushing through this latter distinction. Paul seems inconsistent because *his statements do not in fact fit into that distinction.* The negativeness in his attitude to the law embraces both aspects (getting in and staying in), and the positive statements cannot be confined to the latter either. Whereas my thesis regarding 'works of the law' makes it clear that Paul's criticism was primarily directed at a way of regarding the law and allows the positive thrust of Romans 2 in particular to stand precisely as a counter to that wrong attitude.[29]

Since Hübner and Stuhlmacher have both chided me for taking up from Sanders too uncritically, I hope this clarification serves also for them.

F. F. Bruce, 'Paul and the law in recent research', *Law and Religion*, ed. B. Lindars, Cambridge: James Clarke (1988) 124–5, criticizes me at two points. (9) My exegesis of Galatians 2.16 is defective. 'To translate ἐὰν μή by "except" in this construction seems to me to run counter to Greek idiom' (p. 125). (10) 'Paul's argument throughout Galatians makes it plain that it was not just identity markers that were at issue. Identity markers, for Paul, were optional . . . But if Paul's *Gentile* converts took over Jewish identity markers . . . it was their giving any place to law or law-keeping in the matter of salvation that Paul saw as a subversion of the gospel of free grace' (p. 125).

9. On the force of ἐὰν μή I think it would be generally agreed among grammarians that the phrase is properly exceptive and not adversative.[30] It is true that Moulton and Howard cite a number of examples to demonstrate that εἰ μή or ἐὰν μή can function as equivalent to ἀλλά.[31] But Hort had already pointed out that the force in such cases is not simply 'but', but 'but only'.[32] The point, then, is that there is some degree of ambiguity as to the precise force of the exception – as also, significantly, with the εἰ μή of 1.19. Clearly the exception qualifies the main verb – οὐ δικαιοῦται. This is what is agreed by Paul and his fellow Jewish Christians – that no acquittal is possible except through faith in Jesus Christ. What is ambiguous is the relation of the ἐξ ἔργων νόμου to the ἐὰν μή clause – 'knowing that a person is not justified from works of law but only (that he is justified) through faith in Jesus Christ'. The Jewish Christians evidently believed (as the Antioch incident demonstrated) that 'works of law' continued to be the appropriate if not essential expression of that faith in Jesus Christ, for Jewish Christians at least. But Paul (now) found it necessary to clarify the ambiguity into outright antithesis.[33]

10. Here we are back with the issues already dealt with in the response to Räisänen (point 4 above). As with Räisänen, Bruce seems to ignore the positive role Paul gives to the law 'in the matter of salvation'; how else can one read passages like Romans 2.13–16 and 8.4? Bruce is of course right when he says that Paul seeks to defend and promote his gospel of free grace. But what was threatening that gospel, in Paul's judgement, was not simply law-keeping as such, but law-keeping which made it impossible for Gentiles to experience salvation as Gentiles, that is, a Jewish insistence that only those participate in the promises of the covenant who practise

'the deeds of the law' laid down for the people of the covenant. For Paul, 'the obedience of faith' could not be defined so restrictively.

11. Most recently T. R. Schreiner, 'The Abolition and Fulfilment of the Law in Paul', *JSNT* 35 (1989) 47–74, echoes the same criticism as Stuhlmacher. 'Dunn's attempt to limit "works of law" to these identity markers (circumcision, food laws and observance of certain days) is not successful.'[34] With regard to 'works of law' I refer to my response to Stuhlmacher above, and to the fuller treatment in Chapter 8 below.[35] What is somewhat surprising is that Schreiner's criticism (like that of Westerholm, see pp. 237–40) is in effect directed primarily at the preliminary formulation of the above chapter, and that he has failed to give due acknowledgement to the more careful formulation of Chapter 8 below, even though he cites it in his n. 46 (again like Westerholm). This is all the more surprising since he (unlike Westerholm) has taken the point about the social function of the law as that to which Paul's critique of the law is directed. The laws which Paul specifically excludes are precisely those prctices which separated Jews from Gentiles in the Greco-Roman world, which uniquely characterized the Mosaic covenant and the Jews. 'The nature of that covenant was such that it divided Jews from Gentiles, and thus the covenant was intrinsically nationalistic' (pp. 56–8). But then he rather spoils it by reducing the issue back to one of a distinction between moral and ritual law (pp. 59ff.). In so doing he has fallen into the confusion against which I attempted to give warning in Chapter 7 above (pp. 198, 200 = *BJRL*, pp. 115–16, 118). The fact that Paul's critique of the law produces such a distinction *in practice* is not reason enough for reducing the critique to that distinction. It only works out in these terms because, as I have observed in Chapter 8 (pp. 216–17 = *NTS*, p. 524), social identity is defined and expressed to such a large extent in and through ritual. Paul's objection is not to *ritual* law, but to exclusivist or particularist attitudes which came to expression in and are reinforced by certain rituals. Not the rituals as such, but the attitude behind them, expressed typically as a 'boasting' in works of the law (Rom. 2.17–23; 3.27ff.). Paul does not in fact object to circumcision except as it constitutes a breach of the law by limiting the grace of God to the outwardly circumcised Jew (Rom. 2.25–9), except as it becomes an occasion for 'boasting' (Gal. 6.13).[36]

Notes

1. *NTS* 31 (1985) = *NTS*, p. 545; *Torah and Christ* = *TC*, pp. 172f.
2. *NTS*, p. 546; *TC*, pp. 174f.
3. *NTS*, pp. 546f.; *TC*, p. 176.
4. *NTS*, p. 547; *TC*, pp. 177–8. He is followed here by R. Y. K. Fung, *Galatians*, NICNT, Grand Rapids: Eerdmans (1988) 116 n.
5. Here Räisänen lumps me with Cranfield and refers to his critique of the latter in *Paul and the Law*, WUNT 29, Tübingen: Mohr (1983) 42–50.
6. *NTS*, pp. 548–50; *TC*, pp. 179–84.
7. *NTS*, p. 544; *TC*, p. 171. On two small points Räisänen is in error. (1) *NTS*, p. 550 n. 11 = *TC*, p. 169 n. 6. I do *not* ascribe to Sanders the view that Paul misunderstood Judaism. My point refers to earlier Jewish critiques of Paul –

critiques themselves based on Protestant misreading of Paul and his situation. (2) Despite Räisänen's charge to the contrary (*NTS*, p. 544 = *TC*, p. 170), I *do* note Sanders' recognition of the significance of circumcision, sabbath and food laws (my n. 46).

8. See also J. D. G. Dunn, *Romans*, WBC 38, Dallas: Word (1988) 485.
9. See further Dunn, *Romans* 39–42.
10. See further ch. 9 below.
11. *NTS*, p. 551 n. 31; *TC*, p. 173 n. 2.
12. See above ch. 6 n. 117.
13. cf. J. M. G. Barclay, *Obeying the Truth: A Study of Paul's Ethics in Galatians*, Edinburgh: T. & T. Clark (1988). Since the textual evidence relating to δέ at the beginning of 2.16 is so evenly balanced 'it would be unwise to build much on either reading . . . But we can still tell from the content of 2.16 (Jew and Gentile alike cannot be justified by works of the law) that it modifies the typically Jewish perspective of 2.15 (Jews are distinct from and superior to "Gentile sinners")' (78 n. 9). See also point 9 below.
14. See further ch. 8, including the Additional Note on Westerholm.
15. As Räisänen claims (*NTS*, p. 549; *TC*, p. 182).
16. 'Werke' 131–2. So also R. Yates, 'Saint Paul and the Law in Galatians', *ITQ* 51 (1985) 105–24 (here 107).
17. See Dunn, *Romans* index: 'Boasting', 'Works of law'.
18. Published as 'Paul's Understanding of the Law in the Letter to the Romans', *SEA* 50 (1985) 87–104.
19. *BJRL* 97–100, 102 and n. 46 = ch. 7 above pp. 184–6, 187–8 and n. 46.
20. *Paul and Palestinian Judaism*, London: SCM (1977) 550–2.
21. *Law* 4, 25.
22. *Law* 37.
23. *Law* 78.
24. See further n. 47 above.
25. The criticism is well made by R. H. Gundry, 'Grace, Works, and Staying Saved in Paul', *Bib* 66 (1985) 8–12.
26. *Law* 105.
27. *Law* 4, 77, 86, 122.
28. *Law* 84.
29. See again my *Romans* on Rom. 2, and Introduction pp. 7–8.
30. See E. D. Burton, *Galatians*, ICC, Edinburgh: T. & T. Clark (1921) 121; *BAGD*, ἐάν 3.b.
31. J. H. Moulton and W. F. Howard, *A Grammar of New Testament Greek*, Vol. 2, Edinburgh: T. & T. Clark (1929) 468.
32. F. J. A. Hort, *The Epistle of St James*, London: Macmillan (1909) xvi.
33. See also points 2 and 3 above, in response to Räisänen.
34. 71 n. 46; referring particularly to D. J. Moo, '"Law", "Works of the Law", and Legalism in Paul', *WTJ* 45 (1983) 90–99, and Räisänen's article discussed above. F. Watson, *Paul, Judaism and the Gentiles. A Sociological Approach*, SNTSMS 56, Cambridge University (1986) 198 n. 79 makes a similar criticism.
35. Including the Additional Note on Westerholm; also my *Romans* 153–5.
36. Despite my general agreement with Barclay's thesis, at this point he misses the social dimension of Paul's critical comment – 'they want you circumcised in order that they might boast in *your* flesh' (6.13, my emphasis). In other words, he criticizes them *not* for *self*-glorification (Barclay, *Obeying* 65), but for national aggrandizement – that is, because circumcision will mark the Galatians' full and physical identification with Israel as a people. Cf. my *Romans* 124–5 (on Rom. 2.28–9).

8
Works of the Law and the Curse of the Law
(Gal. 3.10–14)*

The two most recent studies of Paul and the law both show a large
measure of agreement in criticizing Paul's treatment of the law as
inconsistent and self-contradictory. E. P. Sanders argues that
Paul's 'break' with the law gave rise to different questions and
problems, and that his 'diverse answers, when set alongside one
another, do not form a logical whole'.[1] So, in particular, Paul's
'treatment of the law in chapter 2 (of Romans) cannot be harmon-
ized with any of the diverse things which Paul says about the law
elsewhere'; in Romans 2 'Paul goes beyond inconsistency or
variety of argument and explanation to true self-contradiction'.[2]
More thoroughgoing is H. Räisänen, who can see only one way to
handle what Paul says: 'contradictions and tensions have to be
accepted as *constant* features of Paul's theology of the law'.[3] Again
and again he finds himself driven to the conclusion that Paul
contradicts himself. So, for example, with Romans 13.8–10: 'Paul
seems here simply to have forgotten what he wrote in ch. 7 or in
10.4'; '(Romans) 2.14–15, 26–27 stand in flat contradiction to the
main thesis of the section'; Paul puts forward 'artificial and
conflicting theories about the law'.[4] The artificiality and tension is
evident not least in Galatians 3.10–12, where Räisänen finds the
argument of 3.10 to be at odds with the argument of 3.11–12.[5]

Speaking personally, I find such explanations of the text very
unsatisfying. They are not to be ruled out in principle, of course;
but as a way of making sense of the text they must rank as
hypotheses of last resort, second only to speculative emendation of
the text as disagreeable to good exegesis. Basic to good exegesis is
respect for the integrity of the text and, in the case of someone like
Paul, respect for his intellectual calibre and theological competence. Such respect includes a constant bearing in mind of the
possibility or indeed likelihood that the situations confronting Paul
were more complex than we can now be aware of, or include
important aspects which are now invisible to us. Before I resorted

* Delivered as a seminar paper (in briefer form) to the 'Paul and Israel' Seminar at
the SNTS Conference in Basel, August 1984.

to such conclusions therefore I would want to be fully convinced that I had entered as far as possible into the mind and context of Paul's writings. And this is where I suggest both Sanders and Räisänen have fallen short. Despite the labour they have devoted to the subject, despite the illumination which Sanders has brought to our understanding of Palestinian Judaism in relation to Paul, and despite the impressive thoroughness of Räisänen's debate with the secondary literature on the subject, they have both failed to get sufficiently inside the social situation of which 'Paul and the law' were a part. For all that they have turned their backs, quite rightly, on an individualizing exegesis of Paul's theology of justification, they have still failed to grasp the full significance of *the social function of the law* at the time of Paul and how that determines and influences both the issues confronting Paul and Paul's responses.

THE SOCIAL FUNCTION OF THE LAW

Anthropologists and sociologists have made us aware of the fact that any social grouping will inevitably have various features and characteristics which provide the group's self-definition (consciously or unconsciously) and mark it off from other groups. Members of the group will tend naturally to think of the group and of their membership of the group in terms of these features and characteristics, including any distinctive practices and beliefs. Two key words here are *identity* and *boundary*. In particular, ritual (a wide variety of ritual) plays an important part in providing group cohesion and maintaining identity. Thus Hans Mol:

> Rites articulate and reiterate a system of meaning, and prevent it being lost from sight ... They restore, reinforce, or redirect identity. They maximize order by strengthening the place of the individual in the group, or society, and vice-versa by strengthening the bonds of a society *vis-a-vis* the individual. They unify, integrate and sacralize.[6]

Similarly Mary Douglas in her influential study *Purity and Danger* speaks of 'ritual as an attempt to create and maintain a particular culture': 'The rituals enact the form of social relations and in giving these relations visible expression they enable people to know their own society.'[7]

The concept of 'boundary' is closely linked with that of 'identity'. As Mol points out, 'It is precisely the boundary ... which provides the sense of identity'.[8] In particular, the more a group or society feels itself under threat, the more it will tend to emphasize its boundaries. Mary Douglas has noted that 'the body is a model which can stand for any bounded system'. So it is no surprise when anxiety about the purity of the body and of what passes into and out of the body is emphasized at times of danger to the group. She suggests that 'when rituals express anxiety about the body's orifices the sociological counterpart of this anxiety is a care to protect the political and cultural unity of a minority group . . . The anxiety about bodily margins expresses danger to group survival.'[9]

It must immediately be evident how well this analysis fits the Judaism of Paul's day. Douglas herself exemplifies her point by referring to the history of the Israelites in general, since they were always 'a hard pressed minority'.[10] But it is particularly in the post-exilic period and not least in the Maccabean period that the point becomes most clear. For the threat of Syrian assimilation in the second century BCE focused with particular intensity precisely on those bodily rituals which gave Judaism its distinctive identity and marked out its boundaries.

> According to the decree (of Antiochus), they put to death the women who had their children circumcised, and their families and those who circumcised them; and they hung the infants from their mothers' necks. But many in Israel stood firm and were resolved in their hearts not to eat unclean food. They chose to die rather than to be defiled by food or to profane the holy covenant; and they did die. (1 Macc. 1.60–3)

Here the identity and boundary markers are clear – circumcision and the laws of clean and unclean food. It is hardly surprising, then, that the two main issues with which Paul deals in Galatians are precisely the same two areas of concern – circumcision and food laws (Gal. 2.1–14). For ever since the Maccabean period these two sets of legal requirement had been fundamental to the devout Jew's identity as a Jew, as a member of the people whom God had chosen for himself and made covenant with; these two ritual enactments had a central role in marking Israel off from the surrounding nations. And the events described in Galatians 2 took place at a time of renewed and mounting threat to Judaism's national and religious identity – following as they did the attempt of Caligula to defile the Temple (AD 40) and the deteriorating situation in Palestine.[11] Of course, for the devout Jew it was primarily a matter of remaining faithful to the covenant obligations clearly laid down in the Torah (particularly Gen. 17.9–14; Lev. 11.1–23; Deut. 14.2–21). But from a social anthropological perspective it is clear also that what was at stake was a people's identity and self-understanding, and that these rituals were important not least because they served as such clear boundary markers. This is borne out by various comments of Greco-Roman authors of the period which indicate that from the outsider's perspective two of the clearest distinguishing marks of the Jewish race were circumcision and the dietary laws.[12] Wayne Meeks appositely cites Philo in the same connection: 'Israel cannot be harmed by its opponents so long as it is "a people dwelling alone" (Num. 23.9), "because in virtue of the distinction of their peculiar customs they do not mix with others to depart from the way of their fathers" (*Mos.* 1.278)'; and cites the most important of the 'peculiar customs' as circumcision, *kashrut*, sabbath observance, and avoidance of civic rituals which implied recognition of pagan gods.[13] Sanders recognizes the same point when he notes that circumcision, sabbath and food laws 'created a social distinction between Jews and other races in the Greco-Roman world'; similarly Räisänen – 'works of the law are something that *separates* the Jew from the Gentile'.[14] But neither of them follows the insight through far enough.

We should also observe, since it will have a bearing on the later discussion, that it was not simply particular rituals as such which had this identity-affirming, boundary-marking function. The law itself fulfilled this role.[15] After all, had not the law been given to Israel as Israel's special prerogative, given to the chosen people as a mark of God's favour and thus to distinguish them from the other nations? A good expression of this sense of privilege is Baruch's claim that that divine Wisdom whom nobody else knows has been given to Israel:

> She is the book of the commandments of God,
> and the law which endures for ever.
> All who hold her fast will live,
> and those who forsake her will die.
> Turn, O Jacob, and take her;
> walk toward the shining of her light.
> Do not give your glory to another,
> or your advantages to an alien people.
> Happy are we, O Israel,
> for we know what is pleasing to God. (Bar. 4.1–4)

And the boundary function of the law is nowhere more clearly stated than in Aristeas 139, 142:

> [Moses] fenced us round with impregnable ramparts and walls of iron, that we might not mingle at all with any of the other nations, but remain pure in body and soul ... he hedged us round on all sides by rules of purity, affecting alike what we eat, or drink, or touch, or hear, or see.

The same attitude was of course a prominent feature of two of the main sub-groups within Judaism, the Pharisees and the Essenes, since it can be fairly said of them that they both sought to affirm and strengthen the identity of the people of God precisely by emphasizing the law's distinguishing rituals and boundary character.[16]

In short, then, the particular regulations of circumcision and food laws were important not in themselves, but because they *focused* Israel's distinctiveness, made visible Israel's claims to be a people set apart, were the clearest points which differentiated the Jews from the nations. The law was part and parcel of Israel's identity, both as a nation and as a religion. The law was coterminous with Judaism. It was impossible at the time of Paul to conceive of Judaism without the law, scarcely possible for a Jew to conceive of membership of the covenant people apart from the law. All this would have been largely taken for granted by most Jews, so much was it part of the presuppositional attitude of Jewish self-understanding. As soon as this point has been grasped, it at once becomes apparent that Paul's teaching on the law and circumcision must have posed a severe threat to most of his kinsmen's self-understanding and identity, not as individuals, but as Jews, as members of the people marked out as God's by the law. Unless this social, we may even say national and racial, dimension of the issues confronting Paul is clearly grasped, it will be well nigh impossible to achieve an exegesis of Paul's treatment of the law which pays proper respect to historical context.

WORKS OF THE LAW

What I have been pleading for in effect is a shift in perspective – from one dominated by the categories of the Reformation debates, to one properly set within the horizons of the social world of first-century Judaism. When such a shift is carried through it releases a flood of fresh light on the issues confronting Paul and on his response to them. A key example is the phrase τὰ ἔργα τοῦ νόμου, 'the works of the law'. The fact that Paul uses it only in the context of his argument with other Jewish Christians (or Jews) is usually recognized by commentators.[17] But sooner or later (usually sooner) the perspective slips and the assumption begins to dominate the exegesis that by 'works of the law' Paul means the attempt to win God's favour by human achievement, or some such paraphrase. Even Sanders and Räisänen, who consciously distance themselves from Reformation categories, and who show much greater sensitivity to the considerations posed above than has generally been the case, in the end fall back into further variations on the classic Reformation antithesis: ἐξ ἔργων τοῦ νόμου refers to 'entry' requirements, says Sanders, applying his much overworked distinction between 'getting in' and 'staying in'; and Räisänen, referring to the same phrase, argues that Paul misrepresents Judaism 'by suggesting that, within it, salvation is by works ...'[18]

In my view, however, 'works of the law' is precisely the phrase chosen by Paul (as either already familiar to his readers or self-evident to them in its significance), by which Paul denotes those obligations prescribed by the law which show the individual concerned to belong to the law, which mark out the practitioner as a member of the people of the law, the covenant people, the Jewish nation. I gave a first version of this argument in the 1982 Manson Memorial Lecture.[19] This paper constitutes an attempt to broaden and deepen that argument.

(a) For one thing the genitive construction, 'works of the law' has been too little considered and its significance too much taken for granted. But as E. Lohmeyer argued, the phrase ἔργα νόμου is best taken in the sense 'service of the law', 'Dienst des Gesetzes', or in J. B. Tyson's rendering 'nomistic service'.[20] That is to say, service not so much in the sense of particular actions already accomplished, but in the sense of obligations set by the law, the religious system determined by the law. The phrase refers not to an individual's striving for moral improvement, but to a religious mode of existence, a mode of existence marked out in its distinctiveness as determined by the law, the religious practices which demonstrate the individual's 'belongingness' to the people of the law.

Lohmeyer's insight is borne out by the way in which the equivalent phrase is used in the Qumran writings – מעשי תורה, 'deeds of the law'. For it was precisely by reference to his 'deeds', his 'observance of the law' as understood within the community in the day-to-day, year-by-year life of the community, that an individual's membership of the covenant was tested (1QS 5.21, 23; 6.18). Likewise, מעשי תורה was what marked out the community of the end days in its distinctiveness from the outsiders and enemies (4QFlor. 1.1–7).[21]

In terms introduced by Sanders, 'works of the law' is, then, another way of saying 'covenantal nomism' – that which characterizes 'being in' the covenant and not simply 'getting into' the covenant (as Sanders himself put it).[22] And in terms of the preceding analysis, 'works of the law' are Paul's way of describing in particular the identity and boundary markers which Paul's Jewish (-Christian) opponents thought, and rightly thought, were put under threat by Paul's understanding of the gospel.

(b) As I noted in the Manson Lecture, this understanding of 'works of the law' makes best sense of the phrase's use in the contexts in which Paul introduces it. In Galatians 2.16, where he introduces it for the first time (in his extant writings), and uses it no less than three times, ἔργα νόμου most obviously refers back to the issues at the centre of the preceding controversies – circumcision and food laws.[23] That is what was at issue – whether to be justified by faith in Jesus Christ requires also observance of these 'works', whether, as the subsequent discussion makes clear, it is possible to conceive of a membership of the covenant people which is not characterized by precisely these works. The Jerusalem Christians having conceded the argument about circumcision, so

220

far as 'getting in' was concerned, drew the line at the food laws: a membership of the chosen people which did not include faithfulness to the food laws and purity rituals of the meal table was for them too much a contradiction in terms. And Peter, Barnabas and the other Jewish Christians in Antioch evidently agreed, however reluctantly or not – the threat to Jewish identity was too great to be ignored.[24]

So too in Romans. Paul introduces the phrase, somewhat oddly, at the conclusion to the first main part of the exposition (Rom. 3.19–20); again the implication must be that its meaning or reference was either well known or self-evident. Since the second half of the preceding discussion was a refutation of Jewish presumption in their favoured status as the people of the law, the 'works of the law' must be a shorthand way of referring to that in which the typical Jew placed his confidence, the law-observance which documented his membership of the covenant, his righteousness as a loyal member of the covenant. This is confirmed by the way in which in the following paragraphs 'works of the law' are associated with 'boasting' (3.27–8; 4.2), thus explicitly recalling the earlier passage where Paul specifically attacked his own people's presumption as being the people of the law (2.17–20, 23), with circumcision once again serving as the distinguishing mark of 'the Jew' (2.25–9).

(c) The same point emerges from the other prepositional phrases which Paul uses when speaking of the law. In Romans 2.12 the antithesis ἐν νόμῳ/ἀνόμως clearly has the force 'within the law', 'inside the law', and 'without the law', 'outside the law'. This is borne out by the fact that in verse 14 Paul goes on to define the Gentiles equivalently as 'those not having the law'. In other words, the law and the Jewish people are coterminous; the law identifies the Jew as Jew and constitutes the boundary which separates him from the Gentiles.[25] Similarly in Romans 3.19–21 we find the distinction ἐν τῷ νόμῳ and χωρὶς νόμου: the law marks out those inside its boundaries, and their whole religion and lifestyle (works of the law) marks them off from those outside the law.

The phrase ὑπὸ νόμον has the same force, particularly in 1 Corinthians 9.20 and Galatians 4.5, where Paul speaks of the Jews as οἱ ὑπὸ νόμον, 'those under the law', those whose lives as a people are characterized by the authority of the law, by 'works of the law', nomistic service – the law as a banner, loyalty to which gives them their national identity and unity, the law as marking out the extent and boundaries of the covenant people. So in 1 Corinthians 9.20–1 we are not surprised to see the same distinction between Jews and Gentiles defined as between οἱ ὑπὸ νόμον and οἱ ἄνομοι, those under the law and the law-less.[26]

Thus it becomes clearer that the contrast between οἱ ἐκ νόμου and

221

οἱ ἐκ πίστεως in Romans 4.14, 16 is also a sociological as well as theological distinction. A distinction not between two sets of random individuals, one set who think their relation with God depends on human achievement and the other who are justified by faith. But a distinction between what amounts to two definitions of how the offspring, the people promised to Abraham, are to be characterized. The question confronting Paul is this: Are the heirs of Abraham no more and no less than the people marked out by the law, the people whose whole existence as God's people arises out of the law, whose whole national identity comes from the law? Or are they marked out simply by faith, identified simply by faith?[27]

In all these cases a failure to appreciate the social dimensions and national ramifications of what Paul is attacking and what he is affirming will inevitably result in a misconception of his teaching on the law.

(d) To complete this sketch of the language matrix to which the phrase 'works of the law' belongs, we should note also the ideas associated with it. I will refer to four in particular.

(i) As noted above (b), Paul associates 'works of the law' with the 'boasting' of his Jewish interlocutor in Romans (3.27–8; 4.2), clearly recalling the boasting of the 'Jew' in 2.17, 23. Bultmann's influential treatment of the theme understood this in very individualistic terms as a boasting of 'self-confidence'; and Käsemann has continued the line of interpretation by depicting the boasting Jew as the classic type of the pious individual who relies on self-achievement.[28] But clearly what Paul has in mind is the confidence of the Jew as Jew, as member of the people whom God has chosen as his own and to whom he has given the law. He boasts in the law as the long-established mark of divine favour to his own.[29]

(ii) So too the phrase ἐν τῷ φανερῷ, used to describe 'the Jew' and circumcision in Romans 2.28, has often been interpreted in individualistic terms without reference to social context, simply as the outward opposed to the inward. But what Paul has in mind is the Jew visibly marked out as such, circumcision as the public ritual act which gives the individual place within the people so marked out. It is the social function of ritual which is in view, circumcision as a badge of Jewish identity. Precisely because it is an outward visible mark, circumcision serves very effectively as a boundary marker between Jew and Gentile. So too when Paul speaks of the law as γράμμα, what he has in view is precisely the law as the visible definition of the covenant people (Rom. 2.27, 29; 7.6; 2 Cor. 3.6–7).

(iii) Similarly the phrase ἐν σαρκί used in the same passage (Rom. 2.28) denotes not merely the physical as opposed to the spiritual, but also the people of Israel in terms of physical identity and racial kinship.[30] Likewise, 'not of the flesh' stands in parallel to

222

'not of works' in 9.8, 11, precisely because the works of the law demonstrate national identity, constitute national righteousness, the righteousness of those who hold true to the customs given by Moses to Israel. And in Galatians 6.13 the boasting in the flesh which Paul attacks is the boasting of people whose pride in their national identity has been enhanced by the desire of other races to submerge their social and religious distinctiveness in that identity.

(iv) Finally we might note Paul's other criticism of his own people – that 'they sought to establish their own righteousness' (Rom. 10.3). Here too 'their own' is usually taken in the sense, 'their own' as achieved by them, 'a righteous status of their own earning'.[31] But the ἴδιος has more the sense of 'belonging to them, peculiar to them'. That is to say, what is in view is a righteousness which is *theirs and not anybody else's*, 'collective righteousness, to the exclusion of the Gentiles',[32] covenant righteousness, the righteousness of being God's people. They seek to '*establish*' their righteousness, not to create it or achieve it, but to confirm and make secure (στῆσαι) what is already theirs. Here is a good expression of 'covenantal nomism', the claim to a special relationship with God that is secure for all who remain loyal to the covenant. Not surprisingly, the phrase ἐξ ἔργων νόμου appears once again in the same context (9.32) as an equivalent way of describing their mistake; so that once again it becomes evident that 'works of the law' are what Jews do to demonstrate and maintain their standing with God as something peculiar to Israel.

To sum up, the phrase τὰ ἔργα τοῦ νόμου belongs to a complex of ideas in which the social function of the law is prominent. The law serves both to identify Israel as the people of the covenant and to mark them off as distinct from the (other) nations. 'Works of the law' denote all that the law requires of the devout Jew, but precisely because it is the law as identity and boundary marker which is in view, the law as Israel's law focuses on these rites which express Jewish distinctiveness most clearly. The conclusion of the previous section is thus confirmed: 'works of the law' refer not exclusively but particularly to those requirements which bring to sharp focus the distinctiveness of Israel's identity. It is because they have such a crucial role in defining 'Jewishness', membership of the covenant people, that circumcision and food laws feature so prominently in discussion of works of the law and righteousness. What lies behind so much of the debate is the identity crisis which Paul's work among the Gentiles precipitated for his fellow Jewish Christians.[33]

Further confirmation that we are on the right lines is provided by the way in which this perspective helps to 'iron out' two of the puzzling wrinkles in Paul's treatment of the law to which Räisänen in particular has drawn attention.[34]

1. The tension in Paul's language between the law as a negative factor and his continuing positive assessment of the law (contrast in particular Rom. 2.13–15; 3.27, 31; 7.12; 8.4; 9.31–2; 13.8–10).[35] The solution suggested by the above analysis is that it is the law in its social function which draws a large part of Paul's critique.[36] The law as fixing a particular social identity, as encouraging a sense of national superiority and presumption of divine favour by virtue of membership of a particular people – that is what Paul is attacking in the passages mentioned above. Divorced from that perspective, as the law understood in terms of faith rather than in terms of works, it can continue to serve in a positive role. The self-contradictions which Sanders and Räisänen have found are the result of their too blinkered perspective rather than Paul's.

2. The puzzle of why other explanations which propose distinctions within the law (moral and ceremonial law, inward and outward law, core law and law *in toto*) seem to provide partial but only partial resolutions of the tension between Paul's various pronouncements.[37] They are incomplete precisely because they have missed the social function of the law, and the way in which this function focuses on particular ritual requirements. Paul does *not* defend his position by dividing up the law into acceptable and unacceptable elements. For what he is attacking is a particular *attitude* to the law as such, the *law as a whole* in its social function as distinguishing Jew from Gentile. Viewed from a *different* angle, the point of the law as a whole will come into focus in other ways, particularly in faith ('the law of faith' – Rom. 3.28; 9.31–2) and love of neighbour (Rom. 13.10). And, just as important, the requirements which obscure that point will become of secondary relevance as *adiaphora*.

From this perspective the coherence of even such passages as 2 Corinthians 3 and Romans 2 within Paul's theology of the law becomes clearer. When Paul speaks of the 'letter' killing he is not thinking of the law as such, or even of the law understood literally, but of the law as defining the covenant people with the physical visible rite of circumcision (as in Rom. 2.29). It is the law understood in this way which is so destructive of the life of the Spirit.[38] And in Romans 2 what Paul has in view when he speaks of Gentiles doing the law is not some core law as such. His object is rather to undermine Jewish confidence that by *having* the law, by staying *within* the law, their position before God in the final judgement is secure. The fact that there can be a real doing of the law, a real engagement with what the law is about on the part of the Gentiles (2.14–15, 26–7), reveals that confidence to be false and misplaced. Or put the other way round, Jewish boasting in the law should be well and truly punctured by the fact that there are Jews who blatantly disobey some of the law's requirements (2.21–3 – *not*

224

the boundary-defining 'works of the law'), while still Jews and still (presumably) maintaining their covenant identity.[39]

In short, a recognition of the social function of the law, and of 'works of the law' as a summary expression of the law's function as seen from within Judaism, goes a long way towards removing and resolving the contradictions and tensions which have loomed so large for Sanders and Räisänen.

GAL. 3.10–14 – A TEST CASE

In 'The New Perspective on Paul' I was conscious that my argument amounted to little more than an exegesis of Galatians 2.16.[40] Several respondents observed that if my thesis were to gain in credibility it would have to make sense of Galatians 3.10–14. Galatians 3.10–14 does indeed provide a substantial test case, and to it we now turn.

In the preceding paragraphs Paul has reminded his readers of how they began as Christians. He emphasized again the contrast between 'works of law' and 'faith'. They knew well that they received the Spirit and entered upon the continuing experience of the Spirit ἐξ ἀκοῆς πίστεως and not ἐξ ἔργων νόμου, that is, by a response of faith which was not tied to or expressed by the (ritual) observances which characterize Judaism (Gal. 3.2, 5). The warning is clear: as they began, so they should continue (3.3). That is to say, their *continued* life in the Spirit should not be thought to depend on nomistic service, on covenantal nomism, any more than their beginning. Here too, implicit in the argument is the association of 'works of the law' with 'flesh' (ἐξ ἔργων νόμου vv. 2, 5 parallel to σαρκί v. 3). And, once again, neither of these should be reduced to an individualistic striving for self-achievement. On the contrary, as we have now learned to expect, both terms have in view the nationalism of the typical Jewish understanding of God's covenant promise – the Spirit as given to the children of Abraham, understood naturally as the national entity Israel, marked out as God's heirs by law and circumcision of the flesh. Whereas Paul's Gentile readers knew from their own experience that their enjoyment of that promise had not depended and did not depend on their aligning themselves visibly and physically with the native Jew by embracing the ancestral customs of the Jews.

The testimony of their own experience is confirmed by Scripture, which ties together Abraham's faith with the promise to Abraham, the promise which showed that God purposed to bless the Gentiles from the beginning of his covenant relationship with Abraham. As Abraham's faith was what established the covenant in the first place, so οἱ ἐκ πίστεως can quite properly regard themselves as children of Abraham, and in receiving the Spirit ἐκ πίστεως they can know that this is the blessing God purposed from the first when he accepted Abraham in covenant relationship (3.6–9). But if faith is the mark of the people of the promise, what about the law? And what about those who have always taken for granted that it is the law and works of the law which mark out the people of God's covenant? That is the issue to which Paul begins to address himself in Galatians 3.10–14.

Verse 10 'For as many as are ἐξ ἔργων νόμου are under a curse; for it is written, "Cursed is everyone who does not remain within everything that is written in the book of the law to do the same"' (Deut. 27.26). The basic logic of the text is clear: all who are ἐξ ἔργων νόμου are under a curse, *because* they fail to abide by everything that is written in the law. This at once tells us something about οἱ ἐξ ἔργων νόμου in Paul's perspective: (1) to be ἐξ ἔργων νόμου is *not* the same as remaining in the law; (2) to be ἐξ ἔργων νόμου is something which *falls short* of abiding by everything written in the law.

What can Paul mean? The usual answer runs along the following lines: ὅσοι ἐξ ἔργων νόμου refers to those who seek to achieve their own righteousness before God; and in quoting Deuteronomy 27.26 Paul presupposes that it is impossible to fulfil all that the law requires.[41] That is to say, Paul indicts his fellow Jews/Jewish Christians[42] for thinking they could make a claim upon God by keeping the law, something which is simply not possible. However, this exegesis is undercut by several factors. (a) The first clause can no longer be read as an attack on self-achievement. ὅσοι ἐξ ἔργων νόμου are Jews as a whole, precisely in so far as they understand themselves in terms of the law, see their lives as members of God's covenant people characterized by the service which the law prescribes.[43] (b) The idea that Paul in quoting Deuteronomy 27.26 presupposes the impossibility of fulfilling the law is hardly self-evident and has to be read into the argument.[44] (c) The exegesis becomes even more precarious when we realize that it runs at cross purposes with what Paul says elsewhere – with verses 11–12, says Räisänen;[45] and certainly with 5.14, where Paul clearly implies that 'the whole law' *can* be 'fulfilled' by loving one's neighbour as oneself.[46]

The more promising route to the proper exegesis of verse 10 is to recognize that Paul is deliberately denying what his fellow countrymen (and the Judaizers) would take for granted, setting at odds what they equated. That is to say, most Jews of Paul's day would simply assume that to be ἐξ ἔργων νόμου *is* to remain within all that the Torah lays down, *is* to do what the law requires.[47] But Paul denies that equation. To be of the works of the law is *not* the same as fulfilling the law, is *less* than what the law requires, and so falls under the law's own curse. Why so? The answer is given by our

226

not literally, but its intent.

previous exposition of 'works of the law'. Those who are ἐξ ἔργων νόμου are those who have understood the scope of God's covenant people as Israel *per se*, as that people who are defined by the law and marked out by its distinctive requirements.[48] Such an understanding of the covenant and of the law inevitably puts too much weight on physical and national factors, on outward and visible enactments, and gives too little weight to the Spirit, to faith and love from the heart. Such an understanding of the people of God inevitably results in a false set of priorities. On such an understanding of the law, fulfilment of the law will inevitably be judged in terms of these priorities. As Paul well knew from his own past, it was all too possible for the devout and loyal Jew to think of himself as 'blameless' (Phil. 3.6), precisely because he was a devout and loyal Jew, precisely because he was zealous in his observance of the ancestral customs (Gal. 1.14). But Paul now sees all too clearly that such an understanding of the law is *not* all that the law requires. Freed from the nationalistic presuppositions which had previously coloured his own self-understanding and which still coloured the self-understanding of the bulk of his own people, Paul could now see that fulfilment of the law has to be understood in different terms, as something which Gentiles can do without any reference to whether they are inside the law or outside the law (cf. Rom. 2.14–16, 26–9). To cling defiantly to the older view was to diminish the law, to distort the covenant and effectively to destroy its promise. To thus misunderstand the law by giving primacy to matters of at best secondary importance was to fall short of what the law required and thus to fall under the law's own curse (Deut. 27.26). Paul could assume that his readers would recognize his train of thought, precisely because what we now call 'the social function of the law' would be part of the framework of perception for any reasonably well-informed individual of Paul's day when he encountered Judaism, precisely because the restrictiveness of being ἐξ ἔργων νόμου in nationalist and visible terms was well known in Jew/Gentile relationships. That restrictiveness had come into focus with regard to circumcision at Jerusalem (Gal. 2.1–10) and with regard to the food laws at Antioch (2.11–18). In the context of the Galatian situation the train of thought from Galatians 2.16 to 3.10 would not be too difficult to follow.[49]

Verses 11–12 'And that no one ἐν νόμῳ is justified with God is plain, because "The righteous ἐκ πίστεως shall live" (Hab. 2.4). And the law is not ἐκ πίστεως, but "he who does the same will live ἐν αὐτοῖς"' (Lev. 18.5).

Once again Paul sets in antithesis what most of his fellow Jews would regard as equivalent:

ἐν νόμῳ	ἐκ πίστεως
ἐκ πίστεως	ἐν αὐτοῖς

227

In Jewish self-understanding, to be ἐν νόμῳ is to live ἐκ πίστεως (by faithfulness)[50] – in both cases the man who is righteous before God being in view, his righteousness being defined and documented precisely by the two phrases (ἐν νόμῳ, ἐκ πίστεως).[51] To do what the law specifies for the covenant people is to live ἐν αὐτοῖς, to live ἐκ πίστεως. And once again the exegetical key is the recognition of the restrictiveness implied in the two ἐν phrases. Whether they are translated 'in' or 'by' or more vaguely 'in terms of', the point is the same: Paul is referring to the typical Jewish self-understanding of the people of God as circumscribed and defined by the law, as characterized by practice of the law's distinctive features.[52]

However, Paul sets ἐκ πίστεως in contrast to the two ἐν phrases. He thus frees it from functioning simply as a way of defining life ἐν νόμῳ, and gives it independent significance as faith, as trust in and openness to God brought about by the word of preaching, without any reference to the law or its works. Paul need say no more either about 'faith' or about its independence from the social function of the law because his readers had experienced both for themselves in rich measure (3.2–5).[53]

In setting faith and law in such contrast here[54] Paul would not want them to be understood as mutually exclusive; nor would he want to disparage the idea of 'doing the law' as such (cf. Rom. 2.13 and 2.26–7 with Gal. 5.14 and 6.2).[55] Once again it is a question of priorities. For his Jewish kinsmen the law was the more dominant of the two concepts and determined the meaning of πίστις as 'faithfulness', faithfulness in observing the works of the law. But for Paul faith is the primary category and determinative factor (as the Galatians' own experience confirmed). To subordinate it once again to the dictates of covenantal nomism would be to deny their own experience, as confirmed by Scripture. The life of nomistic service validated by Leviticus 18.5 has been superseded by the eschatological life of faith as antitypically foreshadowed by Habakkuk 2.4.

Verses 13–14 'Christ has redeemed us from the curse of the law, having become a curse on our behalf – as it is written, "Cursed is everyone who hangs on a tree" (Deut. 21.23 with 27.26) – in order that the blessing of Abraham might come in Christ Jesus to the Gentiles, in order that we might receive the promise of the Spirit through faith'.

The thought clearly refers back to verse 10, as the formulation of the scriptural passage to align it with the Scripture quoted in verse 10 confirms.[56] Paul must intend 'the curse of the law' to be understood in the light of verse 10. That is to say, the curse of the law is not simply the condemnation which falls on any transgression and on all who fall short of the law's requirements. Paul has in mind the specific short-fall of his typical Jewish contemporary, the

[handwritten margin note: No. Curse refers to 'inability to do the law'.]

228

curse which falls on all who restrict the grace and promise of God in nationalistic terms, who treat the law as a boundary to mark the people of God off from the Gentiles, who give a false priority to ritual markers. The curse of the law here has to do primarily with that attitude which confines the covenant promise to Jews as Jews: it falls on those who live within the law in such a way as to exclude the Gentile as Gentile from the promise. This is confirmed by the second half of Paul's formulation in verses 13–14: the purpose of Christ's redemption from the curse of the law is precisely what we would (now) expect – viz. the extension of the covenant blessing to the Gentiles.[57] The curse which was removed by Christ's death therefore was the curse which had previously prevented that blessing from reaching the Gentiles, the curse of a wrong understanding of the law. It was a curse which fell primarily on the Jew (3.10; 4.5), but Gentiles were affected by it so long as that misunderstanding of the covenant and the law remained dominant.[58] It was that curse which Jesus had brought deliverance from by his death.

This may seem at first a surprisingly narrow understanding of the redemptive effect of Christ's death, especially when a systematized theology of the atonement tends to stress deliverance from the power of sin (and the condemnation of transgression). But Paul's meaning and intention here is in fact quite narrow and specific.

1. He has already taken Deuteronomy 27.26 in a quite specific and narrow sense (v. 10). And the original reference of Deuteronomy 21.23 is very narrow and particular. It is simply because both speak of a curse and both do so in reference to covenant inheritance (Deut. 21.23; 27—28), that he no doubt felt justified in bringing them together as a way of understanding Jesus' death: Jesus' crucifixion could properly have Deuteronomy 21.23 referred to it, as his Jewish contemporaries would agree,[59] and therefore be seen as falling under God's curse, and therefore be related to the curse of Deuteronomy 27.26.[60]

2. The parallel with Galatians 4.4–5 clearly confirms that Paul's thought in both passages is moving along such specific and quite narrowly circumscribed lines:

Christ became a curse	Christ became under the law
to redeem from the law's curse	to redeem those under the law
that we might receive the Spirit.	that we might receive the adoption.[61]

As soon as we recall that 'those under the law' are under the curse of the law (v. 10), the purpose of Christ's redemptive work can be specified quite properly as the removal of *that* curse, as the *no, the curse is more Then That!*

deliverance of the heirs of the covenant promise from the ill effects of the too narrow understanding of covenant and law held by most of Paul's Jewish contemporaries, so that both Jew and Gentile can enter into the fuller scope of the covenant promise. It will be recalled that Ephesians 2.13–16 spells out this understanding of the cross in quite explicit terms – a confirmation from one who treasured the Pauline tradition most dearly (or from Paul himself) that this very specific doctrine of the cross was one of the principal elements in Paul's theology.

3. We should also note how well this accords with what Paul himself states to have been the dominant impact of his conversion – the conviction that he should preach Christ among the Gentiles. Contrary to much speculation, Paul's train of thought does not seem to have been: God raised Jesus from the dead; therefore he could not have deserved to die; therefore the law which condemned him is self-condemned and his death frees those who believe in him from any obligation to obey the law.[62] Of such a train of thought Paul's writings give no evidence.[63] He himself gives central place to the conviction that in Christ God's promise was now open to the Gentiles (Gal. 1.15–16). This suggests that his train of thought was rather: Christ in his death had put himself under the curse and outside the covenant blessing (cf. Deut. 11.26; 30.19–20) – that is, put himself in the place of the Gentile! Yet God vindicated him! Therefore, God is *for* the Gentiles; and consequently the law could no longer serve as a boundary dividing Jew from Gentile. In short, Christ in his death had effectively abolished this disqualification, by himself being disqualified. It is the out-working of this train of thought which we see unfolding in the incidents described in Galatians 2, and climaxing in 2.21: 'If righteousness comes through the law, then Christ died in vain'. Christ's death was effective, in Paul's view, precisely because it broke through the restrictiveness of the typical Jewish understanding of God's righteousness, and demonstrated that the grace of God was now to be experienced apart from the law.[64]

To sum up, then, Galatians 3.10–14 does not run counter to the thesis elaborated in the first two sections of this paper. On the contrary, the thesis enables us to grasp the point and the connection of thought in Galatians 3.10–14 better than other current alternatives, and shows that the tensions perceived by Räisänen in the passage result from the blinkeredness of his perspective rather than from Paul's own thought.

∨ CONCLUSIONS

1. Any attempt to enter sympathetically into the context of Paul's teaching on the law must take into account the social function of

the law at that time. That the law served to *identify* the Jewish people as the people chosen by the one God for himself, and as a *boundary* to mark them off from all (other) nations, would have been a basic assumption of Jewish self-understanding. From such a sociological perspective it also becomes self-evident that Jews (including Jewish Christians) would be particularly sensitive at the points where the boundary seemed to be threatened and consequently their own identity challenged. It is no surprise then that in Galatians 2 it is precisely in circumcision and food laws, two of the most obvious boundary markers, that the larger controversy comes to focus.

2. Within this context 'works of the law' would be understood not simply as 'good works' in general, but as those observances of the law which brought this understanding of the law to expression, nomistic service, covenantal nomism, the observances of the law which ought to characterize the good Jew and set him apart from the Gentile, which show him to be 'within the law', 'under the law', his whole existence determined 'from the law'. It is this attitude which Paul attacks in criticizing Jewish 'boasting', their misplaced emphasis on the outward and physical, their claim to an exclusively Jewish righteousness. It is this attitude which Paul sees as a stunted and distorted understanding of what the law requires, and therefore as falling under the curse of the law (Gal. 3.10). It is an attitude which is at odds with the faith of Abraham and the faith through which the Galatians entered into the blessing promised to Abraham (Gal. 3.11–12).

3. The recognition that what Paul is attacking is a particular and restrictive understanding of the law provides the key to many of the tensions perceived in Paul's writing on the law. Freed from that too narrow understanding of the law, the Jewish Christian (and Gentile) is able to recognize that the law has a continuing positive role, to be fulfilled in love of neighbour. And with the law seen to commend and confirm the right priorities, of faith in God (and his Christ) and love of neighbour, the other priorities which emphasize national distinctiveness can be seen to be false priorities, and the ritual practices involved set on one side as matters of indifference which no one who exercises Abraham's faith and rejoices in the promise given to Abraham should be required to observe.

4. Not least in significance is the way in which our exegesis confirms the dominance of the Jew/Gentile issue in Paul's whole thinking. In his earliest extant teaching on the death of Jesus he asserts that the whole point of Jesus' death on the cross was to remove the boundary of the law and its consequent curse, to liberate the blessing promised to Abraham for all to enjoy (Gal. 2.21; 3.13–14). Just as we now recognize that Paul's teaching on

231

justification by faith was directed to the specific issue of how the righteousness of God might be known by Gentile as well as Jew (however justified later systematic reflection on the doctrine was in enlarging and extending it[65]), so now we need to recognize that his initial teaching on the cross was also specifically directed to the same problem, however justified later Christian reflection was in enlarging and extending the doctrine of the atonement. As Galatians 1.15–16 indicates, the leading edge of Paul's theological thinking was the conviction that God's purpose embraced Gentile as well as Jew, not the question of how a guilty man might find a gracious God. It was round this conviction and as an expression of it that the other central emphases of Paul's theology first took shape.[66]

Notes

1. E. P. Sanders, *Paul, the Law, and the Jewish People* (Philadelphia: Fortress, 1983) 3–4.
2. Sanders, *Law* 123, 147.
3. H. Räisänen, *Paul and the Law* (WUNT 29; Tübingen: Mohr, 1983) 10–11 (his emphasis). A. J. M. Wedderburn, 'Paul and the Law', *SJT* 38 (1985) 613–22, finds Räisänen's analysis for the most part convincing (pp. 621–2).
4. Räisänen, *Paul* 65, 103, 154.
5. Räisänen, *Paul* 94–6, 109.
6. H. Mol, *Identity and the Sacred* (Oxford: Blackwell, 1976) 233.
7. M. Douglas, *Purity and Danger* (London: Routledge & Kegan Paul, 1966) 128; see also earlier 62–5.
8. Mol, *Identity* 57–8.
9. Douglas, *Purity* 124.
10. Douglas, *Purity* 124.
11. See further my 'The Incident at Antioch (Gal. 2.11–18)', *JSNT* 18 (1983) 7–11; reprinted above, ch. 6.
12. Full details in M. Stern ed., *Greek and Latin Authors on Jews and Judaism* (Jerusalem: Israel Academy of Sciences and Humanities, Vol. 1 1974, Vol. 2 1980) – circumcision: Timagenes, Horace, Persius, Petronius, Martial, Tacitus, Juvenal, Suetonius (##81, 129, 190, 194–5, 240–1, 281, 301, 320); food laws: Erotianus, Epictetus, Plutarch, Tacitus, Juvenal, Sextus Empiricus (##196, 253, 258, 281, 298, 334).
13. W. A. Meeks, *The First Urban Christians* (Yale, 1983) 97.
14. Sanders, *Law* 102; Räisänen, *Paul* 171–2.
15. In the ancient world, of course, respect for their ancestral customs (τὰ πάτρια) was a widespread feature of social and national groups; see LSJ πάτριος; R. MacMullen, *Paganism in the Roman Empire* (Yale, 1981) 2–3.
16. 'What marks ancient Israel as distinctive perennially is its preoccupation with defining itself. In one way or another Israel sought means of declaring itself distinct from its neighbours ... The persistent stress on differentiation, yielding a preoccupation with self-definition ... The Torah literature ... raised high those walls of separation ...' 'These laws formed a protective boundary, keeping in those who were in, keeping out those who were not' (J. Neusner, *Judaism: The Evidence of the Mishnah* [University of Chicago, 1981] 69–75).

Hence the Pharisees' stress on ritual purity, to which Neusner has drawn particular attention (*From Politics to Piety* [Englewood Cliffs: Prentice-Hall, 1973] 80, 83–90; also *Judaism* 49–52) and the intensifying of ritual norms at Qumran (e.g. 1QS 3.8–12; 5.8; CD 10.14–11.18; see further J. Riches, *Jesus and the Transformation of Judaism* [London: Darton, 1980] 122–8).

17. See, e.g., Räisänen, *Paul* 187 (also below n. 57), with other references in n. 121. The dispute as to whether Paul in these passages is attacking Judaism or Jewish Christians is important, but not entirely to the point here, since it is the *Jewish* attitude of the Jewish Christians which he confronts.

18. Sanders, *Law* 105, 147 (though elsewhere he treats the phrase in a less restrictive way – pp. 46, 158–9); Räisänen, *Paul* 188–9. Cf. also U. Wilckens, 'Zur Entwicklung des paulinischen Gesetzverständnis', *NTS* 28 (1982) 154–90.

19. 'The New Perspective on Paul', *BJRL* 65 (1983) 95–122; reprinted above, ch. 7. See also K. Kertelge, 'Gesetz und Freiheit im Galaterbrief', *NTS* 30 (1984) 382–94, especially 391.

20. E. Lohmeyer, *Probleme paulinischer Theologie* (Stuttgart: Kohlhammer, n.d.) 33–74 (here 67); J. B. Tyson, '"Works of Law" in Galatians', *JBL* 92 (1973) 423–31 (here 424–5).

21. See further J. D. G. Dunn, *Romans* (WBC 38; Dallas: Word, 1988) 154.

22. Above n. 18. Note also Sanders' attempt to clarify his earlier formulation in *Law* 165–6 n. 38.

23. So correctly Räisänen, *Paul* 259.

24. cf. K. Kertelge, 'Zur Deutung des Rechtfertigungsbegriffs im Galaterbrief', *BZ* 12 (1968) 215.

25. See further Dunn, *Romans* 95–6.

26. See also Gal. 4.4 – Jesus was 'born under the law', that is, a Jew; 4.21 – (some of) the Galatians wish to be 'under the law', that is, in effect, to become Jews. I am not persuaded by L. Gaston, 'Paul and the Torah', *Antisemitism and the Foundations of Christianity*, ed. A. T. Davies (New York: Paulist, 1979) 48–71, who argues that Paul uses the phrase 'under the law' 'to designate the gentile situation' (62–4). See further T. L. Donaldson, 'The "Curse of the Law" and the Inclusion of the Gentiles: Galatians 3.13–14', *NTS* 32 (1986) 95–6; Dunn, *Romans* 339–40.

27. See further Dunn, *Romans* 213–14, 216.

28. R. Bultmann, *TDNT* 3.648–9; also *New Testament Theology* (London: SCM, Vol. 1 1952) 242–3; E. Käsemann, *Commentary on Romans* (London: SCM, 1980) 102; Bultmann's position is defended by H. Hübner, *Das Gesetz bei Paulus* (Göttingen: Vandenhoeck, ²1980), especially 102.

29. cf. particularly, Sanders, *Law* 33, 155–7; disputed by R. H. Gundry, 'Grace, Works and Staying Saved in Paul', *Bib* 66 (1985) 13–16 – 'personal accomplishments', 'self-righteousness'. But see also Dunn, *Romans* 110–11, 185.

30. See further J. D. G. Dunn, 'Jesus – Flesh and Spirit: an Exposition of Romans 1.3–4', *JTS* 24 (1973) 44–9; now also *Romans* 123–5.

31. C. E. B. Cranfield, *Romans* (ICC; Edinburgh: T. & T. Clark, Vol. 2, 1979) 515. Similarly Gundry.

32. G. Howard, 'Christ the End of the Law: the Meaning of Romans 10.4', *JBL* 88 (1969) 331–7 (here 336); similarly Gaston 66; Sanders, *Law* 38. See further Dunn, *Romans* 587–8.

33. A useful parallel is provided from twentieth-century Christianity. In classical Pentecostalism it would generally be agreed that speaking in tongues and the Pentecostal understanding of Spirit-baptism are *not* the most important elements of their faith. But in fact most apologetic writing and most discussion of Pentecostalism has given considerable prominence to these two Pentecostal teachings. The reason is also the reason for the prominence of circumcision and food laws in Gal. 2: in both cases we are dealing with the distinctive features of the group – what marks them off from other even closely related groups. For

anyone wishing to identify himself with classical Pentecostalism in the first half of the twentieth century, the make or break issue was speaking in tongues.

34. My `criticisms in 'The New Perspective' focused principally on Sanders (particularly 201–2).

35. Räisänen, *Paul* 62–73, 101–18.

36. It should be noted that I say 'a large part of his critique'; in this essay I do not attempt to deal with other aspects of the law's function in Paul's thought (particularly Rom. 5.20; 7.7–11). See further Dunn, *Romans* lxxi–lxxii.

37. See particularly Räisänen's discussion (*Paul* 23–8).

38. Räisänen's critique at this point is directed against the equally inadequate view that 'γράμμα means Jewish legalism rather than the Torah', but he has missed the social function of the Torah as a whole (*Paul* 44–6).

39. Sanders' discussion misses the point and thus undermines his own critique (*Law* 123–32). Similarly Räisänen (*Paul* 98–101); Paul attacks the typical Jewish presumption that having the law, being within the law, is what gives assurance of justification (as Räisänen recognizes later – 170); it is that attitude which Paul indicts in Rom. 2.17–24, not 'every individual Jew without exception' (*Paul* 100). I have a fuller treatment relating the contemporary Jewish understanding of the law to the whole argument of Rom. 2 in 'What was the real issue between Paul and "Those of the Circumcision"', *Paulus als Theologe und Missionar und antike Judentum*, hrsg. M. Hengel (WUNT; Tübingen: Mohr, 1990).

40. 'New Perspective' 118–19; above, pp. 200–1.

41. See among recent discussions, H. Hübner, 'Gal. 3.10 und die Herkunft des Paulus', *KD* 19 (1973) 215–31; also *Gesetz* 19–20; A. Oepke/J. Rohde, *Galater* (THNT; Berlin: Evangelische, 1973) 105; H. Mussner, *Galaterbrief* (Freiburg: Herder, ³1977) 225–6; J. Becker, *Galater* (NTD; Göttingen: Vandenhoeck, 1976) 36–7; R. Smend & U. Luz, *Gesetz* (Stuttgart: Kohlhammer, 1981) 94–5; D. Hill, 'Gal. 3.10–14: Freedom and Acceptance', *ExpT* 93 (1981–2) 197; F. F. Bruce, *Galatians* (NIGTC; Exeter: Paternoster, 1982) 157–60; Räisänen, *Paul* 94; D. J. Moo, '"Law", "Works of the Law", and Legalism in Paul', *WTJ* 45 (1983) 96–9; T. R. Schreiner, 'Is Perfect Obedience to the Law Possible? A Re-examination of Galatians 3.10', *JETS* 27 (1984) 151–60; C. K. Barrett, *Freedom and Obligation. A Study of the Epistle to the Galatians* (London: SPCK, 1985) 34; R. Y. K. Fung, *Galatians* (NICNT; Grand Rapids: Eerdmans, 1988) 142. Earlier references in J. Eckert, *Die urchristliche Verkündigung im Streit zwischen Paulus und seinen Gegnern nach dem Galaterbrief* (Regensburg: Pustet, 1971) 77 n. 3.

42. See above n. 17.

43. See above pp. 221–2. Mussner rightly notes recent research's recognition 'wie sehr man gerade im Frühjudentum Bund und Gesetz zusammengedacht hat'. *Galaterbrief* 229 n. 85, referring to Jaubert and Limbeck; add now particularly Sanders.

44. cf. H. Schlier, *Galater* (KEK; Göttingen: Vandenhoeck, ¹³1965) 132; H. Betz, *Galatians* (Hermeneia; Philadelphia: Fortress, 1979) 145; and Sanders' highly individual argument (*Law* 20–5).

45. See n. 5 above.

46. See also Betz's review of the options usually canvassed for v. 10 (*Galatians* 145–6). Betz's own reconstruction of Paul's reasoning (the law was given in order to be broken and to generate sin) is hardly obvious from the text (even allowing for 3.19). It would hardly cut much ice with his readers, and on this point Paul could hardly simply assume that his readers shared his presuppositions (cf. Betz's own observation on p. 141). Moreover, as Hübner points out, such a theology attributes a very perverse motive on the part of God in giving the law (*Gesetz* 27); it is hard to think that Paul would be unaware of such a corollary or would willingly embrace it.

234

47. As Sanders has argued, it is precisely the concern to 'remain within' the framework of the covenant which is at the heart of 'covenantal nomism'.
48. Sanders' failure to appreciate the full force of the phrase ὅσοι ἐξ ἔργων νόμου is mirrored in the weak summary he gives: 'in 3.10 Paul means that those who *accept* the law are cursed' (*Law* 22, my emphasis).
49. G. Howard, *Paul: Crisis in Galatia* (SNTSMS 35; Cambridge, 1979) recognizes the narrowness of Paul's focus in his talk of 'works of the law', and Paul's concern that the law divides Jew from Gentile (especially 53, 62), but he weakens his exposition by arguing that 'being under the law' could be said of Gentiles as well as Jews (60–1); in contrast see p. 221 above.
50. The usual understanding of Hab. 2.4 MT – '. . . will live by his faithfulness'. It is not necessary to the discussion here to resolve the question of whether Paul intended the ἐκ πίστεως to go with ὁ δίκαιος or ζήσεται. See, e.g., the discussion by H. C. C. Cavallin, 'The Righteous Shall Live by Faith', *ST* 32 (1978) 33–43; cf. Dunn, *Romans* 44–6 (on Rom. 1.17).
51. That ἐν νόμῳ (v. 11) is equivalent to ἐξ ἔργων νόμου (v. 10) is plain (Bruce, *Galatians* 161), as also the parallel between 3.11 and 2.16 confirms.
52. See above p. 221–2. Lev. 18.5 'contains one of the fundamental doctrines of the Old Testament and of Judaism' (Betz, *Galatians* 148). By ὁ νόμος in v. 12 Paul means the law understood in this way, as Lev. 18.5 indicates. The term should not be enlarged to mean 'the law' on any and every understanding of the law. The whole argument here clearly relates to a quite specific understanding of the law. In fact the *same* contrast can be posed subsequently by Paul as between 'the law of faith' and 'the law of works' (Rom. 3.27; cf. 9.31–2), precisely because νόμος here is shorthand for ἔργα νόμου (see also above n. 51).
53. In the context of 3.1–9 πίστις must refer primarily to faith exercised by man, rather than God's faithfulness (against Howard, *Paul* 63–4), though a secondary allusion to the latter cannot be entirely ruled out in view of the LXX of Hab. 2.4. That Paul refers Hab. 2.4 to *Christ* (R. B. Hays, *The Faith of Jesus Christ* [SBL Dissertation 56; Chico: Scholars, 1983] 150–7) is still less likely: 3.10–12 is an exposition of the contrast between οἱ ἐκ πίστεως (v. 9) and ὅσοι ἐξ ἔργων νόμου (v. 10).
54. A Christological interpretation of 3.12 (Lev. 18.5 was fulfilled through Christ) ignores the contrast clearly intended here and reads too much into the text (K. Barth, *CD* II/2 245; R. Bring, *Galatians* [Philadelphia: Muhlenberg, 1961] 128–42; Cranfield, *Romans* 522 n. 2).
55. Against Schlier, *Galater* 132–5. As U. Luz and others have noted, it is not the *doing*, but the *not* doing which falls under the law's curse (*Das Geschichtsverständnis des Paulus* [München: Kaiser, 1968] 149).
56. cf. M. Wilcox, '"Upon the Tree" – Deut. 21.22–23 in the New Testament', *JBL* 96 (1977) 87; F. F. Bruce, 'The Curse of the Law', *Paul and Paulinism*, C. K. Barrett Festschrift, ed. M. D. Hooker and S. G. Wilson (London: SPCK, 1982) 30.
57. 'The summary in 3.14 shows where the emphasis of the argument in 3.1–13 falls' (Sanders, *Law* 22). The weakness of Räisänen's atomistic exegesis is illustrated by the weakness of his treatment of 3.13, which ignores the connection between vv. 13 and 14 (*Paul* 59–61, 249–51). This despite the fact that he later notes: 'It is striking how often the polemics against the law as the way to salvation are found in a context where the question of the *inclusion of the Gentiles* is the most important problem (Gal. 2—3, Rom. 3—4, Rom. 9—10)' (*Paul* 176; similarly 187).
58. Commentators are divided on whether ἡμᾶς should be referred only to Jewish Christians (e.g. Betz, *Galatians* 148) or to Gentiles as well (e.g. B. Byrne, '*Sons of God*' – '*Seed of Abraham*' [AnBib 83; Rome: Biblical Institute, 1979] 153). Paul could of course mean that the Gentiles were under the law's curse quite apart from the curse on Jewish restrictiveness, since Gentiles also fall short of

235

all that the law requires in their own way (cf. Rom. 1.18–31). But such a thought is not to the forefront of Paul's mind here (though cf. Gal. 4.8–10). Nevertheless, the baleful effect of Jewish misunderstanding of the law on the Gentiles could be included without too much inexactness in the single thought of both Jew and Gentile requiring deliverance from the curse of the law falsely seen to exclude Gentile *qua* Gentile. To speak of an 'oscillating concept of the law' at this point (Räisänen, *Paul* 19–20) is therefore unwarranted. See now particularly Donaldson, 'Curse' 95–8.

59. See 4QpNah 1.7–8; 11QTempleScroll 64.6–13, and the careful discussion of J. A. Fitzmyer, 'Crucifixion in Ancient Palestine, Qumran Literature and the New Testament', *CBQ* 40 (1978) 493–513, reprinted in *To Advance the Gospel* (New York: Crossroad, 1981) 125–46, especially 129–35, 138–9, with references to earlier literature.

60. The point is perceived by Bruce: 'The curse of Deut. 27.26 was pronounced at the end of a covenant-renewal ceremony and had special reference therefore to the covenant-breaker' (*Galatians* 164). 'The penalty of being hanged on a tree until one dies is prescribed in the Temple Scroll for an Israelite who . . . has been guilty of breaking the covenant-bond. To be exposed "in the sun" was judged in Old Testament times to be a fitting punishment for Israelites who were guilty of covenant violation' ('Curse of the Law' 31).

61. cf. D. R. Schwartz, 'Two Pauline Allusions to the Redemptive Mechanism of the Crucifixion', *JBL* 102 (1983) 260–3. There is no 'discrepancy' between 4.4–5 and 3.13 as Betz asserts (*Galatians* 144 n. 57); both are directed primarily to the soteriological effect of Christ's death (see J. D. G. Dunn, *Christology in the Making* [London: SCM, 1980] 41–2). Cf. further Hays, *Faith* chap. III.

62. So, e.g., the most recent study by H. Weder, *Das Kreuz Jesu bei Paulus* (Göttingen: Vandenhoeck, 1981) 187–93.

63. cf. particularly Sanders, *Law* 25–6; Räisänen, *Paul* 249–51 (but see also above n. 57).

64. Contrast the artificiality of Räisänen's reconstruction of Paul's reasoning: Paul's 'point of departure is the conviction that the law *must not* be fulfilled outside of the Christian community, for otherwise Christ would have died in vain' (*Paul* 118).

65. I refer particularly to K. Stendahl's justly famous essay, 'The Apostle Paul and the Introspective Conscience of the West', *HTR* 56 (1963) 199–215, reprinted in his *Paul Among Jews and Gentiles* (London: SCM, 1977) 78–96; cf. also N. A. Dahl, 'The Doctrine of Justification: its Social Function and Implications', *Studies in Paul* (Minneapolis: Augsburg, 1977) 95–120; W. D. Davies, 'Paul and the People of Israel', *NTS* 24 (1977–78) 4–39, reprinted in his *Jewish and Pauline Studies* (London: SPCK, 1984) 123–52 (here particularly 128); also his review of Betz's commentary, reprinted in the same collection 172–88; Gaston (as n. 26); and, of course, E. P. Sanders, *Paul and Palestinian Judaism* (London: SCM, 1977).

66. See further ch. 4 above. Donaldson, 'Curse' 94, 106, rightly sees that the key to understanding Gal. 3.1—4.7, and 3.13–14 in particular, is to clarify 'the route by which Paul moves from "cross" to "Gentiles"'. But his failure to recognize the social function of the law means that his exegesis of 3.10ff. remains otherwise within the old constraints (see particularly 103–4), leaving the movement of thought between 3.10–14 still unclear and confusing.

Additional Note

1. R. Y. K. Fung, *Galatians* 148 n. 60, criticizes my understanding of the curse of the law 'as having to do "primarily with that attitude which confines the covenant promise to Jews as Jews", as "the curse of a wrong understanding of the law"' (above p. 229 = *NTS*, p. 536), as 'ill-suited to the idea of Christ as the bearer of the curse'. The criticism, however, does not give sufficient weight to two factors.

(a) Paul regards this misunderstanding of the function of the law as a desperately serious matter. If I understand Galatians 3.10 (and Rom. 2) aright, this 'misunderstanding' amounts to a failure to keep the law as God intended, and thus puts those guilty of that misunderstanding under the same curse. The irony is that by assuming those *not within* the *law* are *outside* the *covenant* (and so effectively under God's curse), they actually put *themselves* under that curse; those who insist that the grace of God is tightly restricted when it is not, are in effect confessing that they are not under that grace. As Romans 2—3 argues, over-confidence of covenant security (sin notwithstanding) is a form of unfaithfulness which puts Jews who indulge in such 'boasting' 'under sin'.

(b) In terms of Galatians 3.13, the curse is the curse which falls on the covenant-breaker, the curse of no longer being in covenant relation with God (with all that that means in terms of God's saving righteousness), the curse of being outside the covenant, of being forsaken by God, abandoned by God to the state from which his electing grace had initially drawn them to be his people – in the words of Ephesians, 'strangers to the covenant of promise, having no hope and without God in the world' (Eph. 2.12). It was this forsakenness which Jesus experienced on the cross. The logic of 3.13–14 is that God by vindicating the one thus cursed, thus affirmed that the scope of his covenant love now (the 'eschatological "now"') reaches beyond the old boundaries, to include those previously outside them. He still chooses a 'no people'; he is still the one who 'justifies the ungodly'.

A more penetrating and thoroughgoing rebuttal is offered by S. Westerholm, in his impressive defence of a more traditional Lutheran exposition of Paul – *Israel's Law and the Church's Faith. Paul and his Recent Interpreters*, Grand Rapids: Eerdmans (1988). I will limit my interaction with Westerholm to the issues bearing most immediately on the arguments of Chapter 8.

Westerholm's thesis revolves round the interdependence of 'law' and 'works'. The law (the Sinaitic legislation) is 'based on works' and 'demands works' (p. 106; but the phrases are used repeatedly). But human attempts to meet the law's demand for 'works', to keep God's law, have failed. 'It is Paul's view that the law demands "works" as its condition for life, and Paul's explanation that the law failed as a path to human life (*sic*) because of universal human sin' (p. 173). 'Conversely, since the gospel succeeds where the law has failed, Paul must exclude from his definition of "grace" and "faith" the human activity (*sic* = works!) which doomed the law to failure' (p. 163). 'In Paul's argument it is human deeds of any kind which cannot justify' (p. 134). Hence for Paul, the contrast between law and grace is fundamental: God's righteousness 'is an expression of God's

237

grace to the exclusion of a requirement for deeds, whereas the law demands deeds' (p. 150). And as for Christian ethics, 'Paul consistently argues and assumes that Christians are no longer bound by the Mosaic code. The mark of Christian ethics is life in the Spirit, an ethic which Paul explicitly contrasts with obligation to the law. Paul's refusal to allow the Mosaic law a place in Christian ethics follows immediately from his understanding of the nature of the law' (p. 199).

2. What is particularly disappointing about Westerholm's response is his almost complete failure to take any notice of 'the social function of the law', despite his reference both to 'The New Perspective' (ch. 7 above) and to Chapter 8 above (where it is central to the discussion). Thus he makes the same mistake as Stuhlmacher,[1] of assuming that by 'works of the law' (in my exposition) 'only a few specific statutes', 'a fragment' of the law, are in view (p. 118), ignoring the clarification of Chapter 8 that '"works of the law" denote all that the law requires of the devout Jew . . .' (above p. 223 = *NTS*, p. 531). Consequently Westerholm completely fails to address my point that precisely in the passages he cites, Galatians 2.16, 21, 3.11 and 5.4 (p. 117), it is the law in its social function which is in view, as indicated by the talk of 'Gentile "sinners"' in the context of 2.15ff.[2] and by the ἐν νόμῳ of the last two verses (see above pp. 221, 227–8, 231–2 = *NTS*, pp. 529, 535, 539). And in his treatment of Romans 2 Westerholm misses the point that Paul brings his indictment of the 'Jew' to a climax precisely by reference to circumcision as in itself marking off circumcised from uncircumcised,[3] as focusing what it means to be a 'Jew' in what is visible and ethnically distinctive, in the law as 'letter' (pp. 118–19).[4] Similarly with his exposition of being 'under the law' (pp. 132, 205f.), where clearly (in my view) the sense of obligation to observe its commands is coterminous with the sense of being 'within the law', within the space marked out by its commands.

3. A crucial area of disagreement is whether when Paul speaks negatively of 'works' he means 'works of the law' or 'works in general'. Westerholm is clear that Paul means the latter. The argument centres on Romans 4.1–5, to which Westerholm returns repeatedly. 'The "works" by which Abraham could conceivably have been justified, and of which he might have boasted (4.2), were certainly not observances of the peculiarly Jewish parts of the Mosaic code . . . Not particular works which set Jews apart, but works in general – anything "done" that might deserve a recompense (4.4) or justify pride (v. 2) – are meant . . .' (p. 119).[5]

It is impossible to deal with this argument in detail here. The following points, with reference to the fuller exposition of my *Romans*, must suffice.

(a) The boasting of which Paul speaks in Romans 3.27ff. must surely refer back to the boasting in 2.17, 23. That is to say, it is Jewish pride in status as the people of the one God which Paul has in view (2.17–20). Such is the boasting of those who perform 'the works of the law', not as works of self-achievement, or 'human attempts to keep God's law',[6] but as the pattern of behaviour which attests and maintains membership of the covenant people. Opposed to that, Paul sets 'the law of faith' (3.27): it is the law understood in terms of *faith*, 'the obedience of faith' (1.5), which breaks down the distinction between Jew and Gentile (3.29–30); and it is the *law* understood in terms of faith which establishes the law (3.31).[7]

Hence the treatment of Abraham in Romans 4.1ff. is wholly determined by Paul's attempt to counter the standard Jewish view that Abraham was justified by his faithfulness, that is, as demonstrated by his obedience in the matter of circumcision and the offering of Isaac, his law-keeping (as in Sir. 44.19–21; 1 Macc. 2.52; and already in Gen. 26.5).[8]

(b) As to Romans 4.4–5, that too must not be taken out of context. Paul's objective is primarily to expound λογίζεσθαι. And his main point is that Genesis 15.6 should be understood not in terms of human contract (it uses πιστεύειν, not ἐργάζεσθαι), but in terms of the divine-human relationship (where the correlative to faith is not ὀφείλημα, 'debt', but χάρις, 'grace'). To deduce from this analogy that Paul regards 'working' as wholly negative and 'reward' as entirely excluded for the Christian makes nonsense of Romans 2.10, 13 and 1 Corinthians 3.8, 14. Hence the aim of Paul's critique is more sharply focused and more specifically directed than Westerholm recognizes.

(c) Westerholm's exegesis of Romans 9.30—10.4 is open to similar objection. He recognizes that 9.31 speaks of Israel pursuing the 'law of righteousness' (p. 127), but blurs the point of Paul's critique by taking the phrase as equivalent to 'the righteousness which is based on the law' (p. 145) and by ignoring Paul's own explanation of why Israel failed to reach that law – because they pursued it 'as if it was from works' instead of (as it is) 'from faith' (9.32). Evidently for Paul (despite Westerholm), to follow the law 'from faith' is the right way to 'do' the law. Westerholm also misses the critique of Jewish 'zeal' in 10.2,[9] and so also finds no difficulty in reasserting the more traditional interpretation of 10.3 as directed against self-achieved righteousness (pp. 114–15); whereas the more natural way of taking ἰδίαν δικαιοσύνην is against Jewish concern to establish and maintain righteousness as Israel's and as therefore not open to the Gentiles as Gentiles.[10] That 'as if from works' is all part and parcel of the attitude critiqued in 10.2–3 (and 10.5) seems fairly self-evident from the flow of the argument (9.30ff.).

4. Finally, Westerholm seems to misunderstand a characteristic feature of 'covenantal nomism' and to drive the Lutheran law/gospel antithesis too far into Paul's teaching on judgement and ethics (pp. 150, 163, 173, 199 – cited above, p. 238).

(a) He cites a sequence of Old Testament texts which talk of the life which is a consequence of keeping the law (pp. 145–7). But in characterizing them as speaking of an obedience which 'leads to the possession of life', of the law as 'a path to salvation', he ignores the fact that the principal concern of these texts is to indicate how life should be lived *within* the covenant (covenantal nomism), not to point to a life yet to be attained.

(b) He recognizes that 'divine approval on the day of judgment is the goal of both groups' (Jews and Christians) (p. 145). But in insisting that for Paul 'Christians have *already* been justified' (which is, of course, true) he ignores the fact that for Paul as well as his fellow Jews justification is not a once for all, already over and done with affair. The day of judgement is also about justification/acquittal. But I have already dealt with this point in responding to Räisänen and need say no more about it here.[11]

(c) Most striking of all, Westerholm plays down Paul's talk of judgement according to works (Rom. 2.6ff.; 1 Cor. 3.13ff.). Like his ancestral

239

faith, Paul looked for a quality of life and conduct (works) which would be expressive of the justified (covenant) state. Like his fellow Jews, he saw the law as something to be obeyed, done – 'fulfilled' is his preferred word (Rom. 8.4 – the object of Christ's whole ministry!). The difference is that Paul speaks of an 'obedience of *faith*' (Rom. 1.5; cf. 6.16–17; 10.16; 15.18), of the law properly 'established through faith', 'pursued from faith' (Rom. 3.31; 9.31–2)[12] – faith from start to finish, a walk enabled by the Spirit (Gal. 3.1–5; 5.16f.); he speaks of *love* as the mark of the Christian, in contrast to Jewish 'works' – 'faith working through love' (Gal. 5.6), the law fulfilled in love (Rom. 13.8–10; Gal. 5.14).[13] In contrast Westerholm ignores Romans 1.5 and forces the contrast between 'fulfilling' and 'doing' the law (pp. 201–5), despite once again Romans 2.13–14.[14]

In short, Westerholm's failure is not that he recognizes the close link between 'the law' and 'works'. It is rather that he insists on regarding 'works of the law' as 'works in general', and as such consistently negative for Paul. The result is a disturbing portrayal of a Paul who is essentially enthusiastic and antinomian in his ethics and whose doctrine of final judgement is thrown into disarray. In contrast, to see the link between 'the law' and 'works' in terms of 'the social function of the law', with 'works of the law' recognized as the deeds and lifestyle by which the devout Jew lived within the covenant people and maintained covenant righteousness in distinction from the Gentiles, is to recognize both the continuity and discontinuity between Paul's teaching and his ancestral faith, and the full scope of Paul's teaching on justification/acquittal. The point which Westerholm justifiably wishes to safeguard is *not* thereby lost. Justification remains by faith, from start to finish. But the contrast and the corollary which Paul draws out fits his historical context so much better and makes more consistent sense of all his teaching.

Notes

1. Ch. 7 Additional Note point 6; but Stuhlmacher had not seen the clarification provided on this point by ch. 8 above. Cf. also Schreiner in ch. 7 Additional Note point 11. And contrast J. M. G. Barclay, *Obeying the Truth: A Study of Paul's Ethics in Galatians*, Edinburgh: T. & T. Clark (1988) 82 n. 18 (see also below).
2. See also Barclay, cited in n. 5 below.
3. See also now J. Marcus, 'The Circumcision and the Uncircumcision in Rome', *NTS* 35 (1989) 67–81.
4. See further my *Romans*, WBC 38, Dallas: Word (1988) 123–5.
5. Similarly D. J. Moo, 'Paul and the Law in the Last Ten Years', *SJT* 40 (1987) 296, 298, restating his earlier thesis in 'Law' (n. 41 above); cf. F. Watson, *Paul, Judaism and the Gentiles. A Sociological Approach*, SNTSMS 56, Cambridge University (1986) 199 n. 90. Contrast Barclay, *Obeying*, who argues strongly that in Galatians 'it is clear that Paul is not at all concerned ... to attack "works" as such, only works of *the law*' (94). Thus, in reference to Gal. 2.16: 'The immediate context of the Antioch dispute makes clear that "works of the law" are equivalent to "living like a Jew"' (78); '"the works of the law" appear to be those activities which express Jewish identity ... doing what the law demands is a sign of adopting the Jewish way of life ... "the works *of the law*," that is, maintaining a Jewish life-style' (82).
6. Against Westerholm 166, 169–72.

7. Against Westerholm 123–6, whose failure to give a satisfactory account of 3.31 is one of the weakest points of his whole treatment.

8. Again Westerholm completely fails to inquire into the context and assumptions of the argument in Rom. 4.1ff.

9. See above ch. 4 Additional Note point 1.

10. See above p. 223 = *NTS*, pp. 530–1, and my *Romans* 586–9.

11. See above ch. 7 Additional Note point 1.

12. In citing Deut. 30.12–14 in Rom. 10.6ff. Paul would certainly not have been unaware of how that passage ended – 'that you may do it'! For Paul the word/commandment of God is 'done' in the ῥῆμα and ἀκοή of faith (10.8–11, 17).

13. See further now the well-argued thesis of Barclay, *Obeying*, especially ch. 4.

14. Rom. 2.13–14 is hardly dealt with by Westerholm in 203 n. 18.

9

The Theology of Galatians

My thesis is that Galatians is Paul's first sustained attempt to deal with the issue of covenantal nomism. His argument is basically: (i) that the outworking of God's saving power will be consistent with its initial decisive expression; (ii) that that initial expression of God's covenant purpose was in terms of promise and faith and always had the Gentiles in view from the first; and (iii) that the law, where it is understood in a way which conflicts with that initial expression, has been given a distorted role.

I will begin (§1) by recalling what 'covenantal nomism' means and why it was so important at the time of Paul; then attempt to demonstrate exegetically (§2) that covenantal nomism is the issue underlying Paul's argument in Galatians, and (§3) how Paul deals with it in what I see to be his three-stranded argument; next (§4) I will try to indicate why I think that Galatians is Paul's first full-scale attempt to deal with this issue; and finally (§5) it may be appropriate to indicate by way of corollary the circumstances which probably led up to the letter itself. In all this I take it for granted that however else we may want to speak of and to use 'the theology of Galatians', we must at least start by asking what Paul was saying within the context of his times and of his mission and in relation to the specific situation in Galatia, and what he wanted his Galatian readership and audience to hear and to understand in what he wrote. In the spirit of the seminar[1] I will confine my discussion to Galatians itself and not attempt to underpin or develop the main part of the thesis by reference to any other Pauline text.

§1. 'Covenantal nomism', as coined by E. P. Sanders,[2] is a phrase well-fitted to characterize Jewish self-understanding, or, more precisely, the understanding of the relation between God and his people Israel as it comes to expression consistently (though not uniformly)[3] within Jewish literature, particularly from Deuteronomy onwards.

§1.1 Fundamental to Judaism's sense of identity was the conviction that (i) God had made a special *covenant* with the patriarchs, whose central feature was the choice of Israel to be his peculiar people (e.g. Deut. 4.31; 2 Macc. 8.15; Pss. Sol. 9.10; CD 6.2; 8.18), and (ii) had given the *law* as an integral part of the covenant both to show Israel how to live within that covenant ('This do and you shall live' – Deut. 4.1, 10, 40; 5.29–33; 6.1–2, 18, 24; etc.) and to make it possible for them to do so (the system of atonement).[4] Hence 'covenantal nomism', where the former word emphasizes God's prevenient grace, and the latter cannot and should not be confused with legalism or with any idea of 'earning' salvation.

The typical mind-set of covenantal nomism included a strong sense of special privilege and prerogative over against other peoples (e.g. Bar. 3.36—4.4; Pss. Sol. 13.6–11; Philo, *Mos.* 2.17–25; Jos. *Ap.* 2.277–86). But it also and inevitably meant a reinforcing of the sense of national identity and separateness from other nations (e.g. Jub. 22.16; Ep. Arist. 139, 142; Philo, *Mos.* 1.278).[5] This was evidently a major motivating factor in the reconstitution of Judea after the exile (Ezra 9—10). And the same sense of a basic need to remain loyal to its covenant obligations was obviously one of the most powerful factors in the Maccabean attempt to restore national integrity and to retain national identity. At that time the obligations of covenantal nomism focused on those features of national and religious life which marked out the distinctiveness of the Jewish people – circumcision and food laws (1 Macc. 2.60–3). This was because these demands of the law had become a principal target of Syrian persecution – and for the same reason (they prevented assimilation and integration into a larger international and religious whole). At the same time 'Judaism' first appears in our literature precisely as a protest against such Hellenizing pressure (2 Macc. 2.21; 8.1; 14.38), that is, as a way of marking off the entity of Jewish self-identity from a Hellenism which had swamped and threatened to obliterate such national distinctives. And the verb 'to judaize' is coined to indicate those Gentiles who choose to live their lives in accord with the ancestral customs and practices distinctive of the Jewish nation (Esth. 8.17 LXX; Jos. *War* 2.454, 462–3).[6]

Equally it is evident that these concerns shaped so clearly by the Maccabean national crisis continued to be a dominant factor in the following period. All the literature from then on through the next two centuries bears testimony to a concern to assert, define and defend the boundaries of the covenant, as different groups claimed that it was *their* understanding and practice which was what we might call the *proper* covenantal nomism; that they (alone) were the 'righteous' and 'devout', and the other non-practitioners were 'sinners', disloyal to the covenant, if not apostates, by their failure to keep the law as it should be kept (e.g. Wisd. Sol. 2—5; Jub. 6.32–5; 1 Enoch 1.1, 7–9; 1QS 2.4–5; Pss. Sol. 3.3–12; 13.5–12).[7] In this period circumcision and food laws, together with other specific commandments like sabbath and festivals, remained the clearest identity- and boundary-markers of Judaism as a whole, as indicated by evidence both within and without the corpus of Jewish writings.[8]

All this I would take to be more or less non-controversial – the evidence is clear and consistent. I emphasize it by way of introduction to the particular study of Galatians for the obvious reason that the thrust of Paul's argument regarding these same two features, covenant and law, is unlikely to be understood without an adequate grasp of *the taken-for-granted nature of covenantal nomism within Jewish circles*. The extent to which Paul is actually addressing covenantal nomism has of course yet to be established, but where such a fundamental mind-set was involved (covenantal nomism), any discussion of covenant and law in relation to Judaism was bound to be influenced in greater rather than less degree by that mind-set and its taken-for-granteds.

§1.2 More controversial, I suppose, may be two specific claims which I have already advanced elsewhere,[9] even though they seem to me to follow inevitably from the above. First, the claim that covenantal nomism is so tightly bound up with a sense of national or ethnic identity, that the law became coterminous with Israel, marking out the Jews in their distinctiveness as God's people and in their distinctiveness from others (Gentiles = not God's people).[10] That is to say, however universal the claims made for the law,[11] it never ceased to be the Jewish law; its religious appeal (evident in the many God-fearers who attached themselves in differing degrees to the diaspora synagogues)[12] was never such as could be divorced from its national function as the civil and criminal code of the Jews as a distinct ethnic entity. This 'social function of the law' I believe to be important for our fuller understanding of the mind-set with which Paul is engaging in Galatians.

Second, the claim that the phrase 'works of the law' was a way of describing the same covenantal-nomistic mind-set – 'works of the law' as the praxis which the law of the covenant laid upon the covenant member. This, I believe, is borne out by the use of an equivalent phrase, 'deeds of the law', in the Dead Sea Scrolls, where it describes the obligations laid upon the sectarian by his membership of the Qumran community (1QS 5.21, 23; 6.18; 4QFlor 1.1–7; and an unpublished 4Q text), though whether it was of wider currency or simply a natural way of expressing covenantal obligations we cannot say. In particular, such sense of obligation probably came to particular expression in those commandments which focused the distinctiveness of the claim to be a people set apart by the one God. In the Maccabean crisis that meant specifically circumcision and the food laws; and there are sufficient indications thereafter that wherever Jewish identity came into question the issue of covenantal nomism would focus on these same commandments and on any others which reinforced Jewish distinctiveness. Such deeds/works of the law became the test-cases for Jewish faithfulness.[13]

With one of our key terms thus clarified, we can now turn to Galatians and attempt to explicate the line of argument and emphases Paul employs to meet the challenge confronting his understanding of the gospel among his Galatian converts.[14]

§2. Paul was concerned with the issue of covenantal nomism as it was affecting his converts in Galatia.

§2.1 This becomes clear in Paul's consistent focus on what we might call *the 'second phase'*. It is most explicit in 3.3: what follows from the beginning they have made? how do they think the completion of God's saving work will be achieved? But the same concern lies behind almost every paragraph of the letter, in a whole sequence of variations. What follows from the gospel and its acceptance (1.6–7; 2.14)? What is the outworking of the grace of God (1.6)? For Paul it was apostleship to the Gentiles (1.15; 2.9); for those he opposes it was evidently the law (2.21; 5.4). If the issue of circumcision for Gentiles has been settled (2.1–10), what about the issue of continuing lifestyle, as focused (as also with the Pharisees)[15] in table-fellowship (2.11–14)?

Most persistent of all is the argument regarding the relation of faith and the law. How is (the initial expression of) faith to be correlated with 'works of the law'? The implication of the ἐὰν μή of 2.16a, especially in its context as referring back to the food laws issue at Antioch (2.11–14), is that Jewish Christians thought works of the law (like observance of the dietary laws) were quite compatible with faith in Christ and still a necessary (covenantal) obligation for Jewish believers in Messiah Jesus.[16] But Paul drives that distinction (faith in Christ, and works of law) into an outright antithesis (2.16bc;[17] 3.2, 5, 10–12); to regard the law (covenantal nomism) as the outworking of faith is retrogressive, a stepping back from the freedom of sonship into immature childhood and slavery (3.23—4.11, 21–31). The outworking of faith has to be conceived in different terms from works of the law (circumcision, *et al.*): that is, in terms of the Spirit as against works of the flesh (5.16–26; 6.7–9), a focusing on physical features which would include a nationalistic evaluation of circumcision (3.3; 4.21–31; 6.12–13). It may be conceived in terms of the law – not the law focused in such Jewish distinctives as circumcision, but focused rather in love of neighbour (5.6, 13–14), as exemplified by Christ (6.1–4).[18]

§2.2 The issue underlying all this is covenantal nomism, that is, the issue of whether those Gentiles who had come to faith in the Messiah of the Jews, and who thus claimed a share in the benefits of God's covenant with Israel, needed to live in accordance with the law of Israel, that is, to live in accordance with Jewish customs ('to judaize') or to become proselytes, in order to sustain that claim.[19] That this is the issue has been obscured by several factors.

1. One is the fact that covenantal nomism was such a taken-for-granted for the typical Jewish mind-set that it did not need to be spelt out any more clearly than it is, as indicated above (§1.1).

2. A second is that 'works of the law' have for too long been understood as 'good works by which individuals try to gain acceptance by God'; that fundamental misunderstanding has skewed the whole exegesis of the letter, distorting or concealing the Jewish (as well as Christian) recognition of the priority of God's grace, and losing sight of the corporate dimension of the discussion in an individualistic doctrine of justification by faith.[20]

3. Sanders' own rebuttal of that misplaced emphasis in turn clouded the issue by making *too sharp a distinction between entry* (into the covenant) *and continuance* or maintenance of status within the covenant. 'Justification' (being 'righteoused') was classified as 'transfer terminology',[21] with the implication that that was also where Paul's emphasis on faith belonged, that is, only with the question of entry and not that of continuance (but 5.4 indicates that justification has as much to do with continuance, and 5.5 with final outcome). Consequently *the issue of the continuum between faith and its outworking/corollary was obscured* – whether (covenant) faith comes to expression in (covenant) works of the law (necessarily, inevitably?), or continues to be the basis of continuance (as well as of entry), or what?[22]

4. This last confusion has been the more plausible since so much of the issue in Galatians focuses on circumcision, which seems to reinforce an 'entry into covenant'/'maintenance of status' distinction. But the issue of works of the law first comes to expression as a result of the Antioch incident (2.11–16), where the concern was clearly the maintenance of covenant status on the part of the Jewish Christians in Antioch through faithful observance of the food laws. Moreover, it was not merely circumcision which the Galatian converts were being exhorted to undergo, but circumcision as the beginning of that law observance which was expected of all devout covenant members (4.10; 5.3). At this point it is as well to recall that circumcision was not typically thought of within Judaism as a rite of entry to the covenant, but as one of the commandments by obeying which one expressed one's status as a Jew (or proselyte),[23] the first act we may say of covenantal nomism.

§3. The main thrust of Paul's argument against covenantal nomism has three strands.

§3.1 *The expression of life within the covenant should be consistent with its beginning.*

(a) This is evident from Paul's initial appeal to his readers: what they are doing is to abandon the grace of God which first brought them to faith, in favour of a different gospel (1.6–9). And the appeal is regularly repeated throughout the rest of the letter – 3.1–5, 4.8–11 and 5.1–12. It was by faith that they became participants in the promises of God; their continuing status as such would be maintained in the same way.

(b) Paul equally sees his own experience of being commissioned with the gospel in the same light (1.11—2.10; 2.18–20). Whatever his relationship with Jerusalem after his conversion, and whatever may have passed between himself and the pillar apostles on his two visits there, the crucial fact is that they added nothing to him, but gave full recognition to the grace of God which was the manifest proof of his original commissioning (2.6–9). Similarly he is concerned to make it clear that to have resumed a full-scale observance of the food laws in table-fellowship would have been equivalent to his building again what Christ's death and commissioning had pulled down for him (2.14–21).

(c) Hence also the heart of his argument in chapter 3: that the law neither annuls nor alters the terms of the original covenant promise to Abraham (3.15–20). That is to say, the original promise to Abraham, as given to faith, continues to characterize the covenant and the relationship with God which it sustains; to insist that covenantal nomism with its now traditional check-points was the only way to live for heirs of the promise was to make the promise void.

(d) It is still, of course, necessary to know how faith will work out in practice. Guidance on lifestyle and praxis is still necessary. Hence the final exhortation in 5.13—6.10. And there Paul clearly shows that he sees the law as still having a function. He still believes in a kind of 'covenantal nomism'! But it has markers different from the ancestral customs of the Jews – love and Spirit, not circumcision.[24]

Paul's argument is thus clear. *Ongoing praxis must be a continuing expression of the faith by which his readers first began to function within God's covenant promise and purpose* – a beginning whose divinely given character was self-evident both to Paul and his readers. Stated like this the argument is certainly open to sharp criticism (the law was also given by God; why should works of the law be regarded as an antithesis to faith?), a line of criticism we hardly need James 2.18–26 to spell out for us. But at least its logic is clear. And it is only part of the complete argument.

§3.2 The second strand of Paul's argument is that *God's promise always had the Gentiles in view from the beginning*. This is obviously the point of 3.6–9, where the gospel is focused in the original promise to Abraham, 'In you shall all the nations be blessed' (3.8, following LXX).[25] The point is clear: the original promise is to be offered to those originally in view in it and on the original terms – to the Gentiles, by faith. The covenant promise was not intended solely for Jews.[26]

The following paragraph (3.10–14) has been much disputed and much misunderstood. But it is most obviously to be taken as speaking of a curse understood as a curse on lawlessness, and so as a curse which the law has interposed between the Gentiles (lawless) and their share in the promise. Thus the whole thrust and climax of the paragraph is the opening up of the blessing of Abraham to the Gentiles which Christ achieved by removing that curse in his death (3.13–14). Whatever else is in view, therefore, Paul almost certainly has in mind the law's function in branding the Gentile *per se* as 'sinner' (2.15) – outside Israel, outside the law, therefore sinner and transgressor, and under a curse. *The curse of the law on the Gentile as Gentile is precisely that corollary of covenantal nomism as it had come to be understood in the nationalistic presumption* (we the 'righteous', they the 'sinners') *and ethnic restrictiveness* (inheritance limited to the Jews and proselytes – οἱ ἐξ ἔργων νόμου) *which Paul now contests.*[27]

Similarly with the argument about Christ as Abraham's 'seed' according to the promise (3.16). Its whole point is to enable Paul to make the claim that Gentiles have become partakers of the promise 'in Christ' (3.14, 28–9),[28] through the Spirit (3.14). Paul evidently does not need to debate more fundamental issues of Christology. The centrality of Christ and his death for the gospel (1.4; 2.19–21; 3.1; 4.4–5; 6.12), and the necessity for faith in him (2.16; 3.22–4, 26), were emphases he shared with his readers, and indeed with the 'judaizers'.[29] What Paul needed to emphasize was what we might call the Gentile dimension of his Christology, of his gospel (1.15–16; 2.2–5, 7–8, 15–17; 3.8, 13–14, 16, 27–9; 5.6, 11; 6.14–15), that faith in Christ *continues* to be the means through which *continued* participation in the promise and inheritance of Abraham is maintained. What Paul was concerned about was that the gospel which they took as their common starting-point was actually distorted in its fundamentals if these emphases, outworkings of the gospel and Christology, were not followed through. For the Galatian believers to accept the covenantal nomism which reclaimed the Jewish Christians at Antioch (2.12–14) would be to lose the gospel and Christ (1.6–9; 5.4).

So too Paul evidently felt no need to justify the assumption that the gift of the Spirit was the fulfilment of the promise to Abraham. This must be because the gift of the Spirit to Gentiles was both recognized among the first Christians, and acknowledged as the sure indication of God's acceptance/justifying act (so Gal. 3.2–5; 4.6, 29; 5.5; cf. particularly Acts 10.44–8; 11.15–18; Rom. 8.9, 14).[30] 'This reception of the "Spirit" is the primary datum of the

Christian churches in Galatia.'[31] Here too what Paul needed to emphasize was the gift and continued experience of the Spirit as operating independently of the law and ethnic (fleshly) considerations (3.2–5; 4.3–7, 29; 5.5–6, 18; 6.8).[32] In both cases, the Christology and pneumatology of the letter presuppose a richer and fuller theology as fundamental, but in the letter itself Paul develops only those aspects of immediate importance to the situation of the readers.

We might simply note also how much of Paul's own self-understanding of his commission (that is, of his whole existence as a Christian) was bound up with the conviction that it was now time to reach out to and bring in the Gentiles on equal terms with the Jews (that is, without their ceasing to be 'Greeks' as distinct from 'Jews'). Hence the emphasis in his description of his conversion and calling – 'called ... to preach God's Son among the Gentiles' (1.15–16).[33] Clearly his conviction that he had been called from the first to go to the uncircumcision was bound up with his understanding that the Gentiles were in view from the first expression of the covenant promise. Which of these two came first and gave rise to the other it is not possible now to say.

§3.3 What then was *the purpose of the law*? The question arises inevitably from the line of argument outlined above. The fact that it also arises in 3.19 and 21 may be taken as at least some confirmation that our analysis of Paul's argument so far is on the right lines.

The question arises, obviously, because Paul's treatment of the law as so far outlined has had strongly pejorative features. 'Works of the law' he clearly regards in a very negative light (2.16; 3.2, 5, 10). It is the law which is understood to condemn Gentiles as 'sinners' (2.15), to place a curse on the law-less, which prevents them participating in the covenant promise (3.10–14). But we have also noted that he does see a positive role for the law, at least in that he speaks of loving the neighbour as fulfilling the whole law (5.14). What then is Paul objecting to so strongly?

The answer has already been suggested in the treatment of the curse of the law (in §3.2): Paul objects to covenantal nomism understood as it then was consistently throughout Judaism – that is, covenantal nomism as restricting the covenant to those within the boundaries marked by the law, to Jews and proselytes.[34] This is confirmed by his emphasis on another word used with strong negative overtones – 'flesh' (3.3; 5.19, 24; 6.8). For 'flesh' marks out also a misunderstood relationship with Abraham, or rather a relationship with Abraham in which the emphasis has been misplaced. Hence the allegory of 4.21–31: there is a line of descent from Abraham understood in terms of the flesh – a racial or ethnic or national identity; and that is not the line of promise.[35] To limit

249

participation in the promise to a relationship κατὰ σάρκα is to misunderstand the promise.[36] Hence too the point of 6.12–13: the glorying in the flesh which Paul condemns is a glorying not in human exertion, or in ritual action, but in ethnic identity;[37] to insist that Gentiles must be circumcised is to assume that God's purpose means the triumph of Israel as a nation state, whose supremacy is acknowledged by those who seek to become part of it by their crossing the ritual boundaries which divide Gentile from Jew.[38]

I suspect this also provides the key to the puzzling 3.19 – the law given through angels ('in hand of mediator' probably in apposition to 'ordained through angels', in the light of the next clause). Anyone familiar with the Jewish understanding of the one God's ordering of his creation and of the nations within it, would be familiar also with the idea of God having appointed guardian angels for each state (Deut. 32.8–9; Sir. 17.17; Jub. 15.31–2; 1 Enoch 20.5; Targ. Ps. Jon. on Gen. 11.7–8).[39] The usual corollary in Jewish thought was that God, having appointed angels over other nations, kept Israel for himself, with no mediator interposing. The point Paul is probably making is that to treat the law in such an exclusivist, restrictive way is equivalent to treating the law as though it was given through Israel's guardian angels, or indeed, as though the law itself was Israel's guardian angel (the implication of 4.8–10, coming as it does at the end of 3.23—4.10); hence also the definition of the characteristic state of the Jews as 'under the law' as a ruling power (3.23; 4.4–5, 21; 5.21).[40] To thus regard the law as a national identity marker, as a boundary dividing Jew from Gentile, is in effect to deny the oneness of God.

Even this treatment of the law is not unreservedly negative. There was a positive side to this giving of the law to Israel. It gave the covenant people a way of dealing with sin in the period of time prior to the coming of Christ (3.19).[41] The law (guardian angel) served to direct, govern and protect Israel until the promise could be fulfilled in Christ (3.23—4.7).[42] But now that Christ has come the promise is open to Gentile as well as Jew on the original conditions. Consequently, to put oneself under the oversight of the law in its role as guardian of national rights and prerogatives is to return to childish subserviency and servility, is to deny the fullness of the promise.

The upshot is that Paul is able to pose a different alternative from that usually posed by Judaism. Judaism asserted: within the law = within the covenant. Paul in contrast asserted: within Christ = within the covenant; within the law = outside Christ (5.4).[43]

In short, Paul's attitude to the law in Galatians has regularly been misperceived as more unyieldingly negative than it is. The misunderstanding has been based on a misperception of 'works of the law' as = 'good works', and of 3.10 as requiring perfect compliance with the law.[44] But once the point has been grasped that Paul's chief target is a covenantal nomism understood in restrictively nationalistic terms – 'works of the law' as maintaining Jewish identity, 'the curse of the law' as falling on the lawless so as to exclude Gentiles as such from the covenant promise – then it becomes clear that Paul's negative remarks had a more limited thrust, and that so long as the law is not similarly misunderstood (as defining and defending the prerogatives of a particular group) it still has a positive role to play in the expression of God's purpose and will.[45]

§4. The last main part of my thesis is the claim that *Galatians is Paul's first sustained attempt to deal with the issue of covenantal nomism within the new movement we call Christianity.*

§4.1 The main ground for the claim is that covenantal nomism does not seem to have been an issue before the Antioch incident (2.11–14). Here the relation between 2.1–10 and 2.11–14 is important. What had been settled at Jerusalem (2.1–10) was the issue of circumcision. What emerged at Antioch (2.11–14) was a different issue – food laws. Just how different was at the heart of the disagreement.

If we assume that the 'certain individuals from James' (2.12) had accepted the Jerusalem agreement (however unwillingly, perhaps), then it follows that they must have regarded the agreement not to require circumcision of Gentile converts as permitting a concession, rather than as conceding a principle. This they may well have regarded as simply extending the degree of hospitality to God-fearers which diaspora Judaism had hitherto regularly practised (not least in Syria – Jos. *War* 2.462–3; 7.50–1). That they did not think the principle of covenantal nomism had thereby been conceded is probably indicated by 2.10: almsgiving was such a fundamental expression of covenantal righteousness (Dan. 4.27; Sir. 29.12; 40.24; Tob. 4.10; 12.9; 14.10–11)[46] that Paul's ready agreement to maintain the practice could easily be read as an expression of his own readiness to maintain the principle of covenantal nomism. Moreover, since the tradition of Gentile sympathizers willingly embracing the ancestral customs of the Jews ('judaizing') was so well established (see above n. 6), the men from James may well have assumed that the table-fellowship in Antioch was on a judaizing basis. This would be sufficient to explain why the issue did not emerge earlier from the Jerusalem side.[47]

On Paul's side the agreement at Jerusalem was probably taken as a point of principle. As we might now say, Paul understood circumcision in covenantal nomistic terms (not simply as a rite of entry), as the first act of a continuing compliance to the law. The agreement in Jerusalem would be understood by him as providing a precedent for the downplaying of other boundary-defining, Gentile-excluding commandments. However, if, once again, 2.10 is anything to go by, the issue was not yet so clearly defined for him. He warmly agreed to a continuing emphasis on almsgiving without seeing it as a qualifying of the agreement on circumcision. Perhaps the relief at winning the day on his principal objective made him eager to assent to this one request (requirement?), without sufficient thought for how it would be understood in Jerusalem. Or perhaps the tie-in between covenantal nomism and Jewish ethnic identity had not yet become sharply enough focused for him; after all, any almsgiving by Gentile to Jew could be readily understood within such a mind-set as part of Gentile acknowledgement of Jewish hegemony (Isa. 45.14; 60.5–17; 61.6; Mic. 4.13; Tob. 13.11; 1QM 12.13–15).

Whatever the precise facts on either side, and whatever the shared or differing understandings of the Jerusalem agreement,[48] the Antioch incident itself seems to have come as a surprise to both sides – the men from James surprised at the Jewish Christians' disregard of the food laws to such an extent – Paul surprised that there still was an issue here. At all events, the Antioch incident seems to have been the first major dispute on the issue of food laws, or in more general terms, on the issue of whether covenantal nomism as hitherto understood was still binding on Jewish Christians.

§4.2 2.14–16 does look as though Paul is marking out a step beyond a previously agreed position. Or to be more precise, in these verses Paul seems to be making explicit a theological logic which he may well previously have taken for granted (and so not previously formulated), but which others (even close associates) had not recognized or agreed to, as the Antioch incident demonstrated. What he (now) saw with clarity was that the gospel to Gentile through faith relativized the nationalistic expression of covenantal nomism, and it is this which he (quite possibly for the first time) expressed at Antioch to Peter. Since Peter and the other Jewish Christians at Antioch probably did not accept Paul's argument at that time,[49] Paul uses the opportunity of this letter to Galatia to restate, and presumably to strengthen, the argument used then.

The issue is clearly posed in ethnic terms – Jew and Gentile, 'living like Gentiles', 'judaizing' (2.14). Here the traditional parameters of covenantal nomism are in view – which can be defined simply as 'not living like the Gentiles' (cf., e.g., Jub. 6.35; 15.34; Pss. Sol. 8.13). Likewise the traditional lifestyle of the God-fearer – 'judaizing'. The assumption of the men from James, and of Peter and the other Jewish Christians, is clearly implied: in order for the Jew(ish Christian) to continue to practise his covenantal nomism, the Gentile God-fearer/Christian should be prepared to judaize = live like a Jew. What Paul cannot stomach, however, is that this should be made a requirement for faith. The use of the same verb in 2.3 and 2.14 ('compel') is not accidental. What Paul objects to is that the agreement made in Jerusalem is being set at naught by the *de facto* compulsion of the Jewish Christians' behaviour in regard to table-fellowship at Antioch.

The sense of ethnic boundary and distinctiveness is again to the fore in verse 15 – 'Jews by nature', 'Gentile sinners'. And since 'sinner' indicates the law-less person (e.g. Ps. 27.3; 54.3; LXX; 1 Macc. 1.34; 2.44), again the implication is clear, that the issue focuses on the function of the law as defining the Gentile *per se* as 'sinner' (Ps. 9.17; 1 Macc. 2.48; Pss. Sol. 1.1; 2.1–2; Luke 6.33//Matt. 5.47).[50] To be noted is the fact that Paul expresses himself in traditionally Jewish terms ('we are Jews by nature'): *he speaks as one who is consciously within Judaism,* and conscious of his distinctiveness from the Gentile; he speaks as one within the law, who has traditionally seen the Gentile as outside the bounds marked out by the law, and so by definition a 'sinner'. *Since it is this very distinction which he will be going on to question,* it must be that Paul is trying to argue from an *agreed* position and perspective *within* Judaism in an attempt to lead those who share it into a *new* position and perspective. It is probable also that the movement in self-understanding which he is thereby trying to encourage was a reflection of his own changed self-understanding. But he remains a Jew; *it is still an inner-Jewish dispute.*[51] And he is still able to identify himself with the older mind-set, implying that the full implications of his own changed perspective are still only becoming clear to him.

Hence the much misunderstood opening to 2.16, which I still think has to be read as follows: 'We are Jews by nature . . . knowing that someone is not justified by works of law except (or, but only) through faith in Jesus Christ . . .'[52] Paul continues to locate himself within the Jewish mind-set, but now the traditional Jewish perspective qualified by giving 'faith in Christ' the decisive role.[53] *What is expressed here is the viewpoint of Peter and the other Jewish Christians at Antioch.* They are all at one so far as the gospel call for faith in Jesus Christ is concerned. The Jewish Christian understanding is that this is a fundamental redefinition of covenantal nomism. The life of righteousness *within* the covenant is still defined by works of the law. But that, the Jewish Christians now believe, is not decisive for acceptance by God and final acquittal. Faith in God's Messiah is the primary necessity: 'No one is justified by works of law unless they also believe in Messiah Jesus.'

This is Paul's starting-point, as his own Jewish identity was in verse 15. But he goes on from that to underline the equally evident fact that faith in Christ Jesus has been exercised and has been fully effective *without* works of the law. Experience has demonstrated that God's acceptance is not conditional on covenantal nomism, certainly as so far usually understood. Experience of grace has given sufficient proof that this is how Psalm 143.2 should be understood: 'no one will be justified before God'; and that must include anyone who depends on his Jewish status and praxis for justification, or who thinks of himself as righteous because he lives in accordance with the ancestral customs. Jewish Christians and Galatian addressees should carry this basic insight through in their continuing life together and not return to questions of ethnic ('flesh') and religious ('sinners') distinction (above §3.1).

Here again, therefore, the very structure of the argument seems to indicate a transition in Paul's own thinking and perspective, Paul working through the implications of his understanding of the gospel, Paul forced by the turn of events in Antioch to bring to clear expression consequences and corollaries which he had previously practised without having had to spell out their full theological rationale.

§4.3 A further indication that there has been some development in Paul's own position, or at least in his articulation of it as it related to more traditional Jewish perspectives, is the change in Paul's attitude towards the Jerusalem apostles as it becomes evident in 2.1–10. In this passage the tension between a readiness to accept their authority and a clear distancing of himself from them is quite evident.[54]

On the one hand he readily acknowledges that their reception of his understanding of the gospel would determine whether his work had been or was in vain (2.2). He expresses himself with great care when he describes the actual encounter in Jerusalem (2.3ff.), but the implication of verse 3 is that Paul recognized the Jerusalem authorities' right to require circumcision, if they so chose; his relief that they did not 'compel' Titus to be circumcised is fairly evident. As is his relief that they 'added nothing to him' (2.6), so far as his understanding and preaching of the gospel was concerned. But the implication is the same: he acknowledged thereby that they had a right to make such stipulations. Hence too the readiness to accept the obligation which was actually laid down in verse 10, to remember the poor. There is even an implication that he recognized the pillar apostles' authority to confirm his mission to the Gentiles (2.9 – the right hand of fellowship given in order that Barnabas and Paul should go to the Gentiles, just as Peter and the others should go to the circumcised).

At the same time, Paul also clearly wants to distance himself from the Jerusalem authorities. He describes them as 'those reputed to be of some account', 'those regarded as pillars' (2.6, 9), phrases neatly chosen to indicate that they were highly esteemed, but not necessarily by him. In verse 10 he coyly omits the verb which would have been most appropriate to describe the obligation laid upon him by the pillar apostles, lest, presumably, it seem that he had agreed to an element of traditional covenantal nomism at their behest. Clearest of all is the parenthesis inserted into verse 6: 'what they (the pillar apostles) once were matters nothing to me; God takes no account of human evaluation of status'. Here Paul is almost explicit in his implication that he had once accorded the Jerusalem apostles an authority which he no longer recognized and to which he was no longer willing to submit.

The best way to explain the tension between these rather different attitudes to the Jerusalem authorities is that they reflect different stages in Paul's own career and mission. There was a period when he acknowledged and would have been ready to defer to the authority of Peter and the others. Presumably this was the period when he was active as a member of the church in Antioch. That is to say, during his time both as a teacher in Antioch (if we follow Acts 13.1), and as a missionary commissioned by Antioch (Acts 13.2–3).[55] The decisive factor here, presumably, would be that Antioch saw itself as a daughter church of Jerusalem. Consequently Paul probably attended the Jerusalem consultation (Gal. 2.1–10) as a delegate from Antioch. All during this period, and immediately thereafter, he recognized and operated within the terms of Jerusalem's authority. The degree of mutual acceptance implies that covenantal nomism as such had not yet become an issue.

That issue only came to the surface in the Antioch incident (2.11–14). Whether it would have exploded into outright disagreement at Jerusalem if the pillar apostles had after all tried to 'compel' Titus to be circumcised we cannot tell. Quite likely the answer is Yes. Paul was sufficiently clear-headed on the circumcision issue to fight his corner with the utmost resolution (2.5). *But the acceptance of his argument at that time was probably enough to prevent the issue emerging as a clear-cut either/or : either* covenantal nomism *or* faith. What is clear enough is that when such compulsion was exerted by the men from James, and by the acquiescence of Peter and the other Jewish Christians to what they demanded, at that point Paul drew the line (2.14ff.). And his rejection of the demands of covenantal nomism as they affected the Gentile Christians was at the same time a rejection of the Jerusalem authority which laid them down.

Here again, therefore, there is sufficient indication that the Antioch incident was a decisive factor in the development of Paul's understanding of the gospel: both of how it related to covenantal nomism, and what that meant for Gentile believers in relation to the hitherto unquestioned assumption that covenant membership was bound up with Jewish ethnic identity.[56]

§4.4 To complete the argument I should at least include a brief response to those[57] who claim that Paul's attitude to the law (and so also to covenantal nomism) was a consequence of his Damascus road conversion, and a more or less immediate consequence.[58]

In the first place, I find no evidence to indicate that the Hellenists had already 'abandoned' the law. The only material which explicitly claims to express Hellenist views (Acts 7) is directed against the temple, and not against the law. In Acts 7 the attitude to the law is positive (7.38, 53). That temple and law were tightly bound together is, of course, true (the laws of sacrifice, etc.); hence the formulation of the accusation against Stephen in Acts 6.14. But it requires no argument to claim that the law could be held in high esteem, even when the temple was heavily criticized, or, subsequently, when the temple ceased to be a factor in the life and praxis of Judaism. We cannot assume therefore that what Paul was converted to was a Hellenist rejection of the law.

Paul's persecution of the church was certainly an expression of his zeal for the law (Gal. 1.13–14; Phil. 3.6). This should not be taken as implying a wholesale rejection of the law by the Hellenists who were being persecuted. The key word here is 'zeal'. It indicates the attitude of a zealot, one who wanted to define the boundaries round the covenant more sharply, to mark off the righteous more clearly from the sinner. It expresses an attitude evident in such writings as 1 Enoch 1—5, the Psalms of Solomon and the Dead Sea Scrolls, and also, it would appear, among the Pharisees – a factional or even sectarian attitude, which was prepared to condemn and even to persecute fellow Jews whose loyalty to the ancestral traditions was not so firm and whose practice seemed to question and so to threaten these more tightly drawn boundaries.[59] Thus we should probably envisage a persecution by Paul of Jews who *in their own reckoning* were being properly observant of what the law required – a condemnation of fellow Jews equivalent to that of the Pharisees by the Qumran covenanters, or of the Sadducees by the Psalms of Solomon, or subsequently of the fainthearted by the Zealots.[60]

Paul's own view of his conversion is not of a *conversion* as such, far less of a conversion *from* Judaism, but of a commissioning to go to the Gentiles (Gal. 1.15–16).[61] His acknowledgement of the crucified as Lord did not lead him at once to the conclusion that the law which counted the crucified as accursed was an ass, wholly discredited and disowned by God. Such a line of reasoning appears nowhere in Paul's writing. The theological logic focuses rather on

256

the relation between the curse of the law and the Gentile. For Christ to have died as one cursed by the law meant that he had been put outside the covenant, had become, in effect, like a Gentile. For God to have vindicated this Christ therefore meant that that boundary-line between Gentile and Jew no longer counted with God. God accepted the outsider; his promise could now be accepted by the Gentiles without their coming within the boundary of the law (3.13–14).[62] The seed and principle of Paul's full-blown theology of justification was thus given him from the first; which is why he puts so much emphasis on the 'revelation of Christ' (1.12) in the letter. But evidently the full implications of it were not worked out and did not become clear in these early years – presumably because the ambiguity of God-fearers and proselytes both believing in Jesus *and* willing to judaize to some extent (as they had done before they heard about Jesus) meant that the issue had not yet come into focus. Certainly it is hard to believe that Jewish and Gentile believers in Messiah Jesus had completely abandoned the law in Antioch for a decade or more before it came to the attention of the more conservative brothers in Judea or caused any kind of surprise or comment.[63]

In short, the evidence of Galatians seems to indicate that an evolving situation at Antioch, and a double confrontation with what had hitherto usually been regarded as central in covenantal nomism, brought home to Paul what he now saw always to have been implicit in his initial commissioning to the Gentiles. It is this implication for covenantal nomism which he works out, probably for the first time in such detail, in his letter to his converts in Galatia.

§5. A final corollary may also be drawn with regard to the occasion for the writing of Galatians itself. The passion and urgency of the letter in its restatement of the argument which had failed in Antioch suggests that the letter was written not so very long after that failure. The following sequence of events therefore suggests itself.

Paul was defeated at Antioch (see above n. 49). However compelling the logic of faith which Paul spelled out in his rejoinder to Peter on that occasion, it probably was insufficient to shake Peter himself or to win the Jewish Christians back to the practice they had abandoned. Had Paul been successful it is almost inconceivable that he would not have said so (as he had with regard to the earlier confrontation in 2.1–10), since an agreement in Antioch on Paul's terms would have gone a long way to counter the current threat in Galatia. This defeat at Antioch resulted not only in the transformation in his attitude to Jerusalem (already noted – §4.3), but that would inevitably also include a breach with Barnabas (who had taken the opposite side from Paul in the Antioch incident), and a breach with Antioch itself. Paul leaves Antioch and embarks on a fresh round of evangelism, eventually establishing his base first in Corinth and then subsequently in Ephesus, now in effect an independent missionary, jealous of encroachments on his sphere of work (2 Cor. 10.13–16). It may be indicative of his state of mind following the Antioch incident that at first he had no clear sense of direction (according to Acts 16.6ff.), and that in Thessalonica his preaching evidently avoided any mention of the now controversial teaching on justification and placed the emphasis of the gospel elsewhere.

In the meantime it is likely that the new policy and practice at Antioch would be consolidated, with the terms on which Gentile believers could be accepted within the community of *Christianoi* more carefully defined to enable Jewish believers to maintain their covenantal nomism. It would also be natural for the Antioch believers to assume that the churches established by their missionaries should follow suit; as Antioch followed the lead given from Jerusalem, so it would be expected that the churches of the Antiochene mission should follow the lead given by Antioch. This is probably confirmed by the 'Jerusalem decree' which is addressed specifically to the churches in Antioch, Syria and Cilicia (Acts 15.23), a letter and judgement which, significantly, James later claims as his own (Acts 21.25).[64]

If the churches in Galatia were those established by Paul during his time as a missionary from Antioch, it would follow that delegates would soon be sent to them to inform them of the terms agreed at Antioch. And if the churches in question were established by Paul after the break with Antioch, it would still be natural for Antiochene emissaries to assume that the virtually unanimous consensus at Antioch (Gentiles as well as Jews) should set the pattern for all new churches.[65]

But the crisis in Galatia is over circumcision, not over food laws. This fact can still be contained within the above developing scenario. All we need assume is that some at least from Jerusalem and Antioch used the same logic as Paul, but in the reverse direction. Paul argued in effect that the agreement in Jerusalem regarding circumcision undermined the whole pattern of covenantal nomism as hitherto understood and practised. His opponents no doubt argued conversely that the Antioch incident had confirmed the principle of covenantal nomism, and drew the natural conclusion that circumcision should also be practised, as the first act of covenantal nomism.[66] It looks as though they were remaining faithful to the Jerusalem agreement, at least to the extent that they did not require circumcision as a *sine qua non*. But that would not have prevented them urging it as a logical corollary to a covenantal nomistic perspective, and almost inescapable as such.

Whatever the precise facts of the matter, it is not hard to envisage the resulting sequence of events. Pauline loyalists sent word to Paul of the demands being made by the newly arrived Antiochenes. It would presumably take some time to reach him: since his movements had not followed any predetermined plan the Galatian churches might not have known where to find him; quite possibly it did not arrive till he was already established in Corinth, and after the Thessalonian correspondence. But when it did arrive his reaction was predictable: he exploded in indignation. The importance of restating his understanding of justification by faith became paramount. If the churches of Galatia abandoned him on this score the whole of his missionary work since the Antioch incident would be put in jeopardy (all the more so if the churches in question were in northern Galatia); his gospel would be counted a no-gospel and cut off from its Jewish roots; he would be reckoned simply as a Jewish apostate, and those groups which remained faithful to him would be regarded as comprising an unacceptable syncretistic fringe sect. He had to take a stand, to restate with greater force and detail the argument which had failed at Antioch.

And so he wrote Galatians.[67]

Notes

1. The seminar is that of the Pauline Theology Group of the Society of Biblical Literature, which is working through the Pauline letters in sequence, studying each letter in its own right before attempting any synthesis or overview of the letters so far studied.
2. *Paul and Palestinian Judaism* (London: SCM, 1977) 75, 420, 544.
3. J. J. Collins, *Between Athens and Jerusalem* (New York: Crossroad, 1983) Index 'covenantal nomism'.
4. Rightly emphasized by Sanders.
5. See further my *Romans*, WBC 38 (Dallas: Word, 1988) lxvii–lxxi.
6. Texts cited above ch. 6, pp. 149–50 = AI, pp. 26–7.
7. See further ch. 3 above.
8. See, e.g., the texts cited in my 'The New Perspective on Paul', *BJRL* 65 (1983) 95–122, here 107–10, ch. 7 above and pp. 191–3.
9. 'New Perspective', ch. 7 above; and 'Works of the Law and the Curse of the Law (Galatians 3.10–14)', *NTS* 31 (1985) 523–42, ch. 8 above. The points have been well grasped by J. M. G. Barclay, *Obeying the Truth: A Study of Paul's Ethics in Galatia* (Edinburgh: T. & T. Clark, 1988) 78, 82, cited above, ch. 8 Additional Note, p. 240, n.5.
10. See also T. D. Gordon, 'The Problem at Galatia', *Interpretation* 41 (1987) 32–43 – here 38, and those cited by him. Cf. P. Alexander, 'Jewish Law in the Time of Jesus: Towards a Clarification of the Problem', *Law and Religion. Essays on the Place of the Law in Israel and Early Christianity*, ed. B. Lindars (Cambridge: James Clarke, 1988): 'The centrality of the Torah of Moses to Judaism was the centrality of a national flag' (56).

11. cf. N. Dahl, 'The One God of Jews and Gentiles', *Studies in Paul* (Minneapolis: Augsburg, 1977) 178–91.
12. For details see above pp. 144–7 = AI, pp. 21–3; also my *Romans* xlvii–xlviii.
13. Note the clarification of my earliest statement of this conclusion – particularly ch. 7 Additional Note point 6.
14. This is not to say that Paul accepted his Galatian opponents' frame of reference (a criticism made of the first draft of this paper by J. L. Martyn at the SBL Seminar in Chicago), simply to say that the teaching in Galatians had set an agenda and posed an issue to which Paul had to respond; see also §3 below.
15. J. Neusner, *From Politics to Piety* (Englewood Cliffs: Prentice Hall, 1973); also *Judaism* (University of Chicago, 1981). See also ch. 3 above.
16. See the clarification of the exposition of Gal. 2.16 in ch. 7 Additional Note point 9.
17. See further below, and ch. 7 Additional Note point 3.
18. See particularly Barclay, *Obeying* 125–42.
19. I had formulated this thesis before reading C. K. Barrett, *Freedom and Obligation. A Study of the Epistle to the Galatians* (London: SPCK, 1985) 10 – The theology of the Judaizers 'seems to me to tally in some remarkable ways (though not in every way) with the covenantal nomism of E. P. Sanders'.
20. See further ch. 7 above.
21. E. P. Sanders, *Paul, the Law, and the Jewish People* (Philadelphia: Fortress, 1983).
22. See further ch. 7 Additional Note point 8 above.
23. P. Borgen, 'Observations on the Theme "Paul and Philo"', in *Die Paulinische Literatur und Theologie*, hrsg. S. Pedersen (Aarhus: Aros, 1980) 85–102: 'Philo's and Hillel's understanding has thus been that bodily circumcision was not the requirement for entering the Jewish community, but was one of the commandments which they had to obey upon receiving status as a Jew' (88).
24. See particularly the central thesis of Barclay, *Obeying*: that Paul addresses *both* the issue of identity *and* that of behavioural patterns; that 'a major ingredient in the Galatian dispute is the question of how the members of God's people should live', and that the exhortation of 5.13—6.10 'develops out of and concludes his earlier arguments' (216). Cf. also my *Romans* 705–6.
25. See F. F. Bruce, *Galatians* (NIGTC; Exeter: Paternoster, 1982) 156–7.
26. Martyn in his response to the Chicago version of this paper largely ignored and indeed discounted this horizontal, *Heilsgeschichte* dimension of the whole discussion. Contrast B. R. Gaventa, 'The Singularity of the Gospel: A Reading of Galatians', *SBL 1988 Seminar Papers* (Atlanta: Scholars, 1988) 26; R. B. Hays, 'Crucified with Christ: A Synthesis of 1 and 2 Thessalonians, Philemon, Philippians, and Galatians', *SBL 1988 Seminar Papers* 324ff.; also the contributions by R. Scroggs and D. J. Lull in the same seminar.
27. For a fuller exposition see above ch. 8 and Additional Note point 1. Cf. the main thesis of G. Howard, *Paul: Crisis in Galatia* (SNTSMS 35; Cambridge University, 1979), though I disagree with several subsidiary aspects of Howard's argument.
28. cf. J. C. Beker, *Paul the Apostle* (Philadelphia: Fortress, 1980) 50–2, 96; J. L. Martyn, 'Paul and his Jewish-Christian Interpreters', *USQR* (1987–8) 1–15 (here 3–4).
29. R. B. Hays, 'Christology and Ethics in Galatians: The Law of Christ', *CBQ* 49 (1987) 268–90, rightly notes that in Galatians Christology is 'not the issue' (276).
30. See further my *Baptism in the Holy Spirit* (London: SCM, 1970).
31. H. D. Betz, 'Spirit, Freedom and Law. Paul's Message to the Galatian Churches', *SEÅ* 39 (1974) 145–60 (here 145). Cf. D. J. Lull, *The Spirit in Galatia* (SBLDS 49; Chico: Scholars, 1980); S. K. Williams, 'Justification and the Spirit in Galatians', *JSNT* 29 (1987) 91–100; also *'Promise* in Galatians: A

Reading of Paul's Reading of Scripture', *JBL* 107 (1988) 709–20 – the promise to Abraham is the promise of the Spirit.

32. See now Barclay, *Obeying*, particularly ch. 4, 'The Sufficiency of the Spirit'.
33. See further J. D. G. Dunn, '"A Light to the Gentiles": the Significance of the Damascus Road Christophany for Paul', *The Glory of Christ in the New Testament. Studies in Christology in Memory of G. B. Caird*, ed. L. D. Hurst and N. T. Wright (Oxford: Clarendon, 1987) 251–66, above ch. 4. Cf. also Gordon (n. 10 above) 3. A corollary of this is that Paul's principal concern in Galatians 1—2 was not to defend his apostleship (or apostolic authority) as such (so still G. Lüdemann, *Paulus, der Heidenapostel. Band II. Antipaulinismus in frühen Christentum* [Göttingen: Vandenhoeck, 1983] 145); cf. B. R. Gaventa, 'Galatians 1 and 2: Autobiography as Paradigm', *NovT* 28 (1986) 309–26, and B. Lategan, 'Is Paul Defending his Apostleship in Galatians?', *NTS* 34 (1988) 411–30.
34. Hence also 2.21: if righteousness was still in terms of the law, still included a covenantal nomistic 'us and them' distinction between Jews and Gentiles, then Christ's death was 'in vain' (since it had not ended the covenantal nomistic function of the law as a dividing line which excluded Gentiles as such from the blessings of the covenant promise).
35. The fact that Paul speaks of *two* covenants in Gal. 4.21–31 is an interesting variation on the continuity/discontinuity Paul sees in salvation history. Strictly speaking the 'covenantal nomism' to which Paul objects refers only to the covenant of slavery: the correlative of the covenant of promise is the freedom of the Spirit (3.2–5; etc.).
36. cf. particularly J. L. Martyn, 'A Law-Observant Mission to Gentiles: the Background of Galatians', *Michigan Quarterly Review* 22 (1983) 221–36 (here 231–2); reprinted in *SJT* 38 (1985) 307–24 (here 318–20); also 'Apocalyptic Antinomies in Paul's Letter to the Galatians', *NTS* 31 (1985) 410–24. My exegesis does not exclude the possibility that Paul was reacting to his 'opponents' at this point; so advocated by Martyn and Barclay, *Obeying* 91, and earlier by C. K. Barrett, 'The Allegory of Abraham, Sarah, and Hagar in the Argument of Galatians' (1976), in *Essays on Paul* (London: SPCK, 1982) 154–70, who appositely cites *Jub.* 16.17–18 as an indication of the sort of exposition they would probably have used. Note also 1 Macc. 2.16. See now particularly G. Bouwman, 'Die Hagar- und Sara-Perikope (Gal. 4.21–31)', *ANRW* II.25.4 (1987) 3135–55; and more generally J. M. G. Barclay, 'Mirror-Reading a Polemical Letter: Galatians as a Test Case', *JSNT* 31 (1987) 73–93.
37. W. Schmithals' threadbare hypothesis falls apart here in his argument that the 'glorying in the flesh' is expressed in a Gnostic 'contempt for the flesh' – 'The Heretics in Galatia', *Paul and the Gnostics* (Nashville: Abingdon, 1972) 55. Not Gnostic, but ethnic identity is the issue at this point.
38. This false evaluation of circumcision and flesh means also a failure to recognize the proper function of the law (3.19; 4.8–10) and so also to keep it (3.10; 6.13; cf. Rom. 2.17–29). See also above ch. 8 and Additional Note point 1.
39. R. Meyer, *TDNT* 4.39–41. Cf. T. Callan, 'Pauline Midrash: The Exegetical Background of Gal. 3.19b', *JBL* 99 (1980) 549–67.
40. Here I dispute such views as those of J. W. Drane, *Paul: Libertine or Legalist?* (London: SPCK, 1975) that 3.19 amounts to 'a categorical denial of the divine origin of the Torah' (34), or of H. Hübner, *Law in Paul's Thought* (Edinburgh: T. & T. Clark, 1984), that 3.19 means that the law 'is the product of demonic angelic powers' (24–36), both of which read too much into the text and ignore the context of Jewish thought, where the association of angels in the giving of the law was quite familiar and unthreatening (Deut. 33.2 LXX; *Jub.* 1.29ff.; Philo, *Som.* 1.143; Josephus, *Ant.* 15.136; cf. Acts 7.38, 53; Heb. 2.2); see also S. Westerholm, *Israel's Law and the Church's Faith. Paul and his Recent Interpreters* (Grand Rapids: Eerdmans, 1988) 176–9. A. J. M. Wedderburn,

'Paul and the Law', *SJT* 38 (1985), chides me for denying that Paul is opposed to the law *per se*, by referring to Gal. 3.19 which he thinks does 'seem to express opposition to the law *per se*', though without further explanation (618 n. 11). So too I must register my dissent with Howard, *Paul* 60–1, and L. Gaston, 'Paul and the Torah', *Antisemitism and the Foundations of Christianity*, ed. A. T. Davies (New York: Paulist, 1979) 62–4, who maintain that 'under the law' could include (Howard; though cf. Westerholm 192–5) or even specifically designate (Gaston) the Gentile situation; also with Martyn in the Chicago seminar, who maintained that the phrase 'to be under' meant to be 'under the tyrannical power of something'. But see n. 42 below.

41. I see no grounds within this phase of Paul's argument to take 3.19 ('the law was added for the sake of transgressions') in a negative way (as most modern commentators – e.g. Barrett, *Freedom* 33; Westerholm, *Israel's Law* 178, 182) = to multiply transgressions. That reads Gal. 3.19 too much through the differently slanted and more careful argument of Rom. 5.20. Here Paul is explaining the positive side of covenantal nomism in the period before Christ (see further n. 42 below). Likewise the point of 3.21 is not totally to dismiss the law: the mistake Paul objects to is the assumption that the law fulfils the role of the promise (*giving* life) as well as its own role (*regulating* life within the covenant [2.12], particularly in the period before Christ).

42. See particularly D. J. Lull, '"The Law was our Pedagogue": A Study in Galatians 3.19–25', *JBL* 105 (1986) 481–98; N. J. Young, '*Paidagogos*: the Social Setting of a Pauline Metaphor', *NovT* 29 (1987) 150–76; T. D. Gordon, 'A Note on *ΠΑΙΔΑΓΩΓΟΣ* in Galatians 3.24–5', *NTS* 35 (1989) 150–4. Young sees the emphasis of 3.23–4 as falling on the confining and restrictive rather than either the corrective or protective functions of a pedagogue (171). He concludes: 'Thus the law is "our pedagogue" in the sense that the restrictive regulations which separated Jew and Gentile, which Sinai epitomized, were only temporary. Just as a pedagogue's guardian role finished when the child arrived at maturity, so the legal separation of Jew and Gentile ended with the coming of the new age in Christ' (176). Gordon sees the *paidagogos'* function as guarding and protecting Israel 'from the defiling idolatry of the Gentiles, preserving a community which propagated faith in the God of Abraham until the promise made to Abraham became historical reality' (154).

43. cf. J. H. Neyrey, 'Bewitched in Galatia: Paul and Cultural Anthropology', *CBQ* 50 (1988) 72–100; here particularly 80–3.

44. This is the nub of Hübner's consistent misinterpretation of Paul's treatment of the law in Galatians in his *Law*. His insistence that 3.10 has in view 'the primarily *quantitative* demand of the law that all . . . its stipulations be followed out, so that whoever transgresses against even a single one of these stipulations is accursed' (38) ignores the facts that 'doing what the law requires' includes the provision of atonement for failure (see n. 4 above); and that Paul equally expects 'the whole law' to be 'fulfilled' by believers (5.14). See also Barclay's critique of Hübner at this point (*Obeying* 136–7). Hübner's, of course, is a variant of the normal interpretation of 3.10 (see above n. 41 ch. 8).

45. F. Watson, *Paul, Judaism and the Gentiles. A Sociological Approach* (SNTSMS 56; Cambridge University, 1986), turns Paul's concerns upside down: far from objecting to a covenantal nomism which inevitably means a reinforcement of the boundary between Jew(ish Christian) and Gentile (Christian), Watson thinks Paul's objective was that 'the church should separate from the Jewish community' (64). This thesis recognizes only the discontinuities in Paul's view of *Heilsgeschichte* (promise/law, two covenants) and fails to recognize the continuity of Abraham's seed, of the 'we' which includes Jew and Gentile (3.14; 4.5), of a sonship coming to maturity (3.23—4.5), and of the law fulfilled, as with faith, in love (5.6, 14). The other major flaw in Watson's thesis is that he uses 'Jewish community' in a too undifferentiated and all-inclusive sense.

There were Jews for whom Paul's argument and gospel would mean total separation. But there were others, Jewish Christians, still functioning as Jews in synagogue service, who would go along with Paul (himself a Jewish Christian). And there were no doubt still others, Jews and Jewish Christians, with ambivalent views in between. It was not a case of Paul accepting the boundaries (circumcision, food laws, etc.) as immovable and simply stepping outside of them (contrast 1 Cor. 9.20–1); he was attempting to redraw the boundaries with Gentile Christians inside! See also my critique of Watson in *Romans* index 'Watson'; also my response to Esler above in ch. 6 Additional Note point 10, and to Räisänen above in ch. 7 Additional Note point 4.

46. See further K. Berger, 'Almosen für Israel: zum historischen Kontext der paulinischen Kollekte'. *NTS* 23 (1976–7) 180–204.

47. For the pressures leading to the demand of the men from James see above ch. 6, §2.2, with particular reference to R. Jewett, 'The Agitators and the Galatian Congregation', *NTS* 17 (1970–1) 204–6.

48. I question whether it is right to speak of a 'unilateral reversal of the earlier agreement' on the part of James – so P. J. Achtemeier, *The Quest for Unity in the New Testament Church* (Philadelphia: Fortress, 1987) 54. To similar effect Watson, *Paul* 53–6. Barrett's formulation is probably nearer the mark: 'what agreement there was had probably been inadequately thought through' (*Freedom* 12).

49. That Paul's plea to Peter was unsuccessful is now accepted by most commentators. See, e.g., Achtemeier, *Quest* 59 and those cited by him in nn. 8–9; and see further below.

50. A. Suhl completely ignores this whole dimension of the historical context when he attempts to defend the paraphrase, 'We, of course Jews by nature and not stemming from the Gentiles, are nevertheless sinners (as much as them)' – 'Der Galaterbrief – Situation und Argumentation', *ANRW* II.25.4 (1987) 3102–6.

51. See further K. Haacker, 'Paulus und das Judentum in Galaterbrief', *Gottes Augapfel. Beiträge zur Erneuerung des Verhältnisses von Christen und Juden*, hrsg. E. Brocke and J. Sein (Neukirchen: Neukirchener, 1986) 95–111; also W. D. Davies' critical review of H. D. Betz, *Galatians* (Hermeneia; Philadelphia: Fortress, 1979), in *Jewish and Pauline Studies* (London: SPCK, 1984) 172–88.

52. See further my 'New Perspective', ch. 7 above, with Additional Note points 3 and 9. Also Watson, *Paul* 197 n. 73.

53. I remain quite unconvinced by the now renewedly popular argument that 'the faith of Christ' means 'Christ's faith', rather than 'faith in Christ'. The latter is wholly in line with the sustained thrust of the letter, including the fundamental distinction between (human) faith and (human) works; whereas the former introduces a quite different tack. For example, the fullest recent treatment, R. B. Hays, *The Faith of Jesus Christ* (SBLDS 56; Chico: Scholars, 1983) ch. 4, finds itself drawn into arguing that effectively all the key πίστις references in Gal. 3.1–14 denote the faithfulness of Christ. But the relevant πίστις references of 3.7–9 are bracketed by talk of Abraham's believing and Abraham's πίστις (vv. 6, 9), and are more naturally understood as carrying the same sense of πίστις, that is, 'faith'. And 3.14 is more naturally understood to speak of the mode of *receiving* ('through faith') than of the mode of bestowing. The problem with 'the faith of Christ' interpretation is that to be sustainable it must draw in most other πίστις references, leaving the verbal reference to human believing without a noun counterpart at important points in the argument, the mode of human reception thus unspecified, and references like Gal. 5.5–6 in some confusion. The debate on this phrase was postponed at the Chicago meeting till the Pauline Theology Group reaches Romans. But see also now Barclay, *Obeying* 78 n. 8, and Westerholm, *Israel's Law* 111–12 n. 12.

54. In the following paragraphs I draw on my 'The Relationship between Paul and Jerusalem according to Galatians 1 and 2', *NTS* 28 (1982) 461–78, ch. 5 above.

55. I take 'apostles' in Acts 14.4, 14 in the sense 'emissaries/missionaries' of Antioch (cf. 2 Cor. 8.23; Phil. 2.25), since according to Acts 1.21–2 neither Paul nor Barnabas could be accounted apostles = witnesses of Christ's resurrection (as claimed by Paul for himself – 1 Cor. 9.1; 15.7–11).

56. Watson, *Paul* 31–2, argues that the Gentile mission began as a response to the failure of the Jewish Christian congregation of Antioch in its preaching among the Jews and that it 'involved a more or less complete separation from the Jewish community' (31–2, 36–8). This ignores the evidence of Gal. 2.9 (a conjoint mission – to Jews and Gentiles), of Gal. 2.12a that there was at least initially in Antioch a continuum of Jew, Jewish Christian and Gentile Christian, and treats 1 Cor. 9.21 (present tense) and 2 Cor. 11.24 in a highly tendentious way, not to mention the primary thrust of Rom. 9—11. The implication is that Paul continued to operate within the context of the synagogue so far as possible and sought to maintain the continuum. See also n. 45 above.

57. Particularly S. Kim, *The Origin of Paul's Gospel* (WUNT 2.4; Tübingen: Mohr, 1981) and C. Dietzfelbinger, *Die Berufung des Paulus als Ursprung seiner Theologie* (WMANT 58; Neukirchen: Neukirchener, 1985).

58. What follows supplements the discussion of ch. 4 above.

59. cf. Haacker (above n. 51) 104–7, and my *Romans* 586–7; also ch. 4 Additional Note point 1. Despite Sanders' rejection of the claim that Paul's persecution of the church was tied up with his convictions as a Pharisee, it must be significant to the contrary that Paul uses the same word, 'zeal', to characterize both his commitment to the ancestral customs of his people (that is, as a Pharisee – Gal. 1.14) and his energy in persecution (Phil. 3.6).

60. See also ch. 3 above.

61. See also ch. 4 n. 1 above.

62. See the fuller exposition in ch. 4 above and ch. 8 n. 60.

63. See also ch. 6 Additional Note point 1 above.

64. See also ch. 6 Additional Note point 3 above.

65. This makes better sense than J. Munck's overreaction against the Tübingen school in his argument that Paul was confronted in Galatia only by judaizing *Gentile* Christians – *Paul and the Salvation of Mankind* (London: SCM, 1959) ch. 4. In particular his claim that 'Jewish Christianity carried on its mission only within Israel' (130) is highly suspect (see further n. 36 above).

66. cf. Martyn in n. 36 above.

67. In the much debated question of Galatians' date I therefore tend to side with those who place it early (such as Zahn, J. Weiss and Watson, *Paul* 59–60; cf. Betz), rather than as the earliest (as Burkitt and Bruce), or as written in the middle 50s (e.g. Lightfoot, Kümmel and Suhl), or as one of the latest of Paul's letters (as J. Knox and Beker).

Index of Biblical and Other Ancient Sources

265

Index of Modern Authors

273

275

276

Subject Index

277